Data Communications
From Basics to Broadband

Third Edition

William J. Beyda

University of California Extension, Berkeley
Siemens Information and Communication Networks, Inc.

Prentice Hall
Upper Saddle River, New Jersey 07458

Library of Congress Cataloging-in-Publication Data

Beyda, William J.
    Data communications : from basics to broadband /
  William J. Beyda. -- 3rd edition
      p. cm.
  Includes bibliographical references and index.
  ISBN: 0-13-096139-6
  1. Data transmission systems. I. Title.
TK5105.B485   2000
004.6--dc21   99-14309
                                                         CIP

Publisher: **ALAN APT**
Editor-in-chief: **MARCIA HORTON**
Acquistions editor: **PETRA RECTER**
Production editor: **IRWIN ZUCKER**
Assistant managing editor: **EILEEN CLARK**
Executive managing editor: **VINCE O'BRIEN**
Manufacturing buyer: **PAT BROWN**
Assistant vice president of production and manufacturing: **DAVID W. RICCARDI**
Art director: **HEATHER SCOTT**
Associate creative director: **AMY ROSEN**
Cover designer: **JOHN CHRISTIANA**
Cover image: © **PHOTODISC**

© 2000 by Prentice Hall
Prentice-Hall, Inc.
Upper Saddle River, New Jersey 07458

The author and publisher of this book have used their best efforts in preparing this book. These efforts include the
development, research, and testing of the theories and programs to determine their effectiveness. The author and
publisher make no warranty of any kind, expressed or implied, with regard to these programs or the documentation
contained in this book. The author and publisher shall not be liable in any event for incidental or consequential
damages in connection with, or arising out of, the furnishing, performance, or use of these programs.

Printed in the United States of America

10 9 8 7 6 5 4 3 2 1

ISBN   0-13-096139-6

Prentice-Hall International (UK) Limited, London
Prentice-Hall of Australia Pty. Limited, Sydney
Prentice-Hall Canada Inc., Toronto
Prentice-Hall Hispanoamericana, S.A., Mexico
Prentice-Hall of India Private Limited, New Delhi
Prentice-Hall of Japan, Inc., Tokyo
Prentice-Hall (Singapore) Pte. Ltd., Singapore
Editora Prentice-Hall do Brasil, Ltda., Rio de Janeiro

To Cathy, Joey, and Rachel

Contents

Preface

The prior editions of this book were more successful than I had originally hoped. The book has been adopted at universities around the world, and the second edition is now in its sixth printing. But this industry changes quickly, and with the many advances in data communications, a third edition was required to update certain topics and add new ones for the new millennium.

The goals of the third edition remain the same as those of the first and second. After years of teaching data communications classes, I was still not satisfied with the scope, clarity, and readability of available textbooks. Some textbooks were aimed at advanced electrical engineering students, while others covered only the business aspects of data communications. I sought to create a text that would be accessible to the novice and at the same time challenging to the engineer or technical professional. Those readers desiring a broad overview can simply follow the body of this text, while the more advanced reader can examine concepts in detail inside the special shaded boxes.

Simply stated, I have tried to demystify data communications. I draw on practical examples to explain all technical concepts, as I have found this technique very successful in my teaching experience. This text introduces the language of data communications. It provides a practical understanding of all the relevant terminology, concepts, hardware, software, protocols, architectures, and other information necessary to make the reader literate in data communications. Current and future product offerings are discussed. By the end of the text, the reader should be able to make intelligent decisions on the appropriate design, purchase, integration, and use of data communications equipment and systems.

The text begins with a thorough introduction to telecommunications, an understanding of which is essential in order to appreciate data communications hardware and software designs. The book then progresses logically, from the basic concepts of data communications to transmission and interface standards, as well as to data integrity and security. At that point, it is appropriate to discuss architectures and protocols to tie the components together, leading to a thorough presentation of different networks. The text concludes with a discussion of current and future trends in digital telecommunications, including an in-depth examination of standards currently being developed.

At the end of each chapter, I have provided a summary, as well as a list of newly introduced terms. Exercises are also included to help the reader review the material. A thorough glossary of terms and acronyms, an index, and a topical bibliography will ensure this book's usefulness to the reader as a reference tool long after any courses are completed.

The impact of continuously evolving technologies in this vital industry must not be overlooked. I have therefore focused on both fundamental concepts and practical applications, so that the reader can understand data communications today and also be prepared to understand future advances in technology, products, and standards. The key in developing such a text is not only what to include, but also what to leave out. There are many thicker books on data communications available. Boiling it down to the essentials is what this book is all about.

I believe that I have succeeded in providing a clearer, well-balanced, and more practical approach to data communications.

WHAT'S NEW IN THE THIRD EDITION

The entire book has been revised with the increasing importance of the Internet in the new millennium in mind. Various Internet-access technologies, like Digital Subscriber Line (DSL) and cable modems, are now covered, and the use of ISDN lines for this purpose is also discussed. TCP/IP and related protocols are now presented in much greater detail. This includes an expanded section on the use of SMTP and MIME for electronic mail, HTTP for hypertext, Telnet and Rlogin for remote access, FTP for file transfer, UDP for sending individual packets, SNMP for network management, and SLIP and PPP as data link protocols. S/MIME, SSL, and IPSec are discussed in an expanded treatment of security enhancements that have helped advance the use of the Internet for commercial purposes. The differences between IPv4 and IPv6 are presented as well. Increased coverage is provided to various encryption standards, algorithms, and software. Information regarding the Internet Engineering Task Force (IETF) and its work are now included, and the use of Virtual Private Networks (VPNs) is also presented. Also included is a discussion of the use of client/server architectures to implement Web-based intranets, with Web browsers as the universal client. Thin clients, network computers, and their applications are presented. An expanded comparison of IP and ATM technologies is now provided, and their ability to coexist in the future is considered.

The increasing domination of Ethernet in the LAN environment is now reflected, with additional discussion regarding Fast Ethernet, Gigabit Ethernet, half duplex Ethernet, and full duplex Ethernet. A detailed description of the Ethernet Frame is also provided. Other high-speed LAN standards, including High Speed Token Ring, are presented. The increased use of LAN switches is discussed, and Layer 2 switching, Layer 3 switching, Layer 4 switching, and other switching technologies are compared. Expanded coverage of collision domains and LAN segmentation is also provided. In the area of network management, coverage of SNMP is greatly expanded, and there is a new section discussing RMON. Additional network manager software products are also presented.

In addition, updates are provided in the areas of telecommunications regulation, increased competition, and mergers among carriers. A discussion of changes in area codes and long-distance carrier access codes is also included. A more detailed treatment of cellular telephone standards and technology, including AMPS, ETACS, CDMA, TDMA, and GSM, is now provided as well. The Universal Serial Bus (USB) and Firewire (IEEE 1394) standards are presented. Wave division multiplexing (WDM) is covered, and satellites are now presented in greater detail, with descriptions of the differences between systems orbiting at various altitudes. A description of V.90 56 kbps modems and an explanation of how they differ from conventional analog modems are also provided. Finally, definitions of over 150 new terms and acronyms within the new material have been added to the glossary.

Additional materials for this text can be found on the following website: http://www.prenhall.com/beyda.

ACKNOWLEDGMENTS

The efforts of a few, and the inspiration of many, have led to the successful completion of this book. My father, Joseph D. Beyda, was a constant source of suggestions and moral support during the creation of the first edition, though he did not live to see the later editions. My mother, Barbara M. Beyda, once again applied her considerable editorial skills to ensure the readability of this text. I will always be grateful to my wife Cathy, my son Joey, and my daughter Rachel for their help, patience, and support while I completed this third edition.

Though I left Stanford University with a strong academic and technical foundation, along with a B.S. in electrical engineering and an M.S. in engineering management, it was only upon entering the telecommunications industry that I acquired more practical knowledge. I have been privileged to work with some of the sharpest minds in the industry at Siemens, where we learn from each other every day.

For the last 15 years, I have been teaching introductory classes on data communications at U.C. Berkeley Extension. My students have given me a new perspective on the field, and I am grateful for their insights. Their comments and questions planted the seed for this work. I would like to thank Richard Tsina, chairman of the U.C. Berkeley Extension Engineering program, for his encouragement. Joan Shao, director of the U.C. Berkeley Extension Telecommunications Engineering program, has been especially supportive.

The technical reviewers contributed significantly to the accuracy and readability of this text. Florin Gheorghiu, Charles Okwudiafor, Rich Seifert, and Stan Telson each reviewed significant portions of the revised material. As they are active instructors in the field, their perspective has been invaluable. The editorial and production staff at Prentice Hall has been very helpful as well.

Finally, to the readers of this book, thank you for your feedback over the years and your interest in this field. The information superhighway will need your help to reach its full potential.

C H A P T E R   1

Overview
and Introduction

In order to understand data communications, we should start with a few basic definitions. Communication is often defined as the exchange of information between two individuals using a common set of symbols, signs, or behavior. More specifically, telecommunications usually involves a significant distance between the individuals and some electronic equipment for transmission and reception of the information. Finally, data communications requires that the communicating individuals or devices exchange data in the form of ones and zeroes. Typically, computers and related devices communicate in this manner.

Today, in the so-called "information age," more and more functions in our lives are performed by or with the help of computers. For example, most authors wouldn't even attempt to write a book today with just a typewriter. We have already become adjusted to computerized billings, automated teller machines, and even cars that remember when they're due for their next tune-up. It is only logical that with more and more of society's information stored on computers, we certainly will want to access much of this information and link many of our computers.

The term "data communications" often conjures up images of complex systems; one vendor's otherwise perfectly sound equipment is often unable to communicate with equally expensive counterparts from another vendor, because of seemingly insurmountable compatibility problems. However, data communications need not be such a mystifying topic. After all, data communications really is nothing more than the transmission of ones and zeroes from one place to another. The complexity arises from the various means we use to transmit and receive those ones and zeroes and what we do with them at the destination.

This book attempts to demystify data communications. In fact, half the battle in understanding data communications is getting through all of the jargon and acronyms. Therefore, this book introduces the language of data communications and provides a basic understanding of all the relevant terminology, concepts, hardware, software, protocols, architectures, and other information necessary to allow the reader to achieve literacy in data communications.

The book introduces and explains over 1100 terms and acronyms. Many of these terms are generic in nature. For example, there are thousands of terminals on the market, and what one manufacturer labels a "smart terminal" may be called an automated workstation by another manufacturer. There is a wide variety of terminology in the data communications industry, just as in the auto industry, where there's no clear-cut definition of a "sports car." Throughout this book, we use definitions and examples that represent common usage and practice in the industry.

The information presented here should help put current and future product offerings of the industry in context. By providing a comprehensive overview of many topics, the book prepares the reader for further study of more specific areas, such as local area networks. Finally, the reader should be able to make intelligent decisions on the appropriate design, purchase, integration, and use of data communications equipment and systems.

A LOGICAL PROGRESSION

This book presents topics in a logical order. The following description of the book's chapters may include terminology unfamiliar to some readers; all terms are explained in the respective chapters.

Chapter 2, Understanding Telecommunications, includes an overview of telecommunications, which is required to put data communications in the appropriate context. A basic understanding of telecommunications should help the reader appreciate the purpose and suitability of the different data communications hardware and software discussed in the rest of the book.

Different network topologies, the public network, signaling, divestiture, regulation, call routing, and wireless communications are all presented. Communications service options are compared, including common carrier services and customer-premises equipment.

Chapter 3, Basic Data Communications Concepts, lays the foundation upon which the rest of the book is built. Host computers and terminals are used to illustrate basic principles.

Common character codes are presented and compared. The differences between parallel and serial transmission, asynchronous and synchronous transmission, and simplex, half duplex, and full duplex transmission are all analyzed.

Chapter 4, Data Interfaces and Transmission, discusses data transmission and interface standards. It analyzes in detail the methods used to connect terminals to host computers, whether the terminal is located 20 feet or 2000 miles away.

The ANSI, IEEE, EIA, ECSA, IETF, ISO, ITU (CCITT), and NIST standards organizations are described. The RS-232-C, RS-449, RS-422-A, and RS-423-A standards are compared, and new high-speed standards like USB and Firewire are discussed. The chapter introduces digital and analog bandwidth and examines different transmission media. Baseband transmission and broadband transmission are presented, and various modulation methods are illustrated. Facsimile and fax modems are also discussed.

Chapter 5, Improving Data Communications Efficiency, explains how special devices can maximize the use of communications circuits and minimize the use of computer resources. While the devices described are not prerequisites for communications, they are widely used because they reduce costs and enhance performance.

Front-end processors, port-sharing devices, remote intelligent controllers, line splitters, and multiplexers are described. Different multiplexing methods are compared, and data compression devices are explained.

Chapter 6, Data Integrity and Security, discusses means for preventing errors and protecting data. In any data communications network, there is the possibility of errors occurring during transmission. The prevention or correction of such errors is often referred to as maintaining data integrity. Error detection and correction methods, such as echo checking, parity checking, cyclical parity, the Hamming code, various checksums, and the cyclical redundancy check, are all explained.

As computers take on a larger and larger share of business transactions, the need for data security becomes evident. In this chapter, security goals and measures are explained, including historical and statistical logs, closed user groups, firewalls, callback techniques, and encryption methods.

Chapter 7, Architectures and Protocols, explains how communications architectures and protocols enable host computers, terminals, front-end processors, and other devices to communicate in an orderly manner by defining precise rules and methods for communications.

This chapter introduces the OSI model, along with examples of widely used protocols and architectures. SNA functions are discussed, and the classification of SNA components is presented. We explain polling and selecting and compare ARQ methods. BSC and SDLC are presented as examples of byte-oriented and bit-oriented protocols, respectively. TCP/IP and related protocols are discussed, including SMTP, MIME, Telnet, FTP, HTTP, UDP and SNMP. The IP header itself is also presented in detail.

Chapter 8, Data Transport Networks, describes wide area and local area networks. Data transport networks connect a wide variety of devices located in the same building or across the world, providing the means for transmitting and receiving data.

Packet switching network nodes, IXCs, and PADs are explained. The X.25 standard, along with the related X.3, X.28, and X.29 standards, is presented. PSN routing and services are also described. Local area network topologies are compared, along with the various access methods. Ethernet and token ring networks are analyzed in detail, and the IEEE 802 standards are presented. Internetworking applications involving repeaters, bridges, routers, and gateways are described. The Internet is discussed, along with frame relay, SMDS, CBDS, and wireless data networks. The client/server model of computing is presented, as are thin clients, network computers, and intranets.

Chapter 9, Network Management, describes how harmony in a network can be maintained, ensuring consistent reliability and availability of the network, as well as timely transmission and routing of data.

This chapter introduces network management concepts, as well as specific network management tools. The key functions of network management are presented, and measures of availability, reliability, response time, and throughput are described. Various network management approaches and protocols like SNMP are considered, along with MIBs and RMON. Finally, several diagnostic methods, and the role of specialized test equipment, are analyzed.

Chapter 10, Digital Telecommunications, concludes the book with a discussion of the latest communications technologies and the impact of their possible future implementation. As the 21st century begins, telecommunications and data communications are converging. Digital technology is now being used in almost all types of communications equipment.

This chapter introduces digital PBXs, pulse code modulation, and the T-1 standard. The ISDN standards are explained, including the differences between European and North-American implementations. Equipment classifications and reference points are described, and ISDN services and video transmission are examined. Digital Subscriber Line services and cable modems are discussed. Broadband ISDN and ATM are explained in detail. The chapter also includes discussions about the impact of both Narrowband and Broadband ISDN on the future of data communications.

USING THIS BOOK

This book should be accessible to all readers. Those who have had no prior exposure to computers may need to consult the appendix on the binary number system. Readers who have had some exposure to computers, either through regular use, introductory computer science classes, or other technical training, should be able to follow the body of the text. Throughout the book, many specific topics are examined in detail for the advanced or interested reader; these discussions are placed in special shaded boxes.

In addition, there is a summary at the end of each chapter, to help readers review key ideas and concepts. Terms and acronyms are usually italicized the first time they are introduced or used in a new context, and a list of these terms is provided for review at the end of each chapter. Finally, exercises are provided to help readers review the material further.

For the reader's convenience, a glossary of over 1100 terms and acronyms can be found at the end of the book. A bibliography of useful reference books and publications is also included.

C H A P T E R   2

Understanding Telecommunications

THE IMPORTANCE OF TELECOMMUNICATIONS

The invention of the telephone by Alexander Graham Bell in 1876 has forever altered the way we communicate. It is hard to imagine life without telecommunications. *Telecommunications* is defined as the exchange of information, usually over a significant distance and using electronic equipment for transmission. Our businesses and social lives are highly dependent on the telephone.

We now demand that the telephone network carry more than just our voice conversations. The cost of data communications is the fastest growing segment of most companies' telecommunications budgets. Even though most of this book focuses on data communications, we begin with a discussion of today's telecommunications network.

A basic understanding of telecommunications is necessary to place data communications in the appropriate context. Since almost all data communications networks include or connect to the public telephone network at some point, we start by introducing that aspect of telecommunications.

THE PUBLIC NETWORK

The *public network*, also referred to as the *direct distance dial network*, or *DDD network*, is very familiar to all of us. Each time we pick up our home telephone, we are accessing the public network.

A *network* is simply a group of interconnected devices communicating with each other. These devices can be telephones, as is the case with the public network, or computers, as described in Chapter 3. The word *network* is commonly used today to describe a group of people communicating. In some circles, it is used as a verb: "I networked with a lot of interesting people at that party."

Although the public network allows us to communicate with almost any location on the globe, simple telephone conversations do not require complex equipment. In fact, when Bell invented the phone, he simply had two makeshift telephone instruments (a microphone and a speaker), two wires, and a battery.

Today's analog telephones require a negative 48-volt DC power source. Think of this as 32 "D" batteries attached end to end. Figure 2-1 shows the connection of two telephones. If we have phone conversations only with our neighbor, we could connect our phone to his or hers with two wires, attach a 48-volt power source, and converse forever.

Eventually, we decide that it would be convenient to be able to talk to any of our six neighbors via telephone. We start by running wires to each of the other six houses in our neighborhood. The neighbors could each run wires to their neighbors' houses as well. For neighbors to communicate, the party on each end attaches the correct wires to his or her phone, and one of the parties attaches a power source. Figure 2-2 illustrates this network without power sources. We call this configuration a *mesh network* because there are wires running from each user to all of the other users.

If our neighborhood gets any more populated, there will soon be wires everywhere. In fact, with hundreds of millions of telephone customers in the United States alone, it becomes clear that the mesh network is not an effective solution.

Instead, today's telephone network resembles a *star network*, as shown in Fig. 2-3. In a star network, each user is connected to the central point. In the telephone network, this central point is responsible for providing the power needed for the telephones, as well as for routing the calls to the proper parties.

CENTRAL OFFICES AND LOCAL LOOPS

The *central office* is the term used to describe the hub of our city's telephone network. Each central office is the center of a star network in a particular area. A large city might have several central offices, with each central office handling a portion of the telephone

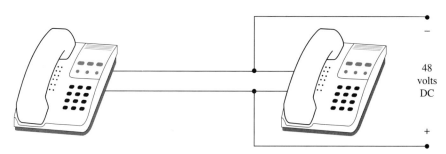

FIGURE 2-1 Basic telephone connection.

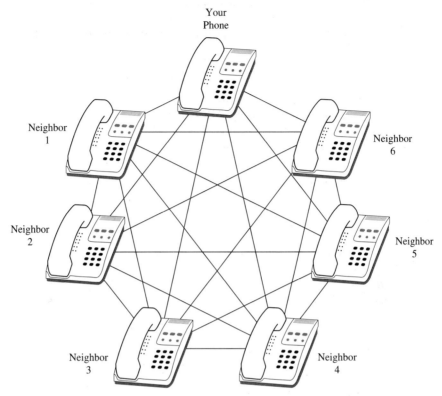

FIGURE 2-2   Mesh network.

lines. Smaller cities might share a central office with other cities. Our local phone company operates the equipment at our central office. Other names for the central office are the *end office* and the *local exchange.*

The pair of wires that runs from the central office into our home or business is known as the *local loop.* Many homes actually have two pairs of wires running from the central office, just in case we decide to install a second telephone line. If we have only a single telephone number, the extra pair of wires remains unconnected at the central office.

The central office provides power for our telephones, routes our calls, and bills us accordingly. The piece of equipment that performs all of this work is known as the *central office switch.* The term *switch* is used often in telecommunications when referring to a device that routes communications to different parties. Originally, these devices were made up of a series of mechanical switches. Today, most central office switches are electronic, or even digital, with no moving parts involved. Digital central offices are more reliable than electromechanical switches, and because they are computer controlled, they are able to offer many special features, such as call forwarding or three-way calling.

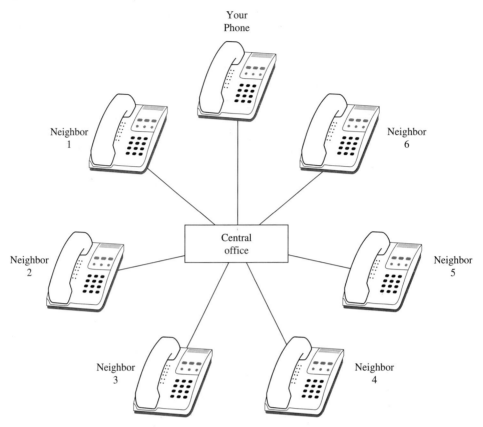

FIGURE 2-3   Star network.

SIGNALING ON A VOICE NETWORK

In the process of routing our calls, the central office performs various *signaling* functions. We first signal the central office when we pick up our phone; this action is known as the *off-hook signal* and tells the central office that we would like to dial. The central office then signals us with a *dial tone*, indicating that we can dial a number.

Another example of a signal that the central office provides us is the *ringing* of our telephone when we are receiving a call. While ringing our telephone, the central office provides the *ringback signal* to the party calling us. Other signals that the central office provides are the *busy signal*, which we get when we call our neighbor and he or she is already using the phone, and the *howler signal*, which is that irritating tone that sounds when we leave our phone off the hook. Some common central office and telephone user signals are listed in Fig. 2-4.

When we dial a number on our phone, we are signaling to the central office our desire to be connected to that phone number. Phone numbers are dialed using *rotary dialing*, also known as *pulse dialing*, or by *Touch-Tone dialing*, also known as *dual tone multifrequency (DTMF) dialing*.

Signal name	From:	To:	Function
Off-hook	User	Central office	Informs central office that user wants to place a call
Dial tone	Central office	User	Informs user that central office is ready to accept dialing
Touch-tones or rotary pulses	User	Central office	Informs central office of call destination
Ringback tone	Central office	User	Informs user that the destination phone is ringing
Ringing voltage	Central office	User	Special voltage sent by central office to cause a phone's bell to ring
Busy signal	Central office	User	Informs user that destination phone is already in use
On-hook	User	Central office	Informs central office that user wishes to disconnect call
Call waiting tone	Central office	User	Informs user that another call is waiting on the line
Flash	User	Central office	A combination of the on-hook and off-hook signals—the user quickly depresses the switch-hook and releases it; often used to pick up a waiting call
Howler tone	Central office	User	Alerts user the phone is off the hook

FIGURE 2-4   Central office and telephone user signals.

Rotary, or pulse, dialing requires the alternate opening and closing of a switch at the end of the local loop at a fixed rate of speed. When we dial the number 8 on a rotary phone, as we release the dial, the dial mechanism returns at a fixed rate of speed, causing the switch to open and close 8 times, one-tenth of a second apart. Special equipment in the central office, often known as a *rotary register*, can detect this switch opening and closing by monitoring the electric current in the local loop. The same opening and closing of the switch can be accomplished by alternately hanging up and picking up our telephone. If we can briefly depress our switch hook eight times, one-tenth of a second apart, without pausing, we will dial the number 8. Most of us aren't this accurate, however, and will pause too long, causing us to dial a 5 and then a 3, for example, instead of an 8.

Touch-tone, or DTMF, dialing works very differently. Each row and column on the DTMF pad has a different tone associated with it. Imagine three different high-pitched tones for the columns and four different low-pitched tones for the rows. A picture of the DTMF pad is shown in Fig. 2-5, along with the frequencies of the associated tones. We explain frequencies in detail in Chapter 4, but for now, just think of frequency as a measure of how high or low a tone's pitch is; the higher the frequency, the higher the pitch. The number 8 on our DTMF pad is in row 3 and column 2. When we push the number 8 on our DTMF pad, our phone produces two tones simultaneously: the row 3 tone and the column 2 tone. It sounds like one tone to our ear, but two separate tones are actually played together in harmony. At the central office, there is a piece of equipment,

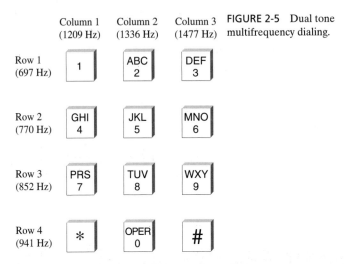

FIGURE 2-5   Dual tone multifrequency dialing.

often known as a *DTMF register*, that listens to those tones and then determines that we sent a row 3 tone and a column 2 tone, and therefore, that we dialed the number 8.

By now, the name *dual tone multifrequency* should make sense; we send two tones at the same time (dual tone), and each can be one of several pitches (multifrequency). Since the name *dual tone multifrequency* is so cumbersome, the simpler name *Touch-tone* has caught on instead. Interestingly enough, the DTMF standard actually provides for a fourth column, allowing 16 different combinations of row and column tones. This 16-number keypad, however, is used only in special applications, and most applications today use the abbreviated 12-key pad (the numbers 1, 2, 3, 4, 5, 6, 7, 8, 9, and 0 and the * and # symbols).

We are so accustomed to hearing the dial tone almost instantly when we pick up the phone that we hardly think of it as a signal to dial; some people don't even listen for it. But if every telephone user attached to our central office picks up the phone at once, not all users will receive the dial tone immediately, as most central offices are not able to provide a dial tone to everyone at once. This is because a dial tone is an indication that there is a piece of equipment in the central office ready to listen to our pulse or DTMF digits. The phone companies don't expect everyone to pick up the phone at once, so they usually don't install enough DTMF and rotary registers to listen to everyone dial at once. If we pick up the phone on Mother's Day and notice a delay in getting a dial tone, that's because so many people are already dialing their phones that there are no rotary or DTMF registers available at the central office to listen to us dial. As soon as a register is available, it is connected electronically to our line and we hear a dial tone.

DIVESTITURE

The methods used for routing calls throughout the telephone network today are largely a result of the U.S. government's antitrust case against *American Telephone & Telegraph*, or *AT&T*. We briefly examine the results of this case as it relates to telephone call routing.

A local phone company, known as a *local exchange carrier*, or *LEC*, operates the central office. These local phone companies include companies formerly controlled by AT&T, known as the *Bell Operating Companies*, or *BOCs*, as well as many *Independent Telephone Companies*, or *ITCs*.

In 1974, the U.S. Department of Justice filed an antitrust law suit against AT&T. At that time, AT&T owned a controlling share of 22 of the 24 BOCs and carried a large majority of America's long-distance traffic; together, these two components were referred to as the *Bell System*. The domination of both the regulated local and long-distance service by AT&T was deemed an unfair monopoly by the U.S. Department of Justice.

AT&T eventually reached a settlement with the government, described in a document known as the *Modified Final Judgment*, or *MFJ*. The MFJ required AT&T to divest itself of the BOCs on January 1, 1984. This *divestiture* is commonly referred to as the *breakup* of the Bell System. AT&T accomplished the divestiture by exchanging its old stock for shares of stock in the new AT&T and the newly formed holding companies we discuss later.

The MFJ allowed AT&T to continue to provide long-distance service. AT&T could enter other businesses, but could not initially provide local telephone service. In addition to relinquishing control of the local phone service, AT&T was forced to compete on an equal basis with other long-distance carriers, known as *interexchange carriers*, or *IECs*.

The newly divested BOCs had to provide *equal access* to all long-distance phone companies, and AT&T had no special priority with its newly divested BOCs. AT&T kept some of the *Bell Labs* research facility and the *Western Electric* manufacturing facility, which produces central office switches, PBXs, and other telephone equipment. A new company, known as *Bell Communications Research*, or *Bellcore*, was formed to act as a research and administrative services company for the newly formed BOCs.

As a result of divestiture, AT&T, often referred to as Ma Bell, was split into many so-called Baby Bells. To allow the newly divested BOCs to remain efficient and achieve economies of scale, they were allowed to group together to form *Regional Holding Companies* (*RHCs*) or *Regional Bell Operating Companies* (*RBOCs*). Figure 2-6 presents a chart of the newly formed BOCs and RBOCs just after divestiture. The RBOCs, in addition to owning their BOCs, could enter other businesses, though they initially could not manufacture equipment or provide long-distance service. Some of the RBOCs have merged since divestiture, and this aspect will be discussed later in this chapter.

As part of the divestiture settlement, each BOC divided itself into several *local access and transport areas*, or *LATAs*. The BOC is responsible for providing customers with access to the public network, and it may also transport calls placed inside the LATA. When a call's destination is outside the LATA, the BOC must only transport the call to the *point of presence*, or *POP*, of a long-distance carrier. This POP is located inside the LATA, and it is the long-distance carrier's responsibility to transport the call to its destination in another LATA. Hence, the BOC's two main functions within its LATA are local access and local transport.

A LATA is usually centered around a major metropolitan area. For example, there is a LATA for the entire San Francisco Bay Area, including the cities of San Fran-

RBOC	BOC	States
Ameritech	Illinois Bell Telephone	Illinois
	Indiana Bell Telephone	Indiana
	Michigan Bell Telephone	Michigan
	Ohio Bell Telephone	Ohio
	Wisconsin Bell	Wisconsin
Bell Atlantic	Bell Telephone of Pennsylvania	Pennsylvania
	Chesapeake & Potomac	Maryland
		Virginia
		Washington, D.C.
		West Virginia
	Diamond State Telephone	Delaware
	New Jersey Bell Telephone	New Jersey
BELLSOUTH	South Central Bell Telephone	Alabama
		Kentucky
		Louisiana
		Mississippi
		Tennessee
	Southern Bell Telephone	Florida
		Georgia
		North Carolina
		South Carolina
NYNEX	New England Telephone	Connecticut
		Maine
		Massachusetts
		New Hampshire
		Rhode Island
		Vermont
	New York Telephone	New York
Pacific Telesis	Nevada Bell	Nevada
	Pacific Bell	California
Southwestern Bell	Southwestern Bell Telephone	Arkansas
		Kansas
		Missouri
		Oklahoma
		Texas
U S WEST	Mountain Bell	Arizona
		Colorado
		Idaho
		Montana
		New Mexico
		Utah
		Wyoming
	Northwestern Bell	Iowa
		Minnesota
		Nebraska
		North Dakota
		South Dakota
	Pacific Northwest Bell	Oregon
		Washington

FIGURE 2-6   RBOCS and BOCS afer divestiture.

cisco, Oakland, and San Jose, spanning many different area codes, including 415, 650, 510, 707, 408 and others. Most of this LATA is served by Pacific Bell, a BOC.

INTRA-LATA CALL ROUTING

If a customer in San Jose places a call within his or her own central office, the call routing is fairly simple. As shown in Fig. 2-7, parties 1 and 2 are both connected to the same central office. Party 1 picks up the phone, waits for the dial tone, and then dials party 2's phone number. The central office looks at the first three digits of the phone number and determines that the called party is in this central office. The central office then checks

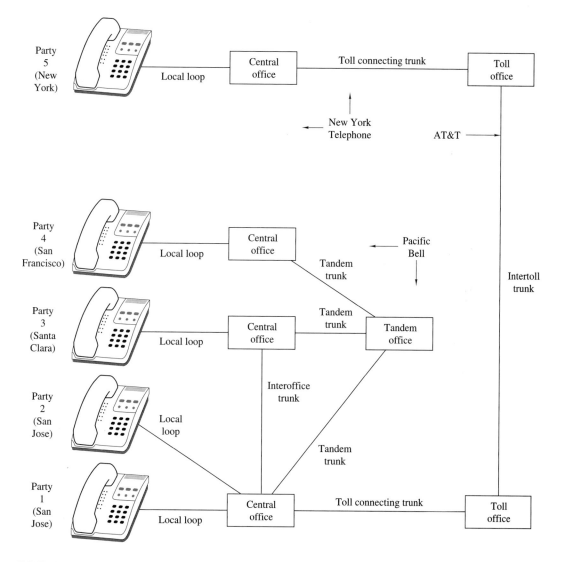

FIGURE 2-7   Call routing.

to see if party 2 is already on the phone. If party 2 is already on the phone, the central office sends party 1 a busy signal. If party 2 is not on the phone, the central office sends party 1 a ringing tone and sends a special voltage to party 2's phone, causing it to ring. This call is placed entirely through Pacific Bell lines and offices.

The central office knows that party 2 is one of its customers because it knows which *office codes* are in its territory. As an example, in the phone number 555-1234, 555 is the *office code*, or *prefix*, and 1234 pinpoints the particular customer in that office code. A central office may have several office codes for its customers.

Suppose that party 1 calls party 3 in Fig. 2-7. Party 3 lives in Santa Clara, another city in the 408 area code and within party 1's LATA, but in a different central office. In this case, the San Jose central office recognizes that the call is destined for the Santa Clara central office by examining the office code. The San Jose central office routes the call to the Santa Clara central office over an *interoffice trunk*, or *IOT*. A *trunk* is another name for a line connecting two switches; an interoffice trunk connects two central office switches in a local area. In this case, the call is routed over party 1's local loop, through one central office, over an interoffice trunk, to another central office, and finally, to party 3's local loop. This call is placed entirely through Pacific Bell lines and offices.

Area codes, which were in use long before divestiture and the concept of LATAs, have nothing to do with whether a call is local or long distance. They represent a certain geographical area, usually determined by the population in that area. Sometimes an area code covers an entire state, as in Wyoming (307). In the case of a large city, multiple area codes are sometimes required, as in New York City (212, 718, and others).

The proliferation of area codes in North America is partly due to the increase in use of cellular phones, pagers, fax machines, and modems, all of which require additional numbers that use up the capacity in a given area code. In addition, with the advent of increased competition among local carriers, large blocks of numbers are assigned to each carrier. A carrier with only a handful of customers might use thousands of phone numbers, because limitations in the existing installed carrier equipment require the allocation of numbers to carriers in large blocks, no matter how few customers a carrier may have. The creation of new area codes is expected to continue in North America for many years, until extra digits will need to be added to the current 10-digit numbering scheme to allow for the addition of new numbers. When new area codes are added, in some cases existing area codes are split geographically, with customers in some locations assigned to new area codes and customers in other locations retaining their old area codes. In other cases, an *overlay* area code is created. In this case, the same geographic area is covered by multiple area codes. Existing customers retain the old area code, but new phone lines on the same block, or even in the same house, may receive a number in the new area code. Although this method has the advantage of minimizing the changes in existing phone numbers, it may require people to dial ten or more digits to reach a number across the street.

Even though area codes affect the numbers we need to dial to reach a particular party, they do not alter the routing process. A call is routed based on whether it is in the LATA or outside the LATA, regardless of area code. Suppose that party 1 in San Jose, within the 408 area code, calls party 4 in San Francisco, as illustrated in Fig. 2-7. This is a call to the 415 area code, but it is still within the San Francisco Bay Area LATA. Party 1 dials the number, and the San Jose central office examines the area code and office code and determines that the destination is a Pacific Bell central office in San Francisco, in the same LATA. Instead of running trunks from every central office in a LATA to every other central office, the local phone company can run *tandem trunks* from all of the central offices into a *tandem office*, as shown in Fig. 2-7. In this case, party 1's call is routed over his or her local loop, through the San Jose central office, through a Pacific Bell tandem office, through the San Francisco central office, and over party 4's local loop. Once again, all of this call routing is done over Pacific Bell equipment and lines in a fraction of a second, and Pacific Bell will bill the customer for the call.

Calls inside a LATA, or intra-LATA calls, are not necessarily what we think of as local calls. The local phone company may label some intra-LATA calls covering great distances as *toll calls*, but they are not true long-distance calls, because they are still intra-LATA. Initially, after divestiture, all intra-LATA calls were routed entirely over the local phone company's equipment, and were billed to the customer by the local phone company, without involving any long-distance carriers. Today, multiple carriers can handle intra-LATA calls in some LATAs.

One constant source of confusion is the fact that not all LATAs are served entirely by one local phone company. For example, in the LATA we have been describing, a group of customers in the town of Los Gatos is served by GTE, an independent phone company, while most of the rest of the San Francisco Bay Area LATA is served by Pacific Bell. In cases like these, the different local phone companies cooperate to ensure that customers receive the same service that a single company would provide.

INTER-LATA CALL ROUTING

What happens when party 1 wants to call a number outside his or her LATA? This is an *inter-LATA*, or *long-distance, call*, and a long-distance carrier must enter the call-routing process. Before divestiture, the call usually would have been placed over AT&T lines. Since divestiture and the advent of equal access, customers are free to choose their long-distance carriers. Figure 2-8 lists some of the long-distance carriers that entered the market for inter-LATA calls after divestiture.

Telephone customers with equal access choose a particular carrier to be their standard, or *default*, long-distance company, through a process known as *presubscription*. Whenever the customer dials an inter-LATA call, the call will be automatically routed over the presubscribed carrier unless the customer dials a special code.

In most areas, a customer must dial a 1 before placing calls to another area code. The presence or absence of this requirement does not affect equal access. Dialing a 1

Carrier	Access code
AT&T	1010288
Allnet/Frontier	1010444
MCI Worldcom	1010222
Sprint	1010333
Telecom* USA (MCI Worldcom)	1010321

FIGURE 2-8   A sampling of long distance carriers after divestiture.

Note: Not all carriers serve all areas, and access codes may vary.

plus the phone number still routes the call over the presubscribed carrier. Dialing a special code, in the format 10*xxxxx*, where *xxxxx* is the carrier code, routes the call over an alternative carrier. A list of carrier codes is also provided in Fig. 2-8. While these codes were initially 5 digits long, they were later lengthened to 7 digits to accommodate additional carriers.

A central office is connected to a long-distance carrier's office, known as a *toll office*, by a *toll connecting trunk*, or *TCT*. A long-distance carrier connects its toll offices all around the country with *intertoll trunks*, in much the same way that the local phone companies connect their central offices with interoffice trunks. Intertoll trunks are also often called *IXCs*, or *interexchange circuits*. Intertoll trunks that can carry many conversations simultaneously are known as *high-usage intertoll trunks*.

We will assume for our example that party 1 has presubscribed to AT&T for his or her long-distance service. Referring to Fig. 2-7, party 1, in San Jose, California, is calling party 5 in New York. This call is clearly outside the San Francisco Bay Area LATA. The call is routed over party 1's local loop, to the San Jose Pacific Bell central office, over a toll connecting trunk, and to an AT&T toll office in California. It is then routed across the country on an AT&T intertoll trunk, to an AT&T toll office in New York, over a toll connecting trunk, to a New York Telephone central office, and out over party 5's local loop. It will be the New York central office's responsibility to provide a busy signal or ringing tone, depending on whether or not party 5 is on the line.

This call routing involves three separate companies: 2 BOCs and one long-distance carrier. This is possible because there are very clear standards for the signaling that must take place between the different offices handling a call. These standards apply to all central offices and all long-distance carriers.

The Pacific Bell central office informs the AT&T toll office of the call originator and the call destination by special signaling. The long-distance company has the choice of billing the customer directly, billing through a third party, such as Pacific Bell, or even billing the customer's credit card. All of this call routing and signaling takes place in a few seconds. Long-distance calls take longer to go through than local calls because these signals have to be passed through many different offices and switches.

Though our example assumes an intertoll trunk between San Jose and New York, this is not necessarily the case. The long-distance carrier is free to route the call to New York through whichever cities it wishes, just as an airline may require passengers traveling between those cities to change planes in Chicago. The long-distance carrier might run all of its trunks into Chicago, routing all calls through a national switching center there. Typically, this routing is done regionally, with several switching centers spread out all over the country. There is an entire hierarchy involving regional and area toll offices, but we won't consider it here because it does not directly affect the customer. In our example, Pacific Bell routes the call to AT&T, and it becomes AT&T's responsibility to get the call to New York using any route it wishes.

REGULATION

Companies that provide voice and data communications transmission services to the general public are known as *common carriers*. These include the local phone companies and the long-distance companies. These common carriers must file *tariffs* for all services they offer with the appropriate regulating bodies. A tariff describes a particular service in detail, along with the rate charged for that service. In some cases, the regulating body may reject a particular tariff—for example, if it feels that the rates are too high.

The *FCC*, or *Federal Communications Commission*, is responsible for regulating all interstate communications in the United States. Thus, the FCC regulates calls that are inter-LATA and interstate, as well as the few calls that are intra-LATA and interstate (where LATAs cross state lines).

Each state has a *PUC*, or *public utilities commission*, responsible for regulating all intrastate phone service. The PUCs regulate all local phone service, all intra-LATA/intrastate calls, and all inter-LATA/intrastate calls.

Each regulating agency reviews and approves tariffs filed for services in its jurisdiction. Since the local phone companies have a basic monopoly on providing phone service within their communities, PUCs are likely to scrutinize rate increases very carefully. The FCC, on the other hand, may allow the long-distance carriers more leeway in pricing new and innovative services, since consumers have equal access to all carriers and can choose the services they prefer.

National issues affecting all of the RBOCs are typically addressed by the FCC. In the postdivestiture environment, the FCC started to require that the RBOCs implement an *Open Network Architecture*, or *ONA*. With an ONA, the public network services are divided into *basic service elements*, or *BSEs*; customers can subscribe to any combination of the BSEs. For example, one BSE might be the ability to forward calls, while another might be conference calling. The customer could select either or both of these BSEs, but would not be forced to take both together as a package. By separating all of the public network's services into BSEs, an *enhanced service provider*, or *ESP*, would be guaranteed access to network services needed to perform special functions. For example, an answering service company is an ESP that would use the call forwarding BSE, combined with its staff of operators or answering machines, to provide a special, or enhanced, service to the customer.

Many countries have their own equivalent of the FCC, often known as a *PTT*, or *postal, telephone, and telegraph administration*. In some countries, the PTT regulates and runs the public network. This system would be the equivalent of the FCC owning, operating, and regulating the predivestiture AT&T, with all of its BOCs.

INCREASED COMPETITION

Divestiture was one of the most sweeping, dramatic changes in American telecommunications history. It unleashed competition in the long-distance industry, and within a decade, it became clear that the formula had worked. Long-distance rates had plummeted to less than 50% of what they had been during AT&T's domination of the market.

Unfortunately, in the process, consumers became increasingly confused with the rich variety of carriers and service options. This confusion may have slowed the continuing deregulation of the industry, but new impetus came from the cable television market.

Due to the increased penetration of cable television in the U.S. marketplace, customers became reliant on certain information sources, such as news and sports networks. Over time, some cable channels became an integral part of American society, and as cable rates increased, angry consumers pressured their government for rate reduction. The FCC, faced with the compelling evidence in the long-distance market, began to encourage competition in the cable industry and actively supported rate reductions.

New switching technologies that make it possible to deliver voice and video on the same network, combined with a trend towards deregulation, are laying the framework for competition between cable television and telecommunications companies. The merging of these technologies into a universal network is the foundation for the *information superhighway*, described in more detail in Chapter 10.

While the FCC and PUCs can generally set the pace for deregulation, the courts and the legislative branch can speed up this process. If traditional regulations continue to be discarded, there is nothing to prevent cable television companies and telecommunications companies from competing on an equal footing. Even within the telecommunications industry, the postdivestiture long-distance companies are offering local service in some areas, and local carriers would like to offer long-distance service. The *Telecommunications Act of 1996* started a new era in regulation, with specific restrictions imposed on phone companies and cable companies alike. Today, increased competition has resulted in several choices of local service for businesses in metropolitan areas. However, business customers outside of major service areas, and many residential customers, still have no choice when selecting a local carrier.

Though the pace of deregulation may vary over the years, it appears unstoppable. Certain regulations will probably remain to guarantee availability and quality of service as well as appropriate standards to protect consumers in terms of fair billing and business practices. Mergers among the original RBOCs, like that between Pacific Telesis and Southwest Bell and between NYNEX and Bell Atlantic, are some examples of consolidation in the industry. While the Telecommunications Act of 1996 placed firm restrictions on mergers between cable companies and local telephone companies, cable companies are free to merge with long-distance carriers. The TCI and AT&T merger is one such example of a combination that may pose a powerful force in the coming decade. It is unlikely that the separation of the cable television and telecommunications industries will still be so well defined in the coming years, and the new combined industry should be dramatically less regulated than in the past.

VOICE COMMUNICATIONS SERVICE OFFERINGS

Many different communications services are available, particularly to the business community, which has large volumes of telephone traffic. One of these services is *WATS*, or *wide area telecommunications services*. WATS is a bulk-rate, long-distance service for users with high call volumes. Traditionally, WATS pricing was done in bands: The United States was divided into several bands, or zones, and the customers paid a per-hour cost for calls to each zone. A California business that placed a lot of calls to the West Coast but very few to the East could subscribe to WATS only for the West Coast bands.

Since divestiture, many long-distance carriers offer services labeled as WATS with different characteristics. Some are simply volume discounts regardless of zone; others are more complex, offering discounts to certain area codes and office codes at certain times. The only safe generalization that can be made about a postdivestiture WATS line is that it offers some discounts for volume long-distance users.

A type of WATS service, *inward-WATS*, is known to most of us as a *toll-free number*, or an *800 number* or *888 number*. The customer agrees to pay for all incoming long-distance calls from certain areas, but at the reduced WATS rates. Another service, known as a *foreign exchange*, is used by a business that wants a phone number in a city other than the one where its offices are located. The business pays a fixed rate for the service, in addition to a mileage charge to the distant area. Calls to and from its customers in that area can then be made at local call rates.

Another way for businesses to save on communications costs is to use *leased lines* to locations they call frequently. A leased line is a permanent connection from one point to another provided by common carriers. In a sense, it is a phone call that never hangs up. The carrier only has to route the call once; after that, all the customer is really renting is a pair of wires from one point to another, along with some amplifying equipment and power. Leased-line services are generally priced by the mile. Whether the line is used frequently or not at all, the monthly price is still the same, because that line has been reserved for the exclusive use of the customer.

For example, a corporation with offices in Santa Clara, California, and Austin, Texas, may discover that it is making many long-distance calls between the two facilities. Rather than continue to pay per-minute rates on the dial-up network, or even per-hour rates through WATS, the customer can opt to lease lines. Leasing lines becomes economical surprisingly fast, often after a few dozen hours of use per month. If the business has an advanced phone system that ensures that the leased lines are used wherever appropriate, the economic benefit is almost guaranteed.

When we pick up our home phone and dial a number, we are accessing the dial-up network. It's up to the common carriers to route our call to the appropriate destination, but we have no control over what route the call takes. Furthermore, every time we place a call to the same number, it may take a slightly different route, depending on what facilities the carriers have available at that instant. This system explains why sometimes we get a good connection and other times the other party is barely audible.

One of the key attributes of the dial-up network is that the flexible routing of calls allows for very high reliability in making connections. For example, a call from San Jose to New York might normally go over a transcontinental intertoll trunk, but if that line is currently out of service, the call could be routed through Chicago. However, with this high reliability in making connections comes the uncertainty of whether or not our next connection will be of high quality.

Leased lines, however, can consistently assure high-quality connections. When a leased line is installed, it must meet a certain specification, such as *voice grade*, suitable for voice communications and most data communications. The customer can even demand a special leased line suitable for high-speed data transmission, known as a *conditioned* leased line. There is an extra charge for the hardware required to meet this improved specification.

A leased-line customer, however, is vulnerable to a service outage on that line's particular wire and hardware. If the line is down, the telephone network will not automatically reroute the call. Either the line must be repaired, another line installed, or a backup call placed on the dial-up network.

The choice boils down to the high reliability and questionable quality of the dial-up network versus the questionable reliability and high quality of a leased line. Of course, the application and priorities of each customer determine which solution is appropriate.

There are many ways to provide leased-line services in higher volumes and at lower costs. These methods include T-1 carrier, satellite, microwave, and fiber optics. We consider these high-volume transmission options in Chapter 4.

ECHO SUPPRESSORS AND CANCELLERS

The dial-up telephone network is equipped with a variety of devices to help stop echoes during normal conversation. The nature of telephone transmission causes some signals to bounce back from the receiving telephone, just as our voices bounce off a canyon's walls and return to our ears.

On a local call, we don't even notice the echo. That is because the party we are talking to is within a few miles of us, and our voice travels at the speed of electricity (almost 300 million meters per second). Our echo returns to our earpiece so quickly that it doesn't even seem to be an echo; it sounds as if the telephone is simply amplifying our voice in the earpiece.

However, long-distance connections can span many thousands of miles. It may take an echo a half second to complete its round-trip back to your telephone. An echo a half second after we have said something is very disconcerting. Several different devices are in use today to help eliminate echoes, including *echo suppressors* and *echo cancellers*.

Echo suppressors work by allowing only a one-way communications path. As soon as we start talking, the path from the other person to us is cut off. If our voice echoes back, it is not transmitted. If the other person begins speaking louder than we do, he or she gets control of the line. This system works well for normal conversation; when we stop talking and the other person begins, his or her voice takes over. If the other person interrupts us midsentence, he or she probably is speaking louder than we are, so we hear him or her. The echo suppressor hears the volume difference and gives the other person the line. Since echoes are going to be softer than the original voice, an echo on the rebound never takes control of the line. Echo suppressors are shown at work in Fig. 2-9.

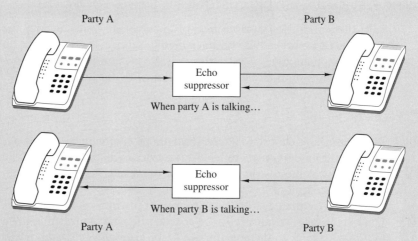

FIGURE 2-9   Echo suppressors.

Echo cancellers are more sophisticated devices. They allow a continuous two-way conversation, but are able to remove your own echo before it returns to your telephone. Echo cancellers are a sophisticated version of acoustical ceiling tiles used to absorb noise. The difference is that echo cancellers are able to detect the difference between true conversation and an echo and selectively absorb only the echo.

Most long-distance carriers install either echo suppressors or cancellers at the end of their equipment. This equipment can be disabled on a particular call by using a special tone. This is useful for certain data communications transmissions, which we review later.

TASI VS. VOICE CALL MULTIPLEXING

Long-distance carriers often combine several calls on the same intertoll trunk using one of two methods. The first method, known as *TASI*, or *time assignment speech interpolation*, allocates a communications path a few milliseconds after the caller begins to speak. This is not noticed during voice transmission, but is often damaging to data transmission, where a few lost milliseconds can result in the loss of precious data. The preferred method, known as *voice call multiplexing*, combines conversations without risking any loss of voice or data. Fortunately, most carriers today use the latter technique.

LEASING SERVICES VS. BUYING CUSTOMER-PREMISES EQUIPMENT

Regardless of the size of a business or the diversity of its telecommunications require-ments, there is always the option of leasing services from others or owning them out-right. Equipment used at the customer's site is known as *customer-premises equipment*, or *CPE*. Many of us already own our own CPE: our home telephones.

CENTREX

Some businesses choose to let the local phone company handle all of their external and internal calls in the central office. This service is called *Centrex*, because the central of-fice is acting as the customer's exchange, or switch. A local loop connects every exten-sion to the central office. The central office interprets the numbers dialed in a special way for the Centrex customer. For example, if employee A in Fig. 2-10 dials the four-digit extension of employee B, the central office recognizes this call as an internal one and routes it back to the appropriate desk. If employee C dials a 9 and then his or her home phone number, the central office recognizes that it is an external call and grants the employee an outside dial tone, without any operator intervention.

Centrex gives a business the appearance of having its own phone system. Em-ployees dial internal calls just by dialing the last few digits of the phone number and don't usually realize that their call is going through the phone company's central office. Centrex is usually very dependable, because central office switches are highly reliable,

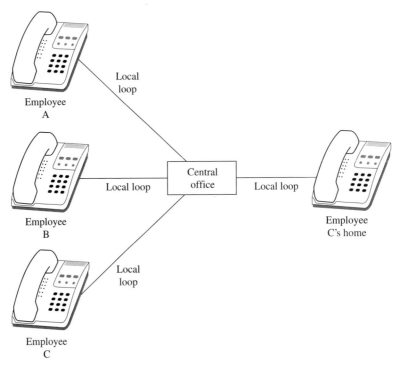

FIGURE 2-10 Centrex service.

with a full-time maintenance and troubleshooting staff. However, the customer must pay a fee for each Centrex line each month, in addition to per-call charges, just as we do for our home telephone service. With Centrex, the customer usually has the option of purchasing or renting the phone instruments.

Today's Centrex services can be tailored to offer some of the same advanced features previously found only in customer-owned systems. However, Centrex is by nature inefficient, since a call destined for a colleague's desk only 10 feet away must take a two-mile round-trip to the central office. In addition, the user relies on the phone company to perform most changes, such as moving telephone locations or changing extensions. Some customers, however, prefer Centrex because they don't have to purchase and maintain a phone system. They are willing to pay higher monthly fees to avoid the initial capital outlay required to purchase a phone system.

KEY SYSTEMS

For some small businesses, *key systems* may provide a suitable telecommunications solution. Early key systems were merely a collection of multiline phones connected with special wiring. These early key systems provided intercom functions, allowing customers to communicate internally over intercom lines. Any external calls were made over local loops.

Early key systems had little or no intelligence, and the user performed all functions manually by pushing the appropriate buttons. To place an external call on early key systems, the user pushed an external-line button on the phone. Similarly, internal conversations were initiated by pressing an intercom button. In addition, calls could be placed on hold using a hold button. Early key systems were limited to only a handful of telephone lines.

Today's key systems are more sophisticated, providing special features such as call forwarding and call transfer. Some of today's key systems can handle up to 150 users.

Key systems are usually compact and use standard electrical power. In addition, they can often be repaired by the customer. Key systems, and the phones attached to them, are usually purchased by the customer, though they can be leased.

Key systems eliminate the inefficiency of Centrex, since an internal call does not go to the central office. A key-system customer does not need a local loop for each telephone, only one for each outside line.

However, most key systems cannot provide many advanced features and are severely limited in their ability to grow beyond 150 lines. For these reasons, medium-sized to large businesses usually do not choose key systems. There is another alternative to Centrex for these customers.

PRIVATE BRANCH EXCHANGE

The *PBX*, or *private branch exchange*, is the most advanced customer-premises equipment telecommunications solution. A PBX acts as a mini–central office, dedicated not to an entire community or town, but to the customer that owns it. The lines running from the PBX to employees' phones are known as PBX *station lines*, and are owned by the customer, not the phone company. A PBX can often accommodate thousands of phones, enough to satisfy the needs of even the largest customers.

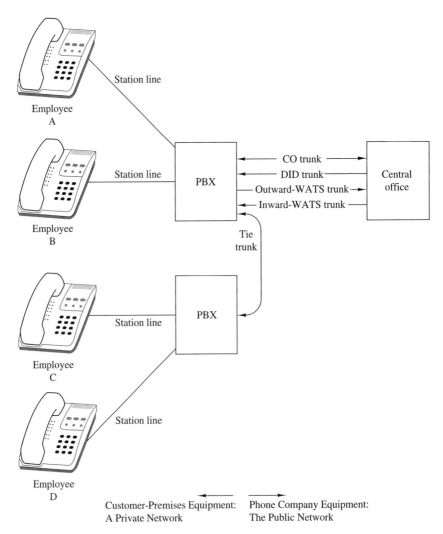

FIGURE 2-11   PBX call routing.

All internal calls are routed through the PBX and never go to the central office. If an employee places an external call, the PBX routes the call off the premises to the central office. For example, in Fig. 2-11, assume that employee A dials employee B. The PBX connects the two parties, and the entire connection is inside the customer's private network. Hence, there are no charges from the central office for this call. In fact, the local phone company doesn't know, or care, that the call took place, because its facilities were not used.

What about external calls? One advantage of a PBX is that a company does not need a local loop for each employee, because only a small percentage of employees make external calls at any given moment. In typical companies, one outside line for every 10 extensions might be sufficient. Special situations require more outside lines. For example, at an airline reservations center, employees spend a majority of their time answering incoming calls from outside lines. Every business has different requirements; the fewer outside lines needed, the more a PBX saves the customer in local loop costs.

We have already mentioned that two switches are connected together using a special type of line known as a trunk. PBXs, therefore, are connected to the central office using trunks. Several different types of PBX trunks are illustrated in Fig. 2-11. An employee gains access to those trunks by dialing a special code, like 9. The PBX can then select the appropriate trunk, based on the call's destination.

The *central office trunk* is the standard trunk used for all external intra-LATA calls and for calls that the central office routes to a long-distance carrier. Incoming calls over a central office trunk must be answered by the customer's *operator*, or *attendant*.

Customers that want incoming calls automatically routed to their employees' desks without going through an operator must rent *direct inward dial trunks*, or *DID trunks*, from the central office. On a DID trunk, the central office actually signals the PBX to which extension an incoming call is destined for, allowing the PBX to route it properly.

An *outward-WATS trunk* is a connection to a discounted long-distance service that we have already mentioned. An *inward-WATS trunk* is the PBX's connection for a *toll-free number*.

Finally, a *tie trunk* is used to connect two PBXs. These PBXs can be at the same or at different locations. An employee on one PBX can place a call to an employee on the other PBX, and it can be automatically routed over these tie trunks. Calls over the tie trunks incur no per call cost, since these lines are leased on a monthly basis.

Early PBXs provided a cost savings simply by reducing the number of local loops. Today's advanced PBXs are loaded with features, which are generally divided into two basic categories, system features and station features.

System features are functions performed and controlled for the entire system, such as voice messaging. A table of popular PBX system features is presented in Fig. 2-12. *Station features* are functions performed for and controlled by each individual user, such as call forwarding. A table of popular PBX station features is shown in Fig. 2-13. Although not all PBXs have all of these features, the system and station features presented in the figures are a representative sample of features provided by most advanced PBXs.

Many advanced PBXs are able to send calls over the least expensive route. This system feature, known as *least-cost routing*, or *route optimization*, has become increasingly sophisticated with the advent of equal access. An advanced PBX can be programmed with the rates of all of the long-distance carriers and can select the cheapest carrier for each call, based on the rate tables and the time of day. This feature can provide considerable cost savings and is often the main reason for purchasing a PBX instead of using Centrex services.

Almost all of today's advanced PBXs are *digital PBXs*. The ROLM CBX, or Computerized Branch Exchange, first installed in 1975, was the first computer-based digital PBX. Digital PBXs are actually computers that treat the telephones and trunks as specialized input and output devices.

Feature name	Function
Automatic call distribution (ACD)	Allows callers to be routed to a group of agents, with calls distributed evenly among all of them. Statistics are available on each agent, including the number of calls, duration, etc. Often used for customer service departments, airline reservationists, etc.
Call detail recording (CDR)	Provides records on each call placed out of the PBX, including the caller, the called party, the duration, time of day, etc. Allows a company to track its telephone costs by department or even by user. Further enhancements allow special account codes to be entered when placing a call to bill it to a particular client or project.
Class of service distinction (COS)	Allows users to be combined into different groups, each with access to different features, and each with different external calling capabilities.
Data switching	Available only on digital PBXs, it allows for switched digital pathways. This provides for sharing of resources, including host computers or modems, among many different terminal devices. Personal computers can also communicate with each other through data switching.
Direct inward dial (DID)	Callers from outside the company can dial directly to employees' desks, or station lines.
Direct inward system access (DISA)	Allows a user away from the office to dial the PBX, enter a special code, and then use the PBX for placing internal and external calls, exactly as if the person were at his or her desk.
Direct outward dial	Users can dial external calls directly, without going through the PBX operator.
Distinctive ringing	Different ring patterns can be provided for different calls. For example, internal calls can be indicated by a single ring; external calls, by two quick rings, etc.
Hunt groups	Allows phones in a department to be assigned to a special group. People calling the departmental number are routed to the first available person in the department's hunt group.
Intercom lines	Allows abbreviated dialing within a department, making it seem that each department has its own system.
Least-cost routing	Automatically routes all external calls over the cheapest route, including WATS lines, tie trunks, foreign exchanges, etc.
Music on hold	Provides a PBX connection to a music source so that callers placed on hold will know they are still connected.
Paging	Provides a PBX connection to a loudspeaker so that users can page someone by dialing a special code and speaking into the telephone.
Remote polling	The computers of the PBX manufacturer's service organization can telephone the PBX on a regular basis, and check the PBX's diagnostic information for any irregularities. A service technician can then be dispatched if necessary, often before the customer is even aware of any problem. In addition, call detail recording information can be collected from the PBX for further analysis.
Route optimization	Same as least-cost routing.
System speed dial	Allows a set of telephone numbers to be programmed into the system. Any system user can then automatically dial one of these numbers by entering a brief code.
Trunk queuing	Users placing an external call when all trunks are busy are queued, or put in line, for a trunk. With some systems the user can hang up, and the system will call back when a trunk is available.
Voice messaging	Provides automated call answering for phones left unattended or phones that are busy. Calls are usually answered by an attached voice messaging system that plays a greeting in the call receivers own voice and then offers several options. The caller can leave a message, which is stored in the system and can be retrieved by the user. Users are usually notified of messages through message waiting lights on their phones, or an interrupted dial tone, known as stutter, or a broken dial tone. Messages can usually be forwarded to other users.

FIGURE 2-12 Popular PBX system features.

Feature name	Function
Account codes	Allows users to key in a special code for each call, ensuring that each call is billed to it particular account. Accounts often represent clients or projects.
Buzz	Allows users to buzz each other as they would on an intercom system.
Camp-on	When a user encounters a busy signal on an internal call, he can camp-on. This is an automated version of waiting for the line to be free. With some systems, the user can hang-up and the system will call back when the called party is free.
Conference calls	Allows users to create telephone conferences, adding multiple users to each conversation.
Do not disturb	Allows users to block incoming calls. Callers receive a busy signal.
Executive override	Allows a high-priority user to interrupt the conversations of others in case of emergency or for urgent messages.
Forwarding	Allows users to forward their incoming calls to another user, or to voice messaging systems.
Hold	Allows users to place calls on hold.
Mute	Allows users to listen to callers without callers hearing them.
Park	Allows users to put calls in progress on hold at another person's extension. For example, a call answered at your desk can be parked at your colleague's desk. You can then go to your colleague's office, get some information, and pick up his phone, continuing your conversation.
Pick	Allows users to answer their phone from another person's desk.
Station speed dial	Allows users to program in their own set of frequently dialed phone numbers, which can later be dialed using a short code. This is similar to system speed numbers, but system speed numbers are preprograrnmed for the entire system.
Transfer	Allows users to transfer a call to other users.

FIGURE 2-13   Popular PBX station features.

One advantage of digital PBXs is their ability to provide a myriad of sophisticated features. In addition, these digital PBXs can use special digital telephones that allow the transmission of voice and data over a single telephone line. Some digital PBXs even have integrated terminals and telephones in a single unit. Further advantages of digital communications are discussed later in the book.

WIRELESS COMMUNICATIONS

The use of telephones and related equipment without cabling is often referred to as *wireless communications*. The simplest type of wireless communications exists in a conventional *cordless* telephone. These single-user devices utilize a handset that is a miniature radio, communicating with a base station connected to the telephone line. Certain radio frequencies, or channels, have been reserved for these devices. Most conventional cordless phones in use today can select from one of several channels to insure clear communications. New frequencies have been added as the use of these devices has increased. The transmission power is relatively low, so they are typically limited to only a few hundred feet in range and are very susceptible to noise.

Wireless communications are also used in the business environment, sometimes in conjunction with a PBX. A good example of this application is a large warehouse, where many employees are somewhere inside a specific building, but none stay in any specific office. If each employee were to carry a simple cordless phone, there might be insufficient range, and the phones would be constantly interfering with each other due to the small number of available channels. One approach to solving this problem involves setting up a series of intelligent base stations, each to cover a particular zone, or *cell*, inside the building. These base stations, and the special handsets that communicate with them, are very intelligent and can switch frequencies during conversations as needed to maintain a clear connection. The base stations are networked to each other, and often to a PBX, and the calls are switched from one base station to the next without the user's intervention. For example, a user can start a conversation through one base station, but as the user walks through the building, another base station senses that the user is nearby. This second base station communicates with the original base station and requests control of the call. The appropriate commands are sent between the two base stations and the handset to coordinate the almost instantaneous switching of the call to the new channel on the new base station. A user walking around the building is unaware of this switch of base stations, even though the connection may switch many times. In this way, users are guaranteed the best possible transmission at any point, because the system automatically switches them to the closest base station with an available channel.

In this example, a building is divided into several cells to create a private wireless communications system. Because these cells are small, this system is often called a *microcellular* phone system. When this technique is employed over a wider area by a commercial carrier and made available to the public, it is called a *cellular* phone system. In this case, the base stations are attached to antennas that may be several stories high, and the cells may cover several miles. The cellular service provider maintains the antennas and transmitters and links the cellular calls with the land-based telephone network. Some of the frequencies set aside for use in commercial cellular systems are assigned to each cell. Neighboring cells are assigned differing frequencies to avoid interfering with each other. Occasionally, users cannot place calls because there are no channels available in the cell they are in. When this begins to occur often, carriers usually add another transmitter with additional frequencies in that area, thereby dividing the original cell into two smaller cells.

In all of our wireless examples, we have assumed that a single frequency, or channel, can serve only one user. However, there are techniques available today for sharing a single channel among many users. The principles of wireless operation remains the same, but additional users can be handled by sharing channels.

Cellular phones, whether portable or vehicle mounted, are of much higher power than the microcellular phones described in the private warehouse application. Unfortunately, the added variables of terrain, weather conditions, large buildings, and other transmission sources all increase the noise on cellular connections. Traditional *analog cellular* phone systems cannot always solve these noise problems, and the noise decreases only if the user moves away from the noise source or is switched to another channel when approaching the next antenna. The two most popular analog cellular standards in use today are *AMPS* and *ETACS*. The *Advanced Mobile Phone Service*, or *AMPS*, was developed by Bell Labs in the 1970s and was first introduced in the U.S. market in 1983. It is still very popular in the United States, South America, Australia, and China. The *European Total Access Communication System*, or *ETACS*, was developed in the mid-1980s and is used throughout Europe. It is similar to AMPS, though there are some differences to accommodate the European phone numbering plan, as well as differences in the radio channels used for transmission.

Digital cellular phone systems that are now being used solve most of the analog systems' noise problems. We discuss other advantages of digital transmission in Chapter 4. The large investment in the installed analog cellular networks probably ensures their continued use in parallel with the newer digital networks. In the United States, the *United States Digital Cellular* standard, or *USDC*, was deployed in the 1990s to allow support of either AMPS or USDC transmission over the same radio channel range. This allowed for a gradual migration of customers from analog to digital by equipping the base stations with both standards. USDC is based on a technology known as *Time Division Multiple Access*, or *TDMA*, in which several conversations utilize a single channel by sharing transmission time on the channel. Its operation is similar in principal to time-division multiplexing, explained in detail in Chapter 5. Another digital cellular standard developed for use in the United States that also uses the same channels as the AMPS system is known as *Code Division Multiple Access*, or *CDMA*. In CDMA, voice signals are spread across many different channels, using a technology known as *spread spectrum*. While major metropolitan areas are equipped with both AMPS and TDMA or CDMA equipment, rural areas still rely on AMPS alone. *Dual-mode* cellular telephones have became popular; these phones first try to connect using the better digital standard (TDMA or CDMA), but fall back to the analog standard if no digital base station is satisfactorily reached.

Meanwhile, the *Global System for Mobile*, or *GSM*, standard was introduced in Europe during the 1990s. It does not try to reuse existing AMPS or ETACS channels; rather, it is an entirely new standard based solely on digital transmission and signaling. It has many advanced signaling features, including allowing the subscriber to insert a *Subscriber Identity Module*, or *SIM*, into any GSM phone. This module identifies the customer to the network, and all GSM calls for this customer are then routed to this handset. The SIM is often provided on a *smart card*, a credit-card-sized device programmed with unique identification and authentication information. A customer could insert this SIM into a hotel phone, a car phone, or a handheld phone, and incoming calls would automatically be routed to the correct location. In addition, outgoing calls from any of these locations would automatically be billed to the customer's account with his or her regular GSM carrier. These convenient features have led GSM to be deployed in numerous countries outside of Europe, with its introduction in many more countries expected in the coming years.

Some satellite-based wireless telephone systems have also been launched that allow practically universal coverage with a single network. These systems tend to be more costly than the land-based cellular systems described here. More details on satellite-based systems are found in Chapter 4. Data from mobile sources, such as laptop computers, can be routed over any of these cellular telephone networks. There are other considerations when trying to transmit data over a wireless network, as well as some special networks designed for data transmission alone. These wireless data transmission issues are discussed further in Chapter 8.

SUMMARY

Understanding the basics of telecommunications is the first step in studying data communications. There are many different network topologies, including mesh and star. The public network, or direct distance dial network, is a series of interconnected star networks. At the center of each star network is a central office, connected to the users by local loops. Users signal the central office of call destinations using rotary pulses or Touch-tones. The central office provides the user with other signals, including a dial tone, a ringback tone, and the busy and howler signals.

The divestiture of AT&T resulted in the formation of the Bell Operating Companies and Regional Bell Operating Companies, many of which have merged in the intervening years. There are also many long-distance carriers now competing for customers' business, all with equal access to the customer. The BOCs have divided their territory into local access and transport areas; routing inter-LATA calls involves interexchange carriers. There are many different trunks used to connect the various central offices and toll offices in the public network. The Federal Communications Commission regulates interstate calls, and the PUCs regulate intrastate calls. Internationally, many countries are regulated by PTTs. Increased competition and further deregulation appears inevitable.

Many voice service options are available to businesses, including outward-WATS, inward-WATS, and leased lines. Some businesses choose to lease basic telephone services by using their phone company's Centrex service. Key systems and private branch exchanges are both examples of customer-premises equipment that can be purchased. Many PBXs can handle thousands of lines and provide a variety of sophisticated features. A PBX can also help reduce a company's telecommunications costs by using the most efficient route. Today's digital PBXs will handle not only voice traffic, but data traffic as well. Wireless communications is an increasingly popular option. From a simple cordless phone to vast cellular phone systems, there are a variety of wireless options to meet users' needs. There are several analog and digital cellular systems in use throughout the world today.

TERMS FOR REVIEW

Advanced Mobile Phone Service	*Basic service element*	*BSE*
American Telephone & Telegraph	*Bell Communications Research*	*Busy signal*
AMPS	*Bell Labs*	*CDMA*
Analog cellular	*Bell Operating Company*	*Cell*
Area code	*Bell System*	*Cellular*
AT&T	*Bellcore*	*Central office*
Attendant	*BOC*	*Central office switch*
	Breakup	*Central office trunk*
		Centrex

Code Division Multiple
    Access
Common carrier
Conditioned line
Cordless
CPE
Customer-premises
    equipment
DDD network
Default
Dial tone
DID trunk
Digital Cellular
Digital PBX
Direct distance dial network
Direct inward dial trunk
Divestiture
DTMF
DTMF register
Dual tone multifrequency
    dialing
Echo canceller
Echo suppressor
800 number
888 number
End office
Enhanced service provider
Equal access
ESP
ETACS
European Total Access
    Communications System
FCC
Federal Communications
    Commission
Foreign exchange
Global System for Mobile
GSM
High-usage intertoll trunk
Howler signal
IEC
Independent Telephone
    Company
Information superhighway
Interexchange carrier
Interexchange circuit
Inter-LATA call

Interoffice trunk
Intertoll trunk
Inward-WATS trunk
IOT
ITC
IXC
Key system
LATA
Leased line
Least-cost routing
LEC
Local access and transport
    area
Local exchange
Local exchange carrier
Local loop
Long-distance call
Mesh network
MFJ
Microcellular
Modified Final Judgment
Network
Off-hook signal
Office code
ONA
On-hook signal
Open Network Architecture
Operator
Outward-WATS trunk
Overlay
PBX
Point of presence
POP
Postal, telephone, and
    telegraph administration
Prefix
Presubscription
Private branch exchange
PTT
Public network
Public utilities commission
PUC
Pulse dialing
RBOC
Regional Bell Operating
    Company
Regional Holding Company

RHC
Ringback signal
Ringing signal
Rotary dialing
Rotary register
Route optimization
Signaling
SIM
Smart card
Spread spectrum
Star network
Station feature
Station line
Subscriber Identity Module
Switch
System feature
Tandem office
Tandem trunk
Tariff
TASI
TCT
TDMA
Telecommunications
Telecommunications Act of
    1996
Tie trunk
Time assignment speech
    interpolation
Time Division Multiple
    Access
Toll call
Toll connecting trunk
Toll-free number
Toll office
Touch-tone dialing
Trunk
United States Digital Cellular
USDC
Voice call multiplexing
Voice-grade circuit
WATS
Western Electric
Wide area
    telecommunications
    services
Wireless

EXERCISES

2-1. Why is the public telephone network a star network rather than a mesh network?

2-2. What functions does a central office perform?

2-3. What are the common signals between the central office and the user during a typical telephone call?

2-4. Explain the differences between rotary and DTMF dialing methods.

2-5. What are the roles of the local exchange carriers and the interexchange carriers, respectively, in inter-LATA calls?

2-6. What is a tariff? What is the difference between the FCC and the PUCs? Which agencies review which tariffs?

2-7. Compare WATS service to leased lines. Which is more useful for a customer who always calls between the same two locations? What about for a customer who calls between many different locations but not often to any one location?

2-8. What are some ways for a business to enable an out-of-town customer to reach it via telephone at reduced cost or no cost? What about for calls from its own out-of-town factory?

2-9. What are the advantages and disadvantages of using the dial-up network versus leased lines?

2-10. Which equipment does the customer provide with Centrex service? What does the local exchange carrier provide?

2-11. What makes Centrex service inherently inefficient?

2-12. How does a PBX's method of handling internal calls differ from Centrex service? How does this affect the customer's central office charges?

2-13. Compare the different types of PBX trunks.

2-14. What is the difference between PBX system features and PBX station features?

2-15. What is the main advantage of the route optimization feature found in advanced PBXs?

2-16. How does a conventional cordless phone differ from a cellular phone?

2-17. What standard is typically used for analog cellular phones in North America? In Europe?

CHAPTER 3

Basic Data Communications Concepts

DEFINING DATA COMMUNICATIONS

Data communications is usually defined as the exchange of digital information between two devices using an electronic transmission system. *Digital* information is another name for ones and zeroes. Therefore, a less formal definition of data communications is the art of sending ones and zeroes from one point to another.

To help illustrate basic data communications concepts, we begin by examining two devices that often need to communicate: host computers and terminals.

HOST COMPUTERS AND TERMINALS

A *host computer*, or *central processing unit* (*CPU*), is at the heart of any data communications network. The host computer can perform numerical calculations, store and retrieve data, and perform a variety of tasks known as *applications*. Examples of host computer *applications software* include word-processing programs, spreadsheets, accounting programs, and payroll programs.

There are many different types of host computers. *Mainframes* are host computers usually serving a large company. *Minicomputers* are host computers usually dedicated to a smaller set of users, perhaps a department or a division. *Microcomputers*, or *personal computers*, usually serve only one user. A *supercomputer* is an extremely fast mainframe dedicated to extensive mathematical calculations.

33

Many data communications networks allow host computers to exchange information with other locally or remotely located devices. One of these devices is known as a *terminal*. Other names for a terminal include *cathode ray tube (CRT)*, *video display terminal (VDT)*, and *display station*. Regardless of the name used, a terminal's basic function is to allow a user to communicate with a host computer. Terminals include a *keyboard* for entering information to be transmitted to the host computer and a *screen* for displaying information received from the host computer.

While some modern computer networks do not even contain terminals today, the simple connection between a terminal and a host computer serves as an ideal starting point for any discussion of basic data communications concepts. More advanced networks build on these concepts, so most of the material presented in the early chapters referring to these terminals will be applicable to the more advanced networks discussed in the later chapters.

Terminals are often classified in one of three ways: dumb, smart, or intelligent. A dumb terminal simply receives data from a host computer and displays it on its screen, and it is unable to modify or change the data it receives. Similarly, any data typed into the keyboard is sent directly to the host computer, without any major modifications by the terminal.

A *smart terminal* usually sends extra information to a host computer, in addition to what the user types. This additional information can include the terminal's address, or location, as well as special information to prevent errors from occurring. The host computer also sends similar information to the smart terminal, including specific instructions regarding when the terminal can send data. The smart terminal is smart enough to interpret these instructions and pass on any actual data to the user. We discuss the rules for smart-terminal communications in detail in Chapter 7.

The difference between an *intelligent terminal* and a smart terminal is very subtle. Intelligent terminals are just like smart terminals, but their behavior can be modified or programmed. After a smart terminal leaves the factory, it never changes its behavior and can never learn to perform new functions. An intelligent terminal can be programmed to perform new functions by many means, including special tapes, cartridges, diskettes, or keyboard commands, depending on the manufacturer.

BITS AND BYTES

Almost all computers and terminals, from the 300-dollar terminal to the multimillion-dollar computer, communicate by sending a series of ones and zeroes to each other. We call each one or zero a *bit* and a group of several (usually eight) ones and zeroes a *byte*. Terminals and computers use the *binary number system* to represent digital information. Readers who have not been exposed to the binary number system before, or who simply need a quick review, should refer to the appendix.

To help simplify our discussion, we first concentrate on dumb terminals. The dumb terminal in Fig. 3-1 is connected to a host computer. Each time the user hits a key on the keyboard, a series of bits is transmitted to the host computer. The host computer receives those bits and then determines which *character* they represent. Characters include letters of the alphabet, numbers, all punctuation marks, and special keys, such as Delete, used by different terminals.

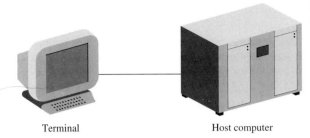

FIGURE 3-1   Terminal and host computer.

Terminal   Host computer

CHARACTER CODES

Each time a user strikes a particular key on the dumb terminal, the terminal must translate it into a series of bits, and the host computer must always recognize that series of bits as representing the same character. There are many ways to represent characters, and these different representations are known as *character codes*.

There are several different character codes in use today. We now examine in detail some of the more popular ones in order of their evolution: Morse, Baudot, EBCDIC, and ASCII.

MORSE CODE

Morse code is one of the first character codes developed. It is a crude, but effective, code for transmitting characters over a telegraph circuit. Morse code was designed with a telegraph operator in mind; the operator sent combinations of a short beep, known as a *dot*, and a long beep, known as a *dash*, to transmit characters. The characters used the most frequently need the fewest dots and dashes for transmission. A table of the Morse code is shown in Fig. 3-2.

Notice in Fig. 3-2 that the letter "A" consists of a dot and a dash, or a short beep followed by a long beep. Every time a telegraph operator sent "dot-dash," the receiving operator knew that the letter "A" was being transmitted. Notice that the letter "R"

A	• —	N	— •	1	• — — — —
B	— • • •	O	— — —	2	• • — — —
C	— • — •	P	• — — •	3	• • • — —
D	— • •	Q	— — • —	4	• • • • —
E	•	R	• — •	5	• • • • •
F	• • — •	S	• • •	6	— • • • •
G	— — •	T	—	7	— — • • •
H	• • • •	U	• • —	8	— — — • •
I	• •	V	• • • —	9	— — — — •
J	• — — —	W	• — —	0	— — — — —
K	— • —	X	— • • —	.	• — • — • —
L	• — • •	Y	— • — —	,	— — • • — —
M	— —	Z	— — • •	?	• • — — • •

FIGURE 3-2   Morse code.

starts out just like the letter "A" but then adds an extra dot at the end. How would the operators distinguish between the letter "A" (dot-dash) followed by the letter "E" (dot) and the letter "R" alone (dot-dash-dot)? Morse code handled this problem by requiring the operator to pause for a short time between letters. "AE" became "dot-dash-pause-dot," and the letter "R" was "dot-dash-dot."

One of the features that makes Morse code unsuitable for computer communications is the extra time required between characters. Why waste the time of an expensive computer by pausing between characters? The small number of different characters that can be transmitted in Morse code is also severely limiting. Clearly, other character codes needed to be developed for computer communications.

BAUDOT CODE

Baudot code is one of the first character codes developed with machines, and not humans, in mind. Baudot code uses ones and zeroes, rather than dots and dashes, to represent characters.

Baudot code addressed the shortcomings of Morse code by using five bits of information for each character. The Baudot code table is presented in Fig. 3-3. As shown in the table, we number the bits in the Baudot character code with the bit on the far left as bit 5 and the bit on the far right as bit 1.

Let's begin by examining the *Lower Case* column in this table. If a user types the letter "A" on a terminal that communicates using Baudot code, the terminal sends five bits, 00011, as shown on the first line of our chart. Assuming that the host computer receiving 00011 also uses the Baudot code, it will then recognize 00011 as the letter "A". Similarly, if the user types the letter "B", 11001 will be transmitted; if the user types the letter "C", 01110 will be transmitted, and so on, as shown in the Baudot table.

What if the user types the number "3"? Notice that the number "3" is in the *Upper Case* column of our chart. The Baudot terminal must now switch to Upper Case to send the number "3". Much as one would hit the Shift Lock key on a typewriter, the terminal sends a special code to the host computer, 11011, to instruct it to switch to Upper Case. This code, known as the *Figures* code, instructs the host computer that all further transmissions will be from the Upper Case column of the chart. In this instance, Upper Case doesn't mean capital letters, but rather a whole new set of characters. Once the host computer has been alerted that future characters are from the Upper Case column, the terminal can send the number "3" by sending 00001.

When the user later strikes a key from the Lower Case column, the terminal will send the *Letters* code, 11111, which instructs the host computer that future transmissions are from the Lower Case column again. This is equivalent to releasing the Shift Lock key on a typewriter.

In addition to the Letters and Figures characters, there are two additional special characters: the *line feed* and *carriage return* characters. A line feed, when sent to a terminal, causes the terminal to advance one line, and a carriage return moves the print head (or cursor) back to the left margin.

Baudot code was used for many years on telex equipment, and some teletype machines still use this code. In fact, the punched tape so familiar to teletype users is a di-

Character		Data bits				
Lower case	Upper case	5	4	3	2	1
A	—	0	0	0	1	1
B	?	1	1	0	0	1
C	:	0	1	1	1	0
D	$	0	1	0	0	1
E	3	0	0	0	0	1
F	!	0	1	1	0	1
G	&	1	1	0	1	0
H	#	1	0	1	0	0
I	8	0	0	1	1	0
J	'	0	1	0	1	1
K	(	0	1	1	1	1
L	)	1	0	0	1	0
M	.	1	1	1	0	0
N	,	0	1	1	0	0
O	9	1	1	0	0	0
P	0	1	0	1	1	0
Q	1	1	0	1	1	1
R	4	0	1	0	1	0
S	BELL	0	0	1	0	1
T	5	1	0	0	0	0
U	7	0	0	1	1	1
V	;	1	1	1	1	0
W	2	1	0	0	1	1
X	/	1	1	1	0	1
Y	6	1	0	1	0	1
Z	"	1	0	0	0	1
Letters (shift to Lower case column)		1	1	1	1	1
Figures (shift to Upper case column)		1	1	0	1	1
Space		0	0	1	0	0
Carriage return		0	1	0	0	0
Line feed		0	0	0	1	0
Blank		0	0	0	0	0

FIGURE 3-3   Baudot code.

rect representation of Baudot code. There are five positions across the punch tape; a hole in the tape represents a one, and no hole represents a zero.

Occasionally, a bit is changed during data transmission. We call this a *bit error*. In Baudot code, there is no way in which the receiving device can tell that a bit error occurred during transmission. The need for *error detection* led to an improvement on the Baudot code known as *International Baudot*. International Baudot adds a sixth bit, known as a *parity bit*, to check for errors. We explain in detail how parity bits work in Chapter 6. Simply stated, a parity bit is an extra bit transmitted in addition to the character code bits. It allows the data to be checked for errors at the receiving end.

The five information bits of Baudot code yield 32 different combinations of ones and zeroes. To represent more than 32 characters, the Letters and Figures characters shift the user into different transmission and reception modes (Upper and Lower Case). Switching back and forth between Upper and Lower Case wastes a computer's time.

For this reason, Baudot code is not often used for high-speed data communications. Later character codes remedied this problem.

EXTENDED BINARY CODED DECIMAL INTERCHANGE CODE

Extended Binary Coded Decimal Interchange Code, known as *EBCDIC*, is an eight-bit character code developed by IBM (International Business Machines Corporation). EBCDIC is a descendant of several older codes, including *Binary Coded Decimal*, or *BCD*, an early code used by computers to represent information internally. BCD led to the development of *Extended Binary Coded Decimal*, or *EBCD*, and finally to EBCDIC.

The eight bits of EBCDIC offer 256 different possible combinations of ones and zeroes. Most EBCDIC implementations, however, do not utilize all of the possible combinations. One EBCDIC implementation is presented in Fig. 3-4. Empty spaces in the chart can be used for other characters and functions needed for other implementations, including foreign language and graphics characters. We number the bits in EBCDIC with the bit on the far left as bit 0 and the bit on the far right as bit 7. To read the EBCDIC chart, simply find a particular character; bits 0, 1, 2, and 3 are found on the left end of the row, and bits 4, 5, 6, and 7 are found at the top of the column.

If a user types the letter "A" on an EBCDIC terminal, the bits 11000001 are transmitted, as shown in Fig. 3-4. Similarly, typing the letter "B" causes 11000010 to be transmitted, typing the letter "C" causes 11000011 to be transmitted, and so on, as shown in the EBCDIC table. There are many special characters in EBCDIC; the abbreviations of those characters relevant to our discussion are also explained in Fig. 3-4. Certain characters, such as the line feed character, simply control printers and terminals. Others, such as the Start of Header (SOH) character, are used extensively in special communications protocols. These special characters are discussed in detail in Chapter 7.

In most cases, EBCDIC is used without parity bits. Usually, groups of EBCDIC characters are sent together, in blocks, and an entire block of characters is checked for errors at once. This technique is explained in detail in Chapter 6. Some variations of EBCDIC do add a ninth bit for parity checking, though in most cases, this bit is removed before transmission.

AMERICAN NATIONAL STANDARD CODE FOR INFORMATION INTERCHANGE

American National Standard Code for Information Interchange, known as *ASCII*, is a seven-bit data code with a single additional parity bit. ASCII (pronounced as-key) was developed by the *American National Standards Institute*, or *ANSI*, as a general-purpose character code. The ASCII table is presented in Fig. 3-5. The seven data bits of ASCII offer 128 different possible combinations of ones and zeroes. We number the bits in ASCII with the bit on the far left as bit 8 and the bit on the far right as bit 1. Bit 8 is the parity bit, and bits 1 through 7 are the data bits.

If a user types the letter "A" on an ASCII terminal, the seven data bits transmitted are 1000001, as shown in Fig. 3-5. Similarly, typing the letter "B" causes 1000010 to be transmitted, typing the letter "C" causes 1000011 to be transmitted, and so on, as shown in the ASCII table. In addition to these seven data bits, a parity bit usually is transmitted.

	4	0	0	0	0	0	0	0	0	1	1	1	1	1	1	1	1
	5	0	0	0	0	1	1	1	1	0	0	0	0	1	1	1	1
Bit	6	0	0	1	1	0	0	1	1	0	0	1	1	0	0	1	1
	7	0	1	0	1	0	1	0	1	0	1	0	1	0	1	0	1
0 1 2 3																	
0 0 0 0	NUL	SOH	STX	ETX	PF	HT	LC	DEL				VT	FF	CR	SO	SI	
0 0 0 1	DLE	DC1	DC2	DC3	RES	NL	BS	IL	CAN	EM			IFS	IGS	IRS	IUS	
0 0 1 0			FS		BYP	LF	EOB	PRE			SM			ENQ	ACK	BEL	
0 0 1 1			SYN		PN	RS	UC	EOT					DC4	NAK		SUB	
0 1 0 0	SP										¢	.	<	(	+	|	
0 1 0 1	&										!	$	*	)	;	¬	
0 1 1 0	-	/									¦	,	%	_	>	?	
0 1 1 1											\	:	#	@	'	=	"
1 0 0 0		a	b	c	d	e	f	g	h	i							
1 0 0 1		j	k	l	m	n	o	p	q	r							
1 0 1 0		~	s	t	u	v	w	x	y	z							
1 0 1 1																	
1 1 0 0	{	A	B	C	D	E	F	G	H	I							
1 1 0 1	}	J	K	L	M	N	O	P	Q	R							
1 1 1 0			S	T	U	V	W	X	Y	Z							
1 1 1 1	0	1	2	3	4	5	6	7	8	9						□	

Note: To read this chart, simply find the character on the chart, then look to the left side of the row for bits 0, 1, 2, and 3, and to the top of the column for bits 4, 5, 6, and 7. This is only one of many possible implementations of EBCDIC.

EBCDIC special characters								
ACK	Acknowledgement	EOT	End of Transmission		PF	Punch Off		
BEL	Bell	ETX	End of Text		PN	Punch On		
BS	Backspace	FF	Form Feed		PRE	Prefix		
BYP	Bypass	FS	File Separator		RES	Restore		
CAN	Cancel	HT	Horizontal Tab		RS	Reader Stop		
CR	Carriage Return	IFS	Information File Separator		SI	Shift In		
DC1	Device Control 1	IGS	Information Group Separator		SM	Start Message		
DC2	Device Control 2	IL	Idle		SO	Shift Out		
DC3	Device Control 3	IRS	Information Record Separator		SOH	Start of Heading		
DC4	Device Control 4	IUS	Information Unit Separator		SP	Space		
DEL	Delete	LC	Lower Case		STX	Start of Text		
DLE	Data Link Escape	LF	Line Feed		SUB	Substitute		
EM	End of Medium	NAK	Negative Acknowledgement		SYN	Synchronous Idle		
ENQ	Enquiry	NL	New Line		UC	Upper Case		
EOB	End of Block	NUL	Null		VT	Vertical Tab		

FIGURE 3-4 EBCDIC code.

There are several *control characters* in ASCII, similar to those used in EBCDIC, and their abbreviations are also explained in Fig. 3-5. Some of these characters, known as *format effectors* (*FE*), perform special display functions on printers and terminals. Other characters, known as *information separators* (*IS*), are used by host computers in storing and retrieving data. Finally, another group of characters, known as *control codes* (*CC*), are used in protocols that we examine in detail in Chapter 7.

Some manufacturers of terminals and host computers have chosen to use their own modified versions of ASCII. Such versions, often known as *extended ASCII*, replace the parity bit with an eighth data bit. This substitution allows for 256 combinations of ones and zeroes, doubling the number of characters that can be represented. Such an extension of the character set allows unusual characters, including foreign language

Bits 7654321	Character	Bits 7654321	Character	Bits 7654321	Character	Bits 7654321	Character
0000000	NUL	0100000	SP	1000000	@	1100000	`
0000001	SOH	0100001	!	1000001	A	1100001	a
0000010	STX	0100010	"	1000010	B	1100010	b
0000011	ETX	0100011	#	1000011	C	1100011	c
0000100	EOT	0100100	$	1000100	D	1100100	d
0000101	ENQ	0100101	%	1000101	E	1100101	e
0000110	ACK	0100110	&	1000110	F	1100110	f
0000111	BEL	0100111	'	1000111	G	1100111	g
0001000	BS	0101000	(	1001000	H	1101000	h
0001001	HT	0101001	)	1001001	I	1101001	i
0001010	LF	0101010	*	1001010	J	1101010	j
0001011	VT	0101011	+	1001011	K	1101011	k
0001100	FF	0101100	,	1001100	L	1101100	l
0001101	CR	0101101	-	1001101	M	1101101	m
0001110	SO	0101110	.	1001110	N	1101110	n
0001111	SI	0101111	/	1001111	O	1101111	o
0010000	DLE	0110000	0	1010000	P	1110000	p
0010001	DC1	0110001	1	1010001	Q	1110001	q
0010010	DC2	0110010	2	1010010	R	1110010	r
0010011	DC3	0110011	3	1010011	S	1110011	s
0010100	DC4	0110100	4	1010100	T	1110100	t
0010101	NAK	0110101	5	1010101	U	1110101	u
0010110	SYN	0110110	6	1010110	V	1110110	v
0010111	ETB	0110111	7	1010111	W	1110111	w
0011000	CAN	0111000	8	1011000	X	1111000	x
0011001	EM	0111001	9	1011001	Y	1111001	y
0011010	SUB	0111010	:	1011010	Z	1111010	z
0011011	ESC	0111011	;	1011011	[	1111011	{
0011100	FS	0111100	<	1011100	\	1111100		
0011101	GS	0111101	=	1011101	]	1111101	}
0011110	RS	0111110	>	1011110	^	1111110	~
0011111	US	0111111	?	1011111	—	1111111	DEL

FIGURE 3-5 ASCII code.

characters, accent marks, and graphic or scientific characters, to be represented in the second set of 128 characters. These extra characters come at the expense of the parity bit and its error detection capabilities, which we consider in Chapter 6.

EQUIPMENT COMPATIBILITY AND CHARACTER CODE COMPARISONS

We have introduced several different character codes with different bit lengths. Clearly, terminals using a particular character code are designed to connect to computers using that same code. But what about the user with a terminal that uses ASCII code and a host computer that uses EBCDIC code? *Code conversion* is required to connect devices using dissimilar character codes, and *protocol conversion* may be necessary as well. These functions are reviewed in more detail in Chapter 5.

Figure 3-6 shows the bit position differences among the various character codes. In most implementations, the lower numbered bit (usually 0 or 1) is transmitted first, followed by the other bits. Remember that the bit-numbering schemes used in the different codes are simply conventions followed in the industry to ensure that transmitting and receiving devices send and receive the bits in identical order. The "P" shown in bit 8 of the ASCII code represents the parity bit.

ASCII control characters			
BEL	Bell	EM	End of Medium
CAN	Cancel	ESC	Escape
DC1	Device Control 1	NUL	Null
DC2	Device Control 2	SI	Shift In
DC3	Device Control 3	SO	Shift Out
DC4	Device Control 4	SUB	Substitute
DEL	Delete		

Control codes			
ACK	Acknowledge	ETX	End of Text
DLE	Data Link Escape	NAK	Negative Acknowledge
ENQ	Enquiry	SOH	Start of Heading
EOT	End of Transmission	STX	Start of Text
ETB	End of Transmission Block	SYN	Synchronous Idle

Format effectors			
BS	Backspace	HT	Horizontal Tabulation
CR	Carriage Return	LF	Line Feed
FF	Form Feed	VT	Vertical Tabulation

Information separators			
FS	File Separator	RS	Record Separator
GS	Group Separator	US	Unit Separator

FIGURE 3-5   ASCII code (*continued*).

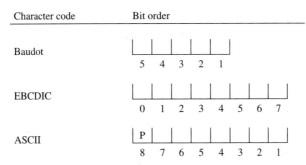

FIGURE 3-6   Bit position differences among various character codes.

Some typical data and parity bit combinations in the different character codes are compared in Fig. 3-7. Notice that there are variations in parity bit implementations even within a single character code. The most common implementation is presented first in each case. Some manufacturers may choose different parity schemes from those shown. Doing so, however, can render their proprietary versions of the character codes incompatible with the rest of the industry.

To the user, it is not really important which character code a terminal is using, as long as the host computer is able to understand the terminal. Character codes merely define exactly which sets of ones and zeroes are transmitted for each character. We now turn to other important data transmission issues.

Character code	Data bits	Parity bits	Total bits
Baudot	5	0	5
International Baudot	5	1	6
ASCII	7	1	8
	8	0	8
EBCDIC	8	0	8
	8	1	9

Note: This chart contains the most commonly used parity/data bit combinations. There are other possible variations.

FIGURE 3-7   Typical data and parity combinations for various character codes.

CHARACTER CODE DESIGN AND TERMINAL IMPLEMENTATION

The most advanced character codes we discussed, ASCII and EBCDIC, both include uppercase and lowercase letters. In the ASCII code chart in Fig. 3-5, notice that the letter "A" is represented by 1000001, while the letter "a" is represented by 1100001. Similarly, the letter "B" is represented by 1000010, and the letter "b" by 1100010. Throughout the alphabet, the only difference between an ASCII letter in lowercase and uppercase is in bit number 6. Uppercase letters have a 0 in bit 6, and lowercase letters have a 1 in bit 6.

This system simplifies the character code implementation on a terminal. Typically, a terminal user will press the shift key to send an uppercase character. Pressing the shift key on an ASCII terminal simply causes bit 6 to be sent as a 0 when another alphabetic key is struck; if the shift key is released, the terminal sends a 1 for bit 6 when another alphabetic key is struck. If the terminal has a Shift Lock or Caps Lock feature, using that feature sets bit 6 to be a 0 all the time.

Similarly, in EBCDIC, as shown in Fig. 3-4, the only difference between the letter "A" and the letter "a" is in bit 1. Uppercase letters in EBCDIC use a 1 in bit 1, and lowercase letters use a 0 in bit 1.

Many ASCII terminal users are familiar with a key known as the *control key*. Users can press the control key, and then hit another alphabetic key, to perform a special function. Pressing the control key causes bit 7 and bit 6 both to be 0.

One special character on the ASCII chart is the BEL character. Most ASCII terminals will sound a short beep when they receive this character. An ASCII terminal user pressing the control key and the "G" key simultaneously will send the BEL character. "G" is normally represented by 1000111, but the control key changes bits 6 and 7 to 0, resulting in 0000111, or the BEL character. Similarly, pressing the control key and the "g" key simultaneously will also send a BEL.

One common function often performed on ASCII terminals with control characters is *XON/XOFF*. In this case, an ASCII terminal can ask the host computer to stop transmitting data by sending the XOFF character, usually the DC3 character. Notice on the ASCII chart that an "S" is usually 1010011. Pressing the control key and the "S" key simultaneously results in 0010011, or the DC3 character. Transmission can be resumed by sending the XON character, usually a DC1. The DC1 character can be sent by pressing the control key and the "Q" key simultaneously.

From this discussion, we can see how character code designers have allowed keyboards to use each key for several functions. Rather than needing hundreds of different keys, special keys like the shift key and the control key allow the size and cost of terminals to be minimized.

PARALLEL VS. SERIAL TRANSMISSION

Though a character code determines which bits need to be transmitted to represent a particular character, it does not define how these bits are to be sent. There are two common methods of data transmission: parallel and serial.

Assume that we have eight bits of information to send from point A to point B. For our example, assume that the eight bits are 01000001. This sequence happens to be the ASCII representation of the letter "A" with a 0 used for the parity bit. How do we send these ones and zeroes?

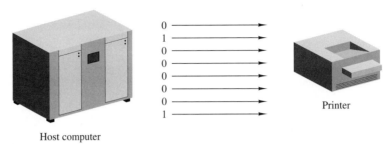

FIGURE 3-8   Parallel data transmission.

One method is to send all eight bits at once. This method is known as *parallel transmission*, as illustrated in Fig. 3-8. This method requires at least eight wires for transmission, one wire for each bit sent. It also requires other wires for functions examined in Chapter 4.

An analogy for parallel transmission can be drawn using cars and highways. If we have eight cars that need to travel between point A and point B, the fastest way to get them there is with an eight-lane highway; all eight cars arrive at their destination at the same time.

The main advantage of parallel transmission is that the entire byte is received at once, since all eight ones and zeroes are sent at the same time. The main disadvantage is the number of wires (or lanes on the data highway) required for transmission.

Another method is to send the eight bits one after another, requiring only one wire for transmission. This method is known as *serial transmission*, as illustrated in Fig. 3-9.

An analogy for serial transmission is a one-lane road, with the eight cars traveling one behind the other. No matter how fast the cars travel, the first car in the line always arrives at the destination before the others. Of course, it is less expensive to build a one-lane highway than an eight-lane highway.

The main advantage of serial transmission lies in minimizing the number of wires (or lanes on the data highway) that are necessary for data transmission. However, some time is wasted, because the byte must be disassembled, sent one bit at a time, and reassembled at the other end.

Both parallel and serial transmission have their places in data communications applications. For example, many personal computers communicate with their printers

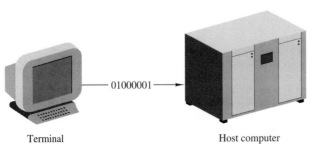

FIGURE 3-9   Serial data transmission.

using parallel transmission. Since printers are usually located within 10 or 20 feet of the personal computer, the extra wires required for parallel transmission are short, and the slight extra cost is more than offset by the added speed.

A user connecting his or her terminal to a host computer two buildings away, however, will most likely use serial transmission. In this case, the additional distance involved makes the cost of parallel transmission prohibitive, and speed is sacrificed for the economical advantage of serial transmission. Only one wire, or channel, is needed for sending data in each direction, thereby lowering the transmission cost.

Since manufacturers expect most terminals to be located some distance from host computers, terminals and host computers almost always communicate using serial transmission. In fact, almost all data communications equipment we consider in the next few chapters use serial transmission. Parallel transmission can be thought of as a special case, or an exception, suitable for short-distance transmission.

Now that we have established that most data communications is accomplished with serial transmission, we can examine the timing of the bit transmission.

ASYNCHRONOUS VS. SYNCHRONOUS TRANSMISSION

There are two common methods in use today for timing serial data transmission: asynchronous and synchronous.

Asynchronous transmission is commonly used by the dumb terminals we mentioned earlier. For our discussion, we assume that our characters are represented by eight bits, including any parity bit. With asynchronous transmission, each device must be set to transmit and receive data at a given speed, known as the *data rate*. The data rate is often measured in *bits per second*, or *bps*. When an asynchronous device sends a byte, it begins by sending a *start bit*, which is always a 0, followed by each of the eight bits in the byte, and then sends a *stop bit*, which is always a 1. These bits add up to form a 10-bit package for transmission. Some asynchronous devices send more than one stop bit, which simply lengthens the number of bits required to send a character.

The asynchronous transmission of the letter "A", followed by the letter "B", from a dumb terminal to a host computer using ASCII code is shown in Fig. 3-10. The terminal user types the letter "A" on the keyboard, and the terminal converts the letter

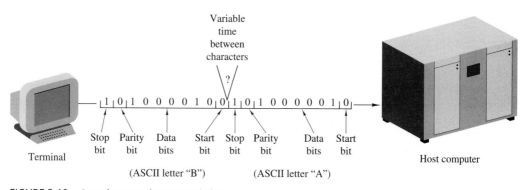

FIGURE 3-10 Asynchronous data transmission.

"A" to the bit sequence 01000001, with a 0 used as the parity bit. If we assume that the terminal is set to transmit at one bit per second, the terminal can send each bit one second apart. The terminal begins by sending the start bit, a 0, for the first second. It then sends the first data bit, a 1, during the next second, followed by the next bit, a 0, and so on. This transmission continues until the start bit, seven data bits, one parity bit, and the stop bit have been sent. The host computer, upon receiving the start bit, is thereby notified to expect seven data bits, one parity bit, and one stop bit. Each of these bits is sent one second apart. The start bit actually starts the host computer's internal stopwatch or clock, and the host then expects to receive the next nine bits one second apart. The stop bit is used to halt the host computer's internal stopwatch. Later, it can be started again by another start bit, sent with the next character. In Fig. 3-10, the next character sent is the letter "B".

To visualize the process of asynchronous transmission, we can pretend that we are using a tennis practice machine that throws balls to us every five seconds. We'll use orange balls to represent zeroes and yellow balls to represent ones. A friend loads 10 balls into the machine, with the first ball an orange one and the last ball a yellow one. We set the machine to start as soon as it is filled with 10 balls; it throws the first ball (an orange ball), or the start ball. After that, we expect a ball (any color) five seconds from now, another ball 10 seconds from now, and so on, until we finally receive the tenth ball, or stop ball (a yellow one), 45 seconds from now. If we don't receive one ball every five seconds and a yellow ball (the stop ball) in 45 seconds, we know that either the machine is not functioning or that one of the balls fell out of the machine.

Similarly, in asynchronous transmission, the only way to know when the next bit is to arrive is to time how long it has been since the start bit was received. If fewer than 10 bits are received, or the stop bit isn't received when expected, either the transmitter is malfunctioning or one of the bits was lost in transmission.

Asynchronous transmission, often known as *start–stop transmission* because of the start and stop bits, is an excellent means for transmitting characters from terminals to host computers. As soon as the user strikes a key, the terminal decides which byte to send for this character and adds the start and stop bits; all 10 bits can be immediately transmitted. In Fig. 3-10, there is a variable time between when the letter "A" and the letter "B" are transmitted. If the user strikes the keys one after another, the characters are transmitted one after the other. If the user types only the letter "A" and then takes a coffee break before typing the letter "B", the terminal is idle and does nothing but wait during that coffee break. The user at the keyboard is like our friend loading the tennis ball machine. We never know when our friend will load the machine, but when the machine has its 10 balls, it will start firing them at us at a fixed rate of speed. Similarly, we don't know when the user will strike a key, but as soon as the user hits a key on the keyboard, the terminal has the 10 bits it needs and will start sending them at a fixed rate.

We've been using data rates of one bit each second, or one every five seconds, to make our examples easier to understand. Actual data rates are more likely to be 110 bps, 300 bps, 1200 bps, 2400 bps, 4800 bps, 9600 bps, 19200 bps, and so on, all the way up to millions of bits per second. Of course, it is essential that the transmitting and receiving devices both be set at the same speed.

Besides asynchronous transmission, the other commonly used form of data transmission is *synchronous transmission*. Here, start and stop bits are not used. There is

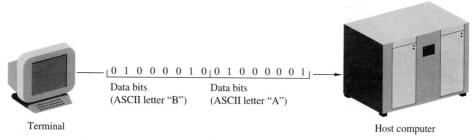

FIGURE 3-11   Synchronous data transmission.

no pause between characters in synchronous data transmission, as shown in Fig. 3-11, and the letters "A" and "B" are sent one after the other. Instead of using start and stop bits, timing is supplied in two ways. The two methods, using sync characters or clock signals, can be used independently, though they are often used in conjunction with each other.

First, synchronous data transmission usually involves large blocks of characters, and special *sync characters* can be sent at the beginning of these data blocks. These sync characters are a special series of bits the receiving device can use to adjust to the transmitter's exact rate of speed.

The second method of timing used in synchronous transmission is *transmit clocks* and *receive clocks*. In this case, separate wires or channels are typically used to send information about the timing of the data being transmitted. The devices transmitting data often send their own timing information on a separate wire from the data, or the clock can be combined with the data using special techniques. The clock signals are a way of saying, "Here comes a bit right now."

We can compare clock signals and sync characters using our tennis ball example. First, to better simulate synchronous data blocks, we will load the machine not with just 10 balls, but with a few hundred. Clock signals are the equivalent of setting the tennis ball machine to operate with an audible signal. Just before the machine throws each ball, it sounds a beep. The beep is our clock signal that lets us know when to expect a ball to be thrown. Similarly, in synchronous data transmission, the transmit clock tells a terminal when to end a bit, and the receive clock warns a terminal when to expect to receive a bit.

Sync characters can be simulated in our tennis ball machine if the first eight balls are always thrown in the same pattern—for example, yellow–orange–orange–orange–orange–orange–orange–yellow. When we receive this pattern of balls, we "sync up," getting used to the pace. We begin our real practice with the ninth ball. Similarly, a sync character is a known pattern of bits. After receiving a certain number of sync characters, a device expects to receive real data.

There is nothing to prevent us from using both a set pattern of eight tennis balls at the beginning of each session, while at the same time using an audible signal. Similarly, many synchronous devices use sync characters initially to "sync up" to the transmission speed and then use clock signals to keep their internal stopwatch in line with the transmitter's stopwatch.

In addition, synchronous transmission is usually governed by protocols, which we explain in detail in Chapter 7. A major feature of these protocols is that data is usually sent in *blocks*, or groups, of characters, not one byte at a time. Most synchronous terminals are smart or intelligent terminals and have an ENTER or XMIT key. As the user types information, the terminal holds all of the data until the user hits the ENTER or XMIT key. Then the terminal places special characters at the beginning and end of the data, according to the protocol, and sends the entire block of characters.

ASYNCHRONOUS VS. SYNCHRONOUS TRANSMISSION EFFICIENCY

Synchronous transmission has an obvious advantage when large blocks of data must be sent: Time is not wasted sending a start and stop bit for each character. For example, as shown in Fig. 3-12, if a block of data contains 1000 characters and 10 special characters need to be used by the synchronous protocol at the beginning and end of the block,

---

Asynchronous transmission efficiency

ABCDEFGHIJKLMNOPQRSTUVWXYZ, etc., ABCDEFGHIJKLMNOPQRSTUVWXYZ

Each character = 8 data bits, 1 start bit, 1 stop bit = 10 total bits

If we need to send 1000 characters,
   then 10000 total bits are sent,
   of which 8000 are data bits   →80% efficiency

If we need to send 40 characters,
   then 400 total bits are sent,
   of which 320 are data bits   → 80%efficiency

If we need to send 20 characters,
   then 200 total bits are sent,
   of which 160 are data bits   →80% efficiency

Synchronous transmission efficiency

*****ABCDEFGHIJKLMNOPQRSTUVWXYZ, etc., ABCDEFGHIJKLMNOPQRSTUVWXYZ*****

Assume that each block of data needs 10 special characters (shown as *)
Each character = 8 data bits

If we need to send 1000 characters,
   we add the 10 special characters,
   for a total of 1010 characters,
   so we send 8080 total bits,
   of which 8000 are data bits   →99. 1% efficiency

If we need to send 40 characters,
   we add the 10 special characters,
   for a total of 50 characters,
   so we send 400 total bits,
   of which 320 are data bits   →80% efficiency

If we need to send 20 characters,
   we add the 10 special characters,
   for a total of 30 characters,
   so we send 240 total bits,
   of which 160 are data bits   →66.7% efficiency

FIGURE 3-12 Synchronous and asynchronous transmission efficiency.

1010 characters need to be sent. If we assume eight-bit characters, 8000 bits out of the 8080 we are sending are actual data bits. This procedure is roughly 99.1% efficient. We consider the special characters, which make up the extra 80 bits, as *overhead* necessary for successful data transmission.

In asynchronous transmission of the same 1000 characters, as shown in Fig. 3-12, we must send 10,000 bits, since each character requires eight bits plus one start and one stop bit. Therefore, since 8000 of the 10,000 bits are data bits and 2000 bits are overhead, asynchronous transmission proves to be only 80% efficient for eight-bit characters.

Note that no matter how many eight-bit characters are sent, asynchronous transmission remains 80% efficient. Synchronous transmission efficiency, on the other hand, depends on the size of the block of characters being sent. The larger the block, the more efficient synchronous transmission becomes. Synchronous transmission of small blocks of data is relatively inefficient. For example, if the user types only one character before hitting the ENTER key, the same 10 special characters may be needed before and after the one data character, leaving an efficiency of eight data bits in 88 transmitted bits, or only 9.1%.

In our example, we chose one start bit and one stop bit for asynchronous transmission and assumed that 10 special characters were necessary in synchronous transmission. For this example, synchronous transmission becomes more efficient than asynchronous transmission for data blocks larger than 40 characters. This is less than the number of characters in a line of a typewritten page. Synchronous terminals are usually smart or intelligent terminals; they are more expensive to build because they must be able to differentiate between actual data and the special synchronous characters, as well as follow special protocols we explain in Chapter 7.

Asynchronous and synchronous transmission are two ways of timing bit transmission once a communications path is available. We must still consider the different types of paths used for communications.

SIMPLEX, HALF DUPLEX, AND FULL DUPLEX COMMUNICATIONS

There are three different types of communications paths for data transmission: simplex, half duplex, and full duplex.

Simplex communications is a one-way transmission path. One device transmits data, and the other device receives data. A student taught by an old-fashioned professor who does not permit any questions is part of a simplex communications path. The professor is talking to the student, but the student does not have the opportunity to speak and ask questions.

Another example of a simplex path is a one-way street. Cars can only pass in one direction on a one-way street; in simplex data communications, ones and zeroes can be transmitted in only one direction.

An example of simplex data communications can be found at most airports. There is usually a central computer, tracking all of an airline's arrivals and departures. Video monitors are placed throughout the airport to display this arrival and departure information. The host computer sends the information to the video monitor, but the monitors do not send any data back to the host computer. This one-way, or simplex, communications path is illustrated in Fig. 3-13.

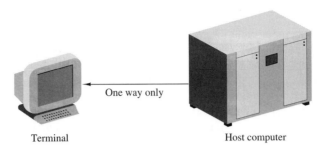

One way only

Terminal

Host computer

FIGURE 3-13 Simplex communications path.

Half duplex communications is an alternating transmission path that goes in two ways, but only one direction at a time. For example, a professor typically conducts class in half duplex fashion. First, the professor lectures for a few minutes and then pauses for a second and waits for students to ask questions. One student asks a question, then the professor answers, another student asks a question, and so on. Only one person, either the professor or a student, is talking at any one time. Most human conversations are conducted in half duplex fashion; first one person speaks, then the other.

Another example of a half duplex path is the reversible commuter lane that is becoming popular in many metropolitan areas, particularly on bridges or in tunnels. In the morning rush hour, cars are permitted to travel into the city in the reversible commuter lane. At some point in the afternoon, the lane is closed for a few minutes to allow it to be cleared. Then the lane is reversed, and cars are allowed to travel out of the city in this reversible commuter lane. This is a half duplex path: first one direction, a short pause, and then the other direction.

An example of half duplex data communications can be found in certain terminals and host computers. First, the user types some information and hits a special key that sends the entire screen to the host computer. The host computer then responds by sending a screen of information back to the terminal. Only one device, either the terminal or the host computer, transmits data at any given time. Typically, a short pause occurs between completion of one device's transmission and the next device's reply. This half duplex communications path is illustrated in Fig. 3-14.

Half duplex transmission is often called *two-wire communications*, because originally one pair of wires was used for half duplex transmission. Since early equipment was unable to both transmit and receive over one pair of wires at the same time, it was necessary for the devices to share the line by alternating.

Full duplex communications is a two-way communications path. Some professors prefer to be interrupted in midsentence if their students have questions. In this case, the professors and students participate in a full duplex communications path. The professor may be talking, but a student may begin speaking at any time. A further example of such a full duplex communications path might be the classic husband–wife argument, where both parties are speaking simultaneously. Each party hears what the other is saying, but both refuse to stop talking.

Another analogy for a full duplex path is a two-way street, with one lane in each direction. Cars can proceed in both directions at the same time, and traffic on one side of the street is unaffected by traffic on the other side of the street.

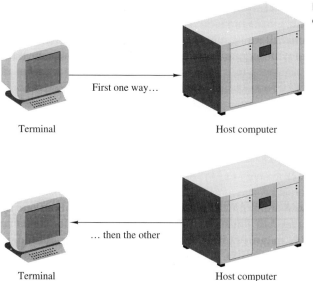

FIGURE 3-14   Half duplex communications path.

An example of full duplex data communications can be found in certain terminals and host computers that have the ability to transmit and receive data at the same time. The terminal does not need to wait for the host computer to stop transmitting before the terminal itself transmits. The same is true for the host computer. This full duplex communications path is illustrated in Fig. 3-15.

Full duplex communications is often referred to as *four-wire communications*, because originally, two pairs of wires were needed for full duplex communications. Early equipment transmitted data over one pair of wires in one direction and received data on the other pair.

Today's equipment is more sophisticated than its predecessors, and full duplex communications is now possible over only one pair of wires. Therefore, simply counting the number of wires leaving a device does not help the user determine whether the equipment is half duplex or full duplex. Unfortunately, the terminology has already caught on, and the terms "two-wire" and "four-wire" are sometimes used today to refer to half duplex and full duplex communications, respectively, regardless of the number of wires actually used for transmission.

Which method is the best: simplex, half duplex, or full duplex? It depends on the application. In the airport example we used earlier, a simplex communications path is

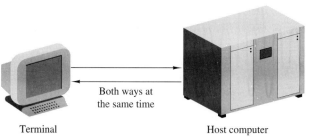

FIGURE 3-15   Full duplex communications path.

perfect for the job of sending information to a video monitor. However, when a terminal is communicating with a host computer, either half duplex or full duplex is necessary, since a two-way communications path is essential.

Half duplex transmission is by nature slower than full duplex. Only one device can transmit at any one time, and the terminals and computers must often wait before they transmit to ensure that the other device has finished transmitting. Clearly, there is an advantage to having a full duplex connection, since either device is able to transmit data all the time. However, it is sometimes easier or cheaper to provide a half duplex communications path, and in most communications, only one party transmits at one time anyway. As a result, some half duplex terminals and host computers are still in use today.

SUMMARY

Data communications is the exchange of digital information, or ones and zeroes, between two devices. Host computers and terminals usually communicate using groups of eight bits, or bytes. Character codes are different methods used by devices to represent information. The two most common character codes, ASCII and EBCDIC, use ones and zeroes to represent characters.

Code and protocol conversion are sometimes required to connect different manufacturers' devices. Even within a character code, some manufacturers may vary their use of parity bits, making some equipment incompatible.

A byte of data can be sent with parallel transmission, all at once, with one bit sent on each of eight separate wires. Serial transmission, however, requires only one wire, and the bits are sent one after another. Serial transmission is more widely used in data communications because the single wire is less expensive.

Asynchronous transmission uses start and stop bits to time serial transmission. Synchronous transmission, on the other hand, uses sync characters and clock signals for timing. Synchronous transmission is more efficient than asynchronous transmission for large blocks of data. Asynchronous transmission, however, is usually less expensive to implement.

Simplex communication provides a one-way communications path. Half duplex is an alternating transmission path; it goes in two ways but only one direction at a time. Full duplex communications is a two-way communications path. The terms *two-wire* and *four-wire* are often used to describe half and full duplex communications, respectively, even though four wires are no longer required for full duplex.

TERMS FOR REVIEW

American National Standard Code for Information Interchange	*ASCII*	*Bit error*
	Asynchronous transmission	*Bits per second*
	Baudot code	*Block*
American National Standards Institute	*BCD*	*Bps*
	Binary Coded Decimal	*Byte*
ANSI	*Binary number system*	*Carriage return*
Applications software	*Bit*	*Cathode ray tube*

CC
Central processing unit
Character
Character code
Code conversion
Control character
Control code
Control key
CPU
CRT
Dash
Data communications
Data rate
Digital
Display station
Dot
Dumb terminal
EBCD
EBCDIC
Error detection
Extended ASCII
Extended Binary Coded
    Decimal

Extended Binary Coded
    Decimal Interchange Code
FE
Figures
Format effector
Four-wire communications
Full duplex communications
Half duplex communications
Host computer
Information separator
Intelligent terminal
International Baudot
IS
Keyboard
Letters
Line feed
Lower case
Mainframe
Microcomputer
Minicomputer
Morse code
Overhead

Parallel transmission
Parity bit
Personal computer
Protocol conversion
Receive clock
Screen
Serial transmission
Simplex communications
Smart terminal
Start bit
Start–stop transmission
Stop bit
Supercomputer
Sync character
Synchronous transmission
Terminal
Transmit clock
Two-wire communications
Upper case
VDT
Video display terminal
XON/XOFF

EXERCISES

3-1.   What is data communications?

3-2.   How do the different types of host computers differ?

3-3.   Describe the different types of terminals.

3-4.   What is the difference between a bit and a byte?

3-5.   What is the major drawback of the Morse code?

3-6.   What technique does Baudot code use to practically double the number of characters represented with five bits? What is the disadvantage of using this method?

3-7.   How does the order of bit transmission in ASCII and EBCDIC codes differ?

3-8.   What are the functions of the XON and XOFF characters?

3-9.   What is the difference between parallel and serial transmission? Which is used more frequently in data communications, and why?

3-10.   How do asynchronous and synchronous transmission differ? Which is better suited to large blocks of characters, and why?

3-11.   Describe the difference between simplex, half duplex, and full duplex communications.

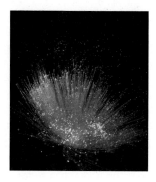

Data Interfaces and Transmission

There are many different ways to connect terminals to host computers. We have already discussed basic data communications concepts, such as full and half duplex communications and asynchronous and synchronous transmission.

We now analyze in detail the methods used to connect terminals to host computers, whether the terminal is located 20 feet or 2000 miles away.

STANDARDS ORGANIZATIONS

Host computer and terminal manufacturers usually conform to certain recognized standards to connect their equipment. Some standards introduced and promoted by one manufacturer are so successful that they become the industry standard. Other standards are formed by *standards organizations*. These organizations are generally chartered to devise standards for a particular industry within certain countries.

Typically, standards are developed by committees with representatives from leading companies in an industry. Certain standards organizations, particularly those covering military products, also have government representation. We now briefly examine the organizations with the most impact on data communications.

The *American National Standards Institute*, or *ANSI*, is an umbrella organization for all of the standards organizations in the United States. ANSI accredits various organizations, which can then submit their standards to ANSI for acceptance as a national standard.

The *Institute of Electrical and Electronics Engineers*, or *IEEE*, is a professional organization of engineers. IEEE consists of many specialized societies whose committees prepare standards in their areas of specialty.

The *Electronic Industries Association*, or *EIA*, is an organization representing many manufacturers in the U.S. electronics industry. The EIA's standards have traditionally been titled *Recommended Standards*, or *RS*, followed by the number of a particular committee. In the last several years the EIA, seeking to ensure the clear identification of its standards, has started using the EIA name instead of "RS" at the beginning of each standard, as in *EIA-232-E*. The RS designation, as in *RS-232-C*, is still used by most people in the industry to refer to standards that were issued before EIA began using the new designation. To avoid confusion, we refer to the more widely used RS designation on these previously issued standards.

The *Exchange Carriers Standards Association*, or *ECSA*, consists of telephone equipment manufacturing companies. ECSA was formed after the AT&T divestiture to continue work on standards previously developed by the Bell System.

The *National Institute of Standards and Technology*, or *NIST*, is a federal organization responsible for producing *Federal Information Processing Standards*, or *FIPS*. Meeting these FIPS is a requirement for many government suppliers. NIST was formerly known as the *National Bureau of Standards*, or *NBS*.

In the United States, most of the standards are only recommendations. With the exception of certain standards regarding interference and safety, the FCC does not regulate the internal workings of equipment, only how it attaches to the public network. Internationally, telecommunications is regulated in most countries by a PTT. PTTs often impose strict requirements on all aspects of communications equipment used in a given country. The PTTs usually represent their countries on international standards organizations. There are two major international standards organizations. The *Consultative Committee on International Telephone and Telegraph*, or *CCITT*, is an international telecommunications standards organization. Its members include the regulating bodies from member countries and leading companies in the field, as well as representatives from other organizations. The CCITT is a committee of a larger organization known as the *International Telecommunications Union*, or *ITU*. Recently issued CCITT standards are now labeled *ITU-Telecommunications Standardization Sector, ITU-T*, or even simply *ITU*. Most of the standards already in existence are known by the widely used CCITT designation. To avoid confusion, we will refer to all of the standards of this organization with the label ITU(CCITT).

In the *International Standards Organization*, or *ISO*, each member country is represented by its own national standards organization. ISO and ITU(CCITT) cooperate on certain standards, but often develop completely different standards for the same technical areas. Membership in both ISO and ITU(CCITT) is possible and often occurs.

The *Internet Engineering Task Force*, or *IETF*, is an international organization open to any individual interested in furthering the development of the Internet architecture. Working groups prepare recommendations and proposals for items important to the operation and evolution of the Internet, which is discussed in more detail in Chapter 8.

These domestic and international standards organizations prepare standards on many topics. We now examine some of those standards used for data communications.

DIGITAL INTERFACE STANDARDS

The point at which one device connects to another is known as an *interface*. An interface standard defines exactly which electronic signals are required for communication between two devices. Some interface standards also define the physical connector to be used.

THE RS-232-C STANDARD

One of the most common interface standards for data communications in use today is EIA's *Recommended Standard 232C*, or *RS-232-C*. RS-232-C defines exactly how ones and zeroes are to be electronically transmitted, including the voltage levels needed as well as the other electronic signals necessary for computer communication.

The ITU(CCITT) has standards similar to EIA's RS-232-C, known as *V.24* and *V.28*. The V.24 standard defines all of the signals described in RS-232-C, and the V.28 standard defines the same voltage levels described in RS-232-C.

RS-232-C voltage levels. What does it mean when we transmit a 1 or a 0? In RS-232-C, ones and zeroes are transmitted using negative and positive voltages. Those readers unfamiliar with the concept of positive and negative voltages should not be concerned; devices can be built that can both send and recognize these different signals.

RS-232-C defines the process of sending a 1, known as a *mark*, as an electronic signal between –3 and –15 volts. It defines the process of sending a 0, known as a *space*, as an electronic signal between +3 and +15 volts. Signals outside these ranges are considered undefined—neither a one nor a zero—and are ignored by the receiver. This signal definition is illustrated in Fig. 4-1.

A terminal communicating according to RS-232-C must therefore be able to send and receive voltages in the range of –15 to +15 volts. For example, to send the ASCII letter "A", with a 0 as the parity bit, or 01000001, an asynchronous RS-232-C terminal must first send (starting from the left) the start bit, a 0, or +15 volts, followed by a 1, or –15 volts, followed by five 0's, or five +15 volt pulses, then another 1, or a –15 volt pulse, followed by a 0, or a +15 volt pulse, and finally the stop bit, or –15 volts. If we assume a transmission rate of one bit per second, then Fig. 4-2 shows the ASCII transmission of

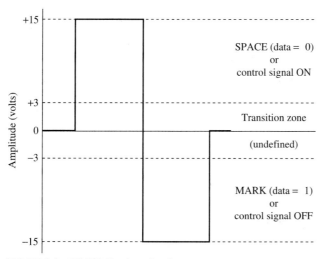

FIGURE 4-1 RS-232-C voltage levels.

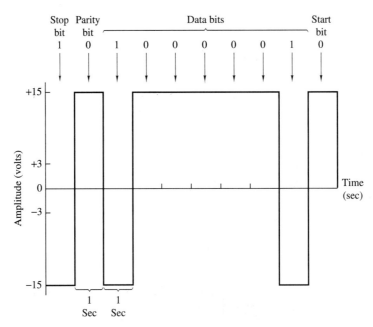

FIGURE 4-2   RS-232-C transmission of the ASCII character "A."

the letter "A". If the letter "A" were to be sent at a faster rate, the time periods in Fig. 4-2 would be shorter. For example, at 1200 bits per second, each of the time periods would be 833 microseconds (1/1200 second) long. Remember that these pulses don't have to be exactly +15 or –15 volts; all voltages in the range of +3 to +15 or –3 to –15 are acceptable. After sending the stop bit, the transmitter remains at the negative voltage until the next character, which begins with a start bit (a positive voltage).

DTEs and DCEs in RS-232-C.   In addition to defining how ones and zeroes are transmitted, RS-232-C also defines other electronic signals useful for communications. RS-232-C assumes that there are two types of interfaces. The first, known as *data terminal equipment*, or *DTE*, is the interface most often found on terminals, host computers, and printers. The second, known as *data circuit-terminating equipment*, or *DCE*, is the interface usually used on devices known as modems and on some multiplexers. DCE is often also referred to as "data communications equipment." Even though RS-232-C defines only the type of interface, we often describe an entire device by referring to its interface; for example, terminals are often called DTEs, and modems are often called DCEs.

The usual purpose of DCEs is to allow DTEs to be located remotely from each other. The DTEs are the data communications equivalent of the people in a telephone conversation. The DCEs are the equivalent of the phones in the conversation; DCEs are simply instruments used to allow DTEs to communicate. This comparison is presented in Fig. 4-3. Notice that a terminal (DTE) can be connected to a remote host computer (DTE) using a pair of DCEs and the public telephone network. RS-232-C defines how DTEs communicate with DCEs, but not how DCEs communicate with each other.

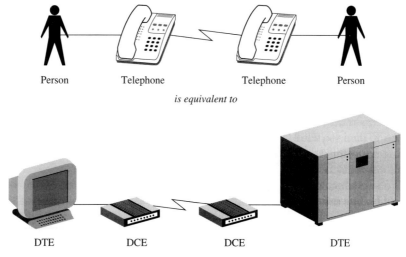

FIGURE 4-3   DTEs and DCEs.

Later in this chapter, we examine the methods DCEs use to communicate with each other.

RS-232-C specifies the signals exchanged between DTEs and DCEs, but not the exact type of physical connector to be used. For most applications, the *DB25* connector, defined in ISO standard number 2110 and illustrated in Fig. 4-4, has become widely accepted. There are two versions of the DB25 connector, male and female. The male connector contains 25 pins, and the female connector contains 25 small receptacles or sockets for these pins.

For an example, consider the standard electrical outlet in our homes. These outlets accept two- or three-prong plugs, depending on whether or not the circuit uses the third grounding prong. A DB25 connector takes this concept one step further, with 25 separate pins. In a standard electrical outlet, there is a specific size for each plug, as well as a specific distance between the prongs. Similarly, the ISO 2110 standard defines the exact size and shape of the DB25 connectors.

Each of the pins and their corresponding sockets are numbered from 1 to 25. These connector pin numbers, the commonly used signal names, and the common abbreviations, which we explain in the upcoming sections, are shown in Fig. 4-5. The EIA and ITU(CCITT) have their own signal abbreviations; although not as commonly used, they are provided in the chart for reference.

There is no technical reason to place certain signals on any particular pin; these conventions are usually followed to allow for compatibility among different vendors'

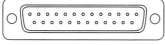

DB25 male connector

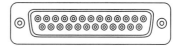

DB25 female connector

FIGURE 4-4   DB25 connectors.

Pin	Abbreviation	Name	Direction	EIA abbreviation	CCITT abbreviation
1	GND	Protective Ground	Both ways	AA	101
2	TD	Transmitted Data	DTE to DCE	BA	103
3	RD	Received Data	DCE to DTE	BB	104
4	RTS	Request to Send	DTE to DCE	CA	105
5	CTS	Clear to Send	DCE to DTE	CB	106
6	DSR	Data Set Ready	DCE to DTE	CC	107
7	SG	Signal Ground	Both ways	AB	102
8	DCD	Data Carrier Detect	DCE to DTE	CF	109
9		Positive Test Voltage	DCE to DTE		
10		Negative Test Voltage	DCE to DTE		
11		Unassigned			
12	SDCD	Secondary Data Carrier Detect	DCE to DTE	SCF	122
13	SCTS	Secondary Clear to Send	DCE to DTE	SCB	121
14	STD	Secondary Transmitted Data	DTE to DCE	SBA	118
15	TC	Transmit Clock	DCE to DTE	DB	114
16	SRD	Secondary Received Data	DCE to DTE	SBB	119
17	RC	Receive Clock	DCE to DTE	DD	115
18		Unassigned			
19	SRTS	Secondary Request to Send	DTE to DCE	SCA	120
20	DTR	Data Terminal Ready	DTE to DCE	CD	108.2
21	SQ	Signal Quality Detect	DCE to DTE	CG	110
22	RI	Ring Indicator	DCE to DTE	CE	125
23	DRS	Data Rate Select	Either way	CH/CI	111/112
24	XTC	External Transmit Clock	DTE to DCE	DA	113
25		Unassigned			

FIGURE 4-5   RS-232-C signals.

equipment. Figure 4-5 also describes the device, a DTE or DCE, that generates each of the signals.

Typically, a cable coming from a DTE device has a male DB25 connector on its end. DCE devices usually have a female DB25 connector to accept the cable from the DTE. RS-232-C limits the maximum length of the cable from a DTE to a DCE to 50 feet. In addition, RS-232-C limits data transmission rates to a maximum of 20,000 bits per second (20 kilobits per second, or 20 kbps). The distance and speed limitation is often exceeded by users without causing operational difficulties, though doing so violates the RS-232-C standard. Manufacturers may refuse to support or service installations that do not comply with the standard.

RS-232-C data signal definitions.   We have already examined how data is transmitted and received using positive and negative voltages. In RS-232-C, the DTE sends data on the *TD*, or *Transmitted Data* pin. In other words, the DTE can provide a positive (+3 to +15 volt) electronic signal on the TD pin to send a 0 (space) or a negative (−3 to −15 volt) electronic signal on the TD pin to send a 1 (mark). TD is usually found on pin number 2 of the DB25 connector.

Similarly, a DTE receives data on the *RD*, or *Received Data* pin. Notice that the pins are named with respect to the DTE. The DCE receives data from the DTE on the TD pin and sends data to the DTE on the RD pin. Also, regardless of whether a device is a DCE or DTE, we almost always refer to pin numbers rather than sockets, since the signal is named with respect to the DTE and the DTE usually uses the male connector with pins. Therefore, even though RD is a signal produced by the DCE, we state that RD is usually found on pin number 3 of the DB25 connector, because that's the corresponding pin number on the DTE's male connector.

RS-232-C ground signal definitions.

Another function needed to ensure proper data transmission is fulfilled by the *Signal Ground*, or *SG* pin. This signal acts as a zero-volt reference for all the other signals. An analogy of a reference voltage can be drawn by looking at the sky on a clear day. A philosophy professor asks, "Is the sky light blue or dark blue today?" Half of the class thinks it's light blue, and the other half thinks it's dark blue. That's because every class member has a different idea of what light and dark really means. If the professor is wearing a navy blazer jacket and asks the class, "Is the sky a darker blue or lighter blue than my jacket?", the entire class will reply, "The sky is a lighter blue." That's because the entire class used the same reference: the professor's jacket.

The Signal Ground in RS-232-C is a zero-volt reference. Signals can be compared to the SG pin; those with higher voltages than the SG pin are positive voltages, and those with lower voltages than the SG pin are negative voltages. When a DTE sends a signal on the TD pin, the DCE compares this voltage to the SG pin to determine whether the data sent was a 1 or a 0. SG is usually found on pin number 7 of the DB25 connector.

There is another ground signal, known as *chassis ground, protective ground*, or *frame ground*, or is simply abbreviated as *GND*. This signal is not necessary for data transmission, but can be used to prevent certain errors. Special shielded cable, designed to reduce interference and electronic noise, can attach its shield to the GND pin. Interference and electronic noise can be generated by large electrical motors, such as those found in elevators or factories, or by ordinary fluorescent lights. With shielded cable, the noise never makes it to the data wires because it runs on the shield, through the GND pin, and through the DTE's or DCE's own electrical ground. This shield should be connected to the GND pin only on one side of the cable, or else it could pose a potential electrical hazard (if the attached equipment is faulty) and violate the *National Electrical Code*. GND is usually found on pin number 1 of the DB25 connector.

RS-232-C timing signal definitions.

In asynchronous transmission, no timing signals are needed. For synchronous transmission, however, there are clock signals provided in RS-232-C. These clock signals are a series of positive and negative pulses, from +15 to –15 volts, that repeat indefinitely and are known as a *square wave*. If the data is being transmitted at 1200 bits per second, there are 1200 complete square waves each second. This process allows the device receiving the clock signal to "sync up" to the data rate of the other device. It is a process of continuous calibration, in which the device receiving the clock signal is constantly adjusting its speed, if necessary, to match

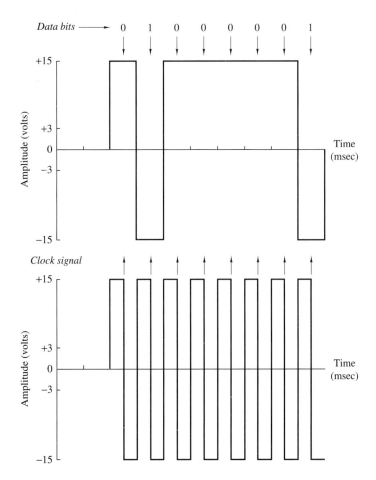

FIGURE 4-6 Using clock signals to time data transmission.

that of the other device. An example of using a square wave as a clock signal to time data transmission is shown in Fig. 4-6.

The *TC* signal, or *Transmit Clock*, is used by the DCE to time the data sent by the DTE on the TD pin in synchronous data transmission. Some DTEs allow the DCE to provide this clock signal. TC is usually found on pin number 15 of the DB25 connector.

The *XTC* signal, or *External Transmit Clock*, is used by the DTE to time the data it sends on the TD pin in synchronous data transmission. Some DTEs insist on providing this clock signal themselves. XTC is usually found on pin number 24 of the DB25 connector.

The *RC* signal, or *Receive Clock*, is used by the DCE to time the data it sends to the DTE on the RD pin in synchronous data transmission. RC is usually found on pin number 17 of the DB25 connector.

RS-232-C control signal definitions. Using the TD, RD, and SG pins, data could be transmitted asynchronously between DTEs and DCEs. Synchronous transmission would also require use of the TC, RC, and XTC pins. However, there are other functions that are usually performed before data is transmitted.

The *control signals* of RS-232-C are used to indicate the status of a given connection. A control signal is said to be *ON*, or *raised*, or *asserted*, or *true* when it is set to between +3 and +15 volts. Similarly, a control signal is said to be *OFF*, or *low*, or *false* when it is set to between –3 and –15 volts. By raising and lowering the control signal voltages, the DTE and DCE can communicate information about the status of a given call and about both devices' readiness to communicate. We begin by describing the most common control signals used in RS-232-C.

When a DTE device is powered on and placed on-line, it asserts the *DTR* signal, or *Data Terminal Ready*. This is an announcement to the DCE that a DTE is attached and ready to begin communications. DTR is usually found on pin number 20 of the DB25 connector.

The *DSR* signal, or *Data Set Ready*, is asserted by the DCE, and indicates that the DCE is powered on and is ready to begin communications. DSR is usually found on pin number 6 of the DB25 connector.

The *RTS* signal, or *Request to Send*, is asserted by the DTE to ask permission to send data. In full duplex, the DTE asserts this signal immediately, because a full duplex device wants a continuous two-way communications path. In half duplex devices, the DTE asserts this signal only when it actually has data to send (for instance, when the Enter key has been hit on a terminal). RTS is usually found on pin number 4 of the DB25 connector.

The *CTS* signal, or *Clear to Send*, is asserted by the DCE in response to RTS when the DCE is able to accept data from the DTE. CTS is usually found on pin number 5 of the DB25 connector.

The *DCD* signal, or *Data Carrier Detect*, is asserted by the DCE to alert the DTE to expect to receive data at any time. In full duplex, DCD remains continuously asserted, since it is a continuous two-way path and data can arrive at any time. In half duplex, DCD is asserted only when data is being sent to the DTE. This signal is often abbreviated as *CD* or *CX*. DCD is usually found on pin number 8 of the DB25 connector.

The *RI* signal, or *Ring Indicator*, is asserted by the DCE to alert the DTE that a remote device wants to initiate communications. RI is usually found on pin number 22 of the DB25 connector.

The control signals we have just analyzed are the most commonly used central signals. There are several less frequently used signals in RS-232-C as well.

The *SQ* signal, or *Signal Quality Detect*, is asserted by the DCE when it believes that transmissions are of high quality and there are no errors occurring. The DCE drops this signal when it determines that the transmission quality has degraded and an error may have occurred. SQ is usually found on pin number 21 of the DB25 connector.

The *DRS* signal, or *Data Rate Select*, can be asserted by either the DTE or the DCE to change the other device's speed under special conditions. Data Rate Select is usually found on pin number 23 of the DB25 connector.

RS-232-C secondary signals.   There are also several secondary signals: *Secondary Transmitted Data* (STD, pin 14), *Secondary Received Data* (SRD, pin 16), *Secondary Request to Send* (SRTS, pin 19), *Secondary Clear to Send* (SCTS, pin 13), and *Secondary Data Carrier Detect* (SDCD, pin 12). These signals are equivalent to their primary counterparts, which we have already considered, but are rarely used by most DTEs and DCEs. Together, these signals provide a second data channel on which data can be transmitted and received independently of the primary channel.

Other RS-232-C signals.   Two other signals described in RS-232-C as "Reserved for Data Set Testing," pins 9 and 10, are usually defined as positive and negative test voltages, respectively. These signals are often useful for troubleshooting.

The remaining three pins, numbered 11, 18, and 25, were left unassigned by the RS-232-C standard. Many manufacturers have used these pins for their own purposes.

In most cases, when signals are not being used by a manufacturer, such as the clocking pins in asynchronous transmission, these pins are simply omitted from the connector to cut manufacturing costs. Some manufacturers who need only a few of the signals described here actually use a smaller connector than the DB25 to economize and save space, though this is only a special case. Still other manufacturers have invented their own functions for the unassigned pins. These variations can make it difficult to connect two different vendors' equipment.

EIA-232-D and EIA-232-E vs. RS-232-C.   *EIA-232-D* and *EIA-232-E* are revisions of the RS-232-C standard that make some minor improvements. The use of connectors and the grounding shield are better defined, and some of the lesser used signals are eliminated. Additional test and loopback signals are provided on previously unassigned pins. Though these improvements make EIA-232-D and EIA-232-E technically superior to RS-232-C, there are so many RS-232-C devices already installed that the new features are seldom used. While the EIA-232-D and EIA-232-E devices can communicate with RS-232-C devices, the new diagnostic features can only be used between the newer devices. In fact, since most RS-232-C devices use nine or fewer signals, these improvements are having little effect on the marketplace.

RS-232-C HANDSHAKING

Now that we are familiar with the basic RS-232-C signals, let's see how they're used in asynchronous communications. The interaction of the RS-232-C signals we have already described is known as RS-232-C *handshaking*.

Assume that we have a terminal (DTE) connected to a DCE, which we refer to as the local DCE, as illustrated in Fig. 4-7. This DCE communicates with another DCE, known as the remote DCE, which is in turn connected to a host computer (DTE).

The terminal is powered up and immediately asserts the DTR signal. The local DCE responds by asserting the DSR signal, thereby establishing communications with the remote DCE. The remote DCE temporarily asserts the RI signal to alert the host

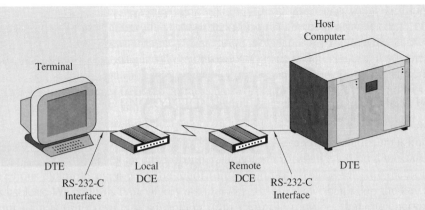

FIGURE 4-7   Connecting DTEs and DCEs with RS-232-C.

computer that another party would like to communicate with it. The host computer, if powered on and ready, then asserts the DTR signal. The remote DCE responds by dropping the RI signal and asserting the DSR signal, completing the connection between the terminal and the host computer.

If the terminal and host computer are communicating using full duplex, they would have asserted the RTS signals almost immediately after receiving the DSR signal from the DCE. The purpose of the RTS signal is to request a transmission path. The DCEs would then respond with the CTS and DCD signals as soon as communications were established (between the DCEs). The CTS signal confirms that a transmission path is available for the DTE to send data to the DCE. The DCD signal confirms that a transmission path is established in the other direction, from the DCE to the DTE. For devices using full duplex, whenever a transmission path is available, it is available in both directions; therefore, the CTS and DCD signals are asserted by both DCEs. Data transmission can now occur between the terminal and host computer, in both directions simultaneously, through the DCEs.

To summarize, in a full duplex connection, the DTEs assert the DTR and RTS signals, and the DCEs assert the DSR, CTS, and DCD signals. Once the connection is established, these signals do not change. Typically, a DTE ends the connection by dropping its DTR and RTS signals.

An interesting function is performed by the DCEs during the connection. The terminal transmits data on the TD pin to the local DCE, which sends the data to the remote DCE using methods we introduce later in this chapter. The remote DCE sends this data to the host computer on the RD pin. Notice that the DCEs have performed a *crossover* of the data signal, much as telephones do for us. When we talk into our telephone mouthpiece (the equivalent of TD), our voice is received in the other party's earpiece (the equivalent of RD). Similarly, the host computer transmits data on TD to the remote DCE, but this data is sent to the terminal by the local DCE on the RD pin.

Half duplex communications differs slightly from full duplex. Although the DTR and DSR signaling is the same, half duplex communications require an alternating transmission path (first one direction and then the other). This is accomplished by the use of the RTS, CTS, and DCD signals.

After the DTR/DSR signal interchange at both the terminal and host computer, one of the DTEs will then want to transmit data—we'll assume it's the terminal. The terminal asserts its RTS signal, and the local DCE informs the remote DCE that data will be arriving shortly. The remote DCE then asserts DCD to the host computer to inform it that data will be arriving shortly. Meanwhile, the local DCE has asserted the CTS signal, indicating that the terminal can now send data. A one-way transmission path has now been established from the terminal to the computer. The computer will not try to send data because it is receiving the DCD signal, implying that data is already on its way. When the terminal finishes sending data, it drops the RTS signal; the local DCE then drops the CTS signal and informs the remote DCE that the transmission is complete. The remote DCE then drops DCD to the host computer. The host computer is now free to assert its RTS signal and start the process all over again in the other direction. This process will repeat indefinitely, first in one direction, then the other, as long as there is still data to transmit.

We have been discussing asynchronous transmission here. Synchronous transmission functions identically, with the addition of the clock signals (TC, RC, XTC) mentioned previously.

CONNECTING A DTE TO ANOTHER DTE IN RS-232-C

While RS-232-C is intended to connect a DTE to a DCE, it is possible to connect two DTEs together using a special cable known as a *null modem cable*. This cable simulates the behavior of the two DCEs and the network between them, usually found in RS-232-C connections. An example of an asynchronous null modem cable is shown in Fig. 4-8.

A signal ground is connected between the two DTEs to provide a reference voltage. DTR and DSR are crossed so that when each DTE raises DTR to indicate that it is on-line, the other DTE sees DSR, indicating that its partner is on-line. When a DTE raises RTS, it sees CTS, giving it permission to send, and the other DTE sees DCD, indicating that data may arrive at any time. Finally, TD and RD are crossed, so when either DTE transmits, the other DTE receives the data.

There are many other variations of null modem cables that will work in different situations. With certain vendors' equipment, it may also be necessary to connect RI to DTR if one of the DTEs is expecting to see an incoming call. When synchronous transmission is used, appropriate clock signals must be connected between the DTEs to provide the timing needed by these devices. The reason for using any type of null modem cable is to convince the attached DTEs that a pair of DCEs and a network are between them so that the DTEs can play their intended role.

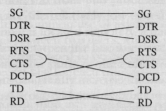

FIGURE 4-8   An asynchronous null modem cable.

RS-449, RS-422-A, AND RS-423-A

The main complaints from the user community about RS-232-C were about its speed limitation (20 kbps), its distance limitation (50 feet), and the lack of standardization on both a particular connector type and pin locations. Realizing the deficiencies of RS-232-C, the EIA later introduced a set of three new standards, known as RS-449, RS-422-A, and RS-423-A.

These new standards share the same basic goal as RS-232-C or any other interface standard. All define a standard method for connecting two devices, one known as a DTE and the other as a DCE. Regardless of the shape of the connector, the number of pins used, or the speed of transmission, a similar set of functions must be provided by all interface standards. For example, "Data Terminal Ready," or the equivalent function with a slightly different name, is found in almost any interface standard.

RS-449 can be thought of as the parent standard, describing the mechanical and functional characteristics of the DTE/DCE interface. *RS-422-A* and *RS-423-A* address the specific details of two different electrical signal characteristics. Together, these three standards were intended as replacements for RS-232-C. However, they are still only in limited use, and RS-232-C devices far outnumber RS-449 devices today.

The RS-449 standard, unlike RS-232-C, defines the exact connector to be used, the *DB37* connector, as presented in Fig. 4-9. The DB37 connector is similar to the

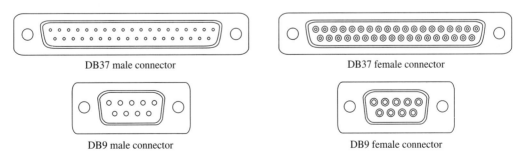

FIGURE 4-9   DB37 and DB9 connectors.

DB25, though it is somewhat larger and has 37 pins. In addition, the RS-449 standard developers realized that the secondary channel of RS-232-C was seldom used, so they opted to place those signals on a separate connector, known as a *DB9* connector, also shown in Fig. 4-9. This 9-pin connector is optional, and if the secondary channel is not needed, it can be completely omitted. RS-449 therefore defines a total of 46 pins, many more than those in RS-232-C; the extra pins allow for added functions and higher data rates, which we explain in the text that follows. The 37-pin and 9-pin connectors are also defined in the *ISO Standard 4902*.

The functions performed by the RS-449 signals are similar to those used in RS-232-C. The RS-449 signals and their RS-232-C equivalents are compared in Fig. 4-10. Notice that some of the RS-232-C functions are also found in RS-449, with slightly different names. For example, Transmitted Data in RS-232-C is the equivalent of Send Data in RS-449. RS-449 also includes additional signals that are not present in RS-232-C. Most

DB9 Connector pin no.	DB37 Connector pin nos.	RS-449 Circuit	RS-449 Description	Category	RS-232-C Equivalent
1	1		Shield		GND
5	19	SG	Signal Ground		SG
9	37	SC	Send Common	II	
6	20	RC	Receive Common	II	
	4,22	SD	Send Data	I	TD
	6,24	RD	Receive Data	I	RD
	7,25	RS	Request to Send	I	RTS
	9,27	CS	Clear to Send	I	CTS
	11,29	DM	Data Mode	I	DSR
	12,30	TR	Terminal Ready	I	DTR
	15	IC	Incoming Call	II	RI
	13,31	RR	Receiver Ready	I	DCD
	33	SQ	Signal Quality	II	SQ
	16	SR	Signaling Rate Selector	II	DRS (DTE)
	2	SI	Signaling Rate Indicator	II	DRS (DCE)
	17,35	TT	Terminal Timing	I	XTC
	5,23	ST	Send Timing	I	TC
	8,26	RT	Receive Timing	I	RC
3		SSD	Secondary Send Data	II	STD
4		SRD	Secondary Receive Data	II	SRD
7		SRS	Secondary Request to Send	II	SRTS
8		SCS	Secondary Clear to Send	II	SCTS
2		SRR	Secondary Receiver Ready	II	SDCD
	10	LL	Local Loopback	II	None
	14	RL	Remote Loopback	II	None
	18	TM	Test Mode	II	None
	32	SS	Select Standby	II	None
	36	SB	Standby Indicator	II	None
	16	SF	Select Frequency	II	None
	28	IS	Terminal in Service	II	None
	34	NS	New Signal	II	None
	3		Undefined		
	21		Undefined		

FIGURE 4-10   RS-232-C and RS-449 signal equivalents.

of these new signals are used for testing and diagnostic purposes; others are necessary for RS-422-A and RS-423-A transmission.

Notice that some of the signals in RS-449 use two pins. These signals are known as *Category I* signals, and the second pin allows for RS-422-A transmission, which we present below. The other signals on the RS-449 interface, which use only one pin, are known as *Category II* signals.

The real technical advantage of the RS-449 standard is found in its methods of electrical transmission of signals, as described in the RS-422-A and RS-423-A standards. These standards can surpass the RS-232-C speed and distance limits, while allowing for compatibility with older RS-232-C devices.

RS-422-A describes a method of *balanced transmission* that can be used for the RS-449 Category I signals. Balanced transmission requires two wires to send data or a control signal, allowing for high data rates and high reliability. Therefore, each of the Category I signals requires two pins. RS-422-A allows a variable transmission rate, according to the distance involved, as shown in Fig. 4-11. The maximum distance varies from 40 feet to 4000 feet, and the maximum speed can reach 10 million bits per second, or 10 *Mbps*.

RS-423-A describes a method of *unbalanced transmission* used for all of the RS-449 Category II signals. Unbalanced transmission sends the signal over one wire, and all signals share a *common return*. There are two of these returns, *Send Common* and *Receive Common*, one for each direction. RS-423-A also allows a variable transmission rate, according to the distance involved, as illustrated in Fig. 4-11. The maximum distance varies from 40 feet to 4000 feet, and the maximum speed can reach 100 kbps.

RS-449 devices can use RS-422-A for their Category I circuits if the added performance is needed. Of course, the extra wires and circuitry costs required for balanced transmission make RS-422-A more expensive than RS-423-A. Therefore, many applications of RS-449 use RS-423-A for their Category I circuits. The balanced transmission has the additional advantage of being less susceptible to noise and interference errors than unbalanced transmission.

Category II circuits, for which performance is generally not an issue, always use RS-423-A. In addition, RS-423-A devices can be attached to RS-232-C devices using a special wiring adapter, since the unbalanced transmission is similar. Of course, then both devices are limited by the RS-232-C distance and speed limitations. RS-449 handshaking is so similar to that used in RS-232-C that we do not elaborate further on the specific RS-449 signals here.

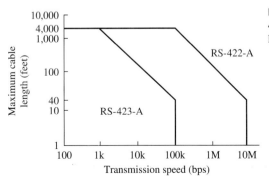

FIGURE 4-11   RS-422-A and RS-423-A speed and distance limitations.

ITU(CCITT) has a set of equivalent standards for RS-449, RS-422-A, and RS-423-A. The functional signals that are shared by RS-232-C and RS-449 are described by the ITU(CCITT) V.24 standard already mentioned. The RS-422-A and RS-423-A transmission standards are similar to the ITU(CCITT) *V.11* and *V.10* standards, respectively.

With the added speed, enhanced distance range, and the other functions of RS-449, RS-422-A, and RS-423-A, why are RS-232-C devices still dominant as the general-purpose data communications interfaces? The distance limitation of RS-232-C can be overcome using inexpensive devices that we consider later. In addition, RS-232-C interfaces are inexpensive to implement, as the components are already in mass production. Finally, RS-232-C devices are already installed in large numbers, and connecting to these devices requires conforming to the RS-232-C standard. Although RS-423-A can connect to RS-232-C, it is more expensive to use a 37-pin connector, and then a converter, than to use a standard RS-232-C interface in the first place. For all these reasons, RS-449 is generally used today only where added speed and longer distances are an absolute necessity.

Although there are many other general-purpose data communications interface standards in use today, RS-232-C is certainly the most common, with all the others trailing far behind.

HIGH-SPEED DESKTOP SERIAL INTERFACES

There are several serial interfaces used in short-distance applications, typically for attaching devices on a desktop to a personal computer. Though none of these interfaces are used extensively in computer networking, they are worth mentioning here so that their functions can be compared to RS-232-C and RS-449. These desktop standards offer speeds much higher than traditional data communications interfaces, as well as the ability to attach many devices to a single computer port. One such standard is the *Universal Serial Bus*, or *USB*, which commonly operates at 12 Mbps. Another standard, *IEEE 1394*, also known as *High Performance Serial Bus* or *Firewire*, operates at speeds up to 400 Mbps. While data communications devices like modems can be attached with these standards, the standards offer very high speeds, and their real benefit is for devices like scanners, printers, and video cameras. Since virtually every PC today has some of these ports, more modems are offering these interfaces for user convenience, even though the speeds they deliver far surpass what modems require.

REMOTE DIGITAL TRANSMISSION

All of the interface standards we have mentioned so far in this chapter are intended for transmission on a user's premises, over a relatively short distance. The user generally owns all of the wiring or cabling between the devices.

But what about terminals accessing host computers across town, across the country, or across an ocean? Our public telephone network's standard voice communications circuits are not well suited to the *digital transmission* we have been discussing. These square waves, however, can be sent over special *digital circuits* provided by the common carriers.

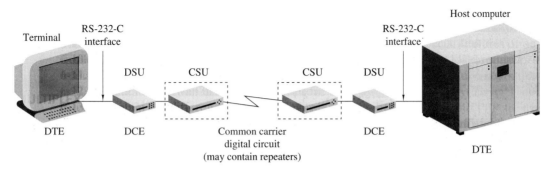

FIGURE 4-12   Typical use of DSUs and CSUs.

Typically, the terminal, or host computer, communicates using one of the standard DTE interfaces we have already examined, like RS-232-C. The DTE is then connected to a special device known as a *digital service unit*, or *DSU*. This DSU uses a DCE interface to communicate with the terminal or host computer and then transmits the data in a special format over the common carrier's digital circuits. Typical use of a DSU is depicted in Fig. 4-12.

Usually the voltage levels required for transmission of data between the DSUs are different from those used by a short-distance interface, like RS-232-C. The DSU is able to convert the signals from the voltage levels used by the terminal to those needed by the digital circuit. Even if RS-232-C is used to connect the terminal to the DSU, the 50-foot limitation applies only to the distance between the DSU and the terminal, not to the distance between the local DSU and the remote DSU.

A *channel service unit*, or *CSU*, is sometimes required at the end of the common carrier's circuit. The trend today, however, is to incorporate the functions of the CSU into the DSU. Since a separate CSU is not always used, it is shown with dashed lines in Fig. 4-12.

The "digital circuit" portion of Fig. 4-12 can span several miles, or several thousand miles, depending on the locations of the host computer and terminal. Special equipment, known as *repeaters*, are placed at regular intervals in the digital circuits to maintain the data signal strength over these long distances and to ensure that it is understandable to the receiving DSU/CSU.

An analogy for the repeater function can be found in the classic firefighter's bucket line. Rather than have one firefighter take the bucket of water up a hill, he hands the bucket to another firefighter, she hands it to the next one, etc. Eventually, the bucket reaches the top of the hill, but the work of sending the water was shared by each firefighter.

A digital repeater simply receives a digital signal (a square wave) and sends it on to the next repeater. In the firefighter's bucket line, some water may spill as the bucket is passed from one firefighter to the next. Similarly, as data is transmitted, it becomes weaker as it gets farther from the repeater. It is the function of the repeater to rejuvenate or regenerate the signal before sending it on. This is the equivalent of each firefighter keeping a spare glass of water at his or her side so that he or she could "top off" the bucket, if necessary, before passing it on.

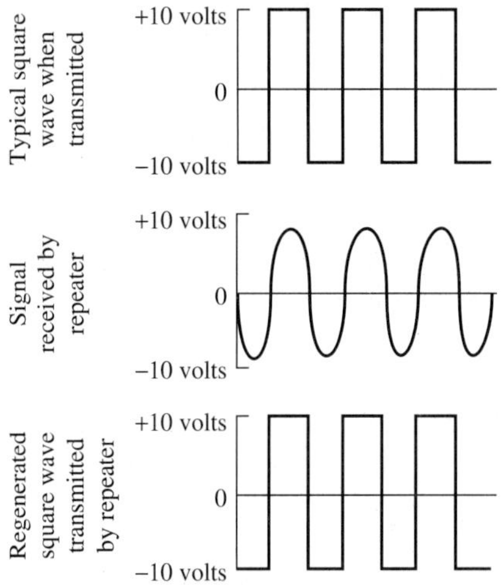

Typical square wave when transmitted

+10 volts

0

−10 volts

Signal received by repeater

+10 volts

0

−10 volts

Regenerated square wave transmitted by repeater

+10 volts

0

−10 volts

FIGURE 4-13   Digital repeaters and square-wave regeneration.

Considering a square wave between −10 and +10 volts as our digital signal, Fig. 4-13 illustrates a repeater's function. The signal deteriorates as it gets farther from the DSU. Before the signal enters the repeater, the highest portion of the signal is barely +9 volts, and it is far from square. The repeater regenerates the signal and sends out a clean square wave at the full 10 volts. The key to using repeaters is that they must be placed close enough to each other so that the signal is still recognizable when it enters the repeater. Without repeaters, the signal would simply fade out, much as a person's voice becomes unintelligible as we walk farther and farther away from the person. These digital repeaters can be separate devices or can be incorporated into the common carrier's switching equipment.

We have already considered the general functions of digital transmission. There are several specific digital transmission options available from common carriers for digital circuits.

DATAPHONE DIGITAL SERVICE

AT&T's *Dataphone Digital Service*, or *DDS*, provides digital circuits for data transmission speeds of 2400 bps, 4800 bps, 9600 bps, 56 kbps, and 64 kbps. The cost of the service varies according to the data speed used. The service can be provided over four wires, and the customer can either lease or own the DSU/CSU, depending on the common carrier. DDS is currently marketed under many different names by other common carriers, and it describes one method of communicating digitally between DSUs.

T-1 CARRIER

T-1 carrier service, available from almost all of the common carriers, is a 1.544-Mbps digital path. For users with lower data rates but with many devices at each location, the T-1 carrier can be divided into 24 separate channels. Since some of the 1.544 Mbps is used for signaling information, the 24 channels can each carry either roughly 64 kbps of digitized voice or 56 kbps of data. T-1 is nothing more than a high-speed method of digital communications between DSUs. We discuss the use of the T-1 carrier and higher speed digital circuits more extensively in Chapter 10. In Europe and other areas, a 2.048-Mbps service known as *E-1* is also popular.

INTEGRATED SERVICES DIGITAL NETWORK

The *Integrated Services Digital Network*, or *ISDN*, is a standard for digital voice and data communications. The data circuit portion of ISDN includes data rates from 16 kbps to 64 kbps for the individual user and typically up to 1.544 Mbps for high-volume transmission. Even higher bandwidth is possible with *Broadband ISDN*. We present ISDN more extensively in Chapter 10.

PACKET DATA NETWORKS

Another method of long-distance data transmission is through the use of packet data networks, including *packet switching* and *frame relay networks*. These networks allow terminals and host computers to connect to other host computers anywhere on the network, which can span thousands of miles. The user has the option of connecting to the same host computer all the time or choosing a different computer with each call, much as we do on the public telephone network. The *Internet* is another packet data network that can transport data around the globe. We examine these and other networks in detail in Chapter 8.

DIGITAL ACCESS

Digital access to the central office can also be provided by *digital subscriber line* services. These services offer digital connections at various speeds to the central office, where the data can then be passed to any network. Another option for local access is provided by *cable modems*. In this case, data is carried by the cable television company to a data network. The Internet is the data network most people connect to with these services. Digital subscriber line and cable modems will be discussed in more detail in Chapter 10.

DIGITAL AND ANALOG BANDWIDTH

A common measure of a communications circuit's usefulness is its *bandwidth*, or carrying capacity. In the digital circuits we have been discussing, bandwidth is simply the capacity in bits per second that can be transmitted. For example, we could say that T-1 is a higher bandwidth circuit than DDS, because T-1 offers a 1.544-Mbps bandwidth, while DDS offers 64 kbps or less.

However, not all communications circuits are digital. In digital transmission, only ones and zeroes are sent and received. Normal telephone lines, like those found in our homes, are designed to carry the wide range of pitches that make up human speech, not ones and zeroes. We call these different pitches *frequencies*. A high-pitched tone is

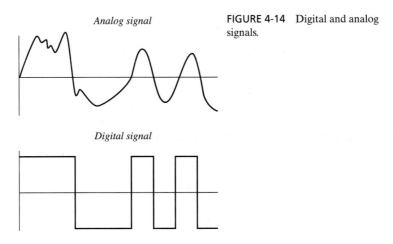

Analog signal

Digital signal

FIGURE 4-14 Digital and analog signals.

therefore also a high-frequency tone, and a low-pitched tone is a low-frequency tone. Human speech, music, and the noise made by a car's engine are all a series of unpredictable sounds, each with its own constantly varying pitch and volume; this type of signal is called an *analog* signal. Whereas digital information is a predictable 0 or 1 (and nothing in between), analog information can vary infinitely over a given range. A comparison between a digital and an analog signal can be found in Fig. 4-14.

There is no way to predict what a person will say on the telephone. We can, however, predict what the average human voice sounds like and what type of equipment will be needed to transmit and receive that voice, whatever it's saying. The analog bandwidth of a communications circuit is the range of frequencies that it can transmit.

How do we determine the frequency of a signal? A perfect tone that maintains its pitch and volume indefinitely looks like a *sine wave* when converted to electrical energy. Notice that a sine wave, as illustrated in Fig. 4-15, repeats itself again and again, and each repetition is known as a *cycle*. Each cycle contains a peak and a valley, and the height of each peak (and depth of each valley) doesn't vary in a perfect sine wave. The height of each peak is known as the *amplitude* of the sine wave; this amplitude is also equal to the depth of each valley. In addition, the time for each

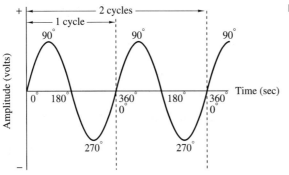

FIGURE 4-15 Sine wave.

complete cycle is also constant and is known as the *period* of the sine wave. The number of cycles of a sine wave in a second is known as its *frequency*. The frequency of a sine wave is therefore measured in *cycles per second*; the term *hertz*, abbreviated *Hz*, is equivalent to cycles per second and is commonly used today.

For convenience, each cycle of a sine wave can be divided into 360 degrees, just like a circle, as shown in Fig. 4-15. Regardless of the frequency or amplitude of a sine wave, it crosses the axis at 0, 180, and 360 degrees (360 is the same as 0, since the sine wave repeats forever). The peak is always at 90 degrees, and the valley is always at 270 degrees. For example, a sine wave of one cycle per second would reach its peak a quarter of a second into its cycle, or at 90 degrees; a sine wave of two cycles per second would reach its peak an eighth of a second into its cycle, but still at 90 degrees.

A standard telephone line adequately transmits tones between 300 Hz and 3300 Hz. As illustrated in Fig. 4-16, the tones near the center of these frequencies are transmitted the best. Most human speech is made up of tones that fall in this range, though a very small percentage of speech falls outside of this range. This situation explains why some people have a "telephone voice," a voice that sounds different on the phone than in person. Another example of the bandwidth limitations of the telephone network can be heard by listening to a radio call-in talk show. The caller always sounds less audible than the host, because only part of the caller's voice reached the radio station: the portion between 300 Hz and 3300 Hz. The telephone lines could support higher frequencies, but economics dictated that the frequencies between 300 Hz and 3300 Hz were sufficient for adequate conversation at a reasonable price. Since the highest frequency passed is 3300 Hz and the lowest is 300 Hz, the bandwidth is the difference, or 3000 Hz.

Why all this concern about telephone line bandwidth when we are studying data communications? In order to transmit ones and zeroes over standard telephone lines, we must first translate them to audible tones. By understanding the bandwidth limitations of the standard telephone line, we can ensure that the tones used can be transmitted reliably.

TRANSMISSION MEDIA

There are many different types of *transmission media* in use in data communications today. Transmission media are the physical paths for carrying information, like a pair of wires.

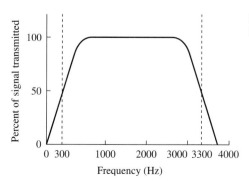

FIGURE 4-16   Telephone channel bandwidth.

A typical local loop between the central office and our home is made up of *twisted pair* wire. Each local loop consists of a pair of wires, continuously twisted throughout its entire length. Typically, the wires are made of copper and coated with an insulating material, and information is transmitted by sending electrical current through the wires. The twisting of the wires helps minimize the effects of certain types of noise on the voice or data transmission. The effects of twisting wire can be illustrated with most modern clock radios. A clock radio's power cord often acts as the antenna for FM reception; if we straighten the power cord, we get the best radio signal reception, and twisting it minimizes the signal received from the surroundings. When transmitting voice or data over wire, we want to minimize the interference received. Therefore, we twist the telephone wire to reduce the amount of signals received from the surroundings; not only does this twisting reduce interference from radio stations, but it minimizes other forms of electromagnetic interference as well.

Twisted pair wire is often used at customer facilities, and also over long distances, to carry voice as well as data communications. Though its bandwidth is limited to 300 Hz to 3300 Hz in the telephone network, this is partly due to the equipment on each end. Higher frequencies can be achieved using special equipment, but twisted pair is generally considered a low-frequency transmission medium. Shielding can be used on twisted pair wire to reduce further the effects of interference and noise, though using it increases the cost. Data rates of 100 Mbps are possible for short distances on customer-owned networks, though 56 kbps is the more accepted maximum over the standard analog telephone network, which is limited by its bandwidth of 300 Hz to 3300 Hz.

The main advantages of twisted pair wire are that it is relatively inexpensive (costing only pennies per foot) and easy to install. The wire is flexible enough to be routed through conduit and on cable trays in office buildings, and each pair of wires is usually less than a sixteenth of an inch in diameter. In many older buildings found in downtown areas of cities, this space requirement is critical, because cables must be run between floors in the narrow space left over in existing elevator shafts. Many pairs of wires are often combined inside a larger cable. In addition, installing twisted pair requires little training, it is readily available, and inexpensive (less than $2) modular phone jacks can be used to make connections. Finally, many buildings are already wired with several twisted pairs in each office to allow for phone lines. Separate twisted pairs can be used for voice and data communications, or the two can be combined on a single twisted pair, as found in advanced digital PBXs.

Another type of cabling often used for data communications, video transmission, and some voice communication is *coaxial cable*, or *coax*. Most cable television systems use coax to connect subscribers. A coax cable usually consists of a single wire in the center surrounded by a core of insulating material, with an outer conductive wrapping, usually a copper cylinder, covered by a final insulating sheath. A cross section of a coax cable is presented in Fig. 4-17, along with a standard coaxial male and female connector. The outer copper cylinder acts as a shield from any external interference; data can be transmitted electronically on the inner wire. Any noise or interference from the surroundings is absorbed by the copper cylinder and sent to the ground. Coax transmits high frequencies, allowing for high data rates, often several hundred Mbps, and it is less susceptible to noise than is twisted pair.

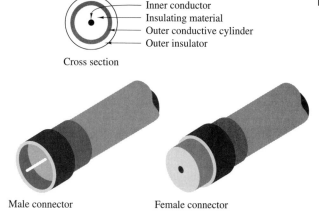

Cross section

Male connector   Female connector

FIGURE 4-17   Coaxial cable.

Coax is slightly more expensive than twisted pair wiring, though the connectors are inexpensive and easy to use with little training. The insulating core does add bulk, however, making the coax cables a quarter inch or more in diameter and far less flexible than twisted pair.

Another type of cable, known as *twinaxial cable*, or *twinax*, is almost identical to coax, except that there are two inner conducting wires. Twinax is used in a few special-purpose applications.

Many manufacturers combine different cables to provide an all-purpose wiring scheme for customer premises. The *IBM Cabling System* and the *AT&T Premises Distribution System* are two such schemes; each includes different types of cable with special shielding to meet particular customer applications.

Fiber optic cable is a popular high-bandwidth transmission medium. Data is transmitted by shining light through a special type of glass fiber. Fiber optic transmission is a modern-day form of the signal lights used to transmit information between ships at sea. The only difference is that in fiber optics, the light travels not through the air, but through glass fiber, and the data rates can exceed a trillion bits per second. One method used to send data through fiber optic cables is simply turning the light on and off. For example, when the light is on, a 1 is transmitted, and when the light is off, a 0 is transmitted. While a single optical channel was traditionally used in fiber optic cable, multiple channels, each on a different color of light, can be used to increase the bandwidth. This technique, known as *wave division multiplexing*, or *WDM*, allows many separate channels of data, each carried by a different color of light in the fiber optic cable. We will discuss multiplexing technologies further in Chapter 5.

Fiber optic cable is far more expensive per foot than coax or twisted pair, but the high bandwidth can still make fiber optics economical for high-volume applications. The cost of installing fiber optic cable is also high, with connections costing far more than coax or twisted pair; special equipment and training are required.

Fiber optic cable is no bulkier than coax and is about as flexible. It is not affected at all by electrical and radio noise and interference, since the fiber optic transmission uses light, not electricity, to send data. This noise immunity makes fiber optics popular with long-distance carriers seeking to provide high-quality voice and data connections. Some local carriers are already choosing this medium, since the added bandwidth of a fiber optic local loop allows them to provide additional services. On the other hand, existing twisted pair local loops are certainly adequate for most voice and data transmission.

Satellite transmission uses radio waves to transmit data. A *satellite dish*, or antenna, known as the *uplink* station, transmits data to the satellite, which orbits the earth. *Transponders* on the satellite then repeat the signal, which is received by another satellite dish, known as the *downlink* station. Satellite transmission is depicted in Fig. 4-18. Conventional satellites typically orbit approximately 22,230 miles above the earth's surface; any satellite dish pointed at the satellite can receive the signal, provided that it is tuned to the proper frequency, much the way we tune in to a radio station.

To help understand satellites, picture a strange mirror orbiting above the earth. Standing in Florida, we shine a very powerful flashlight pointed right at this mirror. This special mirror then reflects the light over the entire country. Our friend in Oregon can then read outside in the light provided by this mirror. We could not light up the whole country with our powerful flashlight without the help of the mirror to reflect the light everywhere. Similarly, the satellite takes our data and repeats it so that everyone within reach of the satellite can receive the signal. We simply point our dish at the satellite and begin transmitting. Since the satellite is so high, the same satellite can transmit data to almost a third of the world; going further simply requires relaying the signal to another satellite. A major advantage of satellites is their ability to communicate from almost anywhere to almost anywhere else.

The bandwidth of satellite transmission depends on the equipment used in the uplink and downlink stations and the number of satellite channels used; each satellite is

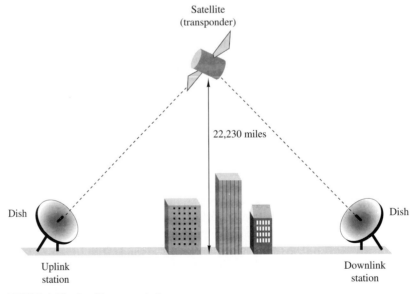

FIGURE 4-18 Satellite transmission.

capable of handling many channels at one time, each of different transmission frequencies. Satellite bandwidth can extend from 64 kbps to many Mbps and is almost unlimited if enough channels are used. Satellite transmission is usually cheaper over long distances than fiber optics or twisted pair, because there is no cabling cost between the two locations. The satellite dishes are a one-time purchase and do not have to be leased monthly from telephone carriers, though the satellite channels must be leased.

However, satellite transmissions are subject to noise and long delays. Since every transmission must go from the ground to the satellite and back to the ground, each transmission takes approximately a 45,000-mile trip. This transmission occurs at roughly the speed of light, so the trip takes a quarter of a second. Sending a message and receiving a response means at least a half-second delay for the round-trip. A half-second wait may seem trivial to us, but a computer might be able to transmit 4800 bits during that time.

The long delays of satellite transmission can produce the so-called "tunnel effect," where annoying echoes are heard during long-distance calls. Though these echoes can be prevented by using echo cancellers, nothing can be done about the delay between transmission and reception. A transcontinental call over twisted pair wire will probably go no farther than 5000 miles, no matter how convoluted the call routing; the same call using a satellite travels nine times farther and therefore can markedly slow down host computers waiting to transmit data.

While these high-altitude satellites have carried voice and data communications for decades, a new breed of satellite, known as a *low-earth orbit* satellite, or *LEO* satellite, has been launched in recent years. These satellites orbit a few hundred miles above the earth. Because they are closer to the earth, more satellites are required to provide global coverage. For example, one such satellite network operates 66 satellites orbiting 485 miles above the earth. Another LEO satellite network operates 48 satellites at an altitude of 736 miles. In between these and conventional satellites falls another type, known as a *medium-earth orbit* satellite, or *MEO* satellite. One of these networks operates 12 satellites at an altitude of 6434 miles. In contrast, a conventional satellite system, based on a *geosynchronous-earth orbit* satellite, or *GEO* satellite, requires only 3 satellites at an altitude of approximately 22,230 miles to cover the globe. This particular altitude is convenient because the satellites orbit at the same speed as the earth rotates, so dish antennas can be aimed once, and the satellite remains in the same relative position. The low-earth and medium-earth orbit satellites are moving with respect to the earth's surface at all times, so these antenna systems are designed to allow for transmission and reception without directly pointing at one particular satellite. The orbiting satellites in these systems hand off calls to one another as they pass near the user. These handoffs are similar in nature to those conducted by a ground-based cellular telephone system, as discussed in Chapter 2.

Satellites are susceptible to noise and interference caused by a variety of sources. Finally, satellite transmission can be heard by anyone with a dish tuning to the right frequency, causing a potential security risk. We discuss methods for minimizing this risk in Chapter 6.

Terrestrial microwave transmission uses radio frequencies similar to those found in satellite transmission. Instead of bouncing radio waves off a satellite, however, the users build tall towers and point the dishes at each other, as illustrated in Fig. 4-19. Alternatively, the dishes can be put on top of buildings, as long as there is a clear *line of sight* be-

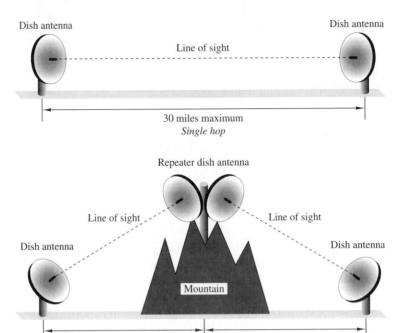

FIGURE 4-19   Terrestrial microwave transmission.

tween the two dishes. If there is an obstruction, like a mountain or building, between the receiver and the destination, another tower can be placed on top of the obstruction and used as a repeater. This additional tower simply receives a signal on one side and transmits it to the other side.

The signals used for microwave transmission can be sent only 20 to 30 miles. Longer distances require using multiple *hops*, with additional towers in between. These intermediary towers act as repeaters, receiving the signal and passing it on. Microwave transmission bandwidth can exceed 250 Mbps.

The key difference between microwave transmission and satellite transmission is that microwave transmission requires a line of sight between the two dish antennas. There can be no obstructions between the two antennas; if we climbed one of the towers on a clear night, we should be able to shine our powerful flashlight at the second tower, and our friend at the top of the second tower would see the light. If the other tower was not the final destination but only a repeater station, our friend would see our flashlight and then point his own flashlight at the next tower.

The cost advantages of microwave transmission lie in relatively short-haul, high-bandwidth applications. The towers and dishes are a one-time purchase cost, there are no satellite channels to lease, and there is currently no shortage of microwave frequencies. Like conventional satellite transmission, there is no cabling cost between the locations, because the signal travels through the air. However, each added hop significantly increases the cost, since every repeater requires a separate tower and two dish antennas, one pointed in each direction. Microwave transmission is subjected to the

Type	Advantages	Disadvantages
Twisted pair wire	Very inexpensive Easy to install Already installed in many locations	Doesn't pass high frequencies well Relatively low bandwidth
Coaxial cable	Shielded Fairly inexpensive Moderately high bandwidth	Bulky and somewhat inflexible
Fiber optic cable	Transmission unaffected by noise Very high bandwidth	Expensive to install Repeaters often required
Satellite	No line of sight needed No cabling needed between sites High bandwidth	Channels must be leased High initial equipment cost Long delays
Terrestrial microwave	No cabling needed between sites High bandwidth	Line of sight needed Towers and repeaters can be expensive High initial equipment cost

FIGURE 4-20   A comparison of transmission media.

same noise and interference as satellite transmission, though it is less likely that we will be encountering interference on a 30-mile route than on a 45,000-mile transmission.

A chart summarizing the different transmission media, and their advantages and disadvantages, is presented in Fig. 4-20.

BASEBAND VS. BROADBAND

There clearly are many different types of transmission media, each suited to certain applications. In addition, there are two methods used to transmit data, baseband and broadband.

In *baseband transmission*, a single data signal is transmitted directly on a wire. The RS-232-C interface, for which a separate wire is used for each signal, is an example of baseband transmission: TD and RD each occupy a separate wire, and the data is transmitted directly on the wires using positive and negative voltages.

Broadband transmission is a technique in which the data to be transmitted are sent using a *carrier signal*, such as a sine wave. Since many different frequency carrier signals can be transmitted simultaneously, more than one signal can be sent on the same wire. This technique is found in cable television, where only a single cable enters our house, but there are many separate signals on that cable; we view the desired station by tuning the particular channel's frequency on our television set or cable box. In data communications, broadband transmission always uses analog signals to send data. We now explain the most common use of broadband transmission in data communications.

MODULATION

The conversion of digital signals to analog form for transmission is called *modulation*, and converting these analog signals back to digital form is called *demodulation*. A device that performs modulation and demodulation is a modulator/demodulator, or a *modem*.

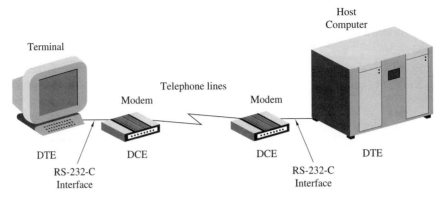

FIGURE 4-21 Using modems in data communications circuits.

Why is the conversion of the signals necessary? Typically, modems are used when the host computer and terminal are in different locations. Most interface standards, like RS-232-C, transmit data using positive and negative voltages, which form square waves. The square waves used in digital transmission cannot be sent over standard telephone lines without first being converted to analog form, because the public telephone network was designed to carry analog signals, like speech. Typical placement of a modem in a data communications circuit is shown in Fig. 4-21. We depict the communications circuit, using common industry practice, as a lightning bolt. The lightning bolt represents the local loops, the central office(s), and any toll offices present in the connection between the two modems.

In some cases, the telephone line between the two modems is permanent, or *leased*. In other cases, the terminal is contacting a different host computer each time or needs to contact the host computer only occasionally. These situations are suitable for a *dial-up*, or *switched circuit*, for which a new telephone call is placed for each connection.

In every dial-up connection there are two modems; the modem that places the call is known as the *originate modem*, and the modem that answers the call is known as the *answer modem*. Some early modems were *originate only* (could only place calls) or *answer only* (could only answer calls). Most of today's modems can both place and receive calls and are known as *originate/answer modems*.

Dial-up modem calls can be placed in two ways. Early modems, known as *dumb modems*, performed only modulation and demodulation. In addition to a modem, a telephone instrument had to be attached to the phone line to place calls. The terminal user picked up the telephone and dialed the number of the answer (remote) modem; after reaching the answer modem, the user could then hang up the phone and hit a "data" button on the originate (local) modem. This put the originate modem in "data mode" and caused it to begin communicating with the answer modem. Some customers used PBXs to automate the dialing process; after dialing the call, instead of hitting a "data" button, a PBX would close a switch connecting a pair of wires coming from the originate modem known as the *mode indicator leads*, or *MI/MIC leads*. The originate modem would recognize this as a signal to enter the "data mode" and begin communicating with the answer modem.

A newer generation of modems, known as *smart modems*, can accept dialing instructions directly from the user of the terminal, dial the call, and perform the necessary modulation and demodulation when the connection is established. Most modems used with personal computers today are smart modems, since the software can instruct the smart modem to dial and disconnect calls. Since the smart modem is able to dial the call itself, using rotary or Touch-tone dialing, a separate telephone instrument is not needed for a smart modem.

Typically, modems convert the square waves that represent ones and zeroes to sine waves for analog transmission. There are many different methods for performing this conversion, each with its own advantages and disadvantages. Both the originate and answer modem must use the same modulation methods for successful data communications. We now explain several popular types of modulation.

AMPLITUDE MODULATION

In one modulation technique, known as *amplitude modulation*, or *AM*, the amplitude, or height, of the sine wave varies to transmit the ones and zeroes. Another name for amplitude modulation is *amplitude shift keying*, or *ASK*, since data is transmitted by shifting amplitudes. The bit pattern 00101001 is being transmitted using amplitude modulation in Fig. 4-22. Notice that the sine wave's amplitude is high when transmitting a 1, and low when transmitting a 0. The duration, or width, of each cycle of the sine wave does not change throughout the transmission; in other words, the frequency doesn't vary. In Fig. 4-22, there are two complete cycles of the sine wave (two peaks and two valleys) for each bit transmitted. The number of complete cycles used to send a bit with amplitude modulation is an arbitrary choice and varies depending on the type and speed of the modem.

If we attached a telephone to a modem using amplitude modulation and listened to it transmit the bit pattern 00101001, we would hear a single tone that never varies in pitch (frequency), but gets louder when transmitting a 1, and softer when transmitting a 0. Of course, we would need very sensitive ears, since most modems transmit several thousand bits per second.

One major disadvantage of amplitude modulation is that telephone lines are very susceptible to variations in transmission quality that affect amplitude. Particularly on long-distance calls, we are accustomed to hearing the volume of a person's voice vary during the course of a conversation. If a modem using amplitude modulation is transmitting a 1 when the telephone connection volume fades, the receiving modem will hear a low-amplitude sine wave and may interpret it as a 0.

We have considered only the transmission of data in one direction at a time. In a full duplex communications circuit, a sine wave of another frequency can be used to si-

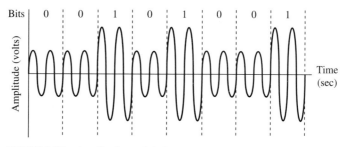

FIGURE 4-22   Amplitude modulation.

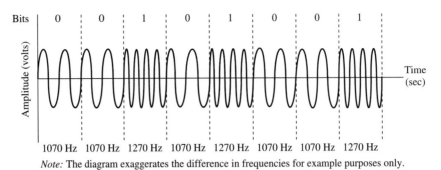

Note: The diagram exaggerates the difference in frequencies for example purposes only.

FIGURE 4-23 Frequency modulation.

multaneously send data in the other direction. The amplitude of this second sine wave also varies to send ones and zeroes in this direction.

FREQUENCY MODULATION

Another technique, known as *frequency modulation*, or *FM*, varies the frequency of the sine wave to transmit data while the amplitude remains constant. Another name for frequency modulation is *frequency shift keying*, or *FSK*, since data is transmitted by shifting frequencies. The same bit pattern, 00101001, is being transmitted using frequency modulation in Fig. 4-23. Notice that the amplitude of the sine wave doesn't vary, but the length of each cycle, and hence the frequency, does. A low frequency (1070 Hz) is used to send a 0, and a higher frequency (1270 Hz) is used to send a 1. If we attached a telephone to a modem using frequency modulation and listened to it transmit the bit pattern 00101001, we would hear a low-pitched tone for each 0 and a higher pitched tone for each 1. The volumes, or amplitudes, of both tones would be the same.

Since the receiving modem recognizes only differences in frequency and is not concerned with the amplitude of the signal, small variations in phone line volume will not cause demodulation errors when using frequency modulation.

If we need to send data in both directions at once, we need two frequencies (one for a 1 and one for a 0) for each direction, for a total of four frequencies. Frequency modulation is often used for 300 bps transmission according to the *Bell 103/113* specification, also known as AT&T 103/113. The originating modem sends a one using a 1270 Hz tone or a zero using a 1070 Hz tone. The answering modem sends a one using a 2225 Hz tone or a zero using a 2025 Hz tone. The ITU(CCITT) *V.21* standard describes a 300 bps modem used internationally with a similar modulation scheme.

PHASE MODULATION

A more sophisticated technique is known as *phase modulation*, or *PM*, because data is transmitted by changing the phase of the sine wave. Another name for phase modulation is *phase shift keying*, or *PSK*, since data is transmitted by shifting phase. A sine wave normally repeats itself indefinitely, with one peak and valley after another. Shifting phase breaks the sine wave abruptly and starts it again a few degrees forward or backward.

We assume 180 degree forward phase shifts for our example, shown in Fig. 4-24. The sine wave continues uninterrupted for two time periods as we transmit zeroes. Then

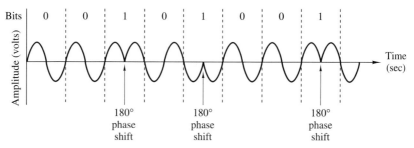

FIGURE 4-24   Phase modulation.

the sine wave stops abruptly at the axis, and we skip forward 180 degrees; in a sine wave, skipping forward 180 degrees moves us halfway across the sine wave, bringing us to the point where the sine wave starts back up to the next peak. In our example, the 180 degree phase shift is used to send ones, and a continuous sine wave is used to send zeroes; this is only one possible way to use phase modulation to transmit data. Notice that the amplitude and frequency of the sine waves stay constant throughout transmission. We simply shift phase during a time period to send a 1, or continue the sine wave uninterrupted to send a 0. The receiving modem can monitor the incoming sine wave and determine if the phase shifted during a particular time period.

A forward phase shift is nothing more than skipping ahead in our sine wave. For example, normally a record player will play an entire album. However, we could lift up the needle and skip a song that we don't enjoy. If we wanted to send data using this method, we could arbitrarily say, "If I skip a song, I'm sending a 1. If I leave the record alone, I'm sending a 0." The receiver must know what song normally comes next on the album in order to determine if a song was skipped. With phase modulation, the receiver knows exactly what the sine wave should look like. If part of the sine wave is skipped, the receiver can recognize this, just as we would recognize that a song was skipped. In our record player example, we skip an entire song; in Fig. 4-24, we skip 180 degrees of the sine wave.

If we need to send data in two directions at once, we use one frequency for each direction. The phases shift on each of these sine waves as necessary to send data. Like frequency modulation, phase modulation is not affected by slight variations in amplitude normally occurring on the telephone network. The main advantage of phase modulation is that only a single-frequency sine wave is used to send both ones and zeroes in each direction. In frequency modulation, separate frequencies are required for sending a one and sending a zero in each direction.

BITS PER SECOND VS. BAUD

So far, we have considered the modulation of only one bit at a time. We have varied amplitude, frequency, or phase to send a one or a zero. In each case, there were two alternatives: a high or low amplitude, a high or low frequency, or a phase shift or no phase shift. We've already discussed the Bell 103/113 standard for 300 bps transmission; for each bit, the transmitting modem needed to decide which frequency to send. The number of these decisions, or possible signal changes in a second, is known as the *baud rate* of a modem. The 300 bps modem described by our example is also a 300 baud modem, because the signal could potentially change 300 times in a second, once for each bit.

Some terminals communicate at much higher speeds, like 9600 bps. However, a telephone circuit's bandwidth does not transmit frequencies higher than 3300 Hz. If we perform only one amplitude, frequency, or phase change in a given cycle, and a single bit is transmitted with each change, we would be limited to 3300 bps. We could build a more sophisticated modem that would recognize an amplitude, frequency, or phase change after half a cycle, but this would still limit us to 6600 bits per second. Clearly, there is a need for faster modulation methods to handle higher speed devices.

What if we could send more than one bit with each shift of amplitude, frequency, or phase? If we wanted to send two bits, that would provide us with four possible combinations: 00, 01, 10, and 11. Therefore, using amplitude modulation, we would need four possible amplitudes; frequency modulation would require four frequencies, and phase modulation would require four phases. When we send two bits in this way, it is known as *dibit modulation*.

One of the most commonly used forms of modulation today is the dibit phase shift keying described by the *Bell 212A* (AT&T 212A) specification. In this specification, the originate modem transmits data using a 1200 Hz sine wave, and the answer modem transmits data using a 2400 Hz sine wave. Phase shifts of 90, 0, 180, and 270 degrees represent the bits 00, 01, 10, and 11, respectively. The bit pattern 01001110 is being transmitted according to the Bell 212A standard in Fig. 4-25. A similar 1200 bps modem standard used internationally is the ITU(CCITT) *V.22*.

With this dibit transmission, the modem could change the signal only every two bits, when it may shift the signal's phase. In this case, Bell 212A described 1200 bps transmission: If 1200 bits are sent in a second, and two bits are sent with each possible signal change, the modem is 600 baud. The terminal and host computer require a certain bit per second rate and are not affected by the baud rate. A terminal transmitting 1200 bits per second functions equally well with a 1200 bps/1200 baud modem or a 1200 bps/600 baud modem.

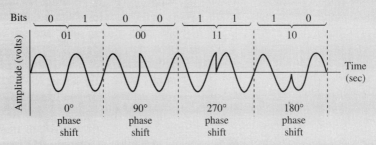

FIGURE 4-25 Dibit phase shift keying using the Bell 212A specification.

Though we have just described dibit modulation, some modems use tribit (three bits at once) or even quabit (four bits at once) modulation. For example, to use tribit phase shift keying, we need to use 45-degree phase shifts to give us the eight possible combinations of three bits: 000, 001, 010, 011, 100, 101, 110, and 111. Quabit phase shift keying would require 22.5-degree phase shifts. These smaller phase shifts require more sophisticated modems to detect the subtle changes.

Since most older modems (300 bps and slower) sent only one bit with each signal change, *bps* and *baud* were equivalent terms and were therefore used interchangeably for many years. Even though today most modems use dibit, tribit, or even quabit modulation, the term *baud* is often mistakenly used instead of *bps*, even by modem vendor sales personnel. For example, the Bell 212A modem, though a 1200 bps/600 baud modem, is often mistakenly referred to as a 1200 baud modem. The easiest way to avoid any misunderstanding when purchasing modems is to specify the bps rate of the host computer or terminal and request a modem that can handle that transmission speed.

MULTISPEED MODEMS

One interesting feature of certain modem specifications is their *multispeed* capability. For example, when a Bell 212A modem begins communications with another modem, it tries to communicate using the 1200 Hz and 2400 Hz tones already mentioned. If the other modem does not provide the appropriate tone, the Bell 212A modem assumes that it has reached a slower modem and tries to communicate using the Bell 103/113 tones we have already presented. In other words, the Bell 212A modem will attempt to communicate at 1200 bps, and if unsuccessful, will fall back to 300 bps. This capability allowed early users of the Bell 212A modem to continue to communicate with older 300 bps modems, yet achieve the increased performance that 1200 bps affords when communicating with other Bell 212A modems. This multispeed capability has become an accepted practice in the industry.

HIGH-SPEED MODEMS

The first widely accepted dial-up 2400 bps modem, described by the *ITU(CCITT) V.22 bis* standard, also included a fallback to the older 1200 bps speed of Bell 212A. The V.22 bis specification is widely used both in this country and internationally for 2400 bps transmission.

High-speed modems often combine two modulation methods to allow for faster transmission rates. The V.22 bis standard achieves 2400 bps by combining changes in phase and amplitude at the same time in a technique known as *quadrature amplitude modulation*. Four bits are sent at once, at 600 baud, for a 2400 bps transmission rate. There are four different phases and four amplitudes, for a total of 16 possible combinations; this allows for all the different possibilities of four bits: 0000, 0001, 0010, 0011, 0100, 0101, 0110, 0111, 1000, 1001, 1010, 1011, 1100, 1101, 1110, and 1111.

The most widely used modulation standard at 9600 bps is the ITU(CCITT) *V.32* standard. This standard also functions at 4800 bps. It utilizes quadrature amplitude modulation with *trellis coding*, which can recover from minor transmission problems. Extra information is sent with the data to allow the receiving modem to detect and correct minor errors. At 14.4 kbps, the ITU(CCITT*) V.32 bis* standard is popular, and at 28.8 and 33.6 kbps, *V.34* is used. A comparison of the various modem standards, and the types of modulation used, is shown in Fig. 4-26.

The ITU (CCITT) *V.90* standard can provide transmission speeds of up to 56 kbps from the central office to the analog-line user, while modulating at V.34 speeds in the other direction. Unlike standard analog modems, which operate on any analog line, this modem requires a digital line connected to a digitally equipped central office on the side transmitting at the higher speed. This digital line, like a T-1 or ISDN line, would normally carry digitized voice. In this case, it will carry signals that look like voice digitized according to the ITU(CCITT) *G.711* standard, but will actually contain computer data. In the high-speed transmission direction, the V.90 modem sends signals through the digital telephone network until they reach the destination central office. At the central office, these signals are assumed to be digitized voice. Therefore, the central office places the analog equivalent of these digital signals on the user's analog local loop. The receiving modem is expecting analog signal levels that mimic the digital ones typically used in the central office. If the line has little noise, the modem will still be able to detect the original signal levels and determine which ones and zeroes they originally represented. An extremely noise-free analog local loop is required on the receiving end to demodulate data at 56 kbps in this manner. In fact, current FCC restrictions in the United States limit this transmission to 53 kbps. In practice, most users connecting with 56 kbps modems approach this rate only sporadically, when the ideal circumstances occur. In the other direction, standard V.34 modulation is used.

Some modem vendors create their own proprietary modulation schemes and do not follow any established standards. The disadvantage is that these modems communicate only with their counterparts manufactured by the same vendor. However, a standard modem, like a V.34 modem, communicates with any V.34 modem, regardless of the manufacturer.

Speed	Standard	Modulation method	Maximum baud rate
300 bps	Bell 103/113	Frequency modulation	300 baud
1200 bps	Bell 212A	Phase modulation	600 baud
2400 bps	V.22bis	Quadrature amplitude modulation	600 baud
4800 bps	V.32	Quadrature amplitude modulation/trellis coding	2400 baud
9600 bps	V.32	Quadrature amplitude modulation/trellis coding	2400 baud
14.4 kbps	V.32bis	Quadrature amplitude modulation/trellis coding	2400 baud
28.8 kbps	V.34	Quadrature amplitude modulation/trellis coding	3429 baud
33.6 kbps	V.34	Quadrature amplitude modulation/trellis coding	3429 baud
56 kbps	V.90	Digital: G.711 Analog: Quadrature amplitude modulation/trellis coding	Digital: 8000 baud Analog: 3429 baud

FIGURE 4-26   Common modem standards.

ERROR-CORRECTING MODEMS

At modem speeds up to 1200 bps, the quality of dial-up phone lines is sufficient to ensure reasonably reliable modem transmission. However, with the advent of 2400 bps modems, the modulation methods became more sophisticated. For example, in the V.22 bis standard, the phase and amplitude both vary, so even slight telephone line noise could cause an error. Most modems operating at speeds of 2400 bps and above have some type of error-correction capability.

Though the higher speed modems use trellis coded modulation, significant line noise can cause more errors than trellis coding can correct. So even these modems need some additional error checking if we want to ensure reliable transmission.

Two approaches are commonly used today to correct for errors between modems, regardless of the speed or underlying modulation methods. The first, known as *Microcom Network Protocol*, or *MNP*, is a commercially licensed error-checking protocol. The second, ITU(CCITT)'s *V.42*, also known as *Link Access Procedure for Modems*, or *LAPM*, is an international standard for error correction. Most modern modems support one or both of these protocols, and users can configure their modems to utilize one of them. Both protocols rely on the receiving modem to detect an error and ask the transmitter to send the data again. The user never sees errors, but may see delays if the modems must halt transmission to retransmit data. The modems will, if necessary, either lower the CTS signal or send an XOFF character to stop the DTE from transmitting while the modem retransmits the prior block. Errors can also be fixed in DTEs or at other places in the network, as discussed in Chapter 6.

DATA COMPRESSION IN MODEMS

Many modems today use data compression. The modems don't send bits any faster, but attempt to send fewer bits by searching for repeated patterns and sending some type of shorthand notation. The receiving modem translates the shorthand back to the original bits, creating the illusion that the two modems are operating at a higher speed.

The fifth version of the previously mentioned MNP standard, known as *MNP 5*, can compress data to half its size under ideal conditions. The ITU(CCITT) *V.42 bis* standard can theoretically compress data to one-fourth its original size under ideal conditions. Since it is hard to predict if the data transmitted will have repeated patterns, compression at these ideal levels should not be expected. In addition, MNP 5 adds some overhead, which actually worsens the transmission of data that is not compressible. V.42 bis, on the other hand, senses if the data is not compressible and suspends operation when it can not improve the data flow.

Compression features are probably the most oversold feature on modems today. Some vendors claim to have a 134.4 kbps modem, when all they have is a V.34 modem operating at 33.6 kbps, with V.42 bis compression, and they are assuming a 4-to-1 compression ratio. This optimistic approach seldom translates to true performance during operation. Data compression is discussed in more detail in Chapter 5.

SHORT-HAUL MODEMS

All of the modems presented thus far have been designed for use over the public telephone network. Occasionally, users may have a large building or campus environment where they need to locate devices a few hundred or even a few thousand feet from each other. If these are RS-232-C devices, the user is limited to 50 feet; any greater distance requires the use of modems. If the user can own or lease wires between these devices, *short-haul modems*, also called *limited-distance modems*, can be utilized.

Short-haul modems transmit data over twisted pair wire, but not through telephone company central offices. They modulate data using frequencies greater than the normal telephone channel bandwidth limit of 3300 Hz. By using these high frequencies, higher transmission rates can be achieved using less expensive hardware. However, the resulting sine waves can be passed over twisted pair wire for only a few miles and cannot be passed through the central office switch. The short-haul modem can transmit for a few miles, and the dial-up modem can transmit around the world, with the help of central offices and toll offices in between. Therefore, a user with a terminal in the basement and a host computer on the fifth floor could connect the two with a pair of short-haul modems and twisted pair wire. This user would have high data rates and no monthly phone line costs.

FACSIMILE, OR FAX, MODEMS

Facsimile, or *fax*, is the electrical transmission of documents over telephone lines. The standards for fax machines are set by the ITU(CCITT). Different standards offer different transmission quality, and this quality, or *resolution*, is measured in lines per inch.

ITU(CCITT) *Group 1* and *Group 2* fax machines were purely analog devices, offering only 100 lines per inch of resolution. Transmission of a typical printed page could take three to six minutes using these techniques.

Modern fax machines employ digital compression technology to shorten the time used for fax transmission. *Group 3* transmission is a common example. Long white spaces or black spaces on a page are described by their dimensions, rather than sent one small dot at a time, as earlier fax machines did. This technique, known as *run length encoding*, reduces the time for transmitting a typical page to under a minute. Group 3 fax typically operates at 4800 bps or 9600 bps and offers 200 lines per inch of resolution.

In a modern fax machine, a scanner converts the document into ones and zeroes, which can be sent by the fax modem. A fax machine contains the scanner, modem, and printer in one unit. Separate fax modems are now available that let any computer with the proper software send and receive faxes as well.

Fax modems use special protocols beyond those found in standard data modems. For example, most fax machines produce a header at the top of each page, indicating the transmitting party and the page number. This information is transferred between the two fax machines, or fax modems, at the start of the transmission.

The *Group 4* standard offers increased resolution and speed, operating at up to 64 kbps with resolutions of up to 400 lines per inch. The higher speeds are seldom used because they are not currently economical for most office communications.

SUMMARY

There are numerous ways to connect terminals to host computers. Many standards organizations, including ANSI, IEEE, EIA, ECSA, IETF, NIST, ITU(CCITT), and ISO, develop specifications for both domestic and international use.

The most commonly used digital interface standard today is EIA's RS-232-C. RS-232-C defines the voltage levels and necessary signals for computer communication between data terminal equipment (DTE) and data circuit-terminating equipment (DCE) interfaces. There are data, ground, timing, and control signals in RS-232-C. Many of these functions are replicated in the seldom-used secondary channel of RS-232-C. The interaction of RS-232-C control signals between the DTE and the DCE is referred to as handshaking. RS-232-C is limited to a distance of 50 feet and a maximum speed of 20 kbps. A null modem cable can be used to connect two DTEs. EIA-232-D and EIA-232-E offer some minor improvements over RS-232-C, but are not having a significant impact.

RS-449 is a more recent standard describing DTE-to-DCE communications; it specifies the interface connector, the necessary signals, and two possible transmission methods. RS-422-A is a method of balanced transmission, with a maximum distance of up to 4000 feet and a maximum speed of 10 Mbps. RS-423-A uses unbalanced transmission, with a maximum distance of 4000 feet and a maximum speed of 100 kbps.

Remote digital transmission over special digital communications circuits requires DSUs and sometimes CSUs at the end of the circuits. Dataphone Digital Service provides digital circuits up to 64 kbps. The T-1 carrier provides a 1.544 Mbps digital path, which can be broken into 24 separate channels. Integrated Services Digital Network is an evolving standard for digital voice and data communications that could provide an all-digital communications network. Packet switching networks, frame relay networks, and the Internet all provide a means for transmitting data to different locations.

A circuit's bandwidth is its carrying capacity. For digital circuits, bandwidth is the number of bits that can be transmitted each second. The bandwidth of an analog circuit is the range of frequencies it can transmit. The bandwidths of different transmission media vary dramatically. Twisted pair, coaxial cable, twinaxial cable, and fiber optic cable are some of the different cabling options. Microwave and satellite transmission media do not require cabling between locations.

In baseband transmission, the data signal is transmitted directly on the wire. Broadband transmission sends data using a carrier signal. Modulation is a common example of broadband transmission, in which digital signals are converted to analog form for transmission over telephone circuits. Modems perform modulation and demodulation and can be used with leased lines or dial-up circuits. Both dumb and smart modems can be used with dial-up lines, and modems can originate calls, answer calls, or both originate and answer calls.

There are many different modulation techniques in use today. In amplitude modulation, a sine wave's amplitude varies to send ones and zeroes. Frequency modulation uses different frequencies to send ones and zeroes. Phase modulation uses shifts in a sine wave's phase to send ones and zeroes. A signal's baud rate is the number of possible changes in a second. If one bit is sent for each signal change, the bit per second rate is the same as the baud rate. Often, the bps rate is faster than the baud rate, because more than one bit is sent with each signal change. Most high-speed modems use dibit, tribit, or quabit techniques. Many modems today have built-in error-correction and data compression features. Short-haul modems are special modems used for short-distance transmission over customer-owned lines, using frequencies outside the bandwidth of the telephone network. Facsimile, or fax, technology electrically transmits documents over phone lines.

TERMS FOR REVIEW

AM
American National
    Standards Institute
Amplitude
Amplitude modulation
Amplitude shift keying
Analog
ANSI
Answer-only modem
ASK
Asserted state
AT&T Premises Distribution
    System

Balanced transmission
Bandwidth
Baseband transmission
Baud rate
Bell 103/113
Bell 212A
Broadband ISDN
Broadband transmission
Cable modems
Carrier signal
Category I
Category II
CCITT

CD
Channel service unit
Chassis ground
Clear to Send
Coax
Coaxial cable
Common return
Consultative Committee on
    International Telephone
    and Telegraph
Control signal
Crossover
CSU

CTS
CX
Cycle
Cycles per second
Data Carrier Detect
Data circuit-terminating
    equipment
Data Rate Select
Data Set Ready
Data terminal equipment
Data Terminal Ready
Dataphone Digital Service
DB9
DB25
DB37
DCD
DCE
DDS
Demodulation
Dial-up
Dibit modulation
Digital circuit
Digital service unit
Digital subscriber line
Digital transmission
Downlink
DRS
DSR
DSU
DTE
DTR
Dumb modem
E-1
ECSA
EIA
EIA-232-D
EIA-232-E
Electronic Industries
    Association
Exchange Carriers Standards
    Association
External Transmit Clock
Federal Information
    Processing Standards
Facsimile
Fax

Fiber optic cable
FIPS
Firewire
FM
Frame ground
Frame relay
Frequency
Frequency modulation
Frequency shift keying
FSK
G.711
Geosynchronous-earth orbit
GEO
GND
Group 1
Group 2
Group 3
Group 4
Handshaking
Hertz
High Performance Serial Bus
Hop
Hz
IBM Cabling System
IEEE
IEEE 1384
IETF
Institute of Electrical and
    Electronics Engineers
Integrated Services Digital
    Network
Interface
International Standards
    Organization
International
    Telecommunications
    Union
Internet
Internet Engineering Task
    Force
ISDN
ISO
ISO Standard 4902
ITU
LAPM
Leased

LEO
Limited-distance modem
Line of sight
Link Access Procedure for
    Modems
Low-earth orbit
Mark
Mbps
Medium-earth orbit
MEO
MI/MIC lead
Microcom Network Protocol
MNP
MNP5
Mode indicator lead
Modem
Modulation
Multispeed
National Bureau of
    Standards
National Electrical Code
National Institute of
    Standards and Technology
NBS
NIST
Null modem cable
Originate-only modem
Originate/answer modem
Packet switching network
Period
Phase modulation
Phase shift keying
PM
Protective ground
PSK
Quadrature amplitude
    modulation
Raised
RC
RD
Receive Clock
Receive Common
Received Data
Recommended Standard
Recommended Standard
    232C

Repeater	*SG*	*Twinax*
Request to Send	*Short-haul modem*	*Twinaxial cable*
Resolution	*Signal Ground*	*Twisted pair*
RI	*Signal Quality Detect*	*Unbalanced transmission*
Ring Indicator	*Sine wave*	*Universal Serial Bus*
RS	*Smart modem*	*USB*
RS-232-C	*Space*	*Uplink*
RS-422-A	*SQ*	*V.10*
RS-423-A	*Square wave*	*V.11*
RS-449	*SRD*	*V.21*
RTS	*SRTS*	*V.22*
Run length encoding	*Standards organization*	*V.22 bis*
Satellite	*STD*	*V.24*
Satellite dish	*Switched*	*V.28*
SCTS	*T-1 carrier*	*V.32*
SDCD	*TC*	*V.32 Bis*
Secondary Clear to Send	*TD*	*V.34*
Secondary Data Carrier	*Terrestrial microwave*	*V.42*
Detect	*Transmission medium*	*V.42 bis*
Secondary Received Data	*Transmit Clock*	*V.90*
Secondary Request to Send	*Transmitted Data*	*Wave division multiplexing*
Secondary Transmitted Data	*Transponder*	*WDM*
Send Common	*Trellis coding*	*XTC*

EXERCISES

4-1. How does the role of standards in the United States differ from that in the rest of the world?

4-2. In the RS-232-C standard, how are ones and zeroes transmitted? How are control signals represented?

4-3. What are the two types of RS-232-C interfaces? Which devices typically fit into each category?

4-4. What is the purpose of the signal ground in RS-232-C? Why is it important?

4-5. Which RS-232-C signals are used only in synchronous transmission? Which of these signals are generated by the DTE, and which by the DCE? What is the purpose of these signals?

4-6. What is the purpose of the control signals in RS-232-C? When is a null modem cable used?

4-7. What does RS-449 define that RS-232-C leaves undefined?

4-8. What are the main differences between the RS-422-A and RS-423-A standards?

4-9. What is the purpose of the DSU/CSU?

4-10. What is the function of a repeater in a digital circuit?

4-11. What are some common digital transmission methods?

4-12.   What is bandwidth? How is analog bandwidth measured? How is digital bandwidth measured?

4-13.   Compare twisted pair wire with coaxial cable. Which is a higher bandwidth medium? Which is already installed in many offices?

4-14.   What is the highest bandwidth cable available today? What is its greatest drawback?

4-15.   Explain the differences between satellite and terrestrial microwave transmission. Which is best suited to shorter distances? Longer distances?

4-16.   What is the difference between baseband and broadband transmission?

4-17.   What is modulation?

4-18.   What are the different types of dial-up modems? How do they originate calls?

4-19.   How does amplitude modulation transmit ones and zeroes? Frequency modulation? Phase modulation?

4-20.   What is the purpose of a short-haul modem? How does it compare with dial-up modems, both technically and economically?

4-21.   How do modern fax machines reduce the time needed for transmission?

4-22.   What is USB?

CHAPTER 5

Improving Data Communications Efficiency

We have already described the minimum hardware components required for data communications. These include terminals, host computers, and sometimes modems and telephone circuits. We now turn to other components that improve the efficiency of data communications, thereby reducing costs and increasing performance.

FRONT-END PROCESSORS

Host computers are well suited to performing numerical calculations, storing and retrieving documents, and accomplishing other tasks in a few millionths of a second. Human terminal operators, however, may type only a few characters in a second. It would be a waste of valuable computer time if the host computer had to spend all of its time monitoring the attached terminals. One of the terminal operators might go on a coffee break, and the host computer would then be tied up with unnecessary monitoring.

A *front-end processor*, or *FEP*, is a communications assistant for the host computer. The front-end processor handles all of the host computer's communications with the outside world, while the host computer concentrates on other things, like calculating this week's payroll deductions. The front-end processor is actually a small, special-purpose computer, dedicated to a single mission. It communicates with the host computer at a very high speed (often several Mbps), while the terminals usually operate at a much lower speed (several kbps). Front-end processors are often referred to as *front ends*.

As an example, consider a brilliant, aloof professor who thinks so fast that she considers speaking with students a waste of time. Rather than asking the class "Do you have any questions?" and then waiting to see if students raise their hands, she hires a teaching assistant. Anyone with questions must write them down and hand them to the teaching assistant as he walks around the room. The assistant writes them all on one page, and he waits patiently for the professor. The professor then grabs the whole page from the assistant, quickly reads it, and writes down all the answers on another piece of paper, which she then hands back to the assistant. It's up to the assistant to walk around the room again, separating each of the answers and handing them to the correct students. The professor is pleased because she didn't even have to deal with the slow-speaking students, and while they digest her answers, she can continue to think great thoughts. The teaching assistant has acted as a front-end processor for the professor; like the host computer, this brilliant professor has better things to do with her time.

In this example, the communication between the students and the teaching assistant occurred at a slow speed, and the communication between the professor and the assistant at a much faster speed. This situation is exactly analogous to the process by which front-end processors communicate. The front-end processor is made up of different logical components, as shown in Fig. 5-1. The *channel interface* connects the front-end processor to the high-speed *input/output channel* of the host computer. The

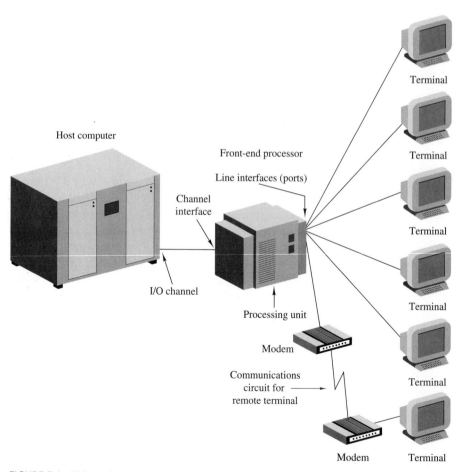

FIGURE 5-1 Using a front-end processor.

processing unit contains the front-end processor's intelligence; it is a special-purpose computer programmed for communications functions. Often, the network control programs are loaded into the processing unit on disk or tape, allowing for future modifications to the software and, hence, the front-end processor's features. Finally, the *line interfaces*, or *front-end ports*, are the relatively low-speed interfaces that usually connect to terminals. If the terminal is located remotely, a pair of modems and a communications circuit can be inserted between the line interface and the terminal.

Since the number of computer ports is often limited by the host computer's architecture, front-end processors can greatly increase the number of terminals that can be attached to a host computer. A front-end processor allows many low-speed devices to share a single high-speed host computer port or channel. Since the channel interface operates at a relatively high speed compared to the line interfaces, the front-end processor may need to hold data destined for the terminals until it can transmit it to the terminals at a slower speed. Holding data in this manner is known as *buffering*.

Some front-end processors schedule terminal communications using special rules, known as *protocols*, which we discuss in detail in Chapter 7. The process by which the flow of communications between a host computer and smart or intelligent terminals is controlled by a front-end processor is known as *polling and selecting. Polling* occurs when the front-end processor asks a terminal, "Do you have any data to send to the host computer?" At this point, a smart terminal might send data or simply answer "No." *Selecting* occurs when the front-end processor asks the terminal, "Can you accept data now?" A smart terminal might then answer "Go ahead" or "Not now, I'm busy." Only smart or intelligent terminals can respond to these messages; dumb terminals cannot be controlled using polling and selecting. The host computer could do the polling and selecting, but it is not necessary to waste a host computer's time on such a tedious, repetitive task when a front-end processor can accomplish it easily and cost effectively.

Returning to the previous analogy, polling is performed by the teaching assistant when he walks around the classroom, collecting papers from students with questions. Selecting would be the approximate equivalent of the teaching assistant distributing the answers. Technically, selecting would require the teaching assistant to ask each student, "Are you ready to receive your answer now?" and then hand the student the answer when the response is positive.

Many front-end processors can perform special functions, varying with each manufacturer and model. One popular function is error detection and correction. Front-end processors with this feature can detect, and sometimes correct, any bit transmission errors that occur. This function is explained in detail in Chapter 6.

Another function that some front-end processors can perform is *data conversion*. This can include *code conversion*, in which the host computer and the terminal device each use a different character code. For example, an ASCII terminal could connect to an EBCDIC host computer using a front-end processor with a code conversion feature. Sometimes, *protocol conversion* is also needed; connecting a dumb asynchronous terminal, which doesn't understand protocols, to a host computer that uses synchronous protocols requires protocol conversion. Finally, *parallel/serial conversion* can be performed by some front-end processors. All of these conversion functions can be performed by separate devices, such as *protocol converters* or *parallel/serial converters*, but it is often less expensive to build these functions directly into the front-end processor.

Front-end processors can be configured differently for each port, allowing different types of terminals to communicate with the same host computer.

Front-end processors can often perform *historical logging* or *statistical logging*. Logging provides a record of the users of the front-end processor, including various information about the users' actions. These two functions are explained in detail in Chapter 6.

Front-end processors are available with many different combinations of the afore-mentioned features. The number of line interfaces that a front-end processor can support varies by manufacturer and host computer model.

PORT-SHARING DEVICES

Though front-end processors allow terminals to share a high-speed host computer channel, sometimes the front-end ports can operate at faster speeds than the attached terminals. Other times, there may be more terminals than front-end ports. A *port-sharing device*, often called a *concentrator*, allows many terminals to share one front-end port, as shown in Fig. 5-2. For example, the front-end port might be operating at 9600 bps, while the four terminals attached to the port-sharing device might each be operating at 2400 bps. In other configurations, all of the terminals might be at 9600 bps, but only one could transmit at any one time. A user with an eight-port front end and 10 terminals might opt for a front end and a port-sharing device, rather than purchasing a second front end. The speeds are chosen for our example arbitrarily, and the concepts described will work at any speed.

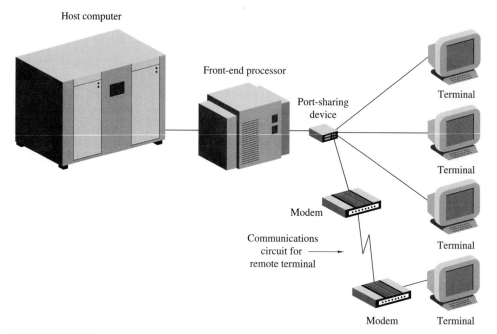

FIGURE 5-2   Using a port-sharing device.

Port-sharing devices are located near the front-end processor and usually require special intelligence in the front end that allows many terminals to communicate through a single front-end port. For example, if polling and selecting were being used, the front-end processor would need to know that there are several terminals attached through a port-sharing device on a particular port; this information allows the front-end processor to send the polling and selecting messages for all of these terminals over a single front-end processor port. This polling and selecting intelligence is usually found in the front-end processor's software. If a terminal is located remotely, then the required pair of modems and a communications circuit are inserted between the port-sharing device and the terminal.

LINE SPLITTERS AND REMOTE INTELLIGENT CONTROLLERS

A *line splitter* performs the same function as a port-sharing device, though line splitters are located remotely from the front-end processor and host computer. The major advantage offered by line splitters is that only one pair of modems, and one communications circuit, is needed for many remote terminals in the same location. Typically, terminal users in a given area of a building might all be attached to a line splitter, which is then connected to a remote front-end processor using a telephone circuit and modems, as shown in Fig. 5-3.

A line splitter's cost can be justified because it reduces the number of modems and telephone circuits needed. Line splitters also require a front-end port that can accept more than one terminal. Just as with port-sharing devices, the front-end processor needs to know that there are several terminals accessing the host through that single

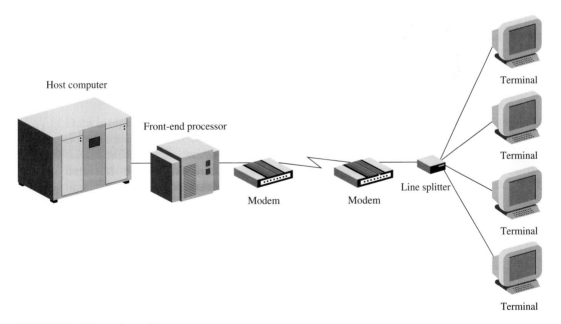

FIGURE 5-3   Using a line splitter.

front-end port so that the proper polling and selecting messages can be transmitted to that port.

A *remote intelligent controller* is just like a line splitter, except that it can also perform some functions of front-end processors. For example, part of the front-end processor's task when communicating to smart or intelligent terminals through a line splitter is to poll the terminals constantly. Since humans type slowly compared to the speed at which a front-end processor can poll, most of the time, the poll is answered with, "No, I have nothing to send now." Normally, a front-end processor sends these polling questions and receives the answers over the single pair of modems to the line splitter, which routes the messages to each of the terminals. If one of the terminals has data to transmit, it still must share time on the modems with all of the other terminals that are simply sending back negative answers to the polling. Remote intelligent controllers, however, can usually perform the terminal polling themselves, so that only real data is passed over the modems to the front-end processor. This frees up the modems for real data transmission and gives the front-end processor more time to concentrate on some of its other ports. The appropriate placement of a remote intelligent controller is shown in Fig. 5-4.

Some manufacturers use names other than "port-sharing device," "line splitter," and "remote intelligent controller" for equipment performing the functions just described. These generic terms, however, serve to describe functions that are common and universal throughout the industry.

All of these methods for improving data communications efficiency, whether with front-end processors, port-sharing devices, line splitters, or remote intelligent controllers, require a special compatibility with the attached host computer or terminals. For example, a front-end processor can be attached only to a host computer that is designed with special high-speed data channels for that purpose. Port-sharing devices, line split-

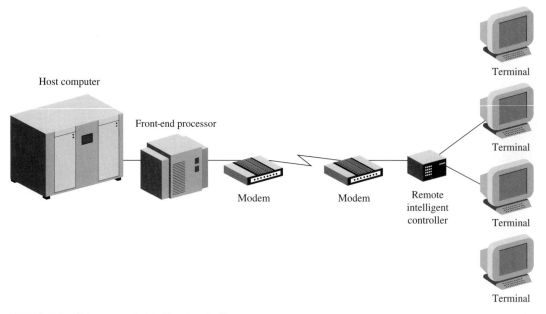

FIGURE 5-4   Using a remote intelligent controller.

ters, and remote intelligent controllers usually require smart or intelligent terminals that can be controlled using polling and selecting. We now turn to other means of improving data communications efficiency that do not require any special features or action on the part of the host computer, front-end processor (if present), or terminal.

MULTIPLEXERS

One of the most widely used devices for improving data communications efficiency is the *multiplexer*, often called a *mux*. A multiplexer allows several devices to share the same communications circuit. This sharing can be accomplished in several ways; for instance, faster modems can be used on the communications circuit, or the communications circuit can be split into several separate channels.

Multiplexing is useful when there are parallel communications paths between two locations. The main advantage of multiplexing, as shown in Fig. 5-5, is that fewer telephone lines and modems are needed. The one-time purchase cost of multiplexers is usually justified over time by the reduction of monthly costs for telephone lines. The main purpose of multiplexers, therefore, is to minimize communications circuit costs.

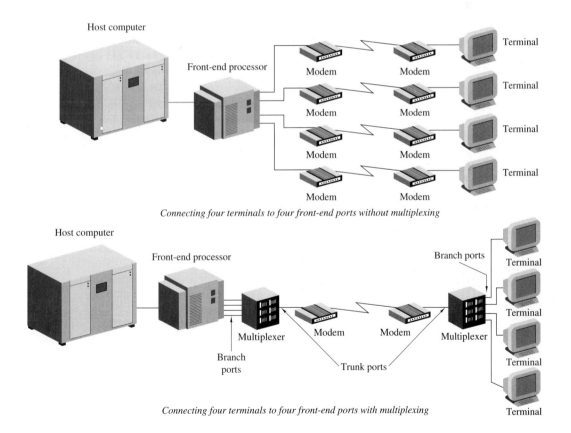

Connecting four terminals to four front-end ports without multiplexing

Connecting four terminals to four front-end ports with multiplexing

FIGURE 5-5   Multiplexing.

Multiplexers are normally used in pairs, with one multiplexer at each end of the communications circuit. The data from several terminals can be sent over a single communications circuit by one multiplexer. At the receiving multiplexer, the data is separated and sent to the appropriate destinations. Multiplexing is a generic technology that is not limited to a particular vendor's hosts or terminals; it can be applied anywhere parallel paths are present.

We often refer to the low-speed ports of a multiplexer as *branch ports* and to the high-speed port as the *trunk port*. Just like a tree, there are many branches (terminals or front-end ports) and only one trunk (connected to the modems). The branch and trunk ports are labeled in Fig. 5-5.

TIME-DIVISION MULTIPLEXING

Multiplexers that share the time on a fast communications circuit among slower devices use a technique known as *time-division multiplexing*, or *TDM*. In our first example of TDM, shown in Fig. 5-6, the four terminals and front-end ports each operate at 2400 bps. The pair of modems between the multiplexers operates at 9600 bps. The four terminals and front-end ports actually share the modem's 9600 bps bandwidth. For convenience, we discuss the transmission of data from the terminals to the front-end ports, though the same principles apply in both directions. In addition, the speeds are arbitrarily chosen for our example, and the concepts described will work at any speed.

Each of the terminals can transmit and receive at 2400 bps, so if all four are constantly transmitting and receiving data, there is a total of 9600 bps transmitted and received by the modems. Since all of the terminals are probably not transmitting all of the time, there is enough bandwidth between the modems to handle this activity. This technique is known as *pure time-division multiplexing* because there is always enough bandwidth to handle the terminals' maximum transmission.

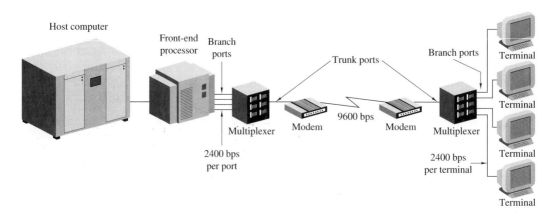

FIGURE 5-6   Time-division multiplexing.

CHARACTER AND BIT INTERLEAVING

How does TDM work? There are two popular methods, known as character interleaving and bit interleaving. The former is the easiest to visualize.

In *character interleaving*, or *byte interleaving*, multiplexing is performed one character at a time. Of course, each character may be made up of eight bits. In Fig. 5-7, each of the terminals is sending a message that we have chosen at random. Terminal 1 sends "Hello," terminal 2 sends "Goodness," terminal 3 sends "Labor," and terminal 4 sends "Nice"; the terminals send these words one character at a time. For convenience, we refer to the multiplexer attached to the terminals as multiplexer A and the multiplexer attached to the front end as multiplexer B.

Multiplexer A, using character interleaving, checks each of its branch ports for characters transmitted by terminals. These characters can be sent, one at a time, over the high-speed trunk port. For example, multiplexer A scans its ports, discovering the characters *H, G, L,* and *N*. Multiplexer A sends *HGLN* over its trunk port to multiplexer B. Multiplexer B then sends the characters to each front-end port at 2400 bps: The *H* to port 1, the *G* to port 2, the *L* to port 3, and the *N* to port 4. Next, multiplexer A sends *eoai* over its trunk port. Multiplexer B sends the *e* to port 1, the *o* to port 2, the *a* to port 3, and the *i* to port 4. This process continues until all of the characters are sent.

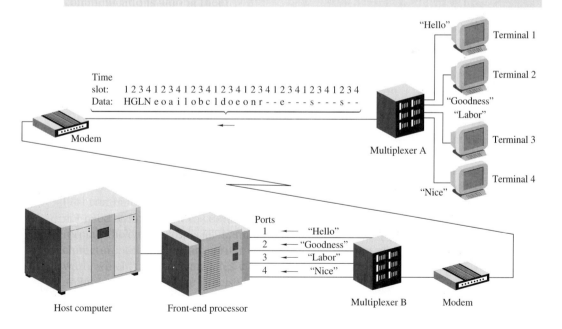

FIGURE 5-7   Character interleaving.

We call this process "character interleaving" because every fourth character transmitted over the multiplexer's trunk ports is destined for the same branch port. It is the equivalent of four lanes on a highway alternately merging into one lane, taking one car from lane 1, one from lane 2, one from lane 3, one from lane 4, one from lane 1 again, and so on. At the end of the road, the one lane splits off into four again, and the first car feeds into lane 1 again, the next to lane 2, the next to lane 3, the next to lane 4, the next to lane 1, and so on. In character interleaving, characters are merged instead of cars. Remember that each character may be made up of eight bits, but the characters are merged in their entirety.

Each of the terminals is allocated one-fourth of the time on the modems in each direction; each time a particular terminal and front-end port pair is communicating is called *a time slot*. In our example, terminal 1 had the first time slot, terminal 2 the second, and so on. At multiplexer B, the character in time slot 1 is sent to front-end port 1, the character in time slot 2 is sent to front-end port 2, and so on. If we used TDM with 10 devices instead of 4 on each end, there would be 10 time slots instead of 4 in each direction.

Notice in our example that terminal 4, with the shortest message ("Nice"), does not use its time slot after it has sent the four characters. We could think of this lack of use as a waste of a time slot, but the vacant time slot does have a purpose. If terminal 4 had a longer word to transmit, it would have been guaranteed enough time slots to do so, because the speed of the trunk port is as large as the sum of the speeds of the branch ports (2400 + 2400 + 2400 + 2400 = 9600). Each terminal and front-end pair is guaranteed enough bandwidth to carry on its communications. If some of the pairs don't use all of their bandwidth, some time slots will go unused, even though the full bandwidth capability is there.

Bit interleaving is another way to accomplish TDM. This method takes one bit from each terminal and sends it on the trunk port. For our example, as shown in Fig. 5-8, we'll assume that there are still four terminals, and terminal 1 sends the ASCII character *A* (01000001), terminal 2 sends a *B* (01000010), terminal 3 sends a *C* (01000011), and terminal 4 sends a *D* (01000100). We ignore any start and stop bits for simplicity in our example. Since we transmit the bit on the right first in ASCII code, the first bit received from terminal 1 is a 1, from terminal 2 is a 0, from terminal 3 is a 1, and from terminal 4 is a 0. Multiplexer A then sends 1010 on the trunk port. Multiplexer B receives these four bits and sends the 1 to front-end port 1, the 0 to front-end port 2, the 1 to front-end port 3, and the 0 to front-end port 4. Rather than sending four characters at a time, as in character interleaving, the multiplexer sends four bits at a time. Each time slot is shorter, containing only one bit instead of an entire character, but there are eight times the number of time slots in a second. The speed of the trunk port still needs to be as great as the sum of the speeds of the branch ports (2400 + 2400 + 2400 + 2400 = 9600). Once again, the speeds are arbitrarily chosen for our example, and the concepts described will work at any speed. Bit interleaving functions identically to character interleaving, except that there is a bit in each time slot instead of a full character, or byte.

Whether bit interleaving or character interleaving is used, an important feature of pure TDM is that the terminals and front-end ports are unaware that their data is being multiplexed over a single communications line. The 2400 bps of data sent by the terminal always arrive at the front end at the rate of 2400 bps. Neither the terminal nor the front-end processor knows that the data was combined with other terminals' data, sped up, then separated and slowed down. The data is still transmitted to the front end at 2400 bps, because a full 2400 bps of bandwidth out of the modem's 9600 bps has been reserved for this connection.

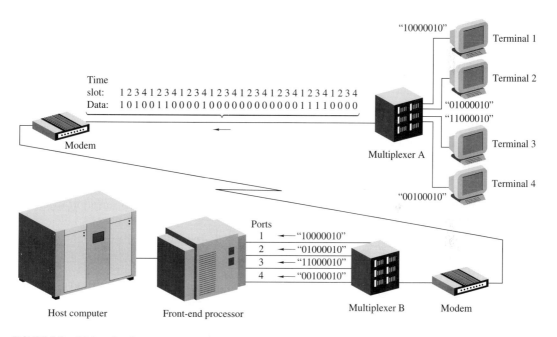

FIGURE 5-8   Bit interleaving.

STATISTICAL TIME-DIVISION MULTIPLEXING

In practice, typical terminal users do not use all of their terminals' bandwidth. Humans take coffee breaks, lunch hours, and long weekends. In addition, terminal users often type at slower speeds than their terminals can transmit, so a few characters may be transmitted, then no characters for a while, then a few more characters, and so on. If we use pure TDM with terminals, some of the time slots are left empty when transmission is not occurring from or to one of the terminals.

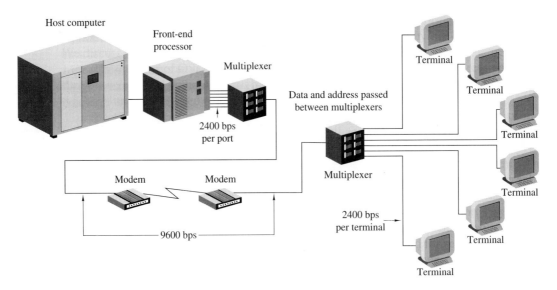

FIGURE 5-9 Statistical time-division multiplexing.

Statistical time-division multiplexing, or *STDM*, takes advantage of the sporadic nature of terminal users and allocates bandwidth to each terminal on the basis of demands and needs. For example, a multiplexer using STDM, often called a *stat mux*, shown in Fig. 5-9, can have a transmission speed in the trunk ports that is lower than the sum of the branch port speeds. In our example, six terminals, each at speeds of 2400 bps, are using a trunk port transmitting at 9600 bps. STDM assumes that not all of the devices are transmitting all the time, which is a very reasonable assumption when terminals are being used.

With pure TDM, the time slots are allocated on a constant basis; one terminal always gets time slot 1, the next, time slot 2, and so on. In STDM, terminals use time slots only when they are actually transmitting data. How does multiplexer B in Fig. 5-9 know which data goes to which front-end port? Typically, a statistical multiplexer sends not only the data, but also an *address*, which indicates which of the ports the data is destined for. In our example, a 3-bit address is used, which would allow for a maximum of eight ports (000, 001, 010, 011, 100, 101, 110, and 111). In STDM, when a terminal is not sending data, no time slots are allocated to it, and other terminals that are sending data can use these time slots.

The term "statistical" refers to the method by which time slots are allocated. A statistical multiplexer decides how many time slots to allocate in the next second based on the amount of data sent by a given device in the last second. Complicated formulas are calculated constantly, so the time slot utilization is forever changing based on the user's most recent demands and probable future needs.

What happens when all users try to transmit at the same time? Clearly, the 9600 bps port cannot handle all 14,400 bps (6 × 2400 bps). Some statistical multiplexers will buffer, or hold the data, until some of the users stop transmitting and there are extra time slots on the trunk port. Other statistical multiplexers are able to stop a terminal from transmitting when there is a shortage of time slots. Once again, the speeds are arbitrarily chosen for our example, and the concepts described will work at any speed.

STDM can be more efficient than pure TDM when there is intermittent transmission from the terminals, because it makes better use of the bandwidth on the trunk port. However, if all of the terminals are constantly trying to transmit, STDM does not provide acceptable transmission time. Not only are there not enough time slots for the terminals' data, but some of the time slots are used up in sending the terminal addresses.

Pure TDM is often described as being *transparent* to the users, meaning that an immediately available transmission path is guaranteed. STDM is not transparent to users, since their data transmission may be delayed.

Clearly, when a guaranteed transmission path is necessary, pure TDM is the only acceptable form of time-division multiplexing. STDM offers a more economical solution through more efficient use of the trunk ports, but with the possibility of transmission delays.

FREQUENCY-DIVISION MULTIPLEXING

Another common type of multiplexing is *frequency-division multiplexing*, or *FDM*. Whereas in time-division multiplexing, many terminals share time on a high-bandwidth link, in frequency-division multiplexing, the terminals continually share the bandwidth by dividing the link into many separate frequencies, or channels.

An example of frequency-division multiplexing can be found in cable television: A single coaxial cable carries all of the television channels simultaneously. Each channel is assigned a separate frequency, which the viewer selects by using the television's tuner. The signals from all of the television stations are multiplexed onto a single link, and each is assigned a different frequency.

In data communications, frequency-division multiplexing transmits the data from each terminal on a different frequency. As shown in Fig. 5-10, the four terminals can communicate with four remote front-end ports by dividing the telephone circuit into four channels. For our example, terminal A communicates with front-end port A over multiplexer channel A, and so on. We choose 1000–1300 Hz for channel A, 1500–1800 Hz for channel B, 2000–2300 Hz for channel C, and 2500–2800 Hz for channel D. As shown in Fig. 5-10, a 0 transmitted from terminal A to front-end port A is sent between the multiplexers on channel A with a 1000 Hz tone; a 1 is sent with an 1100 Hz tone. For data sent in the other direction, from front-end port A to terminal A using multiplexer channel A, a 0 is sent with a 1200 Hz tone and a 1 with a 1300 Hz tone. The other three channels use a similar modulation scheme, as shown in Fig. 5-10. Transmission occurs simultaneously, in full duplex, on all four channels at once, because data is sent using different frequencies for each channel. Although we have chosen four channels for our example, frequency-division multiplexing can be performed with any number of channels; using too many channels, however, makes the cost of the multiplexer prohibitive.

Notice that the multiplexer using FDM is not only sharing the communications path among many users (multiplexing), but it is also converting the digital data to analog form (modulating). A separate pair of modems is not necessary when FDM is used,

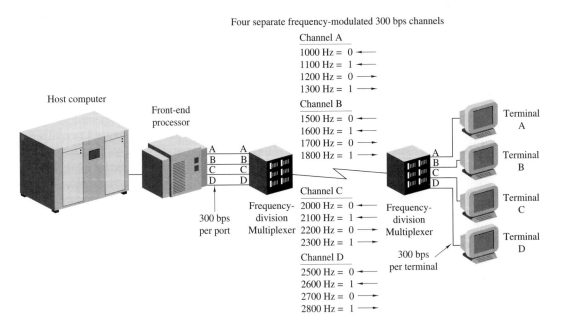

Four separate frequency-modulated 300 bps channels

Channel A
1000 Hz = 0 ←——
1100 Hz = 1 ←——
1200 Hz = 0 ——→
1300 Hz = 1 ——→

Channel B
1500 Hz = 0 ←——
1600 Hz = 1 ←——
1700 Hz = 0 ——→
1800 Hz = 1 ——→

Channel C
Frequency-   2000 Hz = 0 ←——   Frequency-
division   2100 Hz = 1 ←——   division
Multiplexer   2200 Hz = 0 ——→   Multiplexer
              2300 Hz = 1 ——→

Channel D
2500 Hz = 0 ←——
2600 Hz = 1 ←——
2700 Hz = 0 ——→
2800 Hz = 1 ——→

Host computer

Front-end processor

300 bps per port

300 bps per terminal

Terminal A

Terminal B

Terminal C

Terminal D

FIGURE 5-10   Frequency-division multiplexing.

because FDM combines multiplexing and modulation. Having modulation and multiplexing built into the same device may be convenient, but also may be more restrictive in the long run. For example, if advances are made in modem technology, a TDM user could simply purchase a new pair of modems and use the existing TDM multiplexers. An FDM user could only take advantage of new technology by replacing both multiplexers.

Frequency-division multiplexing, like pure TDM, is transparent to the end user. Each user has a full-bandwidth connection at all times. If a particular terminal does not transmit data, time on its channel is wasted. This is the data communications equivalent of a television station when it is off the air; no one else uses that channel either.

Frequency-division multiplexing can be more expensive to implement than time-division multiplexing because each channel requires separate frequencies. The more channels used over a communications circuit, the closer the frequencies are to each other. If the frequencies are too close together, it becomes extremely expensive to build devices to separate the different frequencies. In our example, each channel used four frequencies; if we combined phase-shift keying techniques with frequency-division multiplexing, we would need only two frequencies per channel (one frequency in each direction). However, FDM always requires more frequencies than with a standard single-channel modem, thereby increasing the hardware complexity and costs.

Statistical frequency-division multiplexing, or *SFDM*, is sometimes used to make more efficient use of the channels. However, the complexity and cost for sharing channels usually outweigh the benefits. Unlike STDM, which is a practical and economical alternative to TDM, SFDM is rarely used.

DATA COMPRESSION DEVICES

Data compression is another method commonly used to improve data communications efficiency. The philosophy behind data compression is, "Why send 9600 bps when 4800 bps will do the job?" The typical arrangement of *data compression devices* is shown in Fig. 5-11. The terminal, front end, and modem are usually unaware that compression is taking place. However, some data patterns occur that cannot be compressed. When this happens, the data compression device must be able to buffer incoming data or ask the terminal or front end to stop transmitting while it sends data in an uncompressed fashion. Like multiplexers, data compression devices are used to reduce communications circuit costs. Rather than sharing the communications path, a data compression device manages to send the same information using fewer bits. The net result is a higher effective bandwidth for the user.

Data compression devices can be combined with multiplexers for an even greater communications cost savings. For example, eight 2400 bps terminals connected to a multiplexer using TDM would normally require a pair of 19.2 kbps modems. However, a pair of 2-to-1 data compression devices and 9600 bps modems could be used instead. Alternatively, we could increase to as many as 16 terminals with 19.2 kbps modems and 2-to-1 data compression devices. These concepts apply to any other speed of modems or terminals as well.

Data compression can be achieved in many different ways. One common method is to use a special shorthand notation for transmitting data. If a certain character is sent frequently, the data compression devices may send an abbreviated form of the character. Just as we use "kbps" instead of "kilobits per second" in this book, a data compression device seeks the same efficiency. Another method used is to send only changes to the data. There are many other methods used to compress data, most of which are proprietary. Therefore, the same vendor's data compression devices are typically used at each end of the circuit. Data compression capability may also be included in a modem, as described in Chapter 4.

INVERSE MULTIPLEXERS

Not all data communications applications require minimization of communications circuit costs. In some instances, transmission speed is far more important. For example, as

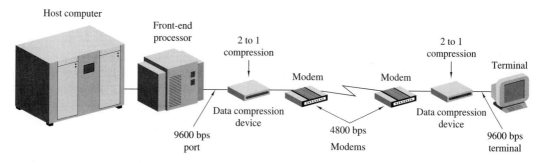

FIGURE 5-11   Data compression devices.

shown in Fig. 5-12, a host computer is located in a nuclear power plant control room. A terminal is located 50 miles away, in a remote control center, and is connected to the host computer through modems and phone lines. It is determined that phone lines in that area can support 9600 bps modems, but any higher speed causes low reliability. Safety considerations dictate that the remote user must be able to receive a screenful of information almost instantly, requiring a 19.2 kbps transmission. We can use two telephone lines and an *inverse multiplexer* to combine the bandwidth of the two telephone lines. Rather than sharing one phone line's bandwidth among many terminals, as is done with the multiplexers discussed previously, we combine the bandwidth of two phone lines for use by a single terminal.

Using the arrangement shown in Fig. 5-12, the host computer could send the word "Warning!" to the inverse multiplexer at 19.2 kbps. The inverse multiplexer would send alternating letters over modems attached to each phone line at 9600 bps. At the other end, the receiving inverse multiplexer recombines the letters, resulting in a 19.2 kbps transmission of the word "Warning!". An inverse multiplexer acts just like a regular multiplexer, except that the high-speed trunk port is attached to the terminals or front ends and the low-speed branch ports are attached to the modems and phone lines.

In this example, the inverse multiplexer's high-speed transmission requires twice as many modems, twice as many phone lines, and a pair of inverse multiplexers. However, in some cases, as in the example previously cited, high-speed transmission is essential and well worth the extra cost.

MULTIDROP CONFIGURATIONS

One type of configuration, known as *multidrop*, is unlike any we have discussed thus far. We have considered only a host computer or front-end port, attached to a single terminal or to a single device, like a line splitter, which could accommodate several terminals. Some host computer architectures, however, can directly accommodate several terminals on the same line. When used locally, these multidrop configurations typically have a single computer or front-end port, with a cable running into the first terminal, then from the first terminal to the second, and so on, as shown in Fig. 5-13. Local multidrop configurations are most advantageous when terminals are located near each other and the front-end processor is located in another room. Rather than running long

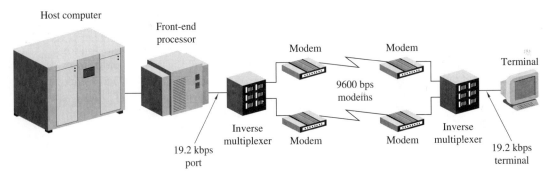

FIGURE 5-12   Inverse multiplexers.

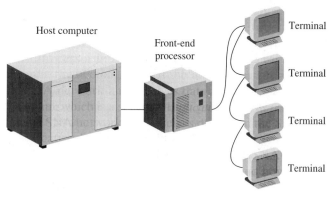

FIGURE 5-13   Local multidrop configuration.

cables from each terminal to the front-end processor, only one long cable and several short ones are needed.

The key to multidrop operation is that the host computer must "address" each message to a particular terminal, and each terminal must be able to determine which messages are destined for it. Similarly, terminals must mark their messages with their "return address" so that the host computer can determine the sender. Polling and selecting are necessary to prevent two terminals from trying to use the line at once. In addition, a host computer can send a *broadcast message* to all terminals on the line by using a special address recognized by all the terminals.

Remote multidrop configurations can also be cost effective. As shown in Fig. 5-14, a company with locations in San Francisco, New York, and Connecticut needs a communications circuit between the West Coast location and each of the East Coast locations. If we used two phone lines and two pairs of modems, the company would pay for two long-distance telephone lines, each about 2500 miles long. However, if we used a multidrop configuration, one 2500-mile line would be needed, and the second line would be only 40 miles long.

A message from San Francisco bound for Connecticut is routed through New York. The message is not displayed on the terminal in New York because it is addressed for Connecticut; we could say that the terminal in New York simply ignored the message.

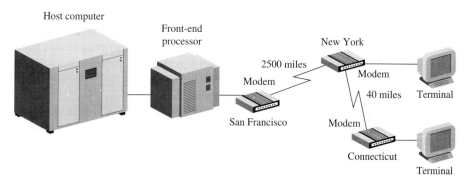

FIGURE 5-14   Remote multidrop configuration.

There is a potential security risk with multidrop configurations, however, since a determined New Yorker could use special monitoring devices to eavesdrop on all of the communications to and from Connecticut.

Clearly, the long-distance communications costs are reduced; however, the multidrop capability must be present in the host computer or front-end processor and in the terminals used. The economic benefits of this configuration vary for each user, depending on the geographic layout of the user's network. There are so many other options for wide area networking, as described in Chapter 8, that multidrop configurations are no longer as popular as they once were.

SUMMARY

There are many different types of components for improving data communications efficiency. Front-end processors assist the host computer in handling input and output tasks. These tasks may include polling and selecting, error detection, error correction, code conversion, protocol conversion, historical logging, and statistical logging.

Port-sharing devices allow many terminals to share a single front-end port. Line splitters perform the same function as do port-sharing devices, but are located remotely from the front-end port. A remote intelligent controller performs the same functions as does a line splitter, but, in addition, performs some tasks normally reserved for a front-end processor. Port-sharing devices, line splitters, and remote intelligent controllers require compatibility with the attached host computers, front-end processors, and terminals.

Multiplexers improve communications efficiency without any special features or actions on the part of the host computer, front-end processor, or terminal. Multiplexers allow many devices to share one communications circuit, thereby minimizing communications circuit costs. Time-division multiplexing splits the communications circuit by allocating time slots to each device. In pure TDM, each terminal has an equal share of the communications circuit and is guaranteed an immediately available transmission path. This is possible as long as the speed of the communications circuit is equal to or greater than the sum of the speeds of the attached devices. TDM can be accomplished using character (byte) interleaving or bit interleaving. In character interleaving, a character occupies each time slot, whereas in bit interleaving, only a single bit is in each time slot. In statistical time-division multiplexing, devices are allocated time slots based on the amount of data recently transmitted. This process is more efficient than pure TDM when the data transmission is sporadic. However, STDM does not guarantee an immediately available transmission path. In contrast to TDM, frequency-division multiplexing divides the communications circuit into several channels, with data being transmitted on all channels simultaneously but on different frequencies. FDM combines modulation and multiplexing, so modems are no longer needed, though the FDM technique can be fairly expensive to implement.

Data compression devices improve communications efficiency by minimizing the number of bits transmitted. Data is often compressed through various abbreviation techniques. Another device, known as an inverse multiplexer, combines the bandwidth of two or more communications circuits to allow for high-speed transmission. Finally, multidrop configurations can be used to minimize communications circuit distances and thereby minimize communications costs.

TERMS FOR REVIEW

Address

Bit interleaving

Branch port

Broadcast message

Buffering

Byte interleaving

Channel interface

Character interleaving

Code conversion

Concentrator

Data compression

Data compression device

Data conversion

FDM

FEP

Frequency-division
*   multiplexing*

Front end

Front-end port

Front-end processor

Historical logging

Input/output channel

Inverse multiplexer

Line interface

Line splitter

Multidrop

Multiplexer

Mux

Parallel/serial conversion

Parallel/serial converter

Polling

Port-sharing device

Processing unit

Protocol

Protocol conversion

Protocol converter

Pure time-division
*   multiplexing*

Remote intelligent controller

Selecting

SFDM

Stat mux

Statistical frequency-division
*   multiplexing*

Statistical logging

Statistical time-division
*   multiplexing*

STDM

TDM

Time-division multiplexing

Time slot

Transparent

Trunk port

EXERCISES

5-1.   What is the main function of a front-end processor?

5-2.   Explain the difference between a front-end processor's channel interface and line interface.

5-3.   Compare a port-sharing device with a line splitter.

5-4.   What is the difference between a line splitter and a remote intelligent controller?

5-5.   What is multiplexing? What is its main purpose?

5-6.   Explain the difference between TDM and FDM.

5-7.   Compare pure TDM with statistical TDM.

5-8.   What is the purpose of a data compression device?

5-9.   When is an inverse multiplexer used?

5-10.   How can a remote multidrop configuration reduce leased-line costs?

CHAPTER 6

Data Integrity and Security

DATA INTEGRITY

In any data communications network, there is the possibility of errors in data transmission. Preventing or correcting these errors is often referred to as maintaining data integrity.

SOURCES OF ERRORS

Errors in data transmission can occur for many reasons, including electrical interference from thunderstorms or from other transmission lines. In addition, power surges or spikes due to faulty equipment can also cause bits to be lost or changed during transmission.

All of us have placed long-distance phone calls where the connection is crystal clear, as if we are talking to someone across the street. If we used modems over a clear connection like that, we would probably never encounter data errors.

But we have also placed phone calls where the connection is terrible, filled with noise, static, echoes, and other sounds. If we used modems over this type of connection, we would likely encounter many errors. Humans can separate static and noise from actual conversation, but modems are easily confused by noise. As we discussed in the section on modulation in Chapter 4, modems may have to detect subtle frequency or phase shifts several thousand times in one second. A "little" static that lasts a half-second can easily obliterate 16.8 kilobits if we're transmitting at 33.6 kbps.

ERROR-CONTROL APPROACHES

Regardless of the source and cause of errors, we need some scheme to protect our data. Such methods of maintaining data integrity are often called error-control approaches. There are four common approaches in use today.

One approach is simply *not to check for errors*. This approach may sound frivolous, but it is used by some of the dumb terminals we introduced in Chapter 3. The device assumes that the terminal operator, and not the terminal itself, is able to catch any errors. In this case, a conscious decision has been made that it's more important to build a cheap terminal than an error-free terminal.

For a human example of this approach, picture a court reporter writing down everything said in a courtroom. A witness uses the word "books" during testimony, but the courtroom is fairly noisy, and the reporter thinks he said "bucks." The reporter writes "bucks" into the court record and doesn't even know he's wrong. Hopefully, whoever reads the court record will notice the error and be able to understand the sentence. That is an example of not checking for errors.

A second approach is *error detection with flagging*. This approach requires that errors be detected, or noticed, when the data is received; it requires no correction of these errors, only an indication that an error exists. Some terminals display a question mark or sound a beep when they receive a character that they believe is in error. These terminals have no idea how to correct errors, but they alert the user that something has gone wrong.

Using the previous example to illustrate this method, the reporter knows that he did not hear the word properly, but thinks that he heard "bucks." He therefore writes down "bucks," circles it, and puts a question mark above it, to alert whoever reads the record later that this word may not be correct. That is an example of error detection with flagging.

A third approach is *error detection with a request for retransmission*. After an error is detected by the receiver, some protocols ask the sender to retransmit the message. A terminal using one of these protocols would check all incoming messages, and if a particular message contained errors, would ask the sender to transmit another copy of the message. The terminal would not display the message on the screen until it was received error free.

Using our courtroom example to illustrate this method, the reporter knows that he didn't hear the word correctly, so he raises his hand and says, "Please repeat that sentence. I didn't quite get it the first time." That is an example of error detection with a request for retransmission.

A fourth approach is *forward error correction*, or *FEC*. In this case, the error is corrected by the receiving device. This method requires sufficient intelligence in the receiving device to determine not only where the error is, but also how to correct it. In most cases, forward error correction is limited. For example, a scheme can be provided to correct 100% of single bit errors, when only one bit in a byte is incorrect, but the same scheme does not correct multiple bit errors in a byte.

Using our courtroom example to illustrate this method, the reporter realizes that he did not hear the word correctly, because "bucks" doesn't make sense in the context of the sentence. The reporter decides that the witness must have said "books" and writes that down instead. That is an example of forward error correction.

IMPLEMENTING ERROR CONTROL: THE TECHNICAL DETAILS

There are many ways to detect errors. The most common methods are echo checking, parity checking, checksums, and cyclical redundancy checks.

ECHO CHECKING

In *echo checking*, the receiving device repeats everything it receives to the transmitting device. If the characters "ABC" are transmitted to a device using echo checking, the receiver then transmits "ABC" back to the sending device. The sender can then determine if the data was received correctly and can retransmit it if necessary.

Since echo checking requires every data bit to be repeated back to the originator, it at least doubles the time required for data transmission. Though this method guarantees that data will be received correctly, it is obviously inefficient and is used only in critical applications. For example, if the command "Lower landing gear" is being sent from an airplane's central computer to the landing gear controller, it is certainly worth repeating the command back and forth a few times to be sure that it has been properly understood.

PARITY CHECKING

Parity checking is the most commonly used error-checking method for asynchronous transmission. As we discussed in Chapter 3, in asynchronous transmission, a user might send 1 character now, 10 characters five minutes from now, no characters for one hour, and then 1000 characters three minutes later. Any error-detection scheme used with asynchronous transmission should be able to check each character as it arrives; it would be foolish to wait for a block of characters to perform a check, since we are not sure that we will receive any more characters.

There are many types of parity checking, including even parity, odd parity, space parity, mark parity, no parity, and ignored parity. Parity checking requires the transmitter to send an extra bit in each character to meet a certain parity requirement. *Even parity* requires an even number of ones in each byte. *Odd parity* requires an odd number of ones in each byte. *Space parity* uses a 0 for every parity bit, and *mark parity* uses a 1 for every parity bit.

Figure 6-1 shows examples of the letters "A", "B", "C", and "D" being transmitted, using ASCII code and even, odd, space, and mark parity.

For a parity-checking example, we use a seven-bit ASCII character, as discussed in Chapter 3. The letter "A" is represented by the seven bits 1000001 in ASCII code. Since

ASCII character	Even parity	Odd parity	Space parity	Mark parity
A	01000001	11000001	01000001	11000001
B	01000010	11000010	01000010	11000010
C	11000011	01000011	01000011	11000011
D	01000100	11000100	01000100	11000100

FIGURE 6-1   ASCII character transmission with different parities.

we are using even parity, there must be an even number of ones sent in every byte. There are already two ones in the sequence 1000001, so the parity bit will be 0, and 01000001 is sent. The receiver counts the number of ones in the byte and assumes that data was received correctly, since there are two 1's in the sequence 01000001. Notice that the parity bit is placed in the leftmost position in ASCII code.

If an error occurs during transmission in the previous example (letter "A", ASCII, even parity, 01000001) and the sequence received is 01001001, the receiver counts the number of ones and determines that there are three ones in the sequence. The receiver recognizes that this outcome is an error, since with even parity, all characters received should have an even number of ones. In this case, even parity is able to detect that there is an error in the byte.

Odd parity functions in the same way as even parity, except that there is always an odd number of ones. The letter "A" using odd parity and ASCII is transmitted as 11000001.

Even and odd parity have several limitations. First, it is critical that both the sending and receiving devices use the same parity-checking method, be it even or odd. It makes no difference which method is used as long as the same method is used by both sender and receiver.

Second, this type of parity-checking detects only an odd number of bit errors in a byte. If an even number of bit errors occurs, parity checking (even or odd) does not detect the error. The only way to be convinced of this point is by repetition. Figure 6-2 shows several examples of transmission errors occurring in the letter "A" to demonstrate this point. If we expect that errors will occur in a random fashion, we have a 50% chance of detecting errors using either even or odd parity.

Space and mark parity are primitive parity-checking methods. In space parity, the sender always uses a 0 for the parity bit and the receiver always looks for a 0. If there is a drastic data error, wiping out enough of the byte to change the parity bit to a 1, space parity will detect the error. Otherwise, as long as the parity bit is 0, the receiving device is oblivious to any error. In fact, if we have only one bit error in the transmission of a byte, there is only a one in eight chance that it is the parity bit, giving us a 12.5% chance of detecting the error. In that case, we have actually detected an error in our parity bit, while our actual data is fine! Mark parity functions in the same manner as space parity

Character "A" sent with even parity	Number of ones sent	Received as:	Number of bit errors	Number of ones received	Is error detected by even parity?
01000001	2	01000001	0	2	No
01000001	2	01100001	1	3	Yes
01000001	2	01110001	2	4	No
01000001	2	01110101	3	5	Yes
01000001	2	01110111	4	6	No
01000001	2	01111111	5	7	Yes
01000001	2	11111111	6	8	No
01000001	2	10111111	7	7	Yes
01000001	2	10111110	8	6	No

FIGURE 6-2 Parity checking and bit errors.

Type of bit	Bit value	Bit number
Data	1	1
	0	2
	1	3
	1	4
	0	5
	1	6
Parity	1	7
	1	8

FIGURE 6-3   Cyclical parity checking.

does; however, a 1 is substituted for the 0. Therefore, space and mark parity work only when a lot of bits are wiped out, and are not really useful for single bit errors.

Ignored parity implies that a 0 is sent as a parity bit and the receiver does not even check the parity bit. This method allows a receiver incapable of parity checking to communicate with another device that is using parity checking. No parity implies that there is no parity bit sent or checked.

CYCLICAL PARITY

Cyclical parity is a less common variation of parity checking, but it increases the odds of detecting errors. Rather than using only one parity bit to detect errors in a byte, cyclical parity uses at least two parity bits. Each parity bit checks some of the bits in the byte. For example, if we wanted to send the six-bit sequence 101101, we could use cyclical parity checking as shown in Fig. 6-3. Bits 1, 3, and 5 are checked with the parity bit in position 7, and bits 2, 4, and 6 are checked with the parity bit in position 8. If we use odd cyclical parity checking, there must be an odd number of ones in bits 1, 3, 5, and 7 and in bits 2, 4, 6, and 8. In this example, bits 7 and 8 must both be 1 to provide an odd number of ones in both bit groups. The only way for errors to slip by this checking scheme is if errors occur in certain combinations of alternating bits.

HAMMING CODE

Hamming code, a forward error-correction code devised by Richard Hamming, allows the receiving device not only to detect a single-bit error, but also to correct it with 100% accuracy. However, because this error-correction ability requires several parity bits, it is not as widely used as other parity methods. Hamming code for a seven-bit ASCII character requires 4 parity bits, for a total of 11 bits. The parity bits are placed in bit positions 1, 2, 4, and 8 (all powers of 2). The data bits are placed in positions 3, 5, 6, 7, 9, 10, and 11 (none of these are powers of 2). Hamming code allows for either even-parity or odd-parity checking; we use even-parity Hamming code for our example.

Figure 6-4 shows the ASCII letter "A", with its seven bits. Notice on the first line of the example that the seven data bits have been placed in the Hamming code data-bit positions. Now we move to line 2 to fill in the parity bits. There must be an even number of ones in the following bit combinations:

ASCII for letter "A" = 1 0 0 0 0 0 0 1

	1		0	0	0		0	0	1	Before parity
—	—	—	—	—	—	—	—	—	—	—	
Bit No.	1	2	3	4	5	6	7	8	9	10	11
	0	0	1	0	0	0	0	1	0	0	1	After parity
—	—	—	—	—	—	—	—	—	—	—	
Bit No.	1	2	3	4	5	6	7	8	9	10	11

FIGURE 6-4 Hamming code.

Bits 1, 3, 5, 7, 9, 11 (checked with parity bit 1)
Bits 2, 3, 6, 7, 10, 11 (checked with parity bit 2)
Bits 4, 5, 6, 7 (checked with parity bit 4)
Bits 8, 9, 10, 11 (checked with parity bit 8)

There are already 2 ones in bits 3, 5, 7, 9, and 11, so a device using Hamming code places a 0 in bit 1 to maintain an even number of ones in bits 1, 3, 5, 7, 9, and 11. There are already 2 ones in bits 3, 6, 7, 10, and 11, so the device places a 0 in bit 2 to maintain an even number of ones in bits 2, 3, 6, 7, 10, and 11. There are no ones in bits 5, 6, and 7, so the device places a 0 in bit 4 to maintain an even number of ones in bits 4, 5, 6, and 7. There is only a single 1 in bits 9, 10, and 11, so the device places a 1 in bit 8 to give us 2 ones in bits 8, 9, 10, and 11.

The resulting sequence, 00100001001, will be transmitted, and the receiving device can check the four parity bits by the same method we used to create them; there should be an even number of ones in every group. If all of the parity checks are correct at the receiving end, then there have been no errors (or there is more than one error).

If a single bit is in error, one or more of the parity checks will fail. Add up the numbers of the parity bits that failed, and the position of the incorrect bit will be found. For example, if bit 6 was switched during transmission from a 0 to a 1, 00100101001 would be received. Parity check 1 would pass (even number of ones), parity check 2 would fail (odd number of ones), parity check 4 would fail (odd number of ones), and parity check 8 would pass (even number of ones). When we add up the numbers of the parity checks that failed (2 + 4 = 6), the result is a clear indication that bit 6 is incorrect. Bit 6 can then be switched from a 1 to a 0, resulting in 00100001001, and the parity bits can be removed, resulting in 1000001, which is the data we sent originally.

Remember, this ingenious method is designed to correct single bit errors. If more than one bit error occurs, the results will not be predictable.

CHECKSUMS

A *checksum* is a generic term referring to a type of error detection used when receiving blocks of characters rather than single characters. Large blocks of data are often sent in synchronous transmission, as we explained in Chapter 3. In a simple example, the transmitting device begins with a checksum equal to zero before transmitting a block of data. As each character in a block is transmitted, the transmitter takes the binary number representing that character (the ones and zeroes) and adds it to the checksum. When the entire block of characters has been sent, the checksum (or a portion of the checksum) is also sent. Meanwhile, the receiver adds up the ones and zeroes that it receives, creating its own checksum. When the checksum arrives, the receiver can then compare it to the checksum it calculated. If these amounts do not match, the receiver knows that an error has occurred. Typically, checksums are used in protocols in which the receiver can ask the sender to retransmit the data if an error has occurred.

CYCLICAL REDUNDANCY CHECK

The *cyclical redundancy check*, or *CRC*, is a variation on the concept of the aforementioned simple checksum. Instead of simply adding up the ones and zeroes, the CRC uses a more complicated mathematical formula, combining division and addition. This formula helps exaggerate errors, preventing them from canceling each other out. In simple binary addition, as in the simple checksum discussed previously, a one changing to a zero in one byte can be hidden by a zero changing to a one in a later byte. Although the CRC is more complicated and expensive to implement, it is more reliable and provides a high degree of data integrity; almost no blocks of characters with an error can slip by a CRC without the error being detected.

SECURITY

Though accurate transmission of data is often essential, in some cases, data security can be even more important.

THE IMPORTANCE OF SECURITY

As computers take on a larger and larger share of business transactions, the need for data security becomes evident. Hardly a check or invoice is written today by medium sized to large corporations without the assistance of computers. Even checks written by hand are probably processed by a computer in the check clearinghouse.

Twenty years ago, it was standard practice for clerks in the accounting department to keep financial records locked away. Similarly, today's computer users are accustomed to utilizing special *passwords* to help "lock up" important information. One common example of a password is the *PIN*, or *personal identification number*, employed in conjunction with our bank card to access an automated teller machine. We tolerate the inconvenience of remembering and using this PIN because we recognize the need to safeguard our bank accounts.

SECURITY CONCERNS

Data communications devices and links are often vulnerable to unauthorized access or intrusion. Many networks, both public and private, include microwave or satellite transmission at one point or another. Anyone with the necessary equipment can eavesdrop on this data, often without the user's knowledge. In addition, phone lines can be tapped, further eroding a data network's security.

There are two common concerns when considering security issues. First, do we expect accidental or intentional intrusions? Precautions taken to prevent someone from stumbling into our network do little to foil a determined intruder.

Second, do we want simply to guard against others eavesdropping on our data, or do we expect someone to attempt to alter the data? Advance knowledge of corporate strategies can be worth millions of dollars to competitors, making eavesdropping a very profitable endeavor for unethical individuals. Similarly, we could all add a few extra zeroes to the end of our bank account balances if we could alter the data on our bank's computer network. There are clearly many motives for breaching a network's security.

SECURITY GOALS

There are several goals to consider when safeguarding data. The *National Institute of Standards and Technology*, or *NIST*, has identified five basic goals for proper data security. A secure data message should be sealed, sequenced, secret, signed, and stamped.

A *sealed message* cannot be modified by an unauthorized party. This is the data communications equivalent of the tamper-proof packaging that is used on many over-the-counter medications today. The receiver will be able to detect if a message has been tampered with.

A *sequenced message* is protected against undetected loss or repetition. This book is an example of a sequenced message; since the pages are numbered, the reader can determine if any pages are missing.

A *secret message* cannot be understood by an unauthorized party. Secret messages are often sent in coded or scrambled form.

A *signed message* includes proof of the sender's identity. A signature on a check is one example; it is recognizable by all, but reproducible only by the sender.

A *stamped message* guarantees receipt by the correct party. Sending a certified letter and requesting a return receipt with the receiver's signature is an example of a stamped message.

SECURITY MEASURES

Most of today's networks do not meet all of these security goals. The level of protection used depends on the value of security in a given application.

Security measures are often distributed throughout data communications networks. These measures can be implemented in host computers, terminals, modems, special security devices, and even transmission facilities.

SECURE TRANSMISSION FACILITIES

One security approach that is often overlooked is the selective use of transmission media. As we discussed in Chapter 4, the characteristics of the various transmission media differ widely. Twisted pair and coax can be tapped easily and cheaply, whereas unnoticed tapping of fiber optic lines requires extensive training and more expensive equipment. Satellite and microwave transmission are also completely vulnerable to tapping by anyone willing to invest in the appropriate receiving equipment. Sometimes the cost involved in making inexpensive services secure is greater than the economic benefits provided. Careful selection of transmission media is the simplest way to improve security.

PASSWORDS

Passwords are the most common form of security. The biggest drawback of passwords is the carelessness of many users. Some users write down passwords where they can be discovered, and others choose a familiar word, like the name of their dog, which can easily be guessed.

Passwords are usually required by the host computer, but can also be required by special security *call-back devices*. These devices help increase the security provided by a password. Remote users attempting to access a host computer using a modem must first enter their password and name into a call-back device attached between the modems and the host. The device then checks the password for accuracy and, if the password is correct, hangs up and calls the location programmed into the call-back device. In this case, an intruder must not only steal a user's password, but must also break into the user's home or office to be there when the call-back device telephones. Some front-end processors, host computers and modems have this call-back feature built in so that a separate call-back device is not necessary. This feature provides increased security, but unfortunately has an important drawback: The call-back device must know in advance where the user will be calling from. A traveling salesman would have a hard time accessing the office computer if it is attached to a call-back device.

Another way to make passwords more secure is to incorporate special hardware into the terminal. For example, an automated teller machine cannot be accessed with a PIN alone; a bank card must be inserted as well.

HISTORICAL AND STATISTICAL LOGGING

Another security method is *historical logging*, a complete recording of all data passed through a particular device. All data passing between a terminal and a host computer can be captured in the historical log. Historical logging is usually performed by host computers or front-end processors, though it can be accomplished at other points in the network as well. The data can be stored on a variety of devices, the most common of which are magnetic tapes or disks.

One example of historical logging is a student taping a professor's lecture. The tape is a complete record of the entire lecture and could be replayed the next week if the student wanted to review a particular topic. Similarly, if a company's personnel computer files have been mysteriously altered, it could replay the historical log in the front-end processor the next day and determine which user changed everyone's salaries, for example. The historical log would contain a complete record of the user's actions. Through review of the log, the user's method of access can be determined, and hopefully the system can be made more secure against future intrusions.

Though this method provides total recall of system events, it also uses a great deal of storage space (disks and tapes). A more efficient but similar method is known as *statistical logging*, whereby statistics are kept on each data port. These statistics might include which users were logged on to which ports, the amount of time users spent logged on, the files accessed, and other information about transactions that occurred. Like historical logging, statistical logging is often performed by host computers or front-end processors, though it can be accomplished by other devices as well.

An example of statistical logging is a student trying to determine which topics a professor considers important. The student records in his or her notebook that the professor spent 10 minutes on topic A, 20 minutes on topic B, and then 10 minutes on topic C. The student can later look back at this record to determine what the professor emphasized. Similarly, the company with the mysteriously altered personnel files could look back at the statistical log to determine which user accessed the salary files. The statistical log would not indicate exactly what was done to the files. The offending user would be identified, but the exact events that occurred would not be recorded.

When comparing statistical and historical logging, remember that by the time a company consults its logs, the security breach has probably already occurred and the damage has been done. A statistical accounting showing which users may have caused the damage is probably just as useful as a play-by-play description of exactly what happened.

CLOSED USER GROUPS

Many networks restrict user access by establishing *closed user groups*, or *CUG*s. A set of users who need to communicate only with each other and do not want other users to access their computers can form a closed user group. For instance, a company may want to allow its branch offices to connect to the corporate computer for sales price information, but at the same time ensure that competitors and customers cannot also access this information. The company can resort to a closed user group to ensure that only its branch offices have this access. Typically, closed user groups are employed with packet switching networks, which we discuss in detail in Chapter 8.

FIREWALLS

Another common security measure is the installation of *firewalls* between networks. A firewall examines data and determines whether to pass it through or to discard it based on a set of predefined rules. Firewalls can be used to provide security, as well as to prevent certain error conditions from spreading to neighboring networks.

Firewalls are usually not separate devices, but rather are functions performed inside existing networking equipment. One example of using a firewall for security purposes would be to place the firewall at the border between a private and public network. The assumption here is that the network at the site putting up the firewall is trustworthy and secure. However, since there is no way to control a network outside one's premises, a method is needed to screen data passing between the two networks for security purposes.

A firewall is not typically used to protect against intruders operating on your own network, though it could be used for this purpose. For example, if the executives of a company were concerned about sensitive communications on the company network, they could create an executive network and connect it with a firewall to the network that the rest of the company uses. In this manner, the executives could communicate with others in the company, but could insure that their executive network remained secure.

Firewalls are often used inside private networks to prevent the proliferation of errors. For example, if one user on a company-wide network was sending a stream of erroneous messages, these messages could fill up the network's capacity. However, if the network is divided into many small department networks, with firewalls in between them, such a problem can be isolated to one department, and the erroneous messages need not be transmitted to the entire company.

There are several different methods used by firewalls to screen data. One technique is known as *packet-filtering*. Packet-filtering can be used when messages are already broken into blocks, or packets, as described in Chapter 8. The origin of the data is checked, along with the destination, and sometimes the type of data is also scrutinized. The packet-filtering firewall is programmed by the network manager with a set of rules describing which users on the private network are permitted to exchange packets with which users on the outside network. Any packets that violate the rules are discarded. Some packet-filtering firewalls can check the type of data, in addition to the address, and can make more refined decisions. For example, electronic mail messages could be accepted from everyone, but file transfers could be accepted only from specifically authorized users or other offices of the same company. This system would allow general electronic mail communications with outside organizations, such as vendors or customers, but would prevent program files containing viruses sent by other organizations from being received. On the other hand, even harmless files from outside organizations would be rejected by this rule, posing an inconvenience to users.

This technique of screening the type of data is not possible with all packet-filtering firewalls, because it requires the firewall to recognize all of the possible formats of user data and to maintain different rules for each. On networks using many different types of applications, it is difficult to program a single firewall with every possible packet format and allowable user address combinations.

Another common approach is to use an *application-level firewall* to check messages only for a particular application. For example, an electronic mail firewall could screen only electronic mail messages. Because it is designed to check only this type of data, it can look for malicious behavior, like repeated messages, or even junk mail. Another firewall might check incoming file transfers to ensure that certain types of files are not accepted, allowing it to exclude viruses. Whereas the packet-filtering firewall screens based on addresses, or perhaps types of data, an application-level firewall can examine the data itself and determine if it is acceptable.

The packet-filtering and application-level examples discussed here are only two of the many possible approaches that can be used to screen data. While no firewall offers an absolute guarantee against network intrusion, it can substantially reduce the risk. The ultimate security measure is to disconnect the private network from the outside world, but doing so precludes users from enjoying the full benefits of networking.

ENCRYPTION AND DECRYPTION

One of the most thorough and effective ways to improve data security is to use *encryption*. Encryption is the coding, or scrambling, of the data before it is transmitted over the communications link. *Decryption* is the decoding, or descrambling, of the received data.

This encryption and decryption can be performed by host computers, front-end processors, or special *encryption devices*. Although these devices actually perform both encryption and decryption, they are commonly referred to as encryption devices.

A terminal can transmit *clear text*, also known as *plain text*, to an encryption device, as shown in Fig. 6-5. The encryption device takes the clear or plain text and scrambles it, or encrypts it, turning it into *cipher text* before sending it on. At the other end of the communications link, the cipher text is decrypted by the encryption device and sent on to the host computer as clear or plain text (as originally transmitted).

The advantage of encryption is that those eavesdropping on the data transmission cannot understand the encrypted data. Encryption allows use of public data networks, and even satellite or microwave links, without fear of security breaches. Of course, almost any code can be broken eventually, given enough time and a powerful-enough computer; the method of encryption chosen determines if it will be practical for an eavesdropper to break a code.

There are several terms describing the process of encryption. An *algorithm* is a set of instructions, in this case for scrambling the data. A *key* is a specific set of codes to be used by the algorithm to perform the encryption.

A child's plastic "code ring" offers a simple example of encryption. Typically, the ring contains the alphabet in proper order on the top row and the alphabet in scrambled order on the bottom. To send a coded message, the user simply finds each letter in the top row and sends the corresponding letter in the bottom row. The receiver must then have an identical ring and decode the message by looking at each letter in the bottom row and finding its counterpart in the top row.

An example of this simple type of encryption is shown in Fig. 6-6. In this example, the encryption algorithm would be "Find the letter in the top row and instead use the corresponding letter in the bottom row." The decryption algorithm is "Find the letter in the bottom row and instead use the corresponding letter in the top row." The key is the two-row alphabet chart. If we changed the order of the letters in the bottom row, we would still use the same algorithm, but we would be using a different key. In this example, the

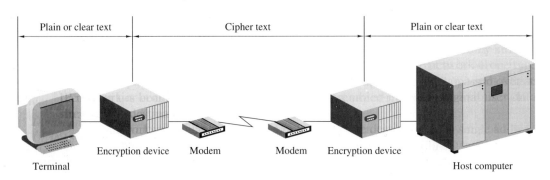

Plain or clear text   Cipher text   Plain or clear text

Encryption device   Modem   Modem   Encryption device

Terminal   Host computer

FIGURE 6-5 Encryption devices.

Clear text:	A B C D E F G H I J K L M N O P Q R S T U V W X Y Z
Cipher text:	Q A Z X S W E D C V F R T G B N H Y U J M K I O L P

FIGURE 6-6 Simple encryption.

phrase "THIS IS SIMPLE ENCRYPTION" would be encrypted as "JDCU CU UCT-NRS SGZYLNJCBG."

Secret keys.   The basis of all encryption systems is that even if the algorithm is known, without the appropriate key an eavesdropper cannot interpret an encrypted message. In the previous example, even with the algorithm, a code ring that is missing the bottom row is useless. We call this type of key a _secret key_; as long as we can keep the key a secret, our data is safe from eavesdroppers. Our example requires that the encryption devices store the entire alphabet and its corresponding code letters. Whereas our example uses only 26 letters, character codes like ASCII and EBCDIC have 128 or 256 characters, respectively. Storing all of these characters and their corresponding coded versions would take a lot of memory space in an encryption device. Therefore, most encryption algorithms and keys are based on mathematical formulas.

One example of an encryption algorithm is "Add the key to the character." The corresponding decryption algorithm is "Subtract the key from the character." For example, as shown in Fig. 6-7, if we choose 0010111 (23 is the decimal equivalent) as our key and want to send the letter "A" in ASCII, which is represented by 1000001 (65 is the decimal equivalent), we will send 1011000 (88 is the decimal equivalent). At the receiving end, the key will be subtracted from 1011000, resulting in the original 1000001, or the letter "A." Readers unfamiliar or uncomfortable with binary math can use the binary-to-decimal conversion charts in the appendix, perform the arithmetic in decimal numbers, and then convert the numbers back to binary numbers to determine what pattern of ones and zeroes is sent.

All subsequent examples in this chapter assume that keys used for encryption and decryption are binary numbers, like 10000001; the encryption algorithms are mathematical formulas that in some fashion combine the key with the data to result in cipher

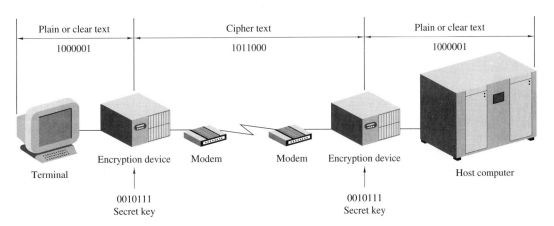

FIGURE 6-7   Secret encryption keys.

text. In some encryption devices, the user can change the key used for encryption or decryption by setting certain switches on the device itself.

The advantage of this type of secret key system is that the key can be changed on a regular basis, to ensure that our data is safe. If the transmitter changes the key, the receiver must be notified, or else the received data will not be decrypted correctly. The new key is often sent over a *secure channel*, if one is available. A secure channel is a communications link that is known to be safe from intrusion. More frequently, a new key is sent by courier, or an arbitrary system can be used. For example, we can agree that our key is the number of words in the first paragraph of column 1 of a particular newspaper's front page that day. As long as the sender and receiver are using the same key and no one else knows what the key is or how the key is determined, the data is relatively safe, and the secret key is effective.

The reason that the data is only "relatively" safe is that any code can be broken, given enough time, computing power, and a little luck. Entire wars have been won or lost by breaking codes. Our example, an addition/subtraction algorithm, would not take long to break. Most algorithms are far more complicated, including multiplication, division, and exponents. As long as the keys are changed frequently enough, these complicated algorithms are more difficult to break. Today's computers are much faster than their counterparts of even five years ago; there is reason to believe that their descendants will be even faster and therefore able to break codes more quickly. New algorithms are constantly being developed to outsmart the faster computers, and these algorithms must continue to evolve to ensure data security.

The Data Encryption Standard and Data Encryption Algorithm.   A need for a standard, general-purpose encryption algorithm for use with secret keys was answered in the mid-1970s by the *Data Encryption Standard*, or *DES*. The DES was originally developed by IBM and later adopted by the National Institute of Standards and Technology. The *American National Standards Institute*, or *ANSI*, adopted the same standard under a different name, the *Data Encryption Algorithm*, or *DEA*. The DES has also been endorsed by the *National Security Agency*, or *NSA*, for protecting information that is sensitive but not classified. Classified information is more likely to be encrypted with a secret algorithm, not a standard one like DES, to make unauthorized deciphering more difficult. The DES is relatively inexpensive to implement, and chips that use DES for encryption and decryption are widely available.

The adoption of the DES set a clear direction for the communications industry. Government agencies and many commercial customers began to demand DES encryption of certain data. DES could be incorporated in an encryption device or in host computers, terminals, modems, or other equipment. The distribution of secret keys would still be up to the individuals transmitting and receiving the data, but at least a standard for encryption devices was established.

A more secure version of DES, known as *Triple DES*, is sometimes used in financial transactions. It executes the DES algorithm three times, thereby increasing the difficulty of breaking the code.

Symmetric and asymmetric keys.   We have already established that secret keys require both users to know which key is being used. The secret keys used in the examples cited so far are based on *symmetric keys*; both the sender and receiver use the same key to encrypt and decrypt the message. In some cases, *asymmetric* keys are used, where the sender and receiver use different keys that are mathematically related in a nonobvious way.

Public keys.   *Public keys* are a common use of asymmetric keys. Though secret keys are easy enough to implement between two users, what if we need to contact many different users, and all of the messages need to be encrypted? It is inefficient to call each person, and make up a new secret key, for each transmission. These calls also jeopardize key security.

The public key encryption method uses asymmetric keys to eliminate this problem. Imagine a company with 100 employees. In the company phone book, in addition to an employee's name and phone number, there is another entry for the employee's unique public key. This public key is used to encrypt messages sent only to that employee. These messages can be decrypted only using that employee's secret key (known only to the employee).

It is assumed that everyone in the company uses encryption devices with the same algorithm. To transmit data to another employee's host computer, we need to enter that employee's public key into the encryption device, as shown in Fig. 6-8. However, the cipher text that emerges can be decrypted only with the receiver's secret key. Everyone knows the public key, but only the particular receiver knows the secret key.

A public key system requires that the algorithm use asymmetric keys; a different key is used to encrypt and decrypt the data. An eavesdropper who tries to decode cipher text with the receiver's public key does not obtain clear text. The public key system is secure because the public keys used to encrypt the data do not also decrypt the data.

All of the encryption methods we have discussed thus far are intended to protect data confidentiality. What about verifying the identity of the sender? A *digital signature* can be obtained by using the reverse of the system just described. If we encrypt data using our secret key, anyone can decrypt it with our public key, as shown in Fig. 6-9. With this method, we lose all data confidentiality, since the key used for decryption is

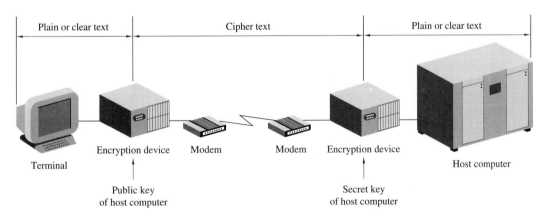

FIGURE 6-8   Data confidentiality using public keys.

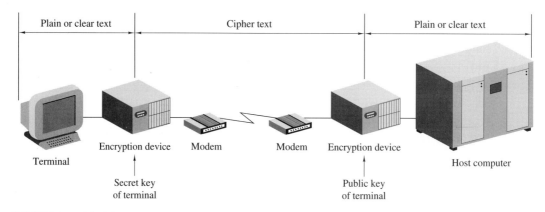

FIGURE 6-9 Digital signatures using public keys.

now public, but we now are assured that no other user can masquerade as us. For example, if someone tries to forge a memo purported to come from us, he or she would need to know our secret key to encrypt the memo properly so that others decrypting the message with our public key would obtain plain text. These digital signatures are often used to issue *digital certificates* to authenticate software. In this manner, a user downloading software from an on-line retailer can verify with the manufacturer the authenticity of this copy of software. Another application of these signatures is a *digital postmark*, in which a trusted third party receives a message and relays it with an authenticated time and date stamp, which is very useful in legal transactions. These applications of digital signatures help make the exchange of electronic messages as effective as the exchange of signed paper documents.

DATA CONFIDENTIALITY AND IDENTITY VERIFICATION

The two systems just described can be combined to obtain both confidentiality and identity verification. We prepare our memo and then encrypt a certain portion, say the last paragraph, using our secret key. Then we encrypt the entire memo again with the receiver's public key. The receiver then uses his or her secret key to decrypt the message. The resulting message will all be in plain text, except for the last paragraph, which we *double encrypted*.

The receiver then decrypts this paragraph using our public key. If the resulting paragraph is then in plain text, it is proof that the message was sent by us; only someone knowing our secret key could have encrypted that paragraph in a way that our public key would decrypt it. This double encryption method requires both parties to agree in advance on which part of the message will be double encrypted.

Hardware, software, and firmware encryption.   In our examples, we used a method known as *hardware encryption*, where a separate encryption device encrypted and decrypted the data. To change the encryption algorithm, the user usually must purchase a new device. The key can often be changed using special switches on the device itself. This method is fairly secure, because it is hard to determine an algorithm by looking at an encryption device.

Host computers and intelligent terminals can perform encryption and decryption themselves if they are appropriately programmed. This process is known as *software encryption*, and no separate encryption devices are needed. The algorithm can be changed simply by changing the software. The keys are usually also contained in the software. However, this method is vulnerable, because anyone obtaining a copy of the software knows not only the algorithm, but also the key, and can decipher all messages.

A compromise between these two methods is *firmware encryption*. In this case, the software containing the algorithm or the keys can be stored on preprogrammed chips that can be inserted into an encryption device. If there are suspected security breaches, a new set of chips, containing new software, can be installed in the encryption device, thereby changing either the algorithm or the key. This method combines the security of hardware encryption with the flexibility of software encryption.

Though software encryption is somewhat more vulnerable than the other methods, its ease of use makes it a common choice, particularly in modern electronic mail systems. In most cases, the details of the encryption technology are hidden entirely from the users. A widely distributed encryption software product is *Pretty Good Privacy*, or *PGP*. It supports several different encryption algorithms. One of the most widely used public key algorithms is the *RSA* algorithm, named after its three inventors, Rivest, Shamir, and Adelman. While the selection of a good algorithm is an important step, it is also critical to choose keys of sufficient length to make code breaking difficult. Since these keys are usually generated from user-selected passwords, both the wise choice of these passwords and the maintenance of their security are vital to any network security system.

SUMMARY

Data integrity and security are both important concerns in today's data communications networks. There are many approaches to error control. Errors can simply be detected and flagged. Another approach is to request retransmission when errors are detected. Sophisticated receiving devices can actually correct some errors, a process that is called forward error correction. Methods for implementing error control include echo checking, parity checking, cyclical parity, the Hamming code, and various checksums, including the cyclical redundancy check (CRC).

Equally important as error control is data security. Ideally, all messages are sealed, sequenced, secret, signed, and stamped. Security measures include the use of appropriate transmission facilities, passwords, historical and statistical logs, closed user groups, firewalls, and encryption.

Encryption is performed using instructions, known as an algorithm, and with a specific code, known as a key. Secret keys can be used for data confidentiality. The DES, or DEA, is a standard secret key algorithm. Public keys can be combined with secret keys to provide not only data confidentiality, but also a digital signature. Digital certificates or postmarks can also be issued. The widely used PGP software supports the RSA algorithm, among others. Finally, encryption can be performed using hardware, software, or firmware methods.

TERMS FOR REVIEW

Algorithm	Double encrypted	Packet-filtering firewall
American National	Echo checking	Parity checking
Standards Institute	Encryption	Password
ANSI	Encryption device	Personal identification
Application-level firewall	Error detection with a request	number
Asymmetric keys	for retransmission	PGP
Call-back	Error detection with flagging	PIN
Checksum	Even parity	Plain text
Cipher text	FEC	Pretty Good Privacy
Clear text	Firewall	Public key
Closed user group	Firmware encryption	RSA
CRC	Forward error correction	Sealed message
CUG	Hamming code	Secret key
Cyclical parity	Hardware encryption	Secret message
Cyclical redundancy check	Historical logging	Secure channel
Data Encryption Algorithm	Key	Sequenced message
Data Encryption Standard	Mark parity	Signed message
DEA	National Institute of	Software encryption
Decryption	Standards and Technology	Space parity
DES	National Security Agency	Stamped message
Digital certificate	NIST	Statistical logging
Digital postmark	NSA	Symmetric keys
Digital signature	Odd parity	Triple DES

EXERCISES

6-1.   Why is data transmission more sensitive than voice transmission to errors?

6-2.   How is error detection with flagging different from error detection with a request for retransmission?

6-3.   What is the advantage of forward error correction over other error-control approaches?

6-4.   What is echo checking?

6-5.   How does even-parity checking detect errors? Odd-parity checking? Is one method better than the other?

6-6.   If errors occur transmitting bits 3 and 4, will even-parity checking detect the error? How about even cyclical parity?

6-7.   What type of bit error does the Hamming code correct?

6-8.   How is a simple checksum different from the cyclical redundancy check?

6-9.   Explain the major goals of proper message security.

6-10. Which transmission media are the most secure? Which are the least secure?

6-11. What is the difference between historical and statistical logging?

6-12. What is a firewall? How does it improve security?

6-13. Explain the difference between clear text and cipher text.

6-14. Compare secret and public keys. How is each used for encryption and decryption?

6-15. What is the difference between symmetric and asymmetric keys?

6-16. What is a digital certificate? A digital postmark?

CHAPTER 7

Architectures and Protocols

We have already discussed host computers, front-end processors, terminals, modems, multiplexers, and many other devices used for data communications. Communications architectures and protocols enable these devices to communicate in an orderly manner, defining precise rules and methods for communications and ensuring harmonious communications among them.

ARCHITECTURES

A *communications architecture* is a manufacturer's strategy for connecting its host computers, terminals, and communications equipment. It defines the elements necessary for data communications between devices. One of the advantages of a well-defined communications architecture is that it cleanly separates the function of communications from the host computer's other functions. Specifically, a communications architecture can describe special functions that the host computer's hardware and software must perform to allow applications programs to communicate with the outside world.

For example, there may be many different types of terminals attached to a single host computer. A programmer writing accounting software for the host computer does not need to know how to communicate with these different terminals. The programmer formats the data in a special manner defined by the host computer's communications architecture; the accounting program then passes the data to the communications software, which, in turn, translates it to a format for each of the different terminals. The architecture defines the precise role of each program; the accounting program calculates profits and losses, and the communications program sends data to the terminals. Similarly, the author of a word processing program doesn't need to understand how particular terminals function; the programmer simply follows the rules spelled out by the communications architecture and then passes the data onto the communications program for further processing.

An analogy for a communications architecture can be found in a televised football game. The referee calls a penalty and uses hand signals to indicate the infraction and the offending team. The announcer sees these hand signals and translates them into words for the television viewers. In this communications architecture, it is the function of the referee to call the penalty and explain it by using hand signals, and the announcer is responsible for translating the hand signals into words and adding further explanation. Similarly, in communications architectures, each piece of hardware and software has its own task, and for communications to occur, they must all function in harmony.

Separating the communications functions of a host computer from its other functions adds flexibility. For example, if we later want to modify our architecture to include other types of terminals and devices, we do not need to modify all of the host computer's software. Since all applications programs communicate through the communications software, only the communications software needs to be modified to accept the new devices. Referring back to our analogy, to televise the same football game in Spain, we would not need to teach the referee to speak Spanish; since only the announcer speaks to the viewers, only the announcer needs to know Spanish.

Thus far in this book, we have considered host computer-to-terminal communications. Users often want to connect host computers to other host computers, to allow them to share information, transfer files, and so on. A communications architecture describes this type of communications, in addition to host computer-to-terminal communications.

Originally, each host computer manufacturer used its own architecture. Unfortunately, although all architectures perform similar functions, they are not always compatible. For example, connecting IBM host computers to each other may be easy; connecting HP host computers to each other may also be easy. Connecting HP host computers to IBM host computers, however, may require special conversion devices that can communicate successfully in both architectures. Before we discuss individual manufacturers' particular architectures, we will consider an international standard that helps us explain the tasks involved in computer communications.

THE OPEN SYSTEMS INTERCONNECTION MODEL

The International Standards Organization (ISO) has developed a universal architecture for computer communications. This standard, known as the *Open Systems Interconnection Model*, or *OSI model*, breaks down the task of communications into seven independent layers, each with its own tasks. OSI's purpose is to permit communications among devices made by many manufacturers. The exact methods for performing these tasks, including the protocols we discuss later in this chapter, are still evolving. Almost all of the major host computer manufacturers have supported the concept of OSI in principle, even though their current product offerings may not all comply with OSI. The *Corporation for Open Systems*, or *COS*, is a nonprofit corporation formed in 1985 consisting of representatives of major host computer manufacturers of that era, including Control Data, DEC, Hewlett-Packard, Honeywell, IBM, NCR, Tandem, Unisys, Wang, Xerox, and others. The corporation's purpose is to facilitate the evolution of intervendor compatibility from a

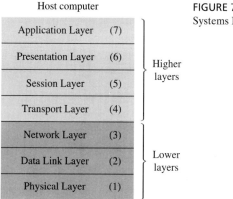

Host computer

FIGURE 7-1   Layers of the Open Systems Interconnection model.

model to a reality. Perhaps the most significant contribution of the OSI model is that it provides all of us with a common language for describing communications tasks and functions.

The seven layers of OSI are shown in Fig. 7-1. Each layer represents a particular function. Sometimes, each function is performed by a separate piece of hardware or software. Other times, a single program may perform the functions of several layers. All of the layers are necessary for communications to occur. The different layer classifications are somewhat arbitrary, and a different standards committee might have chosen to break the communications functions into more or fewer layers. For example, we might describe the process of driving to work as "(1) Open the car door. (2) Sit down. (3) Close the door. (4) Insert the key. (5) Turn the key," and so on. Another person might describe the same process as "(1) Get in the car. (2) Start the car. (3) Put the car in gear," and so on. We are all describing the same task, and both descriptions are correct and accurate; however, each description chooses to break up the process of driving to work into different tasks. Similarly, the ISO–OSI model chooses to divide the function of computer communications into seven layers, though more or fewer layers could easily have been chosen. Rather than examine each layer's functions in detail, we merely highlight its most important functions.

The lowest layer, known as the *Physical Layer*, or *Layer 1*, is responsible for the transmission of bits. The Physical Layer is always implemented using hardware; this layer encompasses the mechanical, electrical, and functional interface. This layer is the interface to the outside world, where ones and zeroes leave and enter the device, usually using electronic signals as specified by interface standards. Examples of Physical Layer standards are RS-232-C, RS-449, RS-422-A, and RS-423-A.

The *Data Link Layer*, or *Layer 2*, assembles the data bits into a block, or *frame*, which is then sent to the Physical Layer for transmission. It is often also responsible for ensuring error-free, reliable transmission of data. The Data Link Layer typically scrutinizes the bits received to determine if errors occurred during transmission. This layer is often able to request retransmission or correction of any errors using protocols such as BSC, SDLC, HDLC, and PPP, presented later in this chapter.

The *Network Layer*, or *Layer 3*, is responsible for setting up the appropriate routing of messages throughout a network. This layer is the only layer concerned with the types of switching networks used to route the data. The routing of data between networks, and through packet switching networks, is also handled by the Network Layer. We discuss packet switching networks further in Chapter 8.

These layers of OSI (Physical, Data Link, and Network) are usually referred to as the *lower layers*. Layers 4 through 7 (Transport, Session, Presentation, and Application) are usually referred to as the *higher layers*, or *upper layers*.

The *Transport Layer*, or *Layer 4*, is responsible for isolating the function of the lower layers from the higher layers. This layer will accept messages from higher layers and break these messages down into messages that can be accepted by the lower layers. For example, a file being transferred may contain thousands of characters; the lower layers may be transmitting data 100 characters at a time, so the Transport Layer breaks the file into many blocks, each 100 characters long. If communications technology changes and longer messages can be accepted in the future, the Transport Layer will need modification, but not other higher layers. The Transport Layer is also responsible for monitoring the quality of the communications channel and for selecting the most cost-efficient communication service based on the reliability required for a particular transmission.

The *Session Layer*, or *Layer 5*, requests that a logical connection be established based on the end user's request. In this case, an end user might be the terminal operator using the computer. For example, if the user wants to transfer a file, the Session Layer is informed of the location of the file on the user's system and the location of the destination file on the remote host computer. Any necessary log-on and password procedures are also usually handled by this layer. The Session Layer is also responsible for terminating the connection.

The *Presentation Layer*, or *Layer 6*, provides format and code conversion services. For example, if the host computer is connected to many different types of printers, each printer may require different character sequences to invoke special features, such as boldface and italics. The Presentation Layer handles all of the necessary formatting. In addition, if files are being transferred from the host computer of one manufacturer to the host computer of another, there may be different file formats, or even different character codes. The Presentation Layer would handle any necessary conversion (e.g., ASCII-to-EBCDIC conversion).

The *Application Layer*, or *Layer 7*, provides access to the network for the end user. The user's capabilities on the network are determined by the Application Layer software, which can be tailored to the needs of the user. Some Application Layer software might permit remote terminals only to access a host computer; other Application Layer software might also permit file transfers. Network management statistics, diagnostics, and other on-line monitoring capabilities can also be implemented in this layer.

We have already mentioned that the Physical Layer must be implemented in hardware. Since this layer is the only part of the model where bits are actually transmitted, it is also the only part of the model requiring hardware implementation. The other layers all manipulate the data in some way, perhaps adding to it or modifying it, but all of these techniques can generally be performed using software. However, since functions can be performed more efficiently and inexpensively by hardware than by software, some functions of the Data Link and Network Layers are sometimes implemented in hardware. The higher layers are almost always implemented in software.

OSI IN ACTION

Few of today's host computers have fully implemented the OSI functions that allow for complete intervendor compatibility. If two host computers used OSI protocols, how would a common transaction, like a file transfer, then take place? We trace a file transferred from an imaginary IBM host computer to an HP host computer, using the OSI model as a reference.

We begin by examining the path of the data through the layers of the IBM host computer. As illustrated in Fig. 7-2, a user of a word processing program on the IBM host computer issues the file transfer command to the Application Layer. The Application Layer then passes the file to the Presentation Layer, which may reformat the data. The data is then passed to the Session Layer, which requests that a connection be provided to the destination host and passes the data to the Transport Layer. The Transport Layer breaks the file into manageable chunks of data for transmission and passes them to the Network Layer. The Network Layer selects the data's route and then passes the data to the Data Link Layer. The Data Link Layer adds extra information to the data so that it can be checked for errors at the receiving end, and passes the data to the Physical Layer. The Physical Layer takes the resulting data stream and transmits it across the physical link to the other host computer.

The data transmitted by the Physical Layer includes not only the file from the Application Layer, but also all of the additional information added by each of the other layers. Each layer performs its function by modifying the data. For example, the Network Layer adds extra bits to the data that specify the route that the data is to take. The data finally transmitted by the Physical Layer could be twice as long as the original data, but each of these extra ones and zeroes performs valuable functions. Each of the receiving host computer's different layers examines the ones and zeroes related to their functions and remove their data before passing the remaining data to the next higher

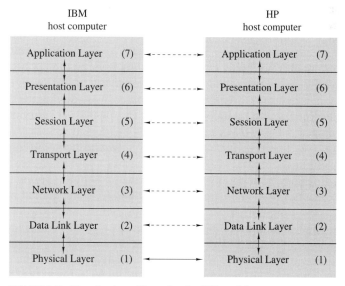

FIGURE 7-2   Transferring a file under the OSI model.

layer. By the time the message reaches the Application Layer on the destination host computer, it is the same length as the message originally sent by the Application Layer on the originating host computer.

The HP host computer's Physical Layer receives the bits and passes them on to its Data Link Layer. The Data Link Layer verifies that no errors occurred and then passes the data on to the Network Layer. The Network Layer ensures that the selected route is proving reliable and then passes the data on to the Transport Layer. The Transport Layer reassembles the small chunks of data into the file being transferred and then passes it on to the Session Layer. The Session Layer determines if the transfer is complete, and if so, may break down the session, in effect ending communications. The data is then passed on to the Presentation Layer, which may reformat it, performing any necessary conversion, and which then passes it on to the Application Layer. The HP host computer's users can then access the transferred information through the Application Layer software.

In this example, the transfer of data went smoothly. What if an error had occurred? For example, if the HP host computer's Data Link Layer detects any errors, it might request that the data be retransmitted. This retransmission request would be sent back over the HP Physical Layer to the IBM Physical Layer, which would pass it on to the IBM Data Link Layer. The IBM Data Link Layer would respond to the retransmission request, since this layer is responsible for error-free transmission. The IBM Data Link Layer retransmits the data to the IBM Physical Layer, which then transmits the data over the physical link. The data is received by the HP Physical Layer and passed on to the HP Data Link Layer. If there are still errors, the entire retransmission process is repeated. If the data is now error free, the file transfer continues as described previously, with the data being passed on to the higher layers.

The OSI model provides for *peer-level communication* between the layers. The Physical Layers of the two host computers are the only parts of the two devices that communicate directly. The other layers communicate indirectly, through the lower layers, and eventually through the Physical Layer. For example, the Data Link Layer on the IBM host computer adds bits to the message for error detection that are interpreted by the HP Data Link Layer. Similarly, each layer on the IBM host computer contributes bits that are interpreted by the corresponding layer on the HP host computer. Although only the Physical Layers communicate directly, all of the layers communicate indirectly with their peers on the other host computer by modifying the data, sending messages for interpretation by their counterparts. This peer-level communication is shown with dashed lines in Fig. 7-2.

Our discussion so far has assumed that two host computers are directly connected to each other. Sometimes, however, in a network with many host computers, there may be intermediary devices between the two host computers trying to communicate. Each device on a network can be referred to as a *node*. For example, a message being routed from a host computer in San Francisco to a host computer in New York might pass through a switching node in Chicago. In Fig. 7-3, there are nodes in New York, San Francisco, and Chicago. The nodes at the far ends of the connection—in this case, in San Francisco and New York—are sometimes referred to as the *destination nodes*. The intermediate devices, known as *intermediate nodes*, support only the first three layers of

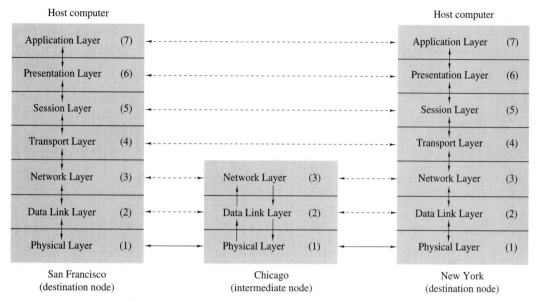

Host computer   Host computer

Application Layer	(7)	<-->	Application Layer	(7)
Presentation Layer	(6)	<-->	Presentation Layer	(6)
Session Layer	(5)	<-->	Session Layer	(5)
Transport Layer	(4)	<-->	Transport Layer	(4)
Network Layer	(3)	<----> Network Layer (3) <---->	Network Layer	(3)
Data Link Layer	(2)	<----> Data Link Layer (2) <---->	Data Link Layer	(2)
Physical Layer	(1)	<----> Physical Layer (1) <---->	Physical Layer	(1)

San Francisco   Chicago   New York
(destination node)   (intermediate node)   (destination node)

FIGURE 7-3   Multiple node communications under OSI.

the OSI model. The node in Chicago must receive the message from San Francisco with its Physical Layer, verify with its Data Link Layer that there are no errors, and then determine, using its Network Layer, the appropriate routing to the destination host computer in New York. Error-correction information is then added back to the message by the Chicago node's Data Link Layer before it is retransmitted to New York by the node's Physical Layer. Intermediate nodes must support the lower three layers, which are necessary for data transmission and routing. The intermediate node may have higher layers, but since it is not the destination device, the message in this case never reaches those layers in the intermediate node. The Network Layer at the host computer in New York recognizes that the message has reached its destination and does not send the message to another node, but instead passes it on to its own higher layers.

TRADITIONAL COMMUNICATIONS ARCHITECTURES

Traditional communications architectures typically have a sole purpose: to allow a single vendor's devices to communicate with each other. Host computers, front-end processors, terminals, and other devices are all linked in accordance with the rules spelled out in a communications architecture. Attachment of devices from other vendors requires the use of special converters and adapters. For example, a Hewlett-Packard terminal might connect to an IBM host computer using a special protocol converter. Typically, a device attached with a converter is limited in its communications capabilities. In our example, the HP terminal might be able to perform basic text communications, but might not be able to perform graphics functions on the IBM host computer.

Since open standards may not be implemented on all devices for many years, we are sometimes still bound by the limitations of traditional communications architectures. Different vendors offer many communications architectures today, but of all the proprietary systems, one, SNA, is by far the most widely used.

SYSTEMS NETWORK ARCHITECTURE

IBM's *Systems Network Architecture*, or *SNA*, introduced in 1974, is one of the most widely used communications architectures in the world. SNA's success is usually attributed to its ability to connect a wide variety of devices, each with different capabilities, in a homogeneous network whose workings are hidden from the end user. SNA allows customers to start with a small network and increase its size in a modular fashion. SNA networks can also be connected to other SNA networks. Finally, SNA includes sophisticated network management functions to simplify fault isolation and problem determination, as well as to provide reports on network usage. We explain these functions in Chapter 9.

Like OSI, SNA functions can be divided into different layers. These layers roughly parallel the OSI model, but some SNA layers perform more or fewer functions than the corresponding OSI layers. The SNA layers are shown in Fig. 7-4, along with a rough approximation of their OSI equivalents.

Because of SNA's flexibility and complexity, a thorough discussion of SNA requires several volumes. We therefore concentrate on some of the basic terminology and language of SNA, as well as its major functions. Since SNA is the architecture of a particular manufacturer (IBM), some of its terminology is slightly different from the terminology used previously in this book. For example, what we have often called "host computers" are known in SNA as *Host Processors*. Similarly, SNA *Workstations* are equivalent to the devices that we have called "terminals."

The structure of SNA.   The components or devices interconnected by an SNA network are known as *Nodes*. The Nodes are connected by data communications *Links*. For instance, a Host Processor and Workstation could be considered Nodes in SNA, and the two Nodes are connected by a communications Link. The *network* includes the components and the communications Links.

SNA layers	OSI layers
Transaction Services	Application Layer
Presentation Layer	Presentation Layer
Data Flow control	Session Layer
Transmission Control	Transport Layer
Path Control	Network Layer
Data Link Control	Data Link Layer
Physical Control	Physical Layer

FIGURE 7-4   SNA layers vs. OSI layers.

SNA clearly separates the network from the users. In other words, the users do not have to understand how the network functions to use the network. For example, assume that an accountant is using a Workstation in an SNA network to access an accounting program on a Host Processor in the same network. There are two *End Users* in this communications path, the accountant and the accounting program. The accountant sends data to the SNA network and receives data from the SNA network. Similarly, the accounting program, which is a specific *Application Program* on the Host Processor, also sends data to the SNA network and receives data from the SNA network. The two End Users, the Application Program and the accountant, are isolated from the routing and transmission of data, which is handled entirely by the SNA network. Neither the accountant nor the accounting program need to understand how the data is routed or transmitted.

Often, there is a *Communications Controller* between the Host Processor and the Workstation, as illustrated in Fig. 7-5. The Communications Controller's responsibilities include routing data through a network and controlling the communications Links. For example, the Communications Controller could be linked to several other Host Processors, allowing the same Workstation user to access several different computers.

Cluster Controllers are often added to allow several Workstations to share a single point of access to the network, as shown in Fig. 7-6. A Cluster Controller is similar in function to the generic remote intelligent controller we presented in Chapter 5. The Cluster Controller is often located many miles from the Communications Controller; the length of the communications Link is not important, and Links can even include telephone circuits and modems.

There are different types of Nodes in SNA, depending on their function. For example, as illustrated in Fig. 7-7, the Host Processor is often referred to as the *Host Node*. A Communications Controller is referred to as the *Communications Controller Node*. A

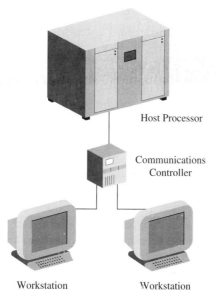

FIGURE 7-5   Using a Communications Controller in an SNA network.

Host Processor

Communications Controller

Workstation   Workstation

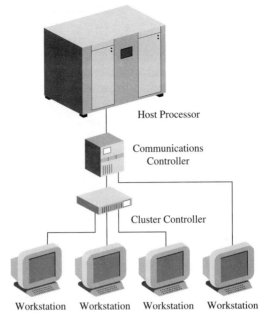

Host Processor

Communications
Controller

Cluster Controller

Workstation   Workstation   Workstation   Workstation

FIGURE 7-6   Using a Cluster Controller in an SNA network.

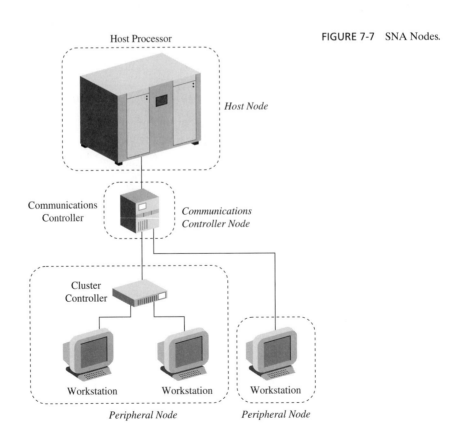

FIGURE 7-7   SNA Nodes.

Host Processor

Host Node

Communications
Controller

*Communications
Controller Node*

Cluster
Controller

Workstation   Workstation   Workstation

Peripheral Node   *Peripheral Node*

Workstation, or a Cluster Controller with several Workstations, is referred to as a *Peripheral Node*. A Peripheral Node is always the source and destination of data. Another type of Peripheral Node is a *Distributed Processor*, which is similar to a Host Processor, though more limited in function.

Network Addressable Units.   The SNA network components we have already discussed can be further broken down into the various functions that they perform. Each Node may contain several *Network Addressable Units*, or *NAUs*. Network Addressable Units have unique addresses, so that data can be routed to a particular NAU. Network Addressable Units are a combination of hardware and/or software in a Node managing a particular function. There are three types of Network Addressable Units: a *Logical Unit*, a *Physical Unit*, and a *System Services Control Point*.

A *Logical Unit*, or *LU*, is the End User's access point to an SNA network. For example, the End User of a Workstation in a Peripheral Node types data on the keyboard, which is then passed to the Logical Unit for routing to its destination, which is a Host Node in the SNA Network. When the data reaches the Host Node, it is passed to the Logical Unit in that Host Node. At the Host Processor, the End User is an Application Program, so the Application Program receives the data from a Logical Unit on the Host Node. Data enters and leaves the SNA network at the Logical Unit.

End Users are not part of the SNA network; they each communicate with the SNA network through the network's Logical Units. When two End Users communicate in SNA through their respective Logical Units, it is known as an LU–LU *Session*, as shown in Fig. 7-8. An SNA session is a communications path through an SNA network.

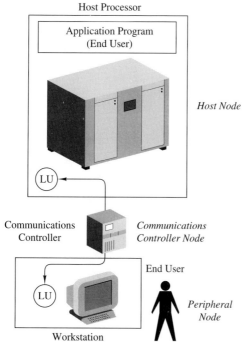

Host Processor

Application Program
(End User)

Host Node

LU

Communications
Controller

*Communications
Controller Node*

End User

LU

*Peripheral
Node*

Workstation

FIGURE 7-8   SNA LU-LU Session between Logical Units in the Workstation and Host Processor.

Workstations that are capable of communicating directly with an SNA network contain a Logical Unit. Some Workstations do not possess sufficient intelligence to communicate directly with the SNA network and are instead attached to a Cluster Controller; in this case, the Cluster Controller contains the Logical Unit, as illustrated in Fig. 7-9. Notice that the Communications Controller does not contain a Logical Unit, because there are no End Users at the Communications Controller Node, and data is only routed through the Communications Controller.

Every Node contains a *Physical Unit*, or *PU*, which manages and monitors that Node's resources. For example, the telephone lines and modems connecting two Nodes are not part of the SNA network. The Physical Unit represents these devices to the network, in much the same way that the Logical Unit represents the End User to the network. A simple SNA network with its Physical Units and Logical Units is shown in Fig. 7-10. Notice that the Workstations connected to the Cluster Controller do not con-

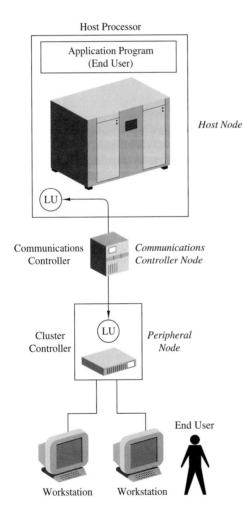

FIGURE 7-9   SNA LU-LU Session between Logical Units in the Cluster Controller and Host Processor.

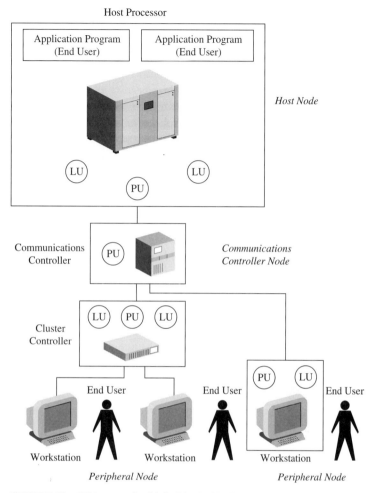

Host Processor

Application Program
(End User)

Application Program
(End User)

Host Node

LU

LU

PU

Communications
Controller

PU

Communications
Controller Node

LU

PU

LU

Cluster
Controller

PU

LU

End User

End User

End User

Workstation

Workstation

Workstation

Peripheral Node

Peripheral Node

FIGURE 7-10   SNA network with its Physical Units and Logical Units.

tain a Physical Unit, because the Cluster Controller is managing that Peripheral Node's physical resources.

Finally, the *System Services Control Point*, or *SSCP*, is a part of the Host Node that acts as a central control point for monitoring and controlling a network's resources. The System Services Control Point communicates with all of the Physical Units in the Network using SSCP–PU Sessions and all of the Logical Units in the Network using SSCP–LU Sessions. The SSCP can communicate with the PUs and LUs, ensuring that they are operating properly; any malfunctions can be logged by the SSCP. Finally, the SSCP can help establish sessions between two LUs, thereby allowing End Users to communicate.

Domains and Subareas.   The SSCP can be thought of as the king of the SNA network, commanding all of the PUs and LUs in its *Domain*. Each domain has only one

SSCP. To establish an LU–LU Session in which each LU is in a different Domain, the SSCPs of each Domain must first communicate through an SSCP–SSCP Session. Two SSCPs and their respective Domains are illustrated in Fig. 7-11.

Domains can be subdivided into *Subareas*, each containing a *Subarea Node* and the resources which that Node controls. Host Nodes and Communications Controllers are both classified as Subarea Nodes. Therefore, as shown in Fig. 7-12, each Host Processor is a Subarea, and each Communications Controller with its attached Workstations and Cluster Controllers are also considered to be a Subarea. Also shown in Fig. 7-12 are the Links between Subarea Nodes. These Links are known as *Transmission Groups*. If there are several Links in a Transmission Group and one should fail, communications are automatically routed over one of the other Links in the Transmission Group.

OTHER COMMUNICATIONS ARCHITECTURES

Almost all computer manufacturers have an architecture for computer communications. It is hard to classify any one architecture as superior to another. Each is designed

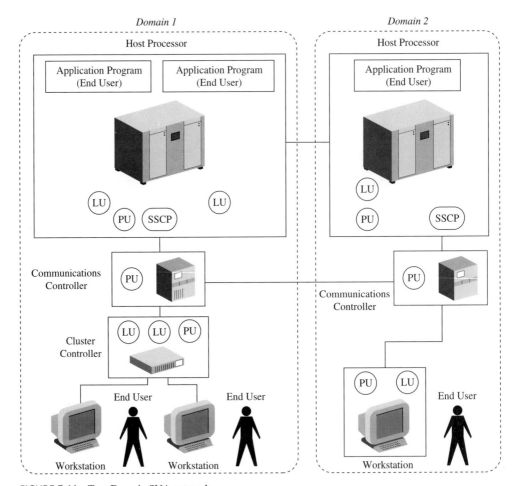

FIGURE 7-11   Two-Domain SNA network.

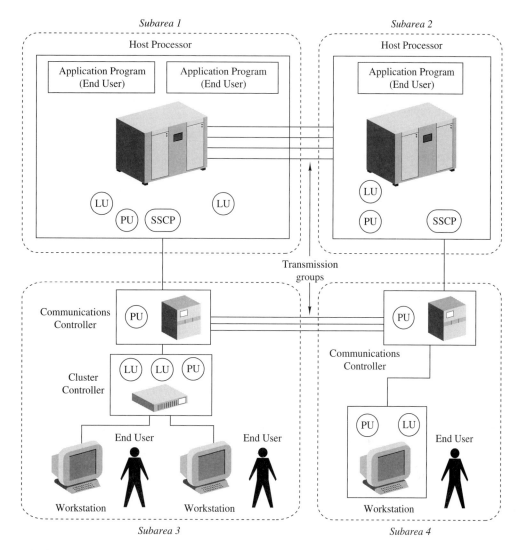

FIGURE 7-12   Subareas and Transmission Groups.

Vendor	Architecture
DEC (Compaq)	Digital Network Architecture (DNA)
Hewlett-Packard	AdvanceNet
Honeywell	Distributed Systems Architecture (DSA)
IBM	Systems Network Architecture (SNA)
Unisys (Burroughs)	Burroughs Network Architecture (BNA)
Unisys (Sperry)	Distributed Communications Architecture (DCA)
WANG	Wang Systems Networking (WSN)

FIGURE 7-13   Proprietary communications architectures..

to allow a particular manufacturer's devices to communicate with each other. Some examples of proprietary communications architectures are listed in Fig. 7-13.

PROTOCOLS

While architectures provide a broad framework for communications, describing how different components can be connected together, *protocols* precisely define the methods used to communicate. Almost all architectures require the use of certain protocols to ensure reliable data transmission. Protocols are a set of rules for transmitting and receiving data between devices. Sometimes called *line disciplines*, protocols spell out the specific character or bit patterns required for communications between two devices.

An example of a human communications protocol can be found in a classroom. Typically, a professor begins a lecture and controls the communications path. If a student wants to communicate, the student must wait until the professor asks, "Any questions?" and then raise his or her hand and wait for permission to communicate. The professor can then call on the student, granting control of the communications line to the student. The student then asks his or her question and grants control of the communications path back to the professor for the response. The protocol in this case is that the student speaks only when called upon; it is customary that the student doesn't interrupt the professor and vice versa. This type of protocol, commonly used in data communications, is known as a *link-level protocol*, because it precisely defines methods for communicating over a link.

POLLING AND SELECTING

Establishing rules for sharing the communications path, known as *communications line control*, is one of the major functions of a link-level protocol. Often, this establishment of rules is accomplished by using polling and selecting methods, mentioned previously in Chapter 5.

Polling occurs when the host computer or front-end processor asks the terminal, "Do you have any data to send?" At this point, a smart terminal might send data, or simply answer "No." *Selecting* occurs when the front-end processor or host computer asks the terminal, "Can you accept data now?" A smart terminal might then answer "Go ahead" or "Not now, I'm busy." Only smart or intelligent terminals can respond to these messages; dumb terminals cannot be controlled by polling and selecting. Protocols define the exact characters or bit patterns that must be sent to perform this polling and selecting.

AUTOMATIC REPEAT REQUEST

Finally, almost all link-level protocols provide for some *error detection and correction* capability. Most link-level protocols use an *automatic repeat request* system known as *ARQ*. In this system, when the receiving device recognizes an error, it automatically requests that the data be retransmitted. Both the transmitting and receiving devices usually detect errors by using a checksum or cyclical redundancy check method, as described in Chapter 6.

There are two common types of ARQ in use today. One type, known as *stop-and-wait ARQ*, requires that the receiver respond to each block of data before the next one can be sent. A human example of stop-and-wait ARQ would be an inexperienced secretary taking dictation; after each sentence spoken by the boss, the secretary may say, "Okay," indicating that the sentence was received and transcribed properly. The boss does not go on to the next sentence until hearing the "Okay." In addition, a secretary who doesn't understand a sentence might ask, "What?". This is a request for the boss to repeat the transmission. Similarly, with stop-and-wait ARQ, a device will not transmit the next sentence until it has received confirmation that the last message was received correctly; it will also repeat messages that were not understood.

In the other method, known as *continuous ARQ*, a device continues sending messages without waiting for confirmation that the last message was received. For example, a boss dictating a letter to a very experienced secretary would probably not pause between sentences to wait for the secretary to say "Okay." We assume that this boss is in the habit of rattling off several sentences at a time, sometimes getting far ahead of the secretary's ability to transcribe. Even though the secretary may continue to say "Okay" after each sentence is transcribed, the boss may already be in the middle of the next sentence. As long as the secretary doesn't say "What?", the boss keeps talking.

There are two types of continuous ARQ protocols; if the secretary asks "What?", there are two possible reactions by the boss. The first, known as *go-back-N continuous ARQ*, would have the boss return to the last sentence the secretary understood and begin retransmitting the misunderstood sentence, as well as any sentences that followed. Another possible response, *selective repeat continuous ARQ*, would require the boss to repeat only the misunderstood sentence; the subsequent sentences would not have to be retransmitted. In either case, the advantage of continuous ARQ protocols over stop-and-wait ARQ protocols is that the sending device does not have to wait for permission from the receiving device before sending the next block of data. With either type of continuous ARQ, as long as no errors occur, data transmission is never delayed. Continuous ARQ, therefore, is more efficient than stop-and-wait ARQ, in which the transmitter must wait for an acknowledgment before proceeding to send the next data block.

COMMON LINK-LEVEL PROTOCOLS

All common link-level protocols allow devices to share a communications path and to detect and correct errors. There are two common classes of link-level protocols, byte-oriented protocols and bit-oriented protocols.

In both types of protocols, the devices must exchange *control information* along with the data transmitted. This control information includes the queries and responses used for polling and selecting, as well as the error-checking information necessary for all types of automatic repeat request. In *byte-*

oriented protocols, also known as *character-oriented protocols*, all control information and data are encoded using entire bytes. *Bit-oriented protocols*, on the other hand, may use single bits to represent both control information and data. Most older protocols were byte-oriented, or character-oriented, and almost all major character sets, including ASCII and EBCDIC, include control characters.

We choose two commonly used link-level protocols, BSC and SDLC, as examples. There are many other link-level protocols in use today, and surely new ones will be proposed in the future. However, these two protocols illustrate classic features. One is byte oriented, and the other is bit oriented; one uses stop-and-wait ARQ, and the other uses continuous ARQ; one allows only half duplex transmission, and the other permits half duplex or full duplex.

BINARY SYNCHRONOUS COMMUNICATIONS

The most widely used byte-oriented or character-oriented protocol is IBM's *Binary Synchronous Communications*, or *BSC* (often referred to as *Bisync*). BSC is a half duplex, stop-and-wait ARQ protocol. It permits point-to-point communications such as a terminal connected to a host computer. BSC also permits multipoint communications.

In multipoint use, there is a single *Control station* and many *Tributary stations*. The Control station can communicate with any of the Tributary stations, and any of the Tributary stations can communicate with the Control station, but the Tributary stations cannot communicate with each other. For example, in Chapter 5, we described a host computer connected to several terminals attached to a line splitter. In this case, the host computer is acting as the Control station and the terminals as Tributary stations.

BSC was originally designed to accommodate three specific character codes: ASCII, EBCDIC, and Transcode. We have already presented ASCII and EBCDIC in Chapter 3; Transcode is a seldom-used six-bit code. The major functions of BSC and other link-level protocols are to share the communications circuit among two or more devices and to ensure error-free transmission. Because BSC uses half duplex transmission, along with stop-and-wait ARQ, it is not well suited to use over satellites or any other transmission media subject to long delays.

For example, if we were to use BSC to communicate over satellites, a block of data, known as a *frame*, would be sent from a host computer over the satellite to a terminal. The message might take a quarter of a second to get to the terminal, at which point the terminal would determine if the frame contains any errors. Assuming that there are no errors, the terminal would send an *acknowledgment* that the frame has been properly received, and this acknowledgment message would go back up over the satellite to reach the host computer, taking another quarter of a second. During this round-trip of a half-second, the host computer is not permitted to send any more data and must wait for the return acknowledgment. We have not even included any line-turnaround time required due to the half duplex nature of the conversation. These delays make BSC unsuitable for satellite transmission.

The BSC frame.   During our discussion of character codes in Chapter 3, we mentioned that special control codes included in character codes were used by certain protocols. BSC uses many of these control codes to permit devices to exchange *control information*, like an acknowledgment message, and to help divide a BSC frame into several parts. We present here only the basic elements of a BSC frame and only a limited number of BSC features. The purpose of this book is not to make the reader fluent in the BSC protocol, but to introduce the types of messages used in a character-oriented protocol.

There are two basic types of BSC frames, one containing user data and the other containing control information. User data frames contain data actually typed by the terminal user or sent from the host computer's applications program. Additional information, known as a *header*, may be included in the user data frame by the BSC protocol, to allow the message to be addresesed to one of several terminals. Some error-checking information may also be included in the user data frame.

The other type of frames, known as control information frames, are passed between the terminal and the host computer to perform polling and selecting, as well as to determine if errors have occurred. A BSC terminal user does not personally type any control information. The terminal itself is programmed to respond to BSC control information, but not to pass this information to the user. A BSC terminal and host computer actually carry on their own private conversation about the data's accuracy and each other's status, without the knowledge or intervention of the terminal user.

For example, the terminal user types data on the keyboard and then hits the ENTER or XMIT (transmit) key. The BSC terminal sends the data, along with a header, to the host computer. The host computer checks the message for errors, and if it is satisfied that none have occurred, sends back the acknowledgment message; this acknowledgment message is control information, which is received by the terminal. The terminal now is certain that its message was received by the host computer, and the message can be erased from its memory; if the host computer had found errors, the terminal would at this point retransmit the message. This exchange of control information occurs between the host computer and terminal, but the terminal does not pass the acknowledgment message to the terminal user. The only way that an end user knows that an error has occurred is if he or she hits the ENTER key again very quickly and doesn't receive a response; this indicates that the terminal may be busy retransmitting the last message.

CHARACTERS IN A BSC FRAME

What characters actually make up a BSC frame? We'll begin with a control information frame, which contains the following characters:

PAD SYN SYN [control information] PAD

The *PAD* character is simply a special pattern of ones and zeroes used at the beginning and end of a frame. The only purpose of the PAD character is to allow time for the transmission line to stabilize. We assume that eight-bit characters are being used for our example, so each PAD character is eight bits in length.

Following the PAD characters are two *SYN* characters, which allow the receiver to "sync up" to the incoming signal and prepare to receive real data. The SYN character can be found in almost all character codes. Since this is a control frame, it contains control information, followed by a PAD character to conclude the frame. Remember that none of these special characters is ever seen by the user, but is each part of the frames sent between the BSC terminal and host computer.

What characters make up control information? That depends on whether we are using BSC for point-to-point or multipoint configurations. Each device is sometimes referred to as a communications *station* in BSC. In point-to-point use, there are only two stations, and the most commonly used control information represents the question "Can I send now?" This question is known as an *enquiry*, and the *ENQ* character is used in the control information portion of the frame. An enquiry frame would be

    PAD SYN SYN ENQ PAD

The device receiving the enquiry can reply with an *ACK0*, a *NAK*, or a *WACK*. An *ACK0* is a type of acknowledgment indicating that the device is ready to receive; a NAK is a negative acknowledgment indicating that the device is not ready to receive; a WACK indicates that the device is temporarily busy but will be ready soon. These three possible responses are

    PAD SYN SYN ACK0 PAD
    PAD SYN SYN NAK   PAD
    PAD SYN SYN WACK PAD

Remember that if we are using an eight-bit character code, the ENQ, ACK0, NAK, and WACK characters may each have an eight-bit representation. If any of these special characters are not available in a character code, a combination of two other characters can be used instead. Assuming that ACK0 was the response, the transmitter can now send data using a data frame, which we will explain in the upcoming discussion. After the data transmission is complete, the transmitter sends an *EOT*, indicating an end of transmission

    PAD SYN SYN EOT PAD

At this point, either of the two devices could ask permission to send, using the ENQ character.

Multipoint use complicates the control information exchanged, because there is now a single Control station and several Tributary stations. Typically, a host computer is the Control station, and the terminals are Tributary stations. The Control station performs all of the polling and selecting in multipoint use. The polling and selecting is performed by using the ENQ character, plus the address of the Tributary station. Selected stations can respond with acknowledgments, indicating their readiness to receive data. Polled stations send data if they have any to send, or otherwise, may indicate that they are done transmitting with a simple EOT message:

    PAD SYN SYN EOT PAD

So far, we have considered only control information. How is data transmitted? After a terminal user hits the ENTER key, the BSC terminal assembles the data into a data frame. A typical data frame in BSC looks like

PAD SYN SYN SOH header STX data ETX BCC BCC PAD

The PAD and SYN characters perform the same functions as previously described. The *SOH* character indicates the start of the header, which contains addressing information. The *STX* character indicates the start of the text, or user data, and is followed by the actual user data. The *ETX* character signifies the end of the data and is followed by two *BCC*s, or block check characters, and a final PAD character. The BCC characters vary with each transmission, containing checksums for error correction, like the cyclical redundancy check (CRC) discussed in Chapter 6. There are other possible data frames that allow control characters to be sent as data, in a special *transparent data mode*. This type of transmission is an exception, however. Most data is transmitted as described in the previous frame.

BSC, like any link-level protocol, is a systematic method for insuring reliable communications over a shared communications link. There is an appropriate query and response for every possible situation, though we have covered only some basic examples. A comparison of these two most common types of BSC frames is presented in Fig. 7-14.

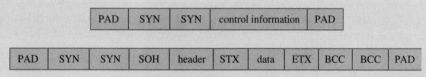

FIGURE 7-14   Binary Synchronous Communications frame..

SYNCHRONOUS DATA LINK CONTROL

One of the most widely used bit-oriented protocols is IBM's *Synchronous Data Link Control*, or *SDLC*. SDLC is similar to the ISO *High-level Data Link Control*, or *HDLC*, which contains some additional features. Other similar protocols are ANSI's *Advanced Data Communications Control Procedures*, or *ADCCP*, and ITU(CCITT)'s *Link Access Procedure'Balanced*, or *LAP-B*. Many vendors have bit-oriented protocols similar to SDLC, but SDLC is probably the most widely used protocol because it is the protocol most often utilized by IBM's popular SNA. The widely used *Point-to-Point Protocol*, or *PPP*, discussed later in this chapter, uses virtually the same frame format as SDLC.

SDLC is most often used in full duplex, though it can be used in half duplex mode. Since it employs go-back-N continuous ARQ, it is suitable for use over satellite links or other transmission media with long delays. With continuous ARQ, the host computer does not have to wait for an acknowledgment of the first message before sending more data.

In a full duplex SDLC link, the transmitter can send data continuously, while simultaneously receiving acknowledgment messages from the receiver. On a half duplex SDLC link, several frames can be sent, at which point the line is turned around and a single acknowledgment message is sent for all of the frames received. This method is more efficient than BSC, in which half duplex must always be used, the line must be turned around after each frame, and each frame is acknowledged separately.

In SDLC, as in BSC, the control information passed between the host computer and terminal never reaches the end user. The user is shielded from all errors by the protocol's ability to correct them, and control information is passed efficiently between stations, using only a few bits. The greatest advantage of SDLC, however, is that it contains continuous ARQ and full duplex capability; this capability allows its use with a wide range of transmission media, regardless of delays. The customer can choose the transmission media based on cost, desired reliability, and bandwidth and does not have to be concerned about the effect of delays on the protocol's performance.

The terminology in SDLC is slightly different from that used in BSC. Rather than using the terms "Control" and "Tributary Stations," SDLC uses *Primary* and *Secondary stations*. All communication is between the single Primary station and the one or many Secondary stations.

The SDLC frame. SDLC, like BSC, also sends data in frames, but data and control information are sent a bit at a time, not a character at time. There are three basic frame formats in SDLC, known as *Information*, *Supervisory*, and *Unnumbered*. As in our discussion of BSC, we consider only the most basic elements of SDLC.

Information Format Frames, or *I-Frames*, are used to send and receive data. *Supervisory Format Frames*, or *S-Frames*, are used to transfer control information, including acknowledgment of the accurate receipt of data. *Unnumbered Format Frames*, or *U-Frames*, are used for special functions, including establishing connections, reporting procedural problems, and performing special cases of data transfer. The I-Frames and S-Frames are most commonly used together to send data and ensure reliable transmission.

The number of frames that can be sent without receipt of an acknowledgment message is either 7 or 127, depending on the number of bits that has been dedicated to count the frames. *Modulo-8* transmission allows 7 frames, while *Modulo-128* transmission allows 127 frames.

BITS IN AN SDLC FRAME

All three frame formats follow the pattern shown in Fig. 7-15. Each type of frame begins with a *Flag*, a pattern of eight ones and zeroes (01111110). Then there is the eight-bit *Address Field*, containing the address of the Secondary station. Since all communication is between a Primary and Secondary station, this address is the destination of a message when the Primary station transmits and the source of the message when the Secondary station transmits. This addressing method allows for proper routing of data to and from Secondary stations in multipoint configurations.

After the address field comes the *Control Field*, which contains either 8 or 16 control bits, depending on the mode of operation. The function of these control bits differs, depending on whether the frame is an I-Frame, an S-Frame, or a U-Frame. After the Control Field is the *Information Field*, which occurs only in certain I-Frames and U-Frames. The Information Field is used to transmit data and is variable in length, depending on the amount of data being transmitted. The length of the Information Field is always a multiple of eight bits.

Next in the frame is the *Frame Check Sequence Field*. The Frame Check Sequence, or *FCS*, contains 16 bits for error checking; the bits are calculated using the cyclical redundancy check (CRC) method presented in Chapter 6. The frame concludes with the ending Flag, also a pattern of eight ones and zeroes (01111110).

Notice that the Flags of SDLC perform a similar function to the PAD and SYN characters in BSC. The FCS is also very similar to the BCC characters used in BSC. Both BSC and SDLC contain addresses. However, the control information in SDLC is passed in a very different manner than in BSC.

Each bit in the Control Field has a special meaning. For example, Supervisory Format Frames are used to acknowledge receipt of data. The SDLC *Receiver Ready*, or *RR*, is similar to the BSC ACK, indicating that data has been successfully received. An SDLC *Reject*, or *REJ*, is similar to a BSC NAK, indicating that a retransmission is necessary. An SDLC *Receiver Not Ready*, or *RNR*, is similar to a BSC WACK, indicating a temporary busy condition. These different conditions are represented by only a few bits in the SDLC Control Field, rather than entire eight-bit characters, as in BSC.

The remaining bits in the Control Field can be used for other functions. For example, in all types of SDLC frames, the Control Field contains a *P/F bit*. The Primary station can require the Secondary station to respond by setting the P/F bit—in this case, the Poll bit. The Secondary station can then transmit data, and when finished, can also set this bit; when the Secondary station sets the P/F bit, it is now the *Final* bit, indicating that transmission is complete. This single bit is used for two functions, compared to the BSC use of eight bits for a single function. This high efficiency is another of the advantages of SDLC.

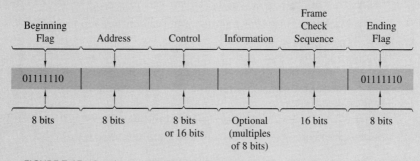

FIGURE 7-15 Synchronous Data Link Control frame.

PROTOCOL CONVERTERS AND CODE CONVERTERS

If two SDLC devices need to communicate, the SDLC protocol ensures reliable and accurate data transmission. What if a dumb asynchronous terminal needs to communicate with a host computer using SDLC? A separate device, known as a *protocol converter*, can act as a translator between the two devices, taking asynchronous data from the terminal, packaging it into SDLC frames, and transmitting it synchronously to the host computer. Data from the host computer is removed from its frame and transmitted asynchronously to the terminal. The same function could be performed for a BSC host computer, as well as almost any other protocol.

In some cases, the terminal may use a different character code from the host computer. A *code converter* can be used to translate the characters from one character code to another. For example, data sent from an ASCII terminal can be translated for reception by an EBCDIC host computer. Sometimes, a *protocol converter* performs both protocol and code conversion. Also, either or both of these conversion functions may at times be performed by front-end processors, as discussed in Chapter 5.

THE TCP/IP PROTOCOL SUITE AND RELATED PROTOCOLS

The *TCP/IP Protocol Suite* is a collection of protocols originally designed for use on a network connecting U.S. government agencies and universities performing research. The TCP/IP Protocol Suite specifies protocols at various levels of the OSI model and covers a wide variety of tasks likely to be performed on an open network.

The *Transmission Control Protocol*, or *TCP*, and the *Internet Protocol*, or *IP*, are at the heart of this suite of protocols. TCP operates at Layer 4 of the OSI model, the Transport Layer. Since it is concerned with reliable delivery of the user's message, TCP retransmits data lost by the lower layers. It is also responsible for establishing and monitoring the entire connection between the users and is called a *connection-oriented protocol*.

IP operates at Layer 3 of the OSI model, the Network Layer. It is concerned with routing and delivering the individual packets, but does not guarantee delivery. For this reason, IP is called an *unreliable service*, offering *best-effort delivery*. It is possible for the IP packets, known as *datagrams*, to be lost due to errors or failed links in an IP network. When TCP is used in conjunction with IP, TCP takes the necessary actions to ensure proper message delivery to the destination. TCP is also responsible for reassembling and resequencing messages at the destination.

Every packet sent by IP is handled independently, even though it may be part of a larger TCP data stream. While TCP monitors the connection, IP handles only individual packets and is therefore called a *connectionless protocol*. An IP network is one type of data transport network discussed in more detail in Chapter 8. All data passed over an IP network is broken into IP datagrams and reassembled into the original user data stream at its destination.

IP networks have the advantage of not limiting the destination to a single address, or *station*. A message can be sent from one user to another; this type of transmission is called a *unicast*. Alternatively, a message can be sent to all users in a particular range of IP addresses using a *broadcast*. In a *multicast*, a subset of the network users are configured to be part of a group which recognizes that a message is for them, while those not in the group ignore the message. While a broadcast group is determined in advance by the numerical value of a station's IP address, a multicast can, in effect, be subscribed to; the user simply chooses to listen to messages with a particular multicast address.

THE IP HEADER

Each IP datagram begins with the *header* shown in Fig. 7-16. The header is at least 20 bytes long and may contain additional optional fields. Following the header is the user data. The entire IP datagram, including the 20-byte header, any optional parts, and any user data, may not exceed 65,535 bytes. Typically, it is limited to far fewer bytes by the underlying transmission link technology.

The first field in the header is a 4-bit *version field*, indicating the version number of IP used in the datagram. It is followed by a 4-bit *IHL*, or *Internet Header Length field*. Since the header may contain optional parts, its length varies; the IHL indicates the length of the header in 32-bit increments. The next 8 bits contain the *type of service field* and signal to the network what type of handling this datagram requires. The options include emphasizing priority, low delay, high throughput, or reliability. Many of these measures of network service are discussed further in Chapter 9. There is no guarantee that the network will be able to fulfill these requests. The *total length field* follows in the next 16 bits, indicating the overall length of the datagram, in bytes.

The total length field is followed by a 16-bit *identification field*, which is used by IP to identify datagrams that originally belonged to a single datagram that was *fragmented* at some point in the delivery process. Fragmentation of datagrams, or breaking them into smaller datagrams, is a common practice in IP networks, and the identification field allows them to be reassembled at the destination. The next 3 bits in the header are referred to as the *flags field*. The first of the three bits in the flags field is currently unused. It is followed by a 1-bit *DF*, or *don't fragment flag*, which is used to instruct the network not to break this datagram down into smaller pieces. The next bit is the *MF*, or *more fragments flag*, which is used to indicate that this datagram is a fragment of a larger datagram and is not the last fragment. The last fragment—or the only fragment, if the datagram has not been broken down—travels without this MF bit set, and since it contains the same identification field as any prior fragments, the network recognizes it as the last fragment of the original datagram. The next 13 bits contain the *fragment offset field*, which is a special way of numbering fragments so that they can be reassembled in the correct order at some point in the future.

The *time to live field* follows in the next 8 bits, indicating the datagram's lifetime. While it is sometimes described in terms of steps, or *hops*, on the network, if a particular device holds on to the datagram for a certain period of time, the time to live field is decreased further. Each time the datagram is passed from one point to another on the network, this hop counter is decreased by at least one, and when it reaches zero, the datagram is discarded. A warning message may then be sent to the originator. Though discarding an old datagram may sound frivolous, this act is an important feature to prevent datagrams from travelling in circles on the network forever. The next 8 bits compose the *protocol field*, indicating the protocol this datagram encapsulates (e.g., TCP). This information allows the destination host to ensure that the datagram will be handled appropriately (e.g., by the TCP software in the host). A 16-bit *header checksum field* follows, to allow error detection on the header itself.

The next 32 bits contain the 32-bit *source address field*, which indicates the station that originated the datagram. It is followed by the 32-bit *destination address field*, describing the station on the network that is to receive the datagram. More details regarding the makeup and use of IP addresses are presented in Chapter 8.

The *options field* was included to allow extensions to IP. If it is used, there are bits to identify the type of user options selected. The IP header must be in 32-bit increments, since the IHL counts headers only in 32-bit increments; therefore, the options bits are often followed by *padding bits*. If the options do not use an increment of 32 bits, additional padding bits are added to round up the number of bits to the next increment of 32. If no options are present, the IHL is set to indicate that there are only 20 bytes (5 × 32 bits) in the header.

When the header is complete, user data follows, up to the length specified in the total length field described previously.

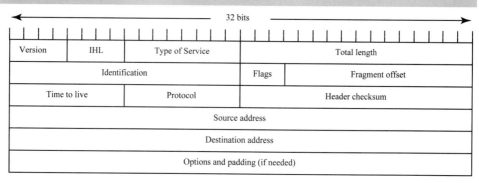

FIGURE 7-16   IP header.

There were many other protocols besides TCP and IP originally included in the TCP/IP Protocol Suite, and dozens have been added in the intervening years; we mention only some of the more commonly used ones here. When people discuss TCP/IP, they are often referring to all of the related protocols, rather than just TCP and IP. The enhancement of these protocols is largely supervised by the Internet Engineering Task Force (IETF) previously discussed in Chapter 4.

Several protocols are involved in the transmission and reception of electronic mail. The *Simple Mail Transfer Protocol*, or *SMTP*, provides a universal format and method for exchanging electronic mail. It was originally designed for seven-bit ASCII text messages, and messages were often limited in size. It was later extended to allow for more advanced operations through the use of the *Multipurpose Internet Mail Extensions*, or *MIME*. MIME is not limited to ASCII text. It also allows attachments to text messages, including binary data files, executable programs, audio files, image files, video files, or any other type of data of any size. In addition, MIME standardizes the formatting of the text portion of the electronic mail messages. The uniform treatment of carriage returns, trailing spaces, and other formatting characters in the text portion of the mail is fully defined in MIME; this helps ensure that mail passing through numerous mail systems will not change during conversions.

The *Telnet* protocol provides a universal method to access a remote host computer through a TCP/IP network. Telnet allows remote users to perform many of the same functions on the remote host as can be performed by a terminal user directly attached to the host. The *Rlogin* protocol is a more advanced remote access procedure than Telnet and is specifically tailored to UNIX-based host computers. Both of these protocols are best suited to remotely accessing text-based applications.

The *File Transfer Protocol*, or *FTP*, allows remote viewing of file directories as well as transfer of files in either direction across a TCP/IP network. The user interface provided is not that of the remote machine, but rather that of the FTP software running on the local machine. For example, a PC user does not need to understand the commands used to operate the file system on a remote UNIX server. FTP hides the UNIX file commands from the user, and the files are transferred, or directories viewed, with the same FTP software commands that would be used if the files were on another PC.

The *Universal Datagram Protocol*, or *UDP*, is utilized to send individual messages in IP packets when the connection-oriented features of TCP are not required. The *Simple Network Management Protocol*, or *SNMP*, spells out methods for exchanging network management information and is discussed in more detail in Chapter 9.

HyperText Transfer Protocol, or *HTTP*, is probably the best known of the high-level protocols used in conjunction with TCP/IP, because it is the protocol most commonly used when accessing the *World Wide Web*. The World Wide Web is a collection of information accessible on the *Internet*, a global IP network discussed in more detail in Chapter 8. HTTP was designed to allow for efficient transfer of information presented in hypertext format, in which users continually bring up one window after another to get more detailed information or go back to the prior window when they are satisfied. The information itself does not have to be text, as the name "hypertext" implies. In fact, HTTP often is used to carry information that is a combination of text, image, audio, video, and other information. Often, this information is presented using *HyperText Markup Language*, or *HTML*, a document format popular on IP networks, although HTTP is able to transfer information stored in any format.

With the growth of open networks, security concerns have increased, and numerous protocols have been spawned to address these issues. A further enhancement to MIME, known as *Secure/Multipurpose Internet Mail Extensions*, or *S/MIME*, adds the exchange of additional information required for public key encryption features, described in Chapter 6. These features include the ability to encrypt mail for secrecy and to sign it digitally for authenticity. The *Secure Sockets Layer* protocol, or *SSL*, adds security functions to data transferred with HTTP, Telnet, or FTP. The *IP Security Protocol*, or *IPSec*, allows companies to safely use normally insecure public data networks to interconnect their sites, as discussed in Chapter 8. The IPSec protocol allows the appropriate encryption techniques to be utilized to protect this private data as it traverses the public data network.

Increasing amounts of voice and video traffic are being sent over modern data networks. Several protocols have been created to improve the performance of these networks when this type of time-sensitive information is sent. One such protocol is *Resource Reservation Protocol*, or *RSVP*. RSVP allows paths to be reserved through a network for high priority data. Though RSVP may ensure that enough bandwidth is reserved, it alone cannot prevent the network from introducing significant variable delays; therefore, RSVP is not very widely used. Other issues associated with sending real-time traffic over data networks will be discussed further in Chapters 8 and 10.

A variety of transmission options is available for Layers 1 and 2 in an IP network, and the choice of which to implement is left to the user. IP is often used with local area networks, which will be discussed in Chapter 8. These local area networks have their own Layer 1 and 2 protocols. When connecting to an IP network using a telephone line as a serial link at Layer 1, two possible options at Layer 2 are *Serial Line Internet Protocol*, known as *SLIP*, and *Point-to-Point Protocol*, known as *PPP*. *Serial Line Internet Protocol*, or *SLIP*, simply sends IP packets one after the other, with an extra byte at the beginning of each packet for framing. There are several different SLIP implementations, and sometimes an extra byte is added after each packet as well. Most SLIP implementations do not offer any error correction or detection, relying on higher layers to deal with problems. SLIP's primary drawback is that it can carry only IP datagrams; it is not able to carry other protocols.

Due to the many different SLIP implementations, as well as SLIP's inherent limitations, the IETF devised *Point-to-Point Protocol*, or *PPP*. PPP supports link error detection and multiple protocols. The IETF built on past protocols in designing PPP. In fact, the PPP frame format is virtually identical to the SDLC/HDLC frame format shown in Fig. 7-15, though the lengths of some of the fields are adapted slightly for the particular application. One modification is that two fields in PPP replace the "Information" field in SDLC, which contained only the user data. The first one or two bytes identify the protocol—for example, IP—and the next field contains the payload, which would include IP packets (or other packets, depending on the protocol being used).

PPP's simplicity and flexibility have made it the protocol of choice when connecting IP networks over telephone lines.

TCP/IP's success can be attributed to several factors. First, the government's communications needs were significant, and the government originally provided funding to develop and refine the technology. The link between government and university research ensured widespread use in the academic community. Since support for TCP/IP was included in most of the popular computer operating systems, it became an easy solution to adopt commercially. In addition, the wide range of protocols, many stretching to the Applications Layer, provides complete solutions for users. From electronic mail to file transfer, the TCP/IP Protocol Suite answered most users' network needs with specific protocols.

This set of specific solutions has helped the TCP/IP Protocol Suite become the most popular standard for universal connection of users in multivendor environments. Is the OSI model still applicable in a TCP/IP dominated world? The OSI model is still very useful because it provides the common language that allowed networking to evolve to its current state. Clear language alone did not yield full interoperability, however, because at each layer the OSI model allows the user to select among many protocols. The TCP/IP Protocol Suite met the users' needs by defining specific protocols for many of these tasks; it took multivendor compatibility out of the model phase and made it a reality.

As with any successful protocol, improvements are always being proposed. Most IP networks today are utilizing IP version 4, also known as *IPv4*. An enhanced version of IP, known as *IPv6*, has been standardized, but its implementation has been slow. It supports longer addresses than IPv4, thereby providing a virtually unlimited supply of addresses. It also provides a shorter header, allowing for faster packet processing. More options are supported, security concerns are better addressed than in the base protocol, and the enhanced service requirements of real-time traffic are handled more effectively. Even with these enhancements, displacing the installed IPv4 equipment would take many years. It is not clear what impact IPv6 will have on the existing IP networks or at what pace it will be deployed.

SUMMARY

A communications architecture is a manufacturer's strategy for connecting its equipment. Most good communications architectures cleanly separate the function of communications from the host computer's other functions. Originally, each manufacturer had its own proprietary communications architecture, but ISO developed a model for discussing communications between devices of all manufacturers. The ISO Open Systems Interconnection (OSI) model breaks down the task of communications into seven independent layers, each with its own roles. The Corporation for Open Systems (COS), a group of major computer vendors, was created to facilitate the implementation of intervendor compatibility.

The seven layers of the ISO model, from lowest to highest, are the Physical Layer, the Data Link Layer, the Network Layer, the Transport Layer, the Session Layer, the

Presentation Layer, and the Application Layer. The tasks of each layer are clearly defined in the OSI model. Even though the actual transmission of data occurs only at the Physical Layer, all of the other layers communicate with their peers on other devices by modifying or adding to the data being transmitted.

IBM's Systems Network Architecture (SNA) is a widely used communications architecture. SNA functions can also be divided into layers—namely, Physical Control, Data Link Control, Path Control, Transmission Control, Data Flow Control, Presentation Services, and Transaction Services. SNA networks are made up of many components, including Host Processors, Workstations, Communications Controllers, Cluster Controllers, and Distributed Processors. SNA networks can be further broken down into different Nodes, including Host Nodes, Communications Controller Nodes, and Peripheral Nodes. Each Node can contain several Network Addressable Units (NAUs), of which there are three basic types: a Logical Unit (LU), a Physical Unit (PU), and a System Services Control Point (SSCP). End Users, such as Workstation users or Application Programs on Host Processors, can communicate with the SNA Network through LUs. A PU exists in each Node to manage the Node's physical resources. An SSCP provides central control and monitoring of a network. Each SSCP is responsible for a certain Domain, which can be further divided into Subareas. Subareas are connected by Transmissions Groups. SNA is only one manufacturer's architecture; many others are also in use today.

Protocols precisely define the methods used for communications between devices. Most link-level protocols provide for polling and selecting. Polling is a request for data transmission, and selecting is a request for data acceptance. Most link-level protocols also use some form of automatic repeat request (ARQ) for error correction. There are different types of ARQ, including stop-and-wait ARQ, in which each frame is acknowledged before the next is sent, and continuous ARQ, in which the next frame can be sent before the previous frame is acknowledged. Continuous ARQ includes go-back-N continuous ARQ, which requires retransmission of all frames sent after an error, and selective repeat continuous ARQ, which requires retransmission only of the frame in error. There are two common classes of protocols, byte-oriented, or character-oriented, and bit-oriented.

IBM's Binary Synchronous Communications, or BSC, is an example of a character-oriented, or byte-oriented protocol. BSC is a half duplex, stop-and-wait ARQ protocol and is therefore not well suited for satellite transmission. BSC frames can contain user data or control information; control information is sent using entire characters. BSC has a single Control station and one or more Tributary stations.

IBM's Synchronous Data Link Control, or SDLC, is an example of a bit-oriented protocol. SDLC can be used in half duplex or full duplex mode and uses go-back-N continuous ARQ; it can therefore be used for satellite transmission. SDLC frames can be Information Format Frames, Supervisory Format Frames, or Unnumbered Format Frames. In all frames, control information is sent by using individual bits. SDLC has one Primary station and one or more Secondary stations.

BSC and SDLC are just two examples of common link-level protocols; many other protocols are also in use today. Devices supporting different protocols can be connected using protocol converters; devices using different character codes can be connected using code converters. The TCP/IP Protocol Suite is a collection of protocols covering a wide variety of tasks likely to be performed on an open network. TCP operates at OSI Layer 4, while IP operates at OSI Layer 3. Some related protocols include SMTP and MIME for electronic mail, Telnet and Rlogin for remote access, FTP for file transfer, HTTP for hypertext, UDP for sending individual packets, and SNMP for network management. S/MIME, SSL, and IPSec are examples of security enhancements that have helped advance the use of the Internet for commercial purposes. At Layer 1 and 2, local area networks are often used as the basis for IP networks. SLIP and PPP are examples of Layer 2 protocols used when sending IP over serial links like telephone lines. IPv4 is so widely used that the newer IPv6 will have difficulty displacing it.

TERMS FOR REVIEW

ACK0
Acknowledgment
ADCCP
Address Field
Advanced Data
    Communications Control
    Procedures
Application Layer
Application Program
Architecture
ARQ
Automatic repeat request
BCC
Best-effort delivery
Binary Synchronous
    Communications
Bisync
Bit-oriented protocol
Broadcast
BSC
Byte-oriented protocol
Character-oriented protocol
Cluster Controller
Code converter
Communications architecture
Communications Controller
Communications Controller
    Node
Communications line control
Connectionless protocol
Connection-oriented protocol
Continuous ARQ

Control Field
Control information
Control station
Corporation for Open
    Systems
COS
Data Link Layer
Datagram
Destination address field
Destination node
DF
Distributed Processor
Domain
Don't fragment flag
End User
ENQ
Enquiry
EOT
ETX
FCS
File Transfer Protocol
Final
Flag
Flags field
Fragment
Fragment offset field
Frame
Frame Check Sequence Field
FTP
Go-back-N continuous ARQ
HDLC
Header

Header checksum field
Higher layers
High-level Data Link
    Control
Hop
Hop counter
Host Node
Host Processor
HTML
HTTP
HyperText Markup
    Language
HyperText Transfer Protocol
Identification field
I-Frame
IHL
Information Field
Information Format Frame
Intermediate node
Internet
Internet Header Length field
Internet protocol
IP
IP Security protocol
IPSec
IPv4
IPv6
LAP-B
Line discipline
Link
Link Access Procedure—
    Balanced

Link-level protocol
Logical Unit
Lower layers
LU
MF
MIME
Modulo-128
Modulo-8
More fragments flag
Multicast
Multipurpose Internet Mail Extensions
NAK
NAU
Network
Network Addressable Unit
Network Layer
Node
Open Systems Interconnection model
Options field
OSI model
PAD
Padding bits
Peer-level communication
Peripheral Node
P/F bit
Physical Layer
Physical Unit
Point-to-Point Protocol
Polling
PPP
Presentation Layer
Primary station
Protocol
Protocol converter
Protocol field

PU
Receiver Not Ready
Receiver Ready
REJ
Reject
Resource Reservation Protocol
Rlogin
RNR
RR
RSVP
SDLC
Secondary station
Secure/Multipurpose Internet Mail Extensions
Secure Sockets Layer protocol
Selecting
Selective repeat continuous ARQ
Serial Line Internet Protocol
Session
Session Layer
S-Frame
Simple Mail Transfer Protocol
Simple Network Management Protocol
SLIP
S/MIME
SMTP
SNA
SNMP
SOH
Source address field
SSCP
SSL

Station
Stop-and-wait ARQ
STX
Subarea
Subarea Node
Supervisory Format Frame
SYN
Synchronous Data Link Control
System Services Control Point
Systems Network Architecture
TCP
TCP/IP
TCP/IP Protocol Suite
Telnet
Time to live field
Total-length field
Transmission Control Protocol
Transmission Group
Transparent data mode
Transport Layer
Tributary station
Type of service field
UDP
U-Frame
Unicast
Universal Datagram Protocol
Unnumbered Format Frame
Unreliable service
Upper layers
Version field
WACK
Workstation
World Wide Web

EXERCISES

7-1. What is a communications architecture?

7-2. Name the layers of the ISO–OSI model. Which are the lower layers and which are the higher layers?

7-3. Explain the functions of each of the layers of the ISO–OSI model.

7-4. What is SNA?

7-5. What connects two Nodes in an SNA network?

7-6. Define the following SNA terms: Host Processor, Workstation, and End User.

7-7. What is the purpose of an SNA Communications Controller? A Cluster Controller?

7-8. What is the difference between a Host Node, a Communications Controller Node, and a Peripheral Node?

7-9. Compare each of the different types of NAUs.

7-10. Compare Subareas and Domains in SNA.

7-11. What is a protocol?

7-12. Explain the difference between polling and selecting.

7-13. What is ARQ? Compare the different types of ARQ.

7-14. What is the difference between a byte-oriented protocol and a bit-oriented protocol?

7-15. What are the different types of basic frames in BSC? In SDLC?

7-16. Is BSC or SDLC better suited for satellite transmission? Why?

7-17. What is TCP/IP? When is it used?

7-18. What was SMTP designed for? What additional capabilities are included in MIME?

7-19. How are ATTP and HTML related?

7-20. What are the advantages of PPP versus SLIP?

C H A P T E R   8

Data Transport Networks

Data transport networks connect a wide variety of devices located in the same building or across the world. In most cases, data transport networks are not limited by a single vendor's architecture or to a single vendor's equipment, because they provide only the means for transmitting and receiving the data. Data transport networks provide only the OSI model's lower layer functions. As long as the two devices can perform the higher layer functions in a compatible manner, they can use data transport networks to perform the lower layer functions of transmitting and receiving the data.

For example, two French-speaking Americans can send letters written in French to each other through the U.S. Postal Service. The mail carriers do not need to understand French, because they only transport the mail. Packet switching networks, frame relay networks, and local area networks are some examples of data transport networks.

PACKET SWITCHING NETWORKS

One popular data transport network often used for long-distance data transmission is a *packet switching network*, or *PSN*. Packet switching networks provide a *switched service*; for example, a terminal user can connect to one host computer now and then connect to a host computer at a different location later. Data is separated into *packets*, or blocks, and sent through the packet switching network to the destination. At the destination, the packets are combined to form the original stream of data.

Packet switching networks provide a *virtual circuit* between two devices, rather than a continuous connection. In other words, when a packet of data is given to a packet switching network, the network routes the data to its destination. However, if no data is being transmitted, there are no transmission resources being wasted on the connection. Compare this system to the telephone network, through which we can call someone and stay on the line, not saying anything, but still tie up a circuit. In a telephone network, we call this act *circuit switching*. We call a packet switching network's connection a *virtual circuit*, because to the users, it appears that they have a virtually continuous connection, and their data always gets to the destination.

Packet switching networks have evolved in recent years. While earlier packet switching networks were based on the *X.25* protocol, the *frame relay* protocol has emerged in recent years as an excellent alternative to X.25. The *Internet* is an even more advanced packet switching network based on the *Internet Protocol (IP)* that has changed the way we communicate electronically. We will discuss all of these protocols and networks later in this chapter. They all share the common principle of breaking data into packets for transmission and reassembling these packets at a later time. We will start our discussion with X.25 packet switching networks and build on these principles with frame relay and IP networks.

Many of today's packet switching networks span great distances. Each location in the network is known as a *switching node*, or simply as a *node*. The switching nodes are connected by *interexchange circuits*, or *IXCs*. A simple packet switching network is presented in Fig. 8-1. These networks can be customer owned, or someone else's packet switching network service can be leased.

Communicating through packet switching networks requires that the devices at each end send data in specially formatted packets. Devices that can communicate by using these packets can be directly attached to a packet switching network. A device known as a *PAD*, or *packet assembler disassembler*, is used to connect devices to an X.25 packet switching network if these devices cannot perform the special packet formatting on their own. A PAD takes data from a terminal or host computer, assembles it in a special packet format, and passes it on to the PSN node. Data coming from the packet switching network is disassembled from its packet by the PAD and can then be routed to the host computer or terminal.

The PAD might be on the premises of the end user or at the packet switching node itself. A PAD that is part of the packet switching node is often called an *internal PAD*, while a PAD on the premises of the end user is often called an *external PAD* or *terminal handler*. Placement of both types of PADs is also shown in Fig. 8-1.

PSNs combine the advantages of many other transmission methods and add some of their own. Packet switching provides the reliability of a dial-up network, because each packet of data can take a different route. For example, a packet of data could be routed directly from San Francisco to New York, or it might be routed through Chicago. If the transcontinental IXC is not functioning, there are still alternative routes for the packets. Packet switching also has the flexibility of the dial-up network, because users can connect to a different host computer with each call.

These networks also provide error detection and correction. Packets are checked for errors during transmission, and if necessary, are retransmitted. The packet switching network guarantees that the data received at the destination node is the same as the data transmitted at the source node. The error detection and correction performed by the packet switching network nodes ensure reliable transmission even if the source and destination devices do no error checking themselves.

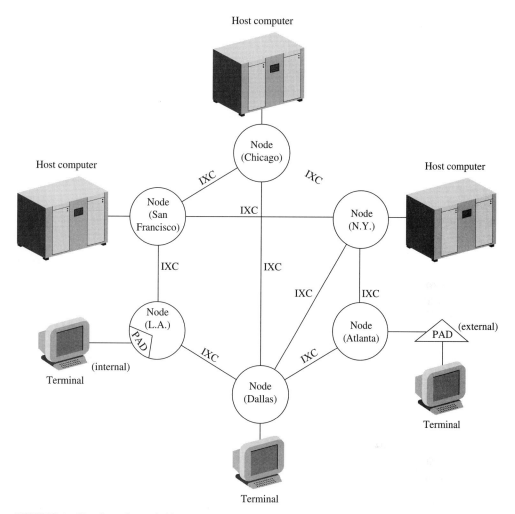

FIGURE 8-1 Simple packet switching network.

PUBLIC PACKET SWITCHING NETWORKS

Packet switching networks that are owned and operated by service providers for use by their customers are known as *public packet switching networks*. These networks often have entire operations staffs monitoring the network's health. This attention provides a high level of service equivalent to the reliability of the public telephone network. Many of these public packet switching networks have nodes and PADs in numerous cities, affording easy access. For example, a traveling salesman could access pricing information in a host computer in the company's home office from anywhere in the country simply by making a local call to the nearest node of the public packet switching network.

One of the first large-scale packet switching networks, known as *ARPANET*, was established to connect U.S. government computing facilities with research universities.

Commercial public packet switching networks are operated by various common carriers; for example, SPRINT and MCI now operate the networks originally known as *Telenet* and *Tymnet*, respectively. Each network uses proprietary methods to communicate between packet switching nodes, but they both support similar interface standards.

Packet switching networks are a very cost effective method of transmitting data. Since no permanent connection is ever established between two devices, users of these networks are typically charged on a per-packet basis. This charge is usually less expensive than comparable dial-up telephone line charges, because the packet switching network effectively shares its bandwidth among many users. For example, the IXCs can be high-bandwidth media, like satellites, microwave, or T-1 circuits. These economies of scale can be passed on to the end users of packet switching networks in the form of lower per-packet costs.

One disadvantage of all packet switching networks, both public and private, is that certain delays may occur, since data may be routed through many nodes before reaching their destination. If an IXC uses satellite transmission, delays are increased even further. A terminal user in San Francisco, communicating with a host computer in New York, might notice a one-second or two-second delay when using the packet switching network. However, the added benefits of low cost, high reliability, flexibility, easy access, and guaranteed error-free transmission usually outweigh the delay problem in most applications.

THE X.25 STANDARD

The first widely deployed standard for connecting to packet switching networks was the ITU(CCITT) *X.25* standard. Packet switching networks do not have to comply with this standard, but many do. The X.25 standard, which describes all of the functions necessary for communicating with a packet switching network, is divided into three levels. These three levels are similar in function to the lower three layers of the OSI model.

The lowest level, known as the *Physical Level*, describes the actual interface; it conforms to the ITU(CCITT) V.24/V.28 standard, which is similar to the EIA RS-232-C standard, discussed in Chapter 4. The second level, or the *Frame Level*, is the ITU(CCITT) LAP-B bit-oriented data-link protocol that handles error detection and correction; it is very similar to the SDLC protocol explained in Chapter 7. The third level, or the *Packet Level*, provides for network-level addressing and call connections.

The X.25 standard defines two types of devices: DTEs, or data terminal equipment, and DCEs, or data circuit-terminating equipment. The packet switching network itself presents an X.25 DCE interface; a host computer or terminal that attaches to the packet switching network presents an X.25 DTE interface. For example, a host computer presenting an X.25 DTE interface would provide a V.24/V.28 type of physical interface, use the LAP-B protocol for transmitting and receiving bits, and then add special packet-level information regarding call setup and addressing.

In addition to the X.25 standard, the ITU(CCITT) developed three standards for describing the operation of an internal PAD. The *X.3* standard defines the PAD's func-

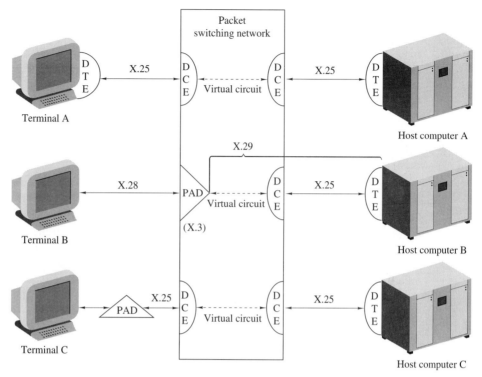

FIGURE 8-2   Interfacing to a packet switching network.

tions and parameters; the *X.28* standard describes the PAD-to-terminal protocol; the *X.29* standard describes the PAD-to-host computer protocol.

The relationship between the X.25, X.3, X.28, and X.29 standards is illustrated in Fig. 8-2. When we discuss the packet switching network interface standards and protocols, we consider the entire network as a single entity, ignoring the various nodes and IXCs inside.

In Fig. 8-2, terminal A and host computer A both communicate to the packet switching network using X.25. Terminal B, however, is not X.25 compatible and must be attached to the packet switching network through a PAD. Terminal B communicates with the internal PAD using the X.28 protocol; the PAD's function and parameters are described by X.3; the PAD communicates with host computer B using the X.29 protocol. Notice that host computer B is X.25 compatible and therefore communicates with the network using X.25. Terminal C is attached to an external PAD on the user's premises. Since the X.25 conversion is done on the user's premises, the packet switching network thinks that terminal C is X.25 compatible. To the packet switching network, the connection from terminal C to host computer C is no different than the connection from terminal A to host computer A. These examples are just a few combinations, and others certainly are possible.

PACKET SWITCHING NETWORK SERVICES

X.25 packet switching networks can provide many optional services. For instance, a *closed user group* allows users to specify that they want to communicate only with certain users. This service is one security measure to ensure that only authorized users can access a particular host computer. For example, a company linking its branch office computers with headquarters could connect all of its computers through the packet switching network in a closed user group; this configuration permits communication among company computers, but prevents others from accessing these computers. Other possible security services include allowing DTEs to accept *incoming calls only* or place *outgoing calls only*, depending on the application.

There are two data transmission related services that can be provided by packet switching networks. *Flow control negotiation* allows the DTEs to specify the size of the packet and other parameters. Another service, known as *throughput class negotiation*, allows the DTE to negotiate for a certain bandwidth on a virtual circuit.

Finally, many packet switching networks provide for *reverse charging*, or *collect calls*. This service is the PSN equivalent of a toll-free number, allowing users to contact a particular DTE, with the receiver paying for the service.

While the aforementioned services are referred to by their X.25 names, similar features are available in almost all packet switching networks.

ROUTING DATA IN A PACKET SWITCHING NETWORK

Perhaps the most interesting facet of packet switching network operation is the routing of data. Earlier, we mentioned that a packet from San Francisco destined for New York might take a direct route or might be routed through a node in Chicago. If we are sending a large block of data through a packet switching network, it will be divided into many packets, or *packetized*. Packets may be of a fixed or variable length, depending on the network. In fact, each packet can take a different route from the source to the destination, though no network tries to do this intentionally.

For example, as shown in Fig. 8-3, packet 1 may leave San Francisco and be routed through Chicago to New York, because the direct transcontinental route to New York may be malfunctioning at that moment. Packet 2, transmitted a tenth of a second later, may take the direct route to New York, because at the moment of transmission, that circuit is available and the other link might be down. Because of the delays involved in routing, it is possible that packet 2 will arrive in New York before packet 1 does.

This method of transmission is analogous to a traveler changing planes in Chicago; not only is the route traveled longer than the direct route, but also there may be some time wasted in Chicago. Traveler 1 may leave San Francisco at 9 AM, change planes in Chicago, and arrive in New York at 7 PM. Traveler 2 may leave San Francisco at 10 AM, take a nonstop flight, and arrive in New York at 6:30 PM. Traveler 2 left later than traveler 1, but arrived in New York earlier. If these travelers were packets, the second 128 bytes of the message would have been received before the first 128 bytes. This sequence of events would be equivalent to reading the second sentence of this chapter before the first. Therefore, the node in New York is holding, or *buffering*, packet 2 until it receives packet 1, and then it sends the packets to the host computer in New

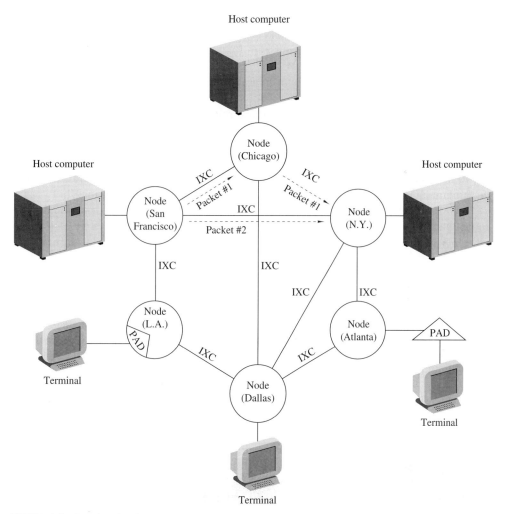

FIGURE 8-3   Routing data in a packet switching network.

York in the proper order. All packets must therefore be *numbered*, and destination packet switching nodes often provide for the *buffering* and *resequencing* of packets. Alternatively, the task of buffering and resequencing can be placed on the user, depending on the network protocol.

FRAME RELAY NETWORKS

One of the most important features of the X.25 packet switching networks we have been describing has been error-free delivery of data to its destination. These packet switching networks were developed in an era when unreliable analog modems and analog phone lines were the usual technology on the links between nodes. For this reason, the X.25 protocol included the necessary error-checking and retransmission procedures to ensure that only perfect data were delivered to the destination. Accomplishing this error checking required overhead bits, as well as processing time in each node, even if no error occurred. Any retransmissions that were necessary added even more delay to the data transmission.

With the increased use of digital phone circuits, the chance of errors occurring on the IXCs was dramatically diminished. One type of data transport network that was developed to take advantage of these reliable IXCs is the *frame relay* network. As in X.25 networks, a virtual circuit is provided. The data are broken into pieces—in this case, known as *frames*—and passed through nodes to their destination. However, the nodes do not correct data errors made by the user, and they assume that the users of the network use their own protocol to check for errors and retransmit if necessary. The main advantage to this network is that errors can be resolved once, between the destination and the source, rather than at every node. This feature dramatically reduces the time needed for data to pass through a frame relay network, particularly in comparison to the time needed for data to pass through an X.25 network.

Another difference is that while X.25 operates at Layers 1 through 3 of the OSI model, frame relay operates only at Layers 1 and 2. As long as the protocols used at Layer 3 and above conform to certain frame relay rules, the nodes in the network do not need to open up the frame, look at the entire contents, and generate a new frame. Instead, the frame relay node checks only the frame's header and routes the data accordingly, without creating an entirely new frame. Since the frame is passed on, or relayed, virtually unchanged, the term *frame relay* is used to describe this technique.

Most of the advantages of packet switching networks are also found in frame relay networks, with the additional benefit of reduced delay and overhead. However, neither packet switching networks nor frame relay networks are suitable for live voice or video transmission, because they lack mechanisms to control delay introduced by the network. While the delay is shorter with frame relay networks, variations in transmission time can wreak havoc with voice or video connections. A newer technology, known as *cell relay*, *Asynchronous Transfer Mode*, or simply *ATM*, addresses these timing issues with the help of a supporting transmission infrastructure. Though not as efficient for pure data transmission as frame relay is, ATM is a good technique to use when a mixture of voice, data, and video traffic needs to be carried. ATM is described in detail in Chapter 10.

THE INTERNET

One very widely used data transport network is the Internet. The *Internet*, with a capital "I," utilizes the TCP/IP protocols. These protocols provide a wide variety of services required in an open network. The Internet began as a network to connect government agencies with universities performing research projects, but has since grown into a large cooperative network, where the users share the operating costs. Many *Internet Service Providers*, or *ISPs*, interconnect their networks using the protocols of the IETF, as described in Chapter 7. Though there are now many commercial users, in addition to governmental and educational users, some of the information accessible from the network has retained the homespun, co-op flavor from its early days.

While the Internet handles the task of delivering data, just as X.25 and frame relay networks do, it has evolved into much more than a data transport network. When people say "the Internet," they are usually referring to the wide range of services and information resources attached to the network, rather than the network itself. Libraries, government agencies, universities, corporations, merchants of all sizes, a variety of information providers, and individuals can be accessed through the Internet. It is also the world's largest public network for transmission of *electronic mail* messages. Another popular application is the use of public bulletin boards, known as *newsgroups*, for exchanging comments, ideas, and information.

The X.25 protocol and frame relay protocol focused solely on delivering data. They were assumed to be a means for large corporations to connect multiple sites, to connect to other corporations, or to simplify remote access to a database. There was no underlying assumption that everyone using an X.25 or frame relay network would use the same Layer 4–7 protocols to provide higher level services. Think of these networks as comparable to an overnight letter delivery service, carrying letters in many different languages to people all over the globe. It doesn't matter that the recipient in France can't understand the contents of the letter bound for Italy, because he or she doesn't need to. The letters to France and Italy can travel on the same intercontinental cargo plane, even though their recipients cannot understand each other's languages, because the addressing meets the standards of the cargo company, and the company understands how to deliver these messages.

While IP networks certainly are capable of carrying traffic with different Layer 4–7 protocols, what makes the Internet so useful is that there are worldwide, agreed-upon standards for performing many common Layer 4–7 functions, as described in Chapter 7. The Internet is not necessarily better or worse at transporting data than X.25 or frame relay. However, the Internet is definitely more useful as a global communications infrastructure because it has a better supporting cast of higher layer protocols than either of these other networks, thereby ensuring that the data can be used around the world, not simply transported there.

One example of a product implementing some of these higher layer protocols is a *browser*. A browser is user software that allows a user to view information, typically stored in HTML format, described in Chapter 7. This information stored around the world on computers connected to the Internet is known as the *World Wide Web*. The fact that most browsers support the same higher layer protocols allows users to access any server attached to the Internet and view the information there. Browsers can be equipped with the public key encryption techniques discussed in Chapter 8 to enhance security, thereby enabling safe on-line banking, credit card transactions, and other commercial uses. Another feature common to most browsers is the ability to take on new functions or features by downloading small applications, sometimes called *applets* or *plug-ins*. For example, a plug-in might allow a browser to play a certain type of audio file that the browser was not originally enabled to handle.

Many people refer to the Internet as the *information superhighway*. Today's Internet, though extremely useful, is certainly not the fastest network imaginable, and it provides only a taste of the advantages of easy access to information. It certainly is an excellent model of an open network. Clearly, a much higher speed infrastructure would offer even greater possibilities. Some networking professionals reserve the term "information superhighway" for a future network that will offer a significant increase in capacity over today's Internet and that will seamlessly carry data, as well as high-quality voice and video traffic. Certainly, today's Internet voice and video transmission quality does not satisfy most users. The Internet's capabilities may be expanded and improved to the point where it can offer these services with high quality in the future.

Other packet-based networks offer alternatives for carrying voice and video traffic. One such high-bandwidth network uses ATM protocols for its underlying transmission infrastructure, as described in more detail in Chapter 10. IP and ATM networks will likely coexist for many years to come.

Most of the networks that we have been discussing are typically used over wide areas and are known as *wide area networks*, or *WANs*. Another type of network, the *local area network*, is used for local data transmission.

LOCAL AREA NETWORKS

A *local area network*, or *LAN*, is a privately owned data communications system that provides reliable high-speed, switched connections between devices in a single building, campus, or complex. Networks that extend outside a single building, campus, or complex are not considered local area networks. Like packet switching networks, local area networks provide switched connections, allowing users to connect to different computers at different times. The transmission speed of local area networks is often many millions of bits per second, providing high-bandwidth connections suitable for almost any application, including lengthy file transfers. The limited geographic area of a local area network usually allows the customer to own all of the wiring; therefore, the speed of the LAN is limited largely by the bandwidth of the transmission media chosen.

Most of today's local area networks are highly reliable, with extremely low error rates. Since few local area networks span more than a mile or two, the probability of transmission errors is much smaller than in a wide area network. Local area networks are typically used to connect desktop computers, known as *personal computers*, with each other or with other host computers; terminals, workstations, and larger host computers can also be connected. A typical application conducted with personal computers over a LAN is the file transfer mentioned previously.

Users of a local area network can exchange files as well as share resources. One example of resource sharing is when several personal computers share a single high-speed laser printer; each user prints infrequently, but may need the special features and speed of the laser printer. The printer may be attached to a personal computer, which also must be attached to the network. We say that this personal computer acts as a *print server* for the network because it provides access to the printing services for other users. Sometimes, an entire department accesses a single file-storage device, such as a high-volume disk attached to one personal computer; this personal computer acts as a *file server*. Providing access to remote resources located off the network is the job of a *communications server*. Typically, a communications server is a personal computer attached to both a modem and the network, thereby allowing network users to use the modem to access remotely located computers and services. There are other specialized server functions that can also be provided on a local area network. The servers may be personal computers used for other functions as well as for their role as a server.

A common approach to computing today is the *client/server* architecture. This approach calls for applications to be distributed around an organization's network on servers that users can access as needed. Rather than running all applications on a single mainframe, users can access programs on servers attached to the network when they need a common database or resource.

Information systems managers have taken advantage of the emerging standards in server platforms to drive down the cost of their computing power. Rather than locking you into a single vendor, as might occur with a mainframe, client/server architecture allows users to select industry-standard platforms for their applications and provides appropriate computational power for applications and users based on their needs. Client/server architectures typically have some part of the program execute on the user's workstation, executing only the database management system centrally. For example, the graphical user interface may be implemented on the client, and the rest of the operations may be performed in the server.

A client that is very simple, requiring relatively little processing power, is sometimes called a *thin client*. A computer with very little processing power and little or no local permanent data storage and that is designed to run thin clients is often called a *network computer*. This type of computer puts the burden on the network to exchange the data between the client and server for almost every operation and makes the network computer the modern-day equivalent of a dumb terminal. In this case, the network computer is typically equipped with a graphical user interface, unlike the dumb terminals of the past.

The widespread deployment of the Internet browser has provided a universal client on almost everyone's desktop. Many organizations have chosen to take advantage of this situation, designing their internal corporate applications based on TCP/IP protocols. This system allows the same browser to access both Internet applications and internal applications. The applications or servers accessible only to clients located inside the company, and inaccessible to external users, are sometimes referred to as the *intranet*.

The flow of data between the clients (users) and servers (databases or applications) can generate a tremendous amount of traffic on modern LANs. This traffic level must be carefully considered when installing and managing local area networks.

Local area networks can be implemented using two different types of control. *Centralized control* requires a single device that controls the entire network. Failure of this controller disables the entire network. Changing the number or configuration of devices on the network requires more than simple rewiring. The central controller needs to be notified of any addition, removal, or moving of devices in the network.

Distributed control, used by many of today's local area networks, requires no central device; instead, all of the devices attached to the network actually run the network. The instructions for transmitting and receiving messages must be built into all of the devices attached to the network, usually utilizing a combination of hardware and software. For example, 10 personal computers in a local area network using distributed control all share the responsibility of running the network; each personal computer usually contains a special network interface card and uses a special network software program.

One advantage of distributed control is that adding another user to the network requires only installing the interface card and software in the new user's personal computer and then attaching the personal computer to the network. There is no central processor or controller that needs to be notified of the addition, because each device speaks for itself on the network and shares in the task of operating the network. These networks can therefore be expanded incrementally; the network hardware cost for 101 users is only 1% more than for a network of 100 users. Companies can start with small networks and enlarge them as their needs increase. There is an upper limit to the number of users on all networks, but this limit varies, depending on the bandwidth of the media, as well as the applications used.

The major disadvantage of distributed control is that if one device attached to the network malfunctions, it can throw the entire network into disarray. Many local area networks make some provision for a centralized monitoring function to shut down network stations that are causing problems.

LOCAL AREA NETWORK TOPOLOGIES

Local area networks can take many different forms or shapes, known as *topologies*. Some of these topologies are illustrated in Fig. 8-4.

In a *mesh network*, each device is connected by a cable to every other device in the network. This configuration may be convenient for small networks, but it becomes awkward and expensive as a network grows to contain more than a few devices.

In a *star network*, all of the devices are connected by cable to a single central point. Some type of a controller is located at this central point; this centralized control requirement is an often-cited disadvantage of star networks. In a star network, all data is routed through the central point.

A *bus network* has many devices connected to a single cable, known as the bus. Typically, there are limitations to the length of the bus in these networks. The point at which a device connects to a bus is known as the *tap*. A *tree network* is similar to a bus network, except that there may be many different branches off the main bus. This configuration allows many closely located devices to attach to the network with only a single tap on the main bus. There is no central control point in a bus or tree network, so new devices can be added simply by tapping onto the network at any point; disconnecting a tap removes a device from the network. Every message placed on a bus travels past all users.

A *ring network* connects all devices in a continuous loop, though it doesn't have to be a perfect circle. Data in a ring network usually flow only in one direction; therefore, data may circle around 90% of the ring to reach a neighboring device. There is no central controller in a ring network either, so devices can be added simply by inserting them anywhere in the ring, or they may be removed from the network by disconnecting them from the ring and closing the ring at that point.

A device known as a *hub* can be used to simplify the wiring of ring or bus networks. In both cases, the hub changes only the physical layout of the network and does

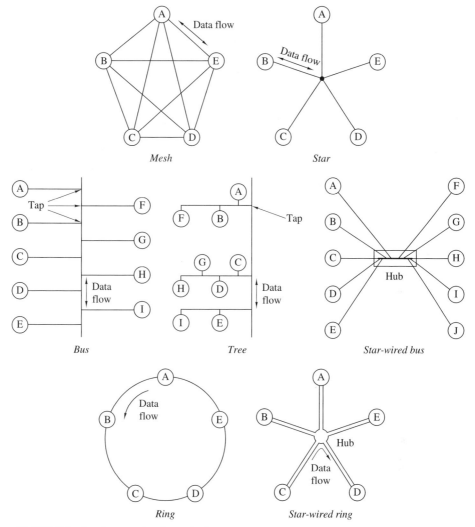

FIGURE 8-4   Local area network topologies.

not affect the way that the network operates. Messages may go from each user to the hub, but once a message is inside the hub, the original bus or ring topology is simulated.

In a *star-wired bus* network, a miniature bus is created inside the hub. Logically, the network is still a bus, and the hub does not route the messages to any specific destination. Every message is sent to the hub, the hub then retransmits each message to every user, and the user determines whether or not to read and process the message, based on the address in the message header. This type of network physically connects the users to a central hub in a star configuration with twisted pair, coax, or fiber optic cable. In fact, you could think of this network as a three-inch bus with 20-foot taps to the users, rather than as a traditional long bus winding through a building, with short taps to each user. In a *star-wired ring network*, a miniature ring is created inside the hub. Data still flows one way in a continuous loop, but between each user, the data return to the hub.

When buildings already have wire running to each office, hubs provide a convenient way to implement bus and ring networks. Users can be removed from or added to the network at the hub, simplifying installation and maintenance. Most hubs can also automatically disconnect a failed device that is generating erroneous data. For these reasons, hubs are quite commonly used.

In the star-wired bus and star-wired ring topologies, the hub is used to maintain the original network design while simplifying the wiring. Devices known as *switching hubs*, or simply as *LAN switches*, do not follow this model; instead, they actually repeat the messages only to the correct user. They create true star networks and are used when traffic and performance requirements demand that stations receive only data destined for them. Switching hubs deliver messages based on their address, acting more like a packet switch than like the standard hubs previously described.

BASEBAND VS. BROADBAND TRANSMISSION

There are two basic types of local area network transmission. *Baseband* local area networks transmit digital signals directly on the cable, while *broadband* local area networks use carrier frequencies to modulate the signal. Whereas baseband LANs allow only a single data conversation or channel at any given time, broadband LANs can be divided into many different channels, allowing for multiple data conversations simultaneously.

Typically, baseband local area networks are less expensive to implement, but they are limited in their capacity and length. Broadband local area networks, though more expensive to purchase and maintain, usually provide higher bandwidth transmission and have less restrictive length limitations. Neither type is clearly superior; the user's applications and cost requirements determine the appropriate choice.

The transmission media chosen depends on whether the LAN is baseband or broadband, as well as on the bandwidth needed. Most local area networks use twisted pair wire or coaxial cable, though some use fiber optic cable for high-speed applications. The relative bandwidths of various transmission media were presented in Chapter 4.

LOCAL AREA NETWORK ACCESS METHODS

When more than one device needs to share a communications line, *access methods* are required to specify which devices can transmit data at any given moment. We have already discussed one such method, known as *polling and selecting*. This technique is not often used in local area networks, since a central controller is required to poll and select the devices.

Some broadband networks use *frequency division*, separating the communications line into many different frequency channels. Some baseband networks employ *time division* techniques, allocating time slots to each device for transmission. These local area network access methods are similar to their point-to-point multiplexing counterparts, frequency-division multiplexing and time-division multiplexing, explained in Chapter 5.

Contention.   Among the most common types of access methods in use today are the *contention* methods. *Ethernet*, a widely used local area network we will discuss later, utilizes contention. The various contention methods allow devices to transmit if the line is free; if the line is busy, devices must wait before transmitting. Contention methods are effective because local area networks use high-bandwidth transmission, and a typical message is relatively short. For example, a 40-page file may contain 120 kilobytes, or 960 kilobits, of data; a 10 Mbps local area network could transmit the entire file in less than a tenth of a second. Since most messages are shorter than a 40-page file and typical devices only use the network occasionally, the network is available most of the time.

Infrequently, two devices transmit at the same time, and a *collision* occurs. Collisions cause data to be lost, and the way the network recovers from a collision depends on the access method. If too many devices are placed on a contention network, many collisions occur and the network's performance deteriorates; a few devices transmitting many large files have the same effect.

One contention method is *random access*, where devices transmit whenever they please. With this method, devices assume that the line is free, because statistically, the network is free most of the time. For this method to succeed, there must be some acknowledgment by the receiver that the message arrived; otherwise, the sender cannot be sure that a collision didn't occur.

If we think of a three-way telephone conference call, random access is the equivalent of individuals who speak whatever is on their minds, without regard to whether anyone else is talking or not. If these individuals don't get an answer, they try speaking again.

A more refined contention method is known as *carrier sense multiple access*, or *CSMA*. In CSMA, the device with data to transmit listens to the network to determine if it is being used. If the network is free, the device transmits the data and waits for an acknowledgment from the receiving device. Once the transmitter begins sending data, other devices, also using CSMA, do not transmit, because they are listening and know that the network is busy. Occasionally, if two devices begin transmitting at exactly the same time, collisions may still occur.

When collisions occur, the transmitted data is garbled and the acknowledgment message is not returned by the receiver. Eventually, after a set time limit, the transmitter gives up waiting for the acknowledgment and retransmits the message. CSMA is an improvement over random access, because at least the transmitter makes an attempt to check if someone else is using the network before sending data. However, the transmitter must still wait for a period of time before deciding that the acknowledgment is not forthcoming due to a collision.

Returning to our three-way telephone conference call example, CSMA is the equivalent of a person who checks to see if anyone is talking, and if not, begins speaking and stops listening. After speaking, this person begins listening again.

CSMA is a type of contention method that uses *collision avoidance* techniques. A further improvement on CSMA adds *collision detection*. In this method, known as *carrier sense multiple access/collision detection*, or *CSMA/CD*, the device not only listens before transmitting but also while transmitting. Ethernet networks, discussed in more detail later, use this CSMA/CD technique. The device first checks to make sure that the network is free and then begins transmitting. If all goes well, the transmitting device hears its own transmission loud and clear. However, if another device begins transmitting at the same instant, both transmitters hear not only their own signals, but both signals, or some mixture of the two. Both of the transmitters hear the collision and immediately stop transmitting. After waiting a certain period of time, the transmitters again attempt to send the message. The process of halting transmission, waiting, and then retransmitting, is known as *backoff*.

The same method is used for the retransmission after a collision: the transmitter listens both before transmitting, to avoid another collision, and during transmission, to detect if another collision occurs. Remember that collisions are relatively infrequent, since they occur only when two devices begin transmitting at roughly the same time.

In our conference call example, CSMA/CD is the equivalent of a person who first listens to be sure that no one else is talking and then begins speaking. This person keeps listening while talking and realizes when someone else starts speaking at the same time. Both people are using CSMA/CD, and both stop talking, back off, and wait a little while before speaking again. Typically, the more aggressive person jumps in almost immediately and starts talking again, while the other person might wait longer.

An essential aspect of CSMA/CD is the determination of how long a device must wait after detecting a collision before attempting retransmission. Clearly, this waiting time must be different for the two transmitters that collided; otherwise, they would continue to repeat their collision forever. For instance, in our conference call example, if two people's statements collided and each person waited exactly 10 seconds after the collision to speak again, the collision would occur again.

These different contention methods regulate when devices can transmit and how they recover from collisions. How do devices know when to receive data? Whether a network is using random access, CSMA, or CSMA/CD, when a device is not trying to transmit data, it must listen to all data on the network. Each message contains a unique address, specifying the intended destination. All devices except the receiver simply ignore the message.

PRIORITY AND RANDOM BACKOFF

It is possible to build devices with different retransmission times, thereby creating a *priority backoff* scheme. After a collision, the device with the shortest retransmission time would always get to retransmit first, and the device with the longest retransmission time would retransmit last. These devices would be the equivalent of aggressive and shy people in a conversation. More typically, a *random backoff* process is used, in which each device picks a random amount of time to back off for each collision. This system ensures fairness and, as long as the devices are good at picking truly random numbers for each collision, practically eliminates the possibility of repeated collisions.

The difference between priority backoff and random backoff is presented in the two diagrams in Fig. 8-5. An "A" represents a transmission completed successfully by device A, a "B" indicates a transmission completed successfully by device B, and an "X" represents a collision between the two devices. As long as each device transmits at a different time, there are no collisions. When a collision does occur, notice that with priority backoff, device A has a higher priority and always gets to retransmit first. In random backoff, sometimes device A gets to retransmit first after a collision, and sometimes device B gets to retransmit first. This random backoff CSMA/CD method is used extensively in Ethernet networks.

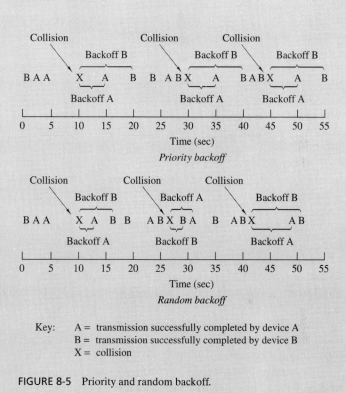

Key: A = transmission successfully completed by device A
        B = transmission successfully completed by device B
        X = collision

FIGURE 8-5 Priority and random backoff.

Token passing.   Another LAN access method, besides the contention methods in widespread use today, is known as *token passing*. A *token* is simply a pattern of ones and zeroes with a special meaning, much like the control information used in the link-level protocols presented in Chapter 7. Two common types of tokens are *free tokens* and *busy tokens*; each is a different pattern of bits. All devices in a token-passing network constantly listen to the network. A device can transmit only when it sees a free token.

We assume a ring topology for our example of token passing because this topology is the easiest to visualize. The various steps of transmission using a *token ring network* are shown in Fig. 8-6. Initially, there is a free token circulating around the ring in Fig. 8-6. This token indicates that the network is free and available for use. A device wanting to transmit data must wait for the free token to reach it.

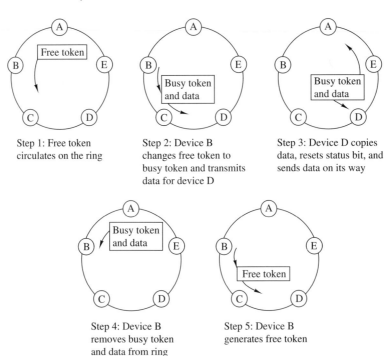

Step 1: Free token
circulates on the ring

Step 2: Device B
changes free token to
busy token and transmits
data for device D

Step 3: Device D copies
data, resets status bit, and
sends data on its way

Step 4: Device B
removes busy token
and data from ring

Step 5: Device B
generates free token

FIGURE 8-6 Operation of a token ring.

In step 2 of Fig. 8-6, device B sees the free token that is circulating and decides to transmit. Device B then changes the free token to a busy token and adds the data to be transmitted, along with the address of the recipient (device D), its own return address, and some bits for error checking and monitoring. This new package of data now circulates on the ring, and any other devices wanting to transmit data have to wait, because there is no free token on the ring. When the data reaches its destination, the receiver (device D) recognizes its address.

As shown in step 3 of Fig. 8-6, device D then copies the data, changing some status bits to indicate that the data was received, and lets the data continue around the ring. When the data reaches the original transmitter, as shown in step 4 of Fig. 8-6, the transmitter removes the data from the ring. The transmitter can then release the network by generating a free token, as shown in step 5. The free token then circulates around the ring as before, and other devices can transmit their data in the same manner. We are now back to step 1, and the network is free again.

The token-passing networks have several features to maintain order in the network. Notice that the data makes a complete circle around the ring, giving the transmitter confirmation that the data was not lost. Also, transmitters cannot monopolize the network; they must generate a free token after a certain time period. One of the devices on the network, known as the *active monitor*, in addition to being a user of the network, is responsible for monitoring the network. An active monitor provides the first free token when the network is started. In addition, if a free token is lost due to a transmission error, the active monitor generates a new free token. Other devices on the network act as *standby monitors*, waiting to step in and fill the role of the active monitor if the current active monitor should fail. Token passing networks are one of the more popular methods in use today.

LOCAL AREA NETWORK STANDARDS

Local area networks provide physical transmission of data, as well as error detection and correction. Therefore, we often think of local area networks as providing the Physical Layer and Data Link Layer functions of the OSI model.

Many of the standards for local area networks were developed by an IEEE committee called *IEEE 802*. This committee divided the Data Link Layer function of local area networks into two main parts. The first, known as *Medium Access Control*, or *MAC*, describes the access methods used in a network, like CSMA/CD or token passing. The second, known as *Logical Link Control*, or *LLC*, describes some other functions that can be used in conjunction with all access methods, like error checking and reliability. Together, the Medium Access Control and Logical Link Control standards describe the way local area networks implement the Physical and Data Link Layers of the OSI model.

Each of the IEEE 802 subcommittees formulates standards on different areas. The *IEEE 802.1* standard provides an overview of local area networks as well as methods of connecting networks and systems management. The *IEEE 802.2* standard describes the Logical Link Control methods that can be used in conjunction with all IEEE 802-compatible networks. The *IEEE 802.3* standard describes the CSMA/CD Bus Medium Access Control method already discussed. The *IEEE 802.4* standard describes the *token bus* method for Medium Access Control; the token bus is a variation on the token ring, which is described by the *IEEE 802.5* standard. The *IEEE 802.6* standard describes Medium Access Control methods for a *metropolitan area network*, or MAN. A metropolitan area network is larger in geographical scope than a classical local area network and is not considered a local area network at all by many experts.

There are other IEEE advisory groups that make recommendations about specific local area network topics that may affect all of the other subcommittees, though they may not result in standards themselves. These groups include the *IEEE 802.7* committee for broadband transmission, the *IEEE 802.8* committee for fiber optics, and the *IEEE 802.9* committee for integrating voice and data on local area networks.

The *Manufacturing Automation Protocol*, or *MAP*, is a user-defined networking standard originally developed by General Motors. The MAP standard describes a token bus network, like IEEE 802.4. MAP is designed to integrate operations on the factory floor by tying together control computers, robot welders, and other intelligent devices that previously operated independently. Many products are already built by automated equipment; the MAP network ties all of this equipment together, allowing an engineer making a design change to communicate the change automatically to the equipment on the production line in seconds. Many users are demanding MAP compatibility for all future factory equipment.

Another user-defined standard, known as the *Technical and Office Products* specification, or *TOP*, was developed by Boeing Computer Services. TOP is similar to MAP, even though it uses the CSMA/CD bus, much like IEEE 802.3. TOP is designed with the office and computing environment in mind, rather than the factory floor.

WIDELY USED LOCAL AREA NETWORKS

There are many different types of local area networks in use today. Two of these, however, have captured the largest share of the market. Equipment compatible with these networks, *Ethernet* and *token ring*, is available from many different vendors.

    Ethernet was originally used by DEC (now Compaq), Intel, and Xerox, among other companies. Ethernet is a bus network, using the CSMA/CD access method found in IEEE 802.3. Ethernet uses baseband transmission, and it initially operated only at 10 Mbps using coaxial cable. The *10BASE-T* standard has become one of the most popular methods of cabling Ethernet networks. It is a 10 Mbps, baseband, IEEE 802.3 standard for transmitting Ethernet over twisted pair wire, hence the name 10BASE-T. It requires the use of hubs in a star-wired bus configuration for half duplex transmission, or LAN switches for full duplex transmission. A fiber version, known as *10BASE-F*, is also available, and higher speed versions will be discussed later.

THE ETHERNET FRAME

The latest version of the Ethernet frame, also known as the IEEE 802.3 frame, is shown in Fig. 8-7. It is the most widely used frame in data communications today.

    The first eight bytes include the seven-byte *Preamble*, followed by a one-byte *Start-of-Frame Delimiter*, or *SFD*. Together, these eight bytes are composed of an alternating series of 62 ones and zeroes, followed by 2 ones, used to indicate the start of the frame. The receiving device can use these early bits to sync up with the transmission speed. In early versions of Ethernet, the preamble was considered to be eight bytes long, with no Start-of-Frame Delimiter, but the bit pattern was the same, so the change is in name only.

    The next fields contain the six-byte *Destination Address*, or *DA*, and the six-byte *Source Address*, or *SA*. The source address refers to the transmitter's identity, and the destination address refers to the intended recipient. These 48-bit fields uniquely identify every Ethernet station on a network. The IEEE assigns blocks of addresses to each vendor, and the vendor is responsible for uniquely identifying each card inside its address block. When a vendor has produced enough cards to exhaust its block of addresses, the IEEE provides it with a new address block. As long as all vendors follow the rules (and they almost always do), every Ethernet device is given a unique address.

    Ethernet provides for sending to users singly or in groups. When the first bit of the 48-bit address is a zero, the address is a unicast address, and the message goes to a single

FIGURE 8-7   Ethernet frame.

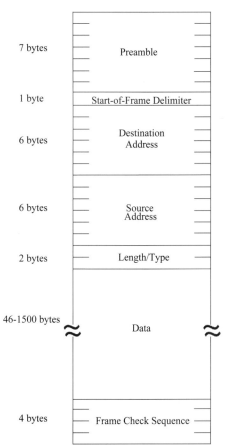

7 bytes — Preamble

1 byte — Start-of-Frame Delimiter

6 bytes — Destination Address

6 bytes — Source Address

2 bytes — Length/Type

46-1500 bytes — Data

4 bytes — Frame Check Sequence

station only. When the first bit of the address is a one, it is a multicast address, and multiple stations are able to receive the message. The most widely used multicast address, known as a broadcast address, is made up of all ones. All stations on the network receive a broadcast message.

The next two bytes contain the *length/type field*. Ethernet is often used today without IEEE 802.2 Logical Link Control. In this case, this two-byte field indicates the type of protocol contained in the Ethernet frame (e.g., IP). When Ethernet is used in conjunction with IEEE 802.2, these two bytes indicate the length of the *data field* that follows in the Ethernet frame, in bytes. In that case, the IEEE 802.2 Logical Link Control is responsible for identifying which higher layer protocol in the receiving device must act on this frame.

To accommodate both methods, the types have been assigned numbers greater than the 1500-byte maximum length of an Ethernet data field. The receiving station, upon reviewing the length/type field, can easily determine if it contains the data field length or the protocol type, since numbers 1500 or less refer to the length and those above 1535 refer to the protocol type (1501–1535 were left unused). In most cases, IEEE 802.2 is not used, and the Layer 3 packets (e.g., IP datagrams) are inserted directly into the data field.

The next field contains the *data*, which can be anywhere from 46 to 1500 bytes long. It is followed by a 4-byte *Frame Check Sequence*, or *FCS*, which is used for error detection of the destination address, source address, length/type field, and data field. It uses a 32-bit Cyclical Redundancy Check, or CRC, as described in Chapter 6.

Using Ethernet with standards like 10BASE-T allows for half duplex operation. In half duplex operation, as with traditional CSMA/CD, ideally only one user transmits at a time. This configuration is suitable when all users are attached to a single cable, like a coaxial cable in a bus network, or when a simple hub is used, as in a star-wired bus. It is also possible to connect two users with a single 10BASE-T connection using half duplex operation.

When a LAN switch, or switching hub, is used to connect each of the devices in a star configuration, there is no need to restrict how many users talk at one time, as long as the switch has sufficient capacity and buffering. With one LAN user attached to each switch port, full duplex operation becomes possible. There is a dedicated path from the switch to the user and from the user to the switch, and either party can transmit at any time. Similarly, two users can be connected to each other using 10BASE-T in full duplex. The same frame format used in half duplex will work in this configuration, but since no one shares his or her transmission link with anyone else, a user can transmit at any time.

One advantage of full duplex, switched connections is that some traffic problems are reduced. If the problem is caused by traffic evenly distributed among many users, switching can eliminate the collisions that occurred on a shared network. If the traffic is concentrated in one place (e.g., when many users are trying to reach a certain server), then a switched infrastructure will not eliminate the problem. In this case, a higher speed link is required to connect that server to the switch. Otherwise, messages would be queued up in a buffer on the switch at the port to which the busy server is connected, so the users would still notice some performance degradation.

Another popular network is the *token ring network*, which uses a star-wired ring configuration. IBM deployed the first popular commercial version. Token passing is accomplished by conforming to the IEEE 802.5 standard. The *IBM Token Ring Network* used baseband transmission to transmit data first at 4 Mbps and later at 16 Mbps, using unshielded twisted pair cable. Even higher speeds are discussed later. While IBM was the first major vendor to get behind the token ring, many other vendors now offer token ring products.

There were additional local area networks in use during the early years of LANs. The *IBM PC Network* was a 2-Mbps network utilizing broadband CSMA/CA. AT&T also had two local area networks. AT&T's *Starlan Network* was a star network based on IEEE 802.3, designed mainly for connecting personal computers in the office environment. AT&T's *Information Systems Network*, or *ISN*, provided connections to a wide variety of devices, including host computers, terminals, and personal computers, by using a combination of local area network and packet switching network transmission methods. Most of these networks have now been replaced by Ethernet or token ring networks.

Literally hundreds of vendors produce devices compatible with Ethernet and the token ring. There are also many different special-purpose, proprietary networks that do not meet any particular standard. Most users, however, prefer a standard network.

HIGHER SPEED LOCAL AREA NETWORKS

Several IEEE standards have been developed to allow operation at 100 Mbps and above. Fast Ethernet is a version of IEEE 802.3 that operates at 100 Mbps. 100BASE-T operates much like 10BASE-T, utilizing Ethernet protocols, twisted pair wire, baseband transmission, and hubs in a star-wired bus architecture. There are also fiber optic versions available.

Gigabit Ethernet operates at a billion bits per second, or 1 gigabit per second (Gbps). While Fast Ethernet simply takes the existing Ethernet protocol and runs it 10 times faster, speeding up is not so simple at gigabit speeds. Half duplex CSMA/CD transmission relies on every station to detect a collision every time one occurs. This requirement limits the maximum distance between stations; the time it takes for a frame to travel this maximum distance must be less than the time it takes to send the shortest possible frame. If the maximum distance exceeded this limit, it would be possible for a station to finish sending a small frame and hear no collision, when in fact, a collision did occur moments later, on the far end of the network. At a billion bits per second, the time to send a small frame would be very short, thereby severely limiting this maximum distance between stations. Special techniques are applied to correct this problem, including allowing stations transmitting very short frames to transmit several frames at a time. Since most users of Gigabit Ethernet are interested in high performance, they are likely to be in a switched, full duplex environment. In this environment, where the connection from the switch to the user is dedicated, rather than shared, collisions are eliminated and the distance issue is no longer relevant.

In all LANs, the rapidly falling prices of LAN switches are bringing switching technology within reach of more users. Though switched LANs do not solve all performance problems by any means, they can provide some relief, depending on the network configuration.

There is one ANSI standard for local area networks that has been deployed for many years. ANSI's *Fiber Distributed Data Interface*, or *FDDI*, uses fiber optics to operate at speeds of up to 100 Mbps per channel using a token ring topology similar to IEEE 802.5. FDDI uses two channels, forming an inner and outer ring. One of the rings is used for normal traffic, and the other ring is used for backup purposes when there is a problem with the primary ring. This high-bandwidth network was originally designed for high-speed mainframe computer communications, as well as many other applications. A version of FDDI that operates on copper cable, known as *Copper Distributed Data Interface*, or *CDDI*, is also available. A recently developed IEEE token ring standard, known as the *High-Speed Token Ring*, or *HSTR*, initially was designed to operate at 100 Mbps over copper cable, though higher speeds of up to 1 Gbps and fiber optic versions are planned.

100VG-AnyLAN is an IEEE 802.12 standard, and it utilizes a *demand priority* scheme that allows certain traffic to be transmitted on a high-priority basis. This approach can improve performance for time-critical traffic on a LAN. This standard also provides mechanisms to facilitate linking Ethernet networks with token ring networks. While 100VG-AnyLAN offers excellent solutions for time-critical traffic, Fast Ethernet has been much more popular.

INTERNETWORKING

When LANs reach their distance limitations or become overcrowded with users or traffic, they must be broken into smaller LANs and connected, or *internetworked*. LANs at multiple locations can also be internetworked if users need to communicate. Many different devices are available to internetwork LANs. The most common are *repeaters*, *bridges*, *routers*, and *gateways*.

REPEATERS

The simplest internetworking device is a *repeater*. A repeater placed between two LANs, as shown in Fig. 8-8, copies every message it hears on LAN #1 to LAN #2 and vice-versa. This device essentially makes the two LANs act like a single LAN. Repeaters operate at Layer 1 of the OSI model, simply receiving and transmitting bits without regard to the content or message address. All traffic is repeated from each LAN onto the other LAN, sometimes unnecessarily. For example, as shown in Fig. 8-8, a message from user A to user C does not need to be sent on LAN #2, but the repeater is unable to recognize this and repeats it anyway.

Repeaters are the least expensive internetworking devices and are typically used to extend a LAN beyond its usual distance limitation. If two LANs connected with a repeater do not have a traffic problem, there is no need for a more complex approach. However, most LANs that are long enough to have reached their distance limitation probably have many users, and there could be advantages to using more sophisticated devices than repeaters.

BRIDGES

A *bridge* can connect two or more networks that use a similar data communications scheme, and specifically, the same addressing method. For example, two Ethernet LANs can be internetworked using a bridge, as shown in Fig. 8-9. The bridge has connections

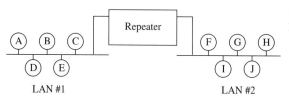

LAN #1   LAN #2

FIGURE 8-8   Internetworking two Ethernet networks with a repeater.

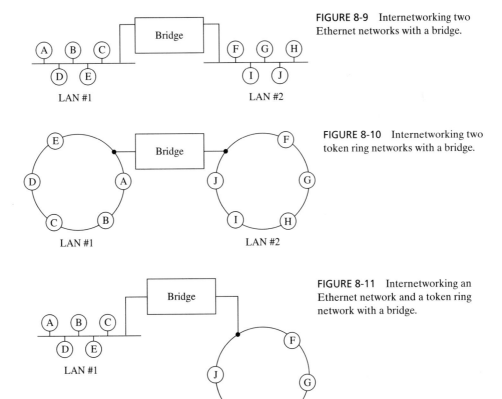

FIGURE 8-9   Internetworking two Ethernet networks with a bridge.

FIGURE 8-10   Internetworking two token ring networks with a bridge.

FIGURE 8-11   Internetworking an Ethernet network and a token ring network with a bridge.

to both networks and listens to all traffic on both networks. Two token rings could also be connected with a bridge, as shown in Fig. 8-10.

In fact, the Ethernet and token ring are both IEEE 802 networks with similar addressing, so they can also be connected to each other with a bridge, with some limitations, as shown in Fig. 8-11. The addressing referred to here is the 48-bit Medium Access Control, or MAC, address, described in the IEEE 802.3 standard for Ethernet or IEEE 802.5 for the token ring. This bridge must switch the data from the Ethernet frame format on one network to the token ring format on the other. If the message is short enough to fit in either format, a bridge theoretically can handle the task. For practical reasons, routers are usually used when connecting Ethernet networks to token ring networks. To simplify our introduction to bridges, we focus on the common case of connecting Ethernet networks. Connecting two token rings with bridges is a similar process with some implementation differences.

In theory, a bridge could be installed and manually configured so that it knows which users are on each network. If party A in Fig. 8-9 sends a message to party C, the bridge knows that both users are on the same network, and the message does not need to be retransmitted on the second network. If, however, the message is from party A to party J, the bridge must retransmit the message on the second network. Only traffic that must reach the other network is transferred there. Bridges operate at Layer 2 of the OSI model, known as the Data Link Layer. A bridge simply checks the address at Layer 2 and retransmits the data on the appropriate port. The message is repeated, if necessary, exactly as it was received. This type of bridge is known as a *transparent bridge* and is commonly used to connect Ethernet networks. It is called "transparent" because it makes all of the decisions about routing messages without requiring the participation of the users or their workstations. There is no higher layer addressing introduced, and no additional information is added to the message to facilitate its delivery. Directing a message based on its Layer 2 address in this manner is sometimes called *Layer 2 switching*.

Bridges are commonly used when a LAN begins to approach its capacity. In this case, splitting the LAN into two smaller LANs with a bridge between them can alleviate the traffic problem, if the users on the two new LANs are carefully distributed. If departments that frequently send messages to each other are grouped on the same LAN, their messages will not need to go through the bridge.

When one Ethernet network is divided into two with a bridge, as in Fig. 8-9, users on opposite sides of the bridge are said to be in separate *collision domains*. Even if user B and user H transmit at the same time, they no longer collide with each other, because they are on two separate LANs. When a particular collision domain becomes overcrowded with traffic, internetworking devices, like bridges, can be used to separate it into many separate collision domains, each with fewer members. This technique is known as *segmenting* the LAN, and the resulting new LANs are often referred to as LAN *segments*.

For example, a 10 Mbps Ethernet with an average traffic load of 50% during the workday probably has certain peak traffic times when response time is unacceptable. This is caused by the increased probability that a user will have to wait to transmit, as well as an increased number of collisions. So if the 5 Mbps average traffic load can be split into two LAN segments, traffic might be reduced to 3 Mbps per LAN. This calculation assumes that of the old 5 Mbps of traffic, 2 Mbps is now between users on the new LAN #1, 2 Mbps is between the users on the new LAN #2, and 1 Mbps needs to be transferred between the LANs. Since the traffic between the LANs must be repeated by the bridge, it will exist on both LANs; therefore, 1 Mbps is added to the 2 Mbps on each LAN for a total average traffic load of 3 Mbps per LAN. An Ethernet network with an average load of 30% of capacity is less likely to have peak traffic problems than one averaging 50% of capacity. Though this example just chooses hypothetical traffic numbers, bridges can be used in most networks to reduce congestion in this way.

Most bridges in use today are able to configure themselves. These bridges, called *adaptive bridges* or *learning bridges*, create a table of user locations by listening to the traffic on all connected networks. When the bridge is first installed, it does not know which users are on which side of the bridge, so it starts by listening to all traffic on connected LANs. When the bridge hears a message, it notices which side it hears it on and checks the return address of the message. This return address is also known as the *source address*. During this learning period, the bridge creates a table showing which users are connected to each LAN based on the source addresses it hears, so it can appropriately direct traffic later on. After a brief learning period, a bridge is ready to operate. However, if some users did not transmit during the initial learning period, the bridge can still learn their location later whenever they first transmit. The bridge always uses the Layer 2, or MAC, address to make its decisions.

For example, in Fig. 8-9, assume that the bridge has completed the learning period and is operating, but still does not know where parties A and C are located because they have not yet transmitted messages. If the next message is transmitted by party A and is destined for party C, the bridge must repeat the message on LAN #2, because it does not know where to find party C. But the bridge does now know that party A is located on LAN #1, because it heard the message on that LAN and party A was listed as the transmitter in the source address field of the message. The fact that the bridge mistakenly repeated the message to LAN #2 is of little consequence. Party C will get the message anyway because it was sent on LAN #1, and no users on LAN #2 will be interested in the message because it is not addressed to them. In this case, a message is repeated unnecessarily, but the bridge learned in the process and now knows where party A is. In fact, once all users have sent a message, the bridge knows where the parties are and can deliver all future messages to them properly. In order for this simple configuration method to function properly, there can be only one active path between any two users. No active duplicate paths between two users can be allowed using this method.

Other techniques used by bridges to ensure that there is only one active path between two users include the *spanning tree protocol*, *source routing*, and a combination of the two methods known as *source routing transparent*. All of these methods allow multiple physical paths to exist, but select only a single path to connect each pair of users. Only if a network link fails do the bridges reconfigure themselves to use a different route. The spanning tree protocol is used when transparent bridges are connecting Ethernet networks, while source routing protocols are used when connecting token ring networks. Bridges using the source routing method are not transparent because they require the user or the user's workstation to select the route. The source routing transparent method, designed to connect token rings with Ethernets, is seldom used. As already mentioned, routers are usually used for connecting Ethernet networks to token ring networks.

While all of the figures discussed thus far assume that the LANs being connected are adjacent to each other, it is possible to use bridges between LANs at different locations. These bridges are then connected by some type of phone circuit; this circuit could be a T-1 line, an analog phone line with modems, or some other data networking service. Bridges used in this manner are often called *remote bridges*. The link between the bridges must be of adequate bandwidth to handle the expected traffic between the LANs, or else bottlenecks will develop at the bridges. Bridges are used in this manner in Fig. 8-12.

The simplicity of bridges becomes more evident when there are more than two LANs being connected, as shown in Fig. 8-13. Each bridge operates in the same manner as when there were only two networks. The bridge listens to the traffic and then decides whether or not to repeat it to the other side. In this example, the bridge between LAN #2 and LAN #3 does not need to consider that on one side there is one network and on the

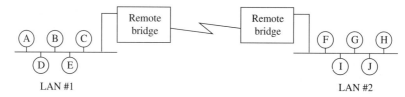

FIGURE 8-12   Internetworking two Ethernet networks with remote bridges.

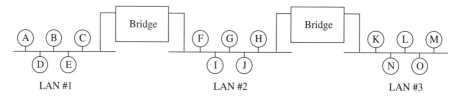

FIGURE 8-13   Internetworking multiple Ethernet networks with bridges.

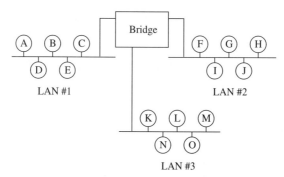

FIGURE 8-14   Internetworking multiple Ethernet networks with a single bridge.

other side there are two. It just knows that users A–J are on one side and users K–O are on the other, and it can repeat the messages accordingly.

Bridges can also have more than two ports, as shown in Fig. 8-14. The bridge still decides where to repeat the messages, based on its knowledge of the users' locations, and the learning techniques and protocols discussed earlier still apply.

There is no difference between a bridge and the LAN switch or switching hub described earlier. The distinction is usually simply made in marketing positioning by the vendor. Both devices switch data based on the Layer 2, or MAC, address. We started our discussion of bridges with the example of dividing a LAN into two segments to reduce traffic issues. A switch with one user on each port creates the smallest possible LAN segments and is known as *microsegmentation*.

In summary, bridges can only connect similar networks using the same addressing method. There must be a unique address for each user on all interconnected networks to enable bridges to use the simple learning methods we have discussed. Bridges are, however, economical internetworking devices and are therefore very popular, in spite of their limitations.

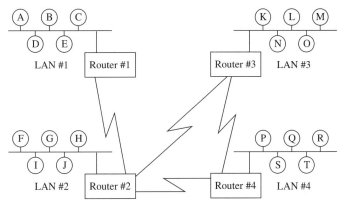

FIGURE 8-15   Internetworking Ethernet networks with routers.

ROUTERS

A *router* can also be used to interconnect LANs. Routers do not require all users on connected LANs to have unique physical addresses, unlike bridges.

Routers, like bridges, can direct messages around link failures when duplicate paths are available. For example, in Fig. 8-15, four LANs are connected using routers. To send a message between LAN #3 and LAN #4, the routers would most likely send the message over the direct line between the two routers. If this line is not functioning, the message might be routed through the router attached to LAN #2.

Routers operate at OSI Layer 3, the Network Layer, and actually contain a virtual map of the network. Directing a message based on its Layer 3 address in this manner is sometimes called *Layer 3 switching*. One typical network protocol is *Internet Protocol*, or *IP*. Users are identified by a Layer 3 address, in addition to the Layer 2 Ethernet or Layer 2 token ring address already assigned to each LAN user. The Network Layer address is a combination of a *network identifier*, or *netid*, and a *host identifier*, or *hostid*. The netid is used to direct the message to the proper network, and the hostid identifies the particular user on the network.

The use of higher level addresses beyond the individual user's Layer 2 address is a significant difference from the approach used by bridges. Bridges keep a table of Layer 2 addresses of all active users on all interconnected networks. A bridge's ability to find a user depends on its ability to send the message in the right direction based on its table of users on all networks. A router knows about all LANs in the internetwork, but only about the specific users on the LANs directly attached to that router. For example, in Fig. 8-15, the router on LAN #1 knows that users A through E are attached to it and knows that it is part of an internetwork containing four LANs. Each of the routers is assigned its own network address, and we call them Routers #1 through #4 for the purpose of our example. Router #1 must only know how to reach Router #4 and does not need to learn separate routes for all of the users on LAN #4. Unlike a bridge, which needs to learn how to reach every specific user, once a router learns how to reach another router, it can reach all of the users on the network served by that router.

Most users are unaware of their actual hostid and netid addresses. Instead, protocols are used to associate nicknames with the actual Network Layer address. For example, a user might send a message to "JohnDoe@LAN4", where John Doe is the user's nickname and LAN4 is the name for the particular router of John Doe's LAN. The user's work-station uses special protocols to translate this nickname into the actual hostid and netid before placing it on the network. Specialized address or directory servers can be attached to the network to help users find the addresses of other users. Though these techniques are not directly associated with routing, most router-based internetworks provide these features to increase usability.

Another example of a router function is connecting networks that carry messages of different sizes. Earlier, we discussed internetworking token ring and Ethernet networks with a bridge, but we added the caveat that the messages transmitted must be small enough to fit on either network. The *maximum transmission unit*, or *MTU*, is the longest message allowed on a network. For example, the MTU may be different on token ring and Ethernet networks. Users in these situations must keep their messages smaller than the maximum transmission unit of all networks through which they pass, if they wish to use simple internetworking technology like a bridge.

Alternatively, a router connecting the networks could split longer messages into shorter ones and reassemble them at the other end of the network. This is a typical function of a router. Routers can consider the MTUs of all networks in the path of the message and break the longer messages down to the appropriate size.

Some routers are capable of handling multiple protocols simultaneously, keeping track of which users expect which type of addresses and handling their messages accordingly. Sometimes, routers can act as *firewalls*, screening and filtering incoming traffic, to help maintain security in an open network. This feature is discussed in more detail in Chapter 6.

Some routers actually look into the Layer 3 packets themselves and examine the Layer 4 protocol being used, to optimize their routing choices and packet prioritization. These routers are sometimes said to be performing *Layer 4 switching*. Even though they are still handling individual Layer 3 packets, this term has unfortunately crept into the industry as router vendors try to distinguish their routers as being of higher performance or smarter than their competition. Some router vendors even claim to be doing higher layer switching, but still, all packets are delivered based on their Layer 3 address. Think of these high-performance routers as Layer 3 routers that simply consider the content of the packets when deciding which to handle first or which route to use.

GATEWAYS

Many routers offer more sophisticated services beyond what would be expected of Layer 3 devices. Though sometimes still referred to as routers, these devices probably fall into a more sophisticated class of devices known as gateways. Two separate networks, each using entirely different communications methods, can be connected using a *gateway*. A gateway may be a dedicated device, similar in function to a protocol converter. Many gateways perform functions found as high as Layer 7 in the OSI model, but certainly higher than Layer 3.

One example of a gateway would be a device connecting a packet switching network with a LAN while providing translation between electronic mail formats, as shown in Fig. 8-16. The packet switching network might be carrying electronic mail in one format, while the LAN users might be utilizing another format. The gateway handles the address translations, message translations, and any other conversion necessary to ensure

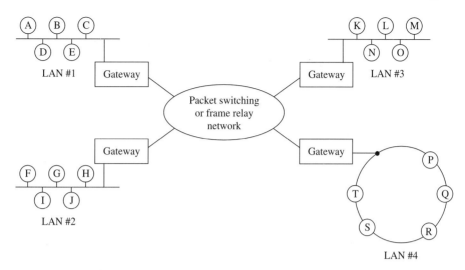

FIGURE 8-16   Internetworking with gateways.

delivery of the mail. A gateway performs any and all functions from Layer 1 through Layer 7 to ensure the compatibility of one or more features on different networks. In this sense, a gateway often acts like a combination of a router and a protocol converter. Unfortunately, the terms "gateway" and "router" are sometimes used interchangeably by vendors.

INTERNETWORKING TRANSMISSION OPTIONS

To simplify our introduction to bridges, we assumed that remote bridges are connected by a simple physical pipe, like a leased digital phone line or an analog line with a pair of modems. Routers and gateways can also operate over such a pipe.

However, if there is not sufficient traffic to justify the use of a leased line, it may be appropriate to turn to commercially available networks to connect your LANs. If a public packet switching network is used between the LANs, a *tunnel* is built through the packet switching network by taking the LAN messages and encapsulating them in the packet switching network's protocol (e.g., X.25). Similarly, data could be tunneled through a frame relay network or other data transport service, if the message is converted to the appropriate protocol before transmission over these networks. At the destination side of the data transport network, the X.25, frame relay, or other protocol is removed, leaving the original message.

IP networks offer another good internetworking choice. Even if the LANs at both sides are using IP as the networking protocol, we may not send the IP packets directly through a vendor's IP network without first protecting them. We may choose to secure the data before sending it across a public IP network like the Internet. In this case, we can build a secure tunnel using the IPSec protocol described in Chapter 7. IPSec uses encryption methods described in Chapter 6, like DES and triple DES, to establish a *virtual private network*, or *VPN*, through the public network. The data can take advantage of the economies of scale of the larger public network, while being kept secure inside the IPSec tunnel. A VPN appears to be a private data network to the user, even though the user's packets ride (in secure form) along with other people's data on a public network. VPNs are similar to the closed user groups provided in X.25 networks.

Another transmission option, defined by Bellcore and offered by carriers today, is *Switched Multimegabit Data Service*, or *SMDS*. Designed specifically with internetworking LANs in mind, it is a *connectionless* service that does not attempt to establish a virtual circuit, but simply delivers individual frames. A similar service, *Connectionless Broadband Data Service*, or *CBDS*, is available in Europe. Both of these services are considered by most experts to be intermediate steps on the way to the ATM service mentioned earlier and described in more detail in Chapter 10.

Each of these configurations provides high-bandwidth transmission within each location through local area networks and takes advantage of the economies found in packet switching, frame relay, the Internet, or other wide area networks.

WIRELESS DATA TRANSPORT NETWORKS

There are many different types of wireless networks available today, and many more are under development. One application of this technology is found in wireless LANs. These LANs allow users in a limited area, typically in the same building, to communicate without cabling.

In some cases, a LAN contains only wireless users, while in other cases, a standard wired LAN, like an Ethernet, has a special hub attached that allows connection to some wireless users. In this method, known as *cable extension*, the special hub contains a low-power radio transmitter and receiver, and similar units are placed in each user's workstation. This approach utilizes the original wired LAN network topology and Medium Access Control protocol, but substitutes radio transmission for cabling to the user's workstation. For example, if an Ethernet network contained a cable extension hub, the standard Ethernet frame would be sent from the hub to the wireless user.

A more sophisticated device known as an *access point* communicates to the wired LAN using the regular protocols, but utilizes a special Medium Access Control on the wireless part of the LAN. One example of such a protocol is described in the *IEEE 802.11* standard. In this case, the data might be sent using standard Ethernet protocols on the wired part of the LAN, but an entirely different MAC would be used on the wireless part of the LAN. The conversion must occur in the access point device. Another type of LAN, known as an *ad hoc* wireless LAN, contains only wireless users, with no cable-based LAN attached.

Although wireless LANs reduce the need for building wiring, the radio transmissions cause an added potential for noise and can be thought of as the data communications equivalent of a cordless phone. The workstation must be within a reasonable distance of the base station, or hub, and transmission quality will vary dramatically, depending on the environment. Wireless LANs that substitute infrared signals for radio waves are also available. Though these infrared LANs are not subject to noise caused by electromagnetic interference, they require a clear line of sight between the transmitter and receiver.

To cover a wider area, there are a variety of private and public options available. There are numerous broadcast networks, in which short data messages are sent in one direction over specific radio frequencies. Good examples of these types of networks are commercial pager networks, in which beepers are activated and the user even receives information like a phone number to call back. Stock quotes are another example of data broadcast in one direction only—to the users.

For those desiring two-way data communications over wide areas, there are several choices. Considering a portable-computer user as an example, one wireless approach is to use the existing cellular telephone network and a special modem. The special modem is able to interact with the cellular phone network's special dialing commands and signals, but once connected, it operates like a normal modem. The transmission and reception capabilities of the user's cellular phone connect this special modem to the cellular network. The cellular network passes the modem signals on to the land-based telephone network, where they will probably reach a standard modem. Unfortunately, signal quality on analog cellular networks is notoriously poor, a problem that could cause frequent retransmissions between error-correcting modems or even cause the connection to be terminated. This situation improves dramatically on digital cellular systems. Though these systems do not guarantee error-free transmission, they bring cellular systems to a level of quality closer to that of the land-based telephone network.

Many cellular carriers and other wireless data providers offer another service called *Cellular Digital Packet Data*, or *CDPD*. This packet data service can operate over the same channels as the existing analog cellular network, much as X.25 networks can operate over analog phone lines using modems. Instead of using a modem and connecting the computer to a cellular phone, the user connects the computer to a special device that combines the modem, radio transmitter/receiver, and other functions. This device operates independently and does not need to be connected to a cellular phone, although it does communicate with the network operated by cellular carrier or other provider. This device formats the data according to the CDPD protocol and encrypts it for security. The CDPD network and mobile device can check the data for errors and request retransmission if necessary. If the destination is not a mobile user, most CDPD networks convert the data back to its original format and then transmit it over standard modems on the land-based telephone network. Most CDPD networks take advantage of spare bandwidth on voice channels in the existing cellular networks, minimizing the cost for transmission. CDPD essentially provides the benefits of a packet switching network for the wireless portion of the connection.

There are many other proprietary schemes used in private networks, and standards continue to evolve in this area. The goal of a universal communications method between wireless devices and land-based networks still seems elusive. There is a broader goal of a *personal communications service*, or *PCS*, in which calls follow a user as the user travels. A single cordless handset that could be used at home, on a mobile basis, and in the office is being widely discussed. At home, the handset would operate as a cordless phone. Outside, or in the car, it would automatically switch to a cellular service, and when you arrive at work, it would talk to your company's PBX. Users could also direct their calls to traditional wired phones when they reach their destination. Although most of the technology for providing this type of service exists, choosing which methods to use and making the service commercially viable are still topics of heated debate.

While many products are marketed today under the name "PCS," some are just a combination of existing services that use conventional digital cellular technology, like the TDMA or CDMA systems described in Chapter 2. The GSM standards also discussed in Chapter 2 offer the most promise as a global infrastructure for carrying this PCS service. Wireless data communications schemes will probably be greatly affected by the evolution of PCS standards in the coming years. Though widespread deployment of PCS is envisioned, it is not yet clear if demand will be sufficient to support this deployment in less developed areas of the world.

SUMMARY

Data transport networks provide the lower layer OSI model functions. Packet switching networks, frame relay networks, the Internet, and local area networks are four examples of data transport networks.

Packet switching networks are often used for long-distance data transmission and provide a virtual circuit between devices. Packets are routed from one PSN node to another node over interexchange circuits. Devices unable to communicate using packets can be attached to an X.25 network with a PAD, which performs the necessary translation. The PAD can be part of the network or completely external and located on the user's premises. PSNs provide the reliability of the dial-up network at a reduced cost, since permanent connections are never established. Packet switching networks can be customer owned or operated by service providers for use by the public. These public PSNs typically charge users on a per-packet basis.

Most early packet switching networks complied with the X.25 standard. This three-level standard specifies the Physical Level, Frame Level, and Packet Level procedures and protocols for connecting to a packet switching network. There are other related standards explaining the PAD function, known as X.3, X.28, and X.29. PSNs can provide additional services, such as closed user groups, incoming or outgoing calls only, flow control or throughput class negotiation, and reverse charging. The routing of data in a packet switching network may cause delays, and packets can arrive out of sequence. Therefore, the destination node must be able to buffer and resequence the packets before transmitting them to the end user.

Frame relay networks are streamlined, more efficient versions of packet switching networks. They take advantage of the reliability of digital links to reduce error checking and to speed the routing of data. Frame relay and packet switching networks are both wide area networks, or WANs. The Internet is a data network based on the Internet Protocol. It connects users with numerous services, including the World Wide Web, electronic mail, and news groups.

A local area network is a privately owned data communications system that provides reliable high-speed, switched connections between devices in a single building, campus, or complex. LAN users typically transfer files or share resources known as servers, and client/server computing is gaining in popularity. LANs can be designed using centralized or distributed control. LANs can also be designed using many different topologies, including a mesh, star, bus, tree, ring, star-wired bus, or star-wired ring. Both baseband and broadband transmission can be used in LANs.

The access methods used in LANs also vary widely. LANs can be designed to use polling and selecting, time division, or frequency division, though contention or token-passing methods are more commonly used. Contention methods include random access, CSMA, and CSMA/CD. The most important aspect of these contention methods is the backoff procedure used; it is typically either priority backoff or random backoff. Token-passing methods use free and busy tokens to control access to the network; active and standby monitor devices help maintain a reliable token-passing network.

The IEEE 802 committee is responsible for many LAN standards, encompassing both Medium Access Control and Logical Link Control. The Ethernet and token ring networks are two of the most widely used LANs. The General Motors Manufacturing Automation Protocol, or MAP, is a user-defined standard for a token bus LAN in the factory environment. Another user-defined standard, Boeing Computer Services' Technical and Office Products specification, or TOP, describes a CSMA/CD bus LAN for the office and computing environment. ANSI's Fiber Distributed Data Interface, Fast Ethernet, 100VG-AnyLAN, and Gigabit Ethernet are among the higher speed standards available today.

Multiple LANs can be connected by internetworking them with a variety of devices. Repeaters operate at OSI Layer 1, bridges at OSI Layer 2, routers at OSI Layer 3, and gateways at higher layers of the OSI model. Repeaters retransmit all messages from one LAN to another and therefore do not need to know the location of individual users. Bridges usually learn the location of users by listening to traffic, and they choose appropriate paths using a variety of protocols. They are ideal for connecting similar networks using similar addressing methods. Routers utilize Layer 3 addresses to direct messages and often use network protocols like the Internet Protocol, or IP. Gateways add higher layer functions, similar to protocol converters. Various LAN switching options are available to further segment LANs and improve performance.

Numerous internetworking transmission options are available, including leased phone lines, packet switching networks, frame relay networks, SMDS, and CBDS. The Internet is one popular network used to internetwork LANs today. VPNs are often built by tunneling through the Internet using the IPSec protocol.

Wireless data networks are increasing in use. Wireless LANs can include only wireless users or a mix of wired and wireless users. Wide area wireless data networks include pager networks and cellular-based networks. These wireless technologies may all lead to a further deployment of personal communications service, or PCS.

TERMS FOR REVIEW

Access method
Access point
Active monitor
Adaptive bridge
Ad hoc
Applet
ARPANET
Asynchronous Transfer
    Mode
ATM
Backoff
Baseband transmission

Bridge
Broadband transmission
Browser
Buffering
Bus network
Busy token
Cable extension
Carrier sense multiple access
Carrier sense multiple
    access/collision detection
CBDS
CDDI

CDPD
Cell relay
Cellular Digital Packet Data
Centralized control
Circuit switching
Client/server
Closed user group
Collect calls
Collision
Collision avoidance
Collision detection
Collision domain

Communications server
Connectionless
Connectionless Broadband
   Data Service
Contention
Copper Distributed Data
   Interface
CSMA
CSMA/CD
DA
Data transport network
Demand priority
Distributed control
Electronic mail
Email
Ethernet
External PAD
Fast Ethernet
FCS
FDDI
Fiber Distributed Data
   Interface
File server
Firewall
Flow control negotiation
Frame
Frame Check Sequence
Frame Level
Frame relay
Free token
Frequency division
Gateway
Gbps
Gigabit
Gigabit Ethernet
Gigabit per second
High-Speed Token Ring
Hostid
Host identifier
HSTR
Hub
IBM PC Network
IBM Token Ring Network
IEEE 802
IEEE 802.1
IEEE 802.2

IEEE 802.3
IEEE 802.4
IEEE 802.5
IEEE 802.6
IEEE 802.7
IEEE 802.8
IEEE 802.9
IEEE 802.11
Incoming calls only
Information superhighway
Information Systems
   Network
Interexchange circuit
Internal PAD
Internet
Internet protocol
Internet service provider
Internetworking
Intranet
ISN
ISP
IXC
LAN
Layer 2 switching
Layer 3 switching
Layer 4 switching
Learning bridge
LLC
Local area network
Logical Link Control
MAC
MAN
Manufacturing Automation
   Protocol
MAP
Maximum transmission unit
Medium Access Control
Mesh network
Metropolitan area network
Microsegmentation
MTU
Netid
Network computer
Network identifier
Newsgroups
Node

Numbered
100BASE-T
100VG-AnyLAN
Outgoing calls only
Packet
Packet assembler
   disassembler
Packet Level
Packet switching network
Packetized
PAD
PCS
Personal Communications
   Service
Personal computer
Physical Level
Plug-in
Polling
Preamble
Print server
Priority backoff
PSN
Public packet switching
   network
Random access
Random backoff
Remote bridge
Repeater
Resequencing
Reverse charging
Ring network
Router
SA
Segment
Segmentation
Segmenting
Selecting
SMDS
Source address
Source routing
Source routing transparent
Spanning tree protocol
Standby monitor
Star network
Starlan Network
Star-wired bus network

EXERCISES

8-1.   What is a virtual circuit in a packet switching network?

8-2.   What are the functions of PSN nodes, IXCs, and PADs?

8-3.   What are the advantages and disadvantages of a PSN?

8-4.   What are the levels of the X.25 standard? What other standards are similar to the lower levels of the X.25 standard?

8-5.   What are the different internal PAD standards?

8-6.   What is a closed user group in a PSN?

8-7.   Explain why packet resequencing may be necessary at the destination node in a PSN.

8-8.   What is a LAN?

8-9.   What is the function of a server? Describe several different servers.

8-10.   What is the difference between centralized control and distributed control in LANs? What are the advantages and disadvantages of each method?

8-11.   Describe the different LAN topologies. Which topology usually requires centralized control?

8-12.   How do baseband LANs differ from broadband LANs?

8-13.   What is an access method?

8-14.   What is contention? What is a collision?

8-15.   Describe random access, CSMA, CSMA/CD, and backoff.

8-16.   Describe how token passing can control access to a LAN. What happens if the free token is somehow lost during transmission?

8-17.   What are the two most widely used LANs today? Which IEEE standards best describe these networks?

8-18.   What is internetworking? Describe the difference between a repeater, a bridge, a router, and a gateway.

8-19.   How does CDPD differ from using a modem over an analog cellular phone line?

8-20.   What is an ISP?

8-21.   What is the World Wide Web?

8-22. How is an intranet different from the Internet?

8-23. What transmission speed is used on the original Ethernet? Fast Ethernet? Gigabit Ethernet?

8-24. What is Layer 2 switching? Layer 3 switching? Layer 4 switching?

CHAPTER 9

Network Management

Any network, whether it is a LAN, a PSN, or an SNA network, is really a collection of individual components working in harmony. *Network management* helps maintain this harmony, ensuring consistent reliability and availability of the network, as well as timely transmission and routing of data.

NETWORK MANAGEMENT FUNCTIONS

Network management can be accomplished by dedicated devices, by host computers on the network, by people, or by some combination of all of these. No matter how network management is performed, it usually includes several key functions: *network monitoring, network control, network troubleshooting,* and *network statistical reporting.* These functions assume the role of network "watchdog," "boss," "diagnostician," and "statistician," respectively. All of these functions are closely interrelated, and often, many or all of them are performed by the same device.

The most important function of network management is *network monitoring.* This function constantly checks on the network and reports on any problems, acting as the network "watchdog." A reported malfunction may be as serious as a completely inoperative communications link to a host computer and might require immediate action. Another possible report might indicate an unusually high error rate between two modems, indicating either modem problems or a possible degradation in the telephone circuit. Such a report would allow the problem to be corrected before the communications link becomes completely inoperative.

Another function of network management is *network control.* This function, acting as the network "boss," allows for the activation and deactivation of network components and features. Deactivating a faulty modem to prevent network users from accessing it is an example of network control. Network control also allows components to be reconfigured; for example, an intelligent terminal might have its address changed using network control.

There is another network management function, known as *network troubleshooting*, that works closely with the network monitoring and control functions. For example, after network monitoring determines that the link to a host computer is not operating properly, the network control feature could be used to deactivate that link. The network troubleshooting function, acting as the network "diagnostician," could then be used to isolate the exact cause of the problem. Diagnostic tests could be run on all of the devices in the communications link, perhaps including the cables, modems, and telephone circuits.

Resolving network operations problems almost always requires a combination of the network monitoring, control, and troubleshooting functions. Even if the network is operating flawlessly, there may still be delays, or resources may be inadequate for the users' data traffic. The *network statistical reporting* function can then be one of the most useful in network management.

The network statistical reporting function, acting as the network "statistician," can pinpoint exactly which parts of a network are being utilized and how often particular components are being used. Overutilization and underutilization problems can be identified and corrected. For example, statistics might reveal that there are not enough communications links between two host computers, because the existing links are constantly busy and data is being delayed. Similarly, infrequently used resources can be identified and taken out of service or used elsewhere.

Working in conjunction with the network monitoring function, information about the performance of specific circuits in a network can be collected. Network statistical reporting can then reveal if the network's overall performance requirements are being met.

SERVICE LEVELS

Some criteria for the successful performance of a network are clear-cut; for example, a link that isn't working at all obviously needs to be reported. But in the case of occasional data errors, how many errors are acceptable? What are the criteria for these subjective network management functions?

The performance of a network is typically judged by comparing it to acceptable *service levels* in several key areas. In some areas, there are industry-accepted standards for reasonable service levels; other areas require the user to specify a service level based on the particular application.

AVAILABILITY

The most important area in which to measure a network's success is its *availability*. We consider the time when it is working properly its *uptime* and the time when the network is not working properly its *downtime*. Availability is the ratio of uptime to total uptime and downtime, as shown in Fig. 9-1. A network that works properly for 99 hours and is then down for 1 hour has an availability of 99%.

Since networks are not likely to fail at a set time each day, we usually deal with the average failure rate of a network. The *mean time between failures*, or *MTBF*, is

$$\underset{(\%)}{\text{Availability}} = \frac{\text{uptime}}{\text{uptime} + \text{downtime}} \times 100\% = \frac{\text{MTBF}}{\text{MTBF} + \text{MTTR}} \times 100\%$$

MTBF = Mean time between failures
MTTR = Mean time to repair

FIGURE 9-1   Availability.

the average time between network failures. Interpreted in a more positive way, MTBF is the uptime, or the average time a network works properly.

In general, the longer the MTBF, the better, though it depends how crucial the component is. For example, the MTBF of a light bulb may be only 1000 hours; this relatively short amount of time is usually acceptable, because light bulbs are easy to replace. However, the MTBF of twisted pair local loops is expected to be many years; that relatively long amount of time is important, because it is not practical to dig up streets to repair telephone wire every few months.

To the network user, the downtime is as important as the uptime. The *mean time to repair*, or *MTTR*, is the average time required to diagnose and correct a problem. The corrective action may be either a repair or a replacement of the defective component. In general, the shorter the MTTR, or downtime, the better. A host computer with an MTBF of nine years may seem outstanding, but if its MTTR is one year, the availability is only 90%. Some components, like modems, are easily and quickly replaced, provided that spares are kept on hand. Because of this low MTTR, a lower MTBF may be tolerated; it may be acceptable that a modem has an MTBF of only one year, since the MTTR may be only one day. The availability of this modem could be 364/365, or 99.7%. A summary of the relationship between MTBF, MTTR, and availability is provided in Fig. 9-1.

The MTBF and MTTR of a network are based on the MTBFs and MTTRs of all of the components in the network. A sophisticated host computer with a long MTBF may sit idle due to a cheap protocol converter with a low MTBF. There is no industry-accepted level of availability for a data communications network; it simply depends on the applications of the end users in a given environment.

The higher a network's availability, the more often the components in the network are functioning properly. However, there are some components that cannot be judged by availability alone. For example, during a thunderstorm, some static may occur on a telephone line. This appearance of static is usually not classified as a failure, since the telephone line is working, although its performance is momentarily degraded, causing a brief period of errors.

RELIABILITY

A data communications network's *reliability* is usually measured by its ability to pass data without errors. Acceptable error rates are usually specified for each communications link in the network. Locally, this link might be a coaxial cable; remotely, the link usually includes telephone circuits and modems.

FIGURE 9-2 Reliability.

$$\text{BERT} = \frac{\text{number of bit errors detected}}{\text{total number of bits received}} = \text{bit error rate test}$$

$$\text{BLERT} = \frac{\text{number of block errors detected}}{\text{total number of blocks received}} = \text{block error rate test}$$

A special test, known as a *bit error rate test*, or *BERT*, can be performed to determine a communications link's reliability. Typically, a known pattern of ones and zeroes is continually transmitted on the link, and proper reception is verified at the other end. If 1000 bits are transmitted and two bit errors are detected, the bit error rate for that circuit is .002. An acceptable bit error rate for modems using voice-grade circuits might be about one bit in a million, or 0.000001. Most modems perform better than this rate under ideal conditions and worse than this rate under poor conditions.

Another measure of reliability, known as a *block error rate test*, or *BLERT*, measures the ability of a link to pass entire blocks of data, rather than just bits. When link-level protocols are used, the BLERT may be more appropriate than the BERT, since these protocols automatically correct errors anyway, using retransmission. The only issue with link-level protocols is how often the blocks need to be retransmitted.

A BLERT is more indicative of actual link reliability when link-level protocols are used, because even if only a single bit error occurs, the entire block of data will need to be retransmitted by the protocol. In addition, a BLERT distinguishes between bit errors spread randomly during transmission and errors that are clustered together in the same block. When link-level protocols are used, randomly dispersed errors are more troublesome, because many blocks may have to be retransmitted. A comparison of BERT and BLERT is presented in Fig. 9-2.

RESPONSE TIME

In some networks, a consistent *response time* is critical. The definition of response time depends on the devices being used. For example, consider a smart terminal connected to a host computer through a network. The time between the instant when the terminal user hits the Enter key and when the reply message is received from the host computer is known as the response time. In this case, response time is really a summation of the time it takes the message to travel from the terminal to the host computer, the processing time at the host computer, and the travel time of the reply. This formula is summarized in Fig. 9-3.

If there are many terminals being polled, three response times are usually considered. There is a *minimum response time*, if the terminal is polled immediately after the user hits the Enter key. The *maximum response time* assumes that the terminal was

FIGURE 9-3 Response time.

Response time = travel time from terminal to host computer +
processing time at host computer +
travel time from host computer to terminal

polled just before the Enter key is hit and therefore must wait until all the other terminals are polled before it gets another chance to transmit. The *average response time* is halfway between the minimum and the maximum response times, assuming that all terminals are using the network equally.

A small local area network might have a response time of only a few hundred milliseconds. On the other hand, a packet switching network with many nodes might have response times of a second or more.

Response time may or may not be important to a user, though for most common applications, a two-second response time is considered adequate. A clerk typing payroll data into a terminal may not mind waiting an extra few seconds for the next screen of information to be transferred from the host computer. However, a nuclear power plant operator needs to communicate with the control computer instantly in an emergency, and even a few seconds can be critical.

THROUGHPUT

Throughput is perhaps even more important than response time as a measure of network transmission speed. Throughput is the net bandwidth of a network; it is a measure of the number of information bits per second that can be accepted and transmitted by a network. This rate is typically less than the transmission speed of the individual links. For example, in a network, a particular communications link with 9600-bps modems may have an average throughput of only 6000 information bits per second, because some of the available bandwidth is used for the extra bits, or *overhead*, associated with protocols. This overhead may include error-checking and addressing information and is necessary for data transmission with protocols, although it is not part of the actual user's data.

Throughput is often referred to as *net bandwidth*, rather than simply *bandwidth*, because it considers only the number of information bits transmitted per second. Bandwidth considers all of the bits transmitted, including the overhead bits.

One standard measure of throughput is calculated using the ANSI formula for *TRIB*, or *transfer rate of information bits*. This formula, shown in Fig. 9-4, provides a throughput rate in bits per second. It calculates the average rate at which users can expect the network to transport actual information bits to their destination. Throughput is an excellent measure of the efficiency of a particular network or communications link.

NETWORK MANAGEMENT APPROACHES

Setting standards for adequate service levels in the availability, reliability, response time, and throughput areas is an important first step in network management. After these thresholds are in place, the next logical step is to judge the network against these levels.

$$\text{TRIB} = \frac{\text{number of information bits transferred}}{\text{time required for the information bits to be transferred}}$$

$$\text{TRIB} = \text{transfer rate of information bits (bits per second)}$$

FIGURE 9-4   Throughput.

Although many different methods are used in network management, there are three basic approaches, using varying degrees of automation.

NONAUTOMATED NETWORK MANAGEMENT

The first approach uses minimal automation and requires users to call a network control center to report problems. There is little or no automated network monitoring and control equipment. However, when network problems are reported, specialized test equipment can be used to isolate the problem. This approach relies on users to monitor the network and report problems, and it requires technicians trained in using the test equipment to isolate and diagnose the problems. This specialized network test equipment is usually portable and can be taken to possible trouble spots in the network. We discuss some different types of network test equipment later in this chapter.

Unfortunately, in a large network, it is often difficult to determine where to place test equipment to start isolating the problem. A typical user might report, "I keep getting disconnected from the computer." There may be 20 links and 10 nodes between the user and the computer. Where does the technician start? It's the equivalent of a driver complaining that there was a pothole somewhere on a 50-mile commute and expecting the highway department to find and repair it.

This minimal-automation approach has the advantage of requiring little or no investment in network management tools. However, the ongoing cost in maintaining the network is high, since problems can be difficult to locate and diagnose. Network problem reporting is completely in the hands of the users, and technicians must isolate and diagnose all problems themselves.

SEMIAUTOMATED NETWORK MANAGEMENT

The second approach uses automatic network monitoring equipment for parts of the network. For example, a host computer might have network management capabilities that trigger alarms when an unusual number of bit errors occur. In this case, automation is used to report a problem, but a technician still must use specialized test equipment with the host computer to isolate and diagnose the problem. The problem could be occurring at the computer, at the end user's terminal, or at any of the links or nodes in between.

This compromise approach takes advantage of built-in network management capabilities already in some devices, without the expense of updating the entire network. Some problems will still be difficult to locate, and the burden of fault isolation and troubleshooting still falls largely on the network technician. A network's reliability is improved somewhat with this approach because problems are detected quickly. However, isolating and troubleshooting many problems will still require much expertise on the part of technicians.

INTEGRATED NETWORK MANAGEMENT

The most advanced network management approach ties all equipment in a network together using special network management protocols. Network management functions are integrated into every component of the network, and software used in one host computer continuously monitors the network; this host computer acts as a control center. Test messages are sent to each device periodically, and any transmission errors are reported to the control center. The control center software may operate on a mainframe, minicomputer, personal computer, or any type of server, depending on the size of the network.

In this integrated approach to network management, a single technician, using the control center host computer, can perform all of the major network management functions. The technician can monitor the network, is instantly alerted to all network problems, and can usually perform network control functions. Typically, diagnostics can be run directly from the control center, and devices can be deactivated or reconfigured if necessary to work around a simple link problem. Many problems will still require that a technician be dispatched to investigate with specialized test equipment, but in almost all cases, the technician at the control center will know about problems before the users do, or at least at the same time.

Many of today's integrated network management tools use graphics extensively to display network status, highlighting problem areas on a map of the network to aid in troubleshooting. Some of these control centers actually use artificial intelligence computer software, known as *expert systems*, to help diagnose and isolate problems. Ideally, a technician's job is simplified by these tools because a defective component is already isolated, or at least the choice is narrowed down to one or two components. The technician can then use the specialized test equipment to determine which of the devices is actually causing the problem.

The integrated network management approach can also provide access at the control center to extensive network statistics on all devices in the network. Such network-wide statistics are almost impossible to compile without an integrated network management approach.

However, it should be noted that with an integrated network management approach, all devices in the network must be compatible with the control center's network management protocols, so they can report their problems and statistics. Clearly, a single vendor could establish network management protocols and implement them in all of its devices. However, for integrated network management to be successful, not all of the equipment needs to be from the same vendor; only compatibility is necessary.

NETWORK MANAGEMENT PROTOCOLS

Several protocols enable the collection of network management information from devices of different vendors. The most popular network management protocol in use today is the *Simple Network Management Protocol*, or *SNMP*. It is part of the TCP/IP Protocol Suite discussed in Chapter 7. SNMP describes a common set of information needed to manage a network, known as the *Management Information Base*, or *MIB*. SNMP also describes the method by which the network *manager* exchanges information with network management *agents* in the devices being monitored. Although limited in its capabilities, SNMP is relatively easy to implement and has been widely accepted by vendors and users alike. As TCP/IP networks proliferate, so will the SNMP protocol. *SNMPv2*, a later version of SNMP, has been generalized to work on non-TCP/IP networks as well and has added some enhancements, though the principles of operation are the same as those of the original SNMP. SNMPv2's enhancements add so much complexity that it has not been widely implemented.

The SNMP agents can report status, or configuration information, about anything contained in the MIB. The MIB also identifies which items the SNMP manager can configure on the remote devices. The simple messages in SNMP can be categorized in three groups: *get*, *set*, and *trap*. The manager can retrieve configuration or status information from the agent by sending a *get* message. The manager can change the configuration or settings of the remote device by sending the agent a *set* message. *Trap* messages are sent by the agent to inform the manager of specific events being monitored at the remote device.

These messages provided by SNMP allow data to be exchanged, but the type of information, and the remote configuration capabilities, may be limited by the MIB. The MIB definition is very flexible, and vendors are free to design their own MIBs. For example, one vendor of networking equipment might choose to offer extensive network management capabilities with a fairly lengthy MIB, while another might offer a small MIB with very little information that can be exchanged. Standards organizations and user groups can also propose standard MIBs for vendors to implement, and one popular MIB is known as the *Remote Network Monitoring* MIB, or *RMON*. RMON was developed by the Internet Engineering Task Force (IETF) to allow for easy monitoring and protocol analysis on Ethernet and token ring LANs.

The first version of RMON, sometimes referred to as *RMON1*, defined some specific traffic statistics and thresholds for reporting certain events. It also provided the ability to capture and filter packets on a remote LAN for viewing at the manager station. Reports about this remote traffic were based on monitoring the MAC address of the LAN stations that were communicating. *RMON2* extended these capabilities by translating the station MAC addresses to higher layer addresses, like IP addresses, as well as monitoring higher level protocols. While RMON1 might report on the overall traffic on a network, RMON2 informed the manager as to which particular types of applications, and which protocols, were making up this traffic. For example, if RMON1 is used to monitor an IP internetwork, a router that carries traffic from other LANs appears to be the source of all traffic from off the local segment, since its MAC address is seen as the origin on the LAN being monitored. RMON2 operates at a higher level, reporting on traffic based on an IP address so that the original source of the traffic coming through the router can be identified. RMON2 is added onto RMON1 and the two MIBs are used together to provide RMON2 functions. RMON1 and RMON2 are just two examples of standardized MIBs; others are sure to be added in the coming years.

ISO has its own protocol for network management, known as the *Common Management Information Protocol*, or *CMIP*. It is far richer and more complex than SNMP, but CMIP is also more costly to implement and operate. For this reason, there is little interest in CMIP, and SNMP is more widely used. While SNMP and CMIP are standard protocols, many vendors also have proprietary protocols for network management.

Most of the network management systems available today support proprietary protocols, as well as some of the standard protocols. Many available software packages can act as the network manager and display the management information conveniently for the user. Hewlett-Packard has a popular network management product, called *OpenView*, that supports a variety of protocols. Another popular product supporting standard protocols is Sun Microsystems' *SolarisNet* (formerly *SunNet) Manager*. Cabletron offers another network management product known as *Spectrum* that also supports numerous protocols. IBM offers host-computer-based network management software known as *Netview*, which can interface to another IBM software product, known as *Netview/PC*. These are two products in IBM's family of *Communications Network Management* (*CNM*) tools. While these products were originally designed to support only Netview protocols, support for other protocols is now included as well. Many other vendors are offering similar products, with a variety of user interfaces and capabilities.

DIAGNOSTIC METHODS

There are several different manual approaches that can be used when diagnosing problems. One of the most common techniques is *loopback testing*, or *echo testing*. Typically, loopback testing is used to test modems or dumb terminals, though other devices can also be tested this way.

For example, a dumb, asynchronous, RS-232-C-compatible terminal can be loopback tested with a specially wired connector. This connector, known as a *loopback plug*, has the Transmitted Data and Received Data pins wired together; in addition, several control signals are connected together to simulate normal operation. If a technician suspects that a terminal is not operating properly, the cable attached to the terminal can be disconnected and the loopback plug attached instead.

The terminal user types characters, which are translated into bits and then sent over the RS-232-C Transmitted Data pin as positive and negative voltages. Since the Transmitted Data pin is wired to the Received Data pin, the terminal receives the characters that it just transmitted. If the terminal is functioning properly, the typed characters are received and then appear on the screen. A typical RS-232-C loopback plug configuration is illustrated in Fig. 9-5; details on the RS-232-C interface itself are provided in Chapter 4.

A loopback test is the equivalent of a person putting one end of a garden hose up to his or her mouth and the other end up to his or her ear; when talking into one end of the hose, he or she hears his or her voice at the other end of the hose.

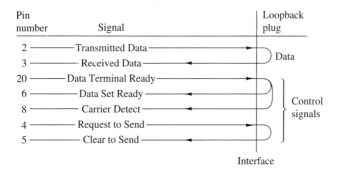

FIGURE 9-5   RS-232-C asynchronous terminal loopback plug.

ANALOG AND DIGITAL MODEM LOOPBACK TESTING

Many modems are designed with internal loopback testing capability because users usually are unable to identify where the problem with a data link lies; the problem could be in the local modem, in the remote modem, or in the phone line itself. The loopback testing capability is usually activated by depressing a switch on the modem or by issuing a special command and can be performed by a user or a technician.

To help isolate modem problems, there are two types of modem loopback testing, the *local analog loopback test* and the *remote digital loopback test*. Neither test verifies all of a modem's functions, but the two combined reveal almost any modem problem. Modems usually have switches, or commands, to activate each test. To understand these two tests, we take a brief look inside a modem.

As shown in Fig. 9-6, square waves from a DTE (perhaps a terminal), in normal operation, enter the modem's *decoder* circuitry. At this point, the square waves are translated into an internal representation of ones and zeroes used by the modem. The *modulator* circuitry then translates these ones and zeroes into an analog signal, usually a sine wave. This analog signal is then sent out on the telephone line.

At the receiving modem, the sine waves enter the *demodulator* circuitry, where they are translated into ones and zeroes. This digital data then enters the *driver* circuitry, which produces a square wave at the appropriate voltage levels.

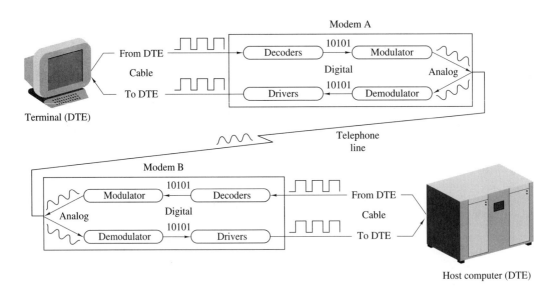

FIGURE 9-6   Normal operation of a modem.

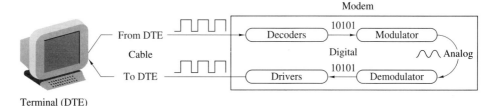

FIGURE 9-7   Local analog loopback test.

If a modem uses an RS-232-C interface, its decoders must be able to receive and interpret RS-232-C square waves, and its drivers must be able to transmit these waves. Similarly, another type of interface could be used simply by changing the decoder and driver circuitry.

In the local analog loopback test, a terminal is attached to a single modem with a cable, as illustrated in Fig. 9-7. When the local analog loopback switch is depressed, the analog signal is looped back before ever leaving the modem. In a successful test, a user types a key on the terminal, the terminal generates a square wave, the data enters the modem and reaches the decoders, and the data is then converted to digital form and sent to the modulator, where it is converted to analog form. The analog sine wave is then looped back into the demodulator—hence the name *analog loopback*.

In the demodulator, the analog signal is converted back to digital form and passed on to the driver, where it can be translated back to a square wave with the appropriate voltage levels and sent back to the terminal.

The character then appears on the terminal screen, and the test is complete. This test verifies the operation of almost all of one modem's components. Some parts of the modem, including some of the wiring from the modulator/demodulator circuitry to the phone jack are not tested, however; nor is the phone line itself tested. "Local" refers to the fact that the analog loopback test can be performed locally without another modem and without any phone line. A successful analog loopback test confirms that a modem's decoders, drivers, modulators, and demodulators are probably functioning properly; it also confirms that the terminal and cable are working.

A remote digital loopback test can test the phone line itself as well as parts of the modem not covered in the local analog loopback method. In this case, two modems, a terminal, a cable, and a phone line are required, as shown in Fig. 9-8. The remote digital loopback switch is pressed on modem A; modem B is in normal operation mode. The terminal user strikes a key and the data is sent by modem B in analog form to modem A, where it enters the demodulator and is translated to digital form. The digital signal is looped back; hence the name *digital loopback*.

The digital signal enters the modulator and is translated back into analog form and sent back over the phone line to modem B and the terminal. A successful test confirms

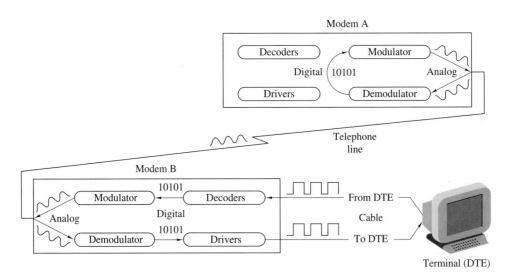

FIGURE 9-8 Remote digital loopback test.

the operation of the terminal, the phone line, all of modem B, and the modulator/demodulator circuitry of modem A. The term *remote* in this case simply means that another modem is required at the other end of a telephone line.

By using the local analog loopback and the remote digital loopback testing capabilities of most modems, many obvious problems can be isolated without specialized test equipment. Intermittent problems, and problems caused by large volumes of data, will not usually be detected by these tests. Also, it is sometimes difficult to determine whether problems lie in the data link or in the attached equipment, such as host computers. These cases still require specialized data communications test equipment.

DATA COMMUNICATIONS TEST EQUIPMENT

Regardless of which network management approach is chosen, specialized test equipment is sometimes necessary to isolate and confirm the cause of a problem. Networks using the integrated network management approach seldom need to use specialized test equipment, while networks managed without automation almost always need this equipment to resolve network problems.

THE BREAKOUT BOX

The simplest form of data communications test equipment is called a *breakout box*. A breakout box typically can be attached at a data communications interface, perhaps between a terminal and a modem. A breakout box contains light bulbs, called *LEDs*, or *light-emitting diodes*, to monitor interface signals. For example, an RS-232-C breakout box might contain 25 LEDs, one for each signal on the DB-25 connector. A positive voltage might cause the LED for that signal to light; a negative voltage might cause it to turn off. In this way, the status of control signals can be monitored. Data being transmitted by the terminal causes the Transmitted Data LED to flash on and off, but at a rate much too fast to be read by humans.

The main purpose of the LEDs on a breakout box is to allow monitoring of the control signals, which typically are either on or off and do not change as frequently as the data signals. Breakout boxes can therefore be used to determine if a particular device is presenting a DTE or DCE interface, based on the status of the control signals. This knowledge helps users connect this device to other devices.

Breakout boxes get their name from their switches and jumper wires, which allow technicians to "break out" individual signals. For example, in normal position, all switches are closed and signals are passed straight through the breakout box. However, the switches for the Transmitted Data and Received Data signals can be opened and wires used to cross these signals. In this way, custom cables can be tested to determine the most suitable configuration for connecting two devices. The "breaking out" of signals in this manner is known as interface modification.

Some breakout boxes contain a small battery for use in testing cables. A simple continuity test can be performed on each wire in a cable; a lit LED indicates that a wire is conducting electricity, and an LED that doesn't light indicates that a wire is broken.

To summarize, a breakout box is often used for monitoring control signals, DTE/DCE determination, interface modification, and cable testing.

THE DATASCOPE OR PROTOCOL ANALYZER

A more sophisticated device is a *datascope*, or *protocol analyzer*. Like a breakout box, a datascope can be placed in the data communications circuit for monitoring purposes. The datascope generally has all of the features of a breakout box, including switches and jumper wires, and can perform all functions of a breakout box. However, a datascope also has its own display screen to allow technicians to observe the data being transmitted and received.

Datascopes are often called protocol analyzers because they let users see not only the data typed at a terminal, but also the special control information added by a protocol. Only the actual data typed by the terminal user, or sent by the host computer, appears on the terminal screen; however, all transmitted data, including the control information, is visible on the datascope's display screen, and this information can aid in troubleshooting network problems.

In addition to monitoring the data transmitted, many datascopes have features that allow data to be trapped in memory when certain conditions or errors occur. When used for troubleshooting intermittent conditions, datascopes can be left in place and configured to sound alarms when protocol errors are detected. Some datascopes, when attached to a phone line, can call a remote office when errors are observed.

Most datascopes can perform the bit and block error rate tests (BERT or BLERT) we mentioned earlier. Typically, after a communications problem is isolated and repaired, a datascope is used to run a BERT or BLERT to verify that the problem is corrected.

Some datascopes can even be programmed to simulate or mimic the operation of host computers. For example, a datascope can be programmed to poll a smart terminal to test its operation.

Since datascopes typically contain their own microcomputers, their features are limited only by the software used in them. When a datascope is attached to a LAN, it is sometimes called a *sniffer*. The RMON2 MIB used with SNMP, as described earlier, provides many monitoring features in remote LANs without requiring the user to physically attach test equipment to each LAN. But in some difficult troubleshooting cases, attaching a datascope to the network may be the only way to accurately detect the problem.

ANALOG TEST EQUIPMENT

Finally, since almost all data communications networks include analog telephone circuits at some point, *analog test equipment* is often used. For example, analog test equipment can determine if a particular analog leased line is providing the expected bandwidth. A wide variety of analog test equipment exists today and is capable of measuring distortion, noise, loss, gain, and many other analog circuit characteristics.

SUMMARY

Network management helps maintain network harmony, ensuring consistent availability and reliability, as well as timely transmission and routing of data. Network monitoring, network control, network troubleshooting, and network statistical reporting are the key functions of network management. These functions assume the role of network "watchdog," "boss," "diagnostician," and "statistician," respectively.

Appropriate service levels need to be established for a network in the areas of availability, reliability, response time, and throughput. Availability is the ratio of a network's uptime to its total uptime and downtime. Uptime is also called the mean time between failures, or MTBF; downtime is also called the mean time to repair, or MTTR. Reliability is often measured by using a bit error rate test (BERT) or a block error rate test (BLERT). Response time is the time between the instant when a user strikes the Enter key and when the reply message is received from the host computer. This time period includes the round-trip travel time as well as any processing time at the host computer. If there are many terminals being polled, there will be a minimum, average, and maximum response time. Throughput is a measure of the net bandwidth of a network. The ANSI standard measure of throughput is known as the transfer rate of information bits, or TRIB. TRIB is the ratio of the number of information bits transferred to the time required for these bits to be transferred.

There are several different approaches to network management, including nonautomated, semiautomated, and integrated network management. Nonautomated network management relies on people to report, isolate, diagnose, and correct problems. Semiautomated network management relies on automation to report many problems, but still requires people to isolate, diagnose, and correct problems. Integrated network management employs automation to report, isolate, diagnose, and assist technicians in correcting network problems. Many vendors use an integrated network management approach; examples of programs that provide such an approach are Netview and Netview/PC, both part of IBM's family of Communications Network Management (CNM) tools. Simple Network Management Protocol, or SNMP, is the most widely used network management protocol. Many devices and software products support SNMP. Remote Network Monitoring, or RMON, is a standardized MIB providing network managers with many useful capabilities. The ISO standard Common Management Information Protocol (CMIP) is less popular.

One simple diagnostic method in use today is loopback testing. Dumb asynchronous terminal loopback testing can be accomplished with a simple loopback plug, while modem loopback testing capability is typically built into the modem itself. There are two common types of modem loopback tests, the local analog loopback test and the remote digital loopback test. A combination of these tests can verify the operation of the different parts of a modem, including the decoders, drivers, modulators, and demodulators, as well as the terminal, cable, and phone line itself.

Sometimes, specialized data communications test equipment is needed to solve problems. The breakout box is used for monitoring control signals, DTE/DCE determination, interface modification, and cable testing. The datascope, or protocol analyzer, is a more sophisticated device that can perform all of the functions of a breakout box, as well as monitor data on a display screen. Using a datascope, a technician can view protocol control information, set alarms, trap data, perform tests, and program complex simulations. For telephone line problems, analog test equipment is used to measure distortion, noise, loss, gain, and other analog circuit characteristics.

TERMS FOR REVIEW

Agent	Light-emitting diode	Protocol analyzer
Analog test equipment	Local analog loopback test	Reliability
Availability	Loopback plug	Remote digital loopback test
Average response time	Loopback testing	Remote Network Monitoring
BERT	Management Information	Response time
Bit error rate test	Base	RMON
BLERT	Manager	RMON1
Block error rate test	Maximum response time	RMON2
Breakout box	Mean time between failures	Service level
CMIP	Mean time to repair	Set
CNM	MIB	Simple Network
Common Management	Minimum response time	Management Protocol
Information Protocol	Modulator circuit	Sniffer
Communications Network	MTBF	SNMP
Management	MTTR	SNMPv2
Datascope	Netview	SolarisNet Manager
Decoder circuit	Netview/PC	Spectrum
Demodulator circuit	Network control	SunNet Manager
Downtime	Network management	Throughput
Driver circuit	Network monitoring	Transfer rate of information
Echo testing	Network statistical reporting	bits
Expert system	Network troubleshooting	Trap
Get	OpenView	TRIB
LED	Overhead	Uptime

EXERCISES

9-1.   Explain each of the key functions of network management.

9-2.   What is the difference between availability and reliability?

9-3.   What is MTBF? MTTR? When is a short MTBF acceptable?

9-4.   What is response time?

9-5.   What is throughput? Why is it sometimes referred to as net bandwidth?

9-6.   Compare the different network management approaches.

9-7.   Which of the network management approaches is the most economical to implement initially? In the long run?

9-8.   Does integrated network management require that all of the equipment in the network be supplied by a single vendor? Why or why not?

9-9.   Why is SNMP so popular?

9-10.   What are the major uses of a breakout box?

9-11.   What are the major uses of a datascope? Why is it sometimes called a protocol analyzer?

9-12.   What are some differences between RMON1 and RMON2?

C H A P T E R   1 0

Digital Telecommunications

This book began with a discussion of telecommunications and went on to examine various aspects of data communications. Basic data communications concepts, transmission, interfaces, efficiency, security, integrity, architectures, protocols, transport networks, and network management were all considered at length.

As the 21st century begins, telecommunications and data communications are converging. In Chapter 2, voice communications technology is presented as a predecessor to data communications. In fact, many of today's voice communications systems depend on digital equipment. Both customer-premises equipment and transmission facilities are increasingly using digital technology.

DIGITAL CUSTOMER-PREMISES EQUIPMENT

The PBX, discussed in Chapter 2, is perhaps the most widespread customer-premises equipment in use today. Almost all major PBX vendors are currently offering digital PBXs; voice is *digitized*, or translated from analog form into ones and zeroes. We present a method for digitizing voice later in this chapter.

Typically, a *digital phone* converts the voice into digital form for transmission to the PBX. A digital phone should not be confused with the DTMF or rotary phones described earlier, which are analog voice communications devices that send dialing signals using tones or pulses. Digital phones use ones and zeroes to transmit voice as well as signaling information. Computer data can also be transmitted through a digital phone as well.

For example, a digital phone equipped for both voice and data communications allows a personal computer user to place a voice call to one person while simultaneously transferring files to the personal computer of another person. This integration of voice and data in a single device, the digital phone, is shown in Fig. 10-1.

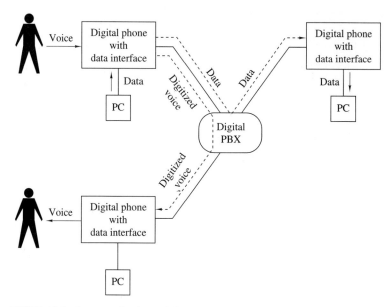

FIGURE 10-1   Integrated voice and data in a digital PBX.

Another device, known as an *integrated voice/data terminal*, or an *IVDT*, usually combines the capabilities of a digital phone with those of a terminal. Many of today's digital PBXs can be equipped with IVDTs.

While digital PBXs can be used to integrate voice and data, some data communications applications demand extremely high bandwidth. For this reason, the LAN, discussed in Chapter 8, is the more popular data communications solution. LANs can be connected to PBXs, allowing LAN users access to host computers, terminals, and modems attached to the PBX; PBX users can also access devices on the LAN. Both LANs and PBXs can be connected to packet switching or frame relay networks for economical long-distance data communications. These connections are shown in Fig. 10-2.

As discussed in Chapter 2, *facsimile*, or *fax*, was originally an analog communications method for transmitting an image of a printed page. Newer digital facsimile machines convert the image into ones and zeroes, allowing the possibility of high-speed

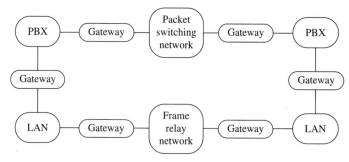

FIGURE 10-2   Interconnecting PBXs and Data Networks.

facsimile transmission over digital communications networks, including PBXs, LANs, PSNs, frame relay networks, and other digital transmission facilities.

Transmission of moving images, known as *video transmission*, was originally only an analog technology, like fax. Conventional cable television is an example of analog video transmission. Digital transmission of video is now possible, though it requires a very high digital bandwidth, as we will discuss later in this chapter.

DIGITIZING VOICE USING PULSE CODE MODULATION

In Chapter 4, we explained various modulation methods that allow us to transmit data over analog telephone lines. When digital customer-premises equipment and transmission facilities are used, it becomes necessary to transmit analog signals, like voice, over digital communications facilities; this requires the reverse approach, since the analog signals must now be converted to digital signals for transmission.

Normal telephone conversation can be digitized by using a technique known as *pulse code modulation*, or *PCM*. In PCM, an analog signal is converted to a digital signal for transmission; typically, the analog signal is sampled 8000 times a second, and an eight-bit representation of the signal is recorded for each *sample*, for a total of 64 kbps. Think of a sample as an audio equivalent of a snapshot of the signal at a given moment; if someone is speaking and we freeze his or her voice at a given instant, we can assign a number that represents the amplitude of the voice signal at that moment. If we do this 8000 times per second, we can then transmit these numbers in binary form; at the other end, we can reconstruct the voice by converting the digital representation back into an analog signal. A simplified, four-bit version of PCM is shown in Fig. 10-3.

The receiver cannot detect any interruptions in the voice, because there are so many samples each second. This is the same principle as that on which movies are based. The camera really records many individual snapshots each second on the moving film. When the film is replayed on a projector, it appears that motion is continuous, because the eye cannot detect the slight jumpiness in the motion between each frame.

HIGH-BANDWIDTH DIGITAL TRANSMISSION FACILITIES

High-bandwidth digital transmission facilities are playing a major role in communications today. In Chapter 4, we briefly mentioned *T-1 carrier* service. The T-1 standard, developed by AT&T, provides a 1.544 Mbps digital path now available from all of the common carriers. The electrical characteristics, including the voltage levels for T-1 bit transmission, are specified by the *DS-1* standard. Typically, the 1.544 Mbps is divided into 24 separate channels, using time-division multiplexing.

T-1 frames.   Data is transmitted in *frames*, each 193 bits long; 8000 frames are transmitted each second in a T-1 carrier (1,544,000/193 = 8000). A typical T-1 frame is illustrated in Fig. 10-4. Notice that each of the 24 channels transmits eight bits per frame; in addition, one bit per frame is a *framing bit*, used for *synchronization*, and sometimes for error checking. The 8000 frames per second include 8 kbps of synchronization and 24 channels each of 64 kbps, adding up to a total of 1.544 Mbps. Each of these 24 channels can be used for either data or digital voice communications.

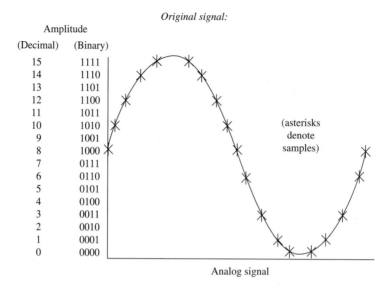

Converted to digital form:

1000 1010 1100 1110 1111 1111 1110 1100 1010 1000 0110 0011 0001 0000 0000 0001 0011 0110 1000

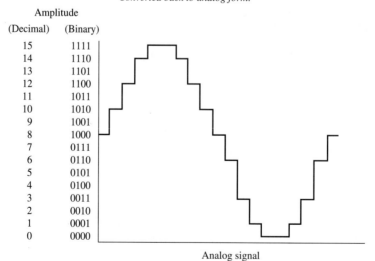

FIGURE 10-3 Pulse code modulation.

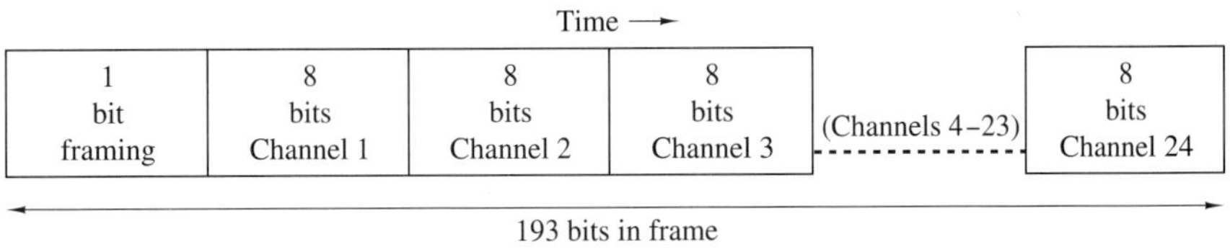

Time ——▶

1 bit framing	8 bits Channel 1	8 bits Channel 2	8 bits Channel 3	(Channels 4–23)	8 bits Channel 24

◀———————— 193 bits in frame ————————▶

FIGURE 10-4   T-1 Frame.

T-1 SIGNALING

In Chapter 2, we discussed signals passed through the communications network. These analog signals included on-hook, off-hook, some dialing signals, and so on. Since T-1 is a digital transmission method, these signals must be passed by using a few bits of the 1.544 Mbps. The 8 kbps of synchronization information is required to separate one frame from the next; however, a bit can occasionally be "stolen" from one of the 24 channels for signaling purposes. One of the most common T-1 signaling methods, known as *robbed-bit signaling*, allows signaling to occur simultaneously with digitized voice or data transmission.

If a particular channel has a bit robbed for signaling, this channel only has seven bits left instead of eight during this frame. With digitized voice, losing an occasional sample does not affect voice quality, since there are 8000 samples per second; this change is equivalent to a speck of dust on one frame of a movie film each second.

However, if a T-1 channel is used to transmit computer data, the bit robbed for signaling purposes will cause data errors. Therefore, when actual data, rather than digitized voice, is transmitted via T-1 carrier, only seven bits per channel should be used for actual data; the eighth bit can be used for signaling, when necessary. With 8000 frames a second, and seven actual data bits per channel in each frame, this process results in an effective data rate of 56 kbps per channel. With an analog line and modems, it is very difficult to achieve 56 kbps reliably, and rates closer to 33.6 kbps are more typical. Therefore, the guaranteed 56 kbps capacity of a T-1 data channel is still a significant advantage to data communications users.

Ironically, with robbed-bit signaling, a digital transmission medium appears to provide 64 kbps per channel for digitized voice, but only 56 kbps per channel for data. In reality, the same bandwidth exists in both cases, but data transmission will fail at 64 kbps with robbed-bit signaling, while voice transmission will not be noticeably impaired. The difference is that a missing bit is always noticed in data transmission.

There have been several generations of T-1, known as *T-1/D1*, *T-1/D2*, *T-1/D3*, *T-1/D4*, *T-1/D5*, and so on. The "D" part of the T-1 standard specifies exactly how the 1.544 Mbps can be subdivided into separate channels—the voice digitization and signaling methods used. T-1 continues to evolve as user requirements change.

T-1 applications.   By combining T-1 carrier with PCM, 24 voice conversations can be simultaneously transmitted over a single T-1 circuit, which requires only two twisted pairs. With analog voice transmission, 24 pairs would be required. This 12-to-1 advantage does not come without a price, however. In T-1 transmission, repeaters need to be used after a certain distance to prevent the signal from fading, as discussed in Chapter 4. In addition, special digital transmission equipment is required at each end of a T-1 circuit. Analog transmission requires amplifiers and devices known as *loading coils*, instead of digital repeaters.

Even with the added costs of T-1 repeaters and other digital equipment, a T-1 circuit may cost only as much as a dozen analog leased lines, depending on the distance involved. In this case, T-1 offers 24 connections for the price of 12, over only 2 pairs of wires instead of 24 pairs; this results in a 2-to-1 price advantage and a 12-to-1 advantage in terms of wiring requirements. Also, a digital circuit, because of its many repeaters, is less likely to be affected by small amounts of noise. For this reason, a digitized long-distance voice circuit is usually free of any static. In an analog circuit, static and other noise is usually amplified and carried with the signal.

A common application of T-1 is presented in Fig. 10-5, where two PBXs, each at a different site, are connected using a T-1 circuit through a central office. This configuration allows a customer to provide 24 channels between the two PBXs for far less than the cost of 24 analog leased lines. Our figure shows 24 phones at each PBX, implying digitized voice communications on all of the T-1 channels. However, some of these channels could be used to transmit digitized voice, while others are being used simultaneously to transmit data.

T-1 multiplexers and submultiplexing.   Though voice can be neatly digitized into 64 kbps channels, there are many data communications devices that operate at lower speeds, such as 9600 bps terminals. Usually, the T-1 transmission rate of 1.544 Mbps is

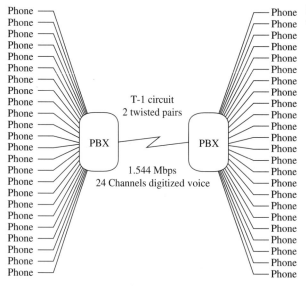

FIGURE 10-5   Connecting PBXs with a T-1 circuit.

broken into 24 separate channels using a device known as a *T-1 multiplexer*. Any of these channels can be further broken down by *submultiplexing*. Since we have agreed that for data transmission, 56 kbps is the limit of a T-1 channel, then five 9600 bps terminals could be submultiplexed onto a single channel with bandwidth to spare. Submultiplexed in this manner, the entire T-1 circuit could carry 120 simultaneous 9600 bps terminal-to-host-computer connections, all on two pairs of wires. Users who need less than T-1's full 24 channels can often subscribe to *fractional T-1* from a carrier at a reduced rate.

Voice and data compression.   Even greater economies can be achieved by using a more efficient method than standard PCM to digitize voice. There are methods that can digitize voice using only 32 kbps, 16 kbps, or 8 kbps. As technology improves, these numbers will be driven even lower. However, there is already a great deal of 64-kbps PCM equipment installed, and compatibility is often more important than efficiency in telecommunications.

Data compression, explained in Chapter 5, can also be used in conjunction with T-1 circuits. This combination can greatly increase the effective bandwidth for certain applications.

Beyond T-1 speeds.   While T-1 offers a 1.544 Mbps digital path, there are other, less widely used, higher bandwidth standards. *T-1C* has a bandwidth of 3.152 Mbps and offers 48 channels. *T-3* offers 672 channels and a 44.736 Mbps bandwidth. However, few companies need 672 channels between two locations; clearly, one or more T-1 lines provides ample bandwidth for all but the largest organizations. The bandwidth of the T-1C and T-3 standards are not exact multiples of the T-1 bandwidth, because they require extra bits for framing and synchronization. Examples of some North-American transmission standards are shown in Fig. 10-6.

DIGITAL NETWORKS

Today, digital customer-premises equipment is often combined with digital transmission facilities to form a completely digital private telecommunications network. For example, a company with digital phones attached to digital PBXs at two locations can connect the two PBXs by using a T-1 circuit.

Many companies still use analog equipment in at least part of their network. For example, most digital PBXs today still use some analog lines for central office trunks. In addition, almost all residential customers still use analog telephone service. The

Digital signal type	Carrier type	Data rate	Number of channels
DS-1	T-1	1.544 Mbps	24
DS-IC	T-I C	3.152 Mbps	48
DS-2	T-2	6.312 Mbps	96
DS-3	T-3	44.736 Mbps	672
DS-4	T-4	274.176 Mbps	4032

FIGURE 10-6   Some North American digital transmission standards.

technology is available, however, to create an entirely digital public telecommunications network, serving businesses of all sizes, as well as residential customers.

INTEGRATED SERVICES DIGITAL NETWORK

The *Integrated Services Digital Network*, or *ISDN*, is a set of standards for a digital network carrying both voice and data communications. Today, most residential and some small business communications are carried over analog local loops. Only midsize and larger businesses with high volumes of telecommunications traffic currently use T-1 carrier. ISDN extends the advantages of digital transmission to all users, large and small, by including many different sizes of digital transmission paths.

The ITU(CCITT) took the lead in defining international ISDN standards. The ISDN standards are really a collection of many standards, specifying interfaces for connecting to the public network, as well as a set of services that the network will provide to users. By standardizing interfaces through ISDN, the ITU(CCITT) hopes to make end-to-end digital connections between all devices a reality. Communications networks operated in different countries can all be connected under ISDN standards, allowing for a worldwide integrated digital network. In addition, ISDN provides special services to the users, such as call forwarding, voice mail, and calling-party identification. How fast ISDN will be welcomed by different countries, and by the users within those countries, is still not known.

We discuss only the more common ISDN standards here. Variations are occurring in different countries; in fact, even in the United States, services differ regionally. However, the fundamental interfaces should be the same, allowing device portability and universal attachment within large regions. This fundamental similarity is equivalent to today's modular jack, which is accepted as the universal method for attaching a telephone to the public network. Ideally, ISDN will allow terminals, computers, and telephones to attach to the network with similar ease.

ISDN CHANNELS

To accommodate large and small users, ISDN provides different sizes of transmission paths, known as *channels*. These channels can be combined in different ways to satisfy user requirements.

The *B-channel*, also called the *bearer channel*, is a 64-kbps digital channel. The B-channel can carry user data or digitized voice.

The *D-channel* is a digital channel used to carry signaling information. The capacity of the D-channel can be 16 kbps or 64 kbps, depending on the type of circuit used. These bits are reserved for signaling information, such as on-hook and off-hook status, dialing information, busy signals, and so on, and are also used in T-1 signaling. However, most T-1 transmission uses *in-band signaling*, where the signaling bits are interspersed in the same channels as the data bits. ISDN uses *out-of-band signaling*, or *common-channel signaling*, meaning that a separate channel (the D-channel) is used for the signaling bits.

Since most signaling typically occurs at the beginning and end of a connection, the D-channel may be idle most of the time. Therefore, certain low-priority user data can also be passed on the D-channel when it is free. A typical example of low-priority data for the D-channel might be electronic mail sent in a packet format; there is usually no urgent need for rush delivery, so these messages can be sent when the D-channel is available, rather than using the high-speed B-channel.

The B-channel and D-channel are the basic building blocks of ISDN transmission, although there are several other channels already defined. The *A-channel* is similar to today's analog telephone circuit and provides a means for analog signals to be carried in an ISDN. Since not everyone discards his or her analog customer-premises equipment overnight, some method of carrying analog signals will still be necessary; hence, the need for the A-channel. Another channel, known as the *C-channel*, provides a low-speed (up to 16 kbps) data channel for older, pre-ISDN data devices, such as many dumb terminals. A summary of these ISDN channel types is provided in Fig. 10-7.

THE BASIC-RATE INTERFACE

ISDN provides service to residential and business users with the *basic-rate interface*, or *BRI*. This interface consists of two B-channels and a single D-channel. Usually, one B-channel is used for digitized voice, the other B-channel is used for high-speed data, and the D-channel is used for signaling and low-speed data packets. The basic-rate interface is commonly referred to as *2B+D*.

In the basic-rate interface, the D-channel can carry 16 kbps of signaling information, and each B-channel can carry 64 kbps of data or digitized voice, for a total of 144 kbps. However, an additional 48 kbps is used for overhead, which includes synchronization and framing bits. Therefore, the basic-rate interface requires 192 kbps of digital transmission capacity, even though the effective bandwidth is actually 144 kbps.

The basic-rate interface is intended to provide voice and data transmission to the office desktop or the home for the typical individual user. A 64 kbps data transfer rate is adequate for basic terminal and PC applications, although as processor speeds increase, a higher bandwidth may be desirable. The basic-rate interface provides the user with simultaneous voice and data communications capability, along with advanced signaling capability. The 64 kbps data rate is far superior to traditional data transmission, which uses modems and analog lines; much of the signaling information in the basic-rate interface is not available to the user in today's public network. Certainly, the basic-rate interface is a marked technological improvement over today's analog local loops.

Channel	Type	Bandwidth	Typical use
A	Analog	Voice grade	Voice
B	Digital	64 kbps	Digitized voice or high-speed data
C	Digital	Up to 16 kbps	Low-speed data
D	Digital	16 or 64 kbps (depending on circuit type)	Signaling or data packets

FIGURE 10-7   ISDN channel types.

THE PRIMARY-RATE INTERFACE

ISDN also provides a higher bandwidth service for business users, known as the *primary-rate interface*, or *PRI*. This interface normally is used to connect PBXs to central offices, PBXs to PBXs, PBXs to LANs, and LANs to LANs and in other high-bandwidth applications. The primary-rate interface consists of either 23 or 30 B-channels for user data and a single 64-kbps D-channel for signaling.

In North America and Japan, where T-1 transmission is already popular, the *23 B+D* method is used. Since the capacity of each of the 23 B-channels is 64 kbps and the D-channel capacity is also 64 kbps, existing T-1 transmission equipment that transmits 24 channels of 64 kbps each can also accommodate this primary-rate interface. Since a separate D-channel is used for signaling, no bits are taken from the B-channel for this purpose, and each B-channel has a full 64-kbps capacity, unlike the channels in T-1. A framing arrangement similar to that found in T-1 transmission is used in this version of the primary-rate interface. Therefore, there are 24 channels each of 64 kbps and an additional 8 kbps used for framing, for a total of 1.544 Mbps.

In Europe, where high-speed digital transmission is done today using 2.048 Mbps, the *30 B+D* arrangement is used. Though at first this arrangement may seem to cause a fundamental incompatibility between North-American and European networks, this is not the case. Each country, or continent, can use its own methods for digital transmission, as long as gateways exist to connect the different networks. It certainly makes sense to maximize the use of existing digital transmission equipment between central offices and toll offices in each country, and the two different primary-rate interfaces permit this.

OTHER CHANNEL ARRANGEMENTS

The A-channel and C-Channel can be combined in a *hybrid interface* to allow users without ISDN phones and terminals to receive at least some of the ISDN features. These users will have voice and data communication, but will not have access to some of the ISDN services.

Name	Channel composition	Bandwidth needed	Typical use
Basic-rate interface	2 B + D	192 kbps	Desktop or residence use: one digitized voice and one data channel
Primary-rate interface	23 B + D	1.544 or	PBX to PBX, PBX to CO, PBX to LAN, LAN or to LAN
	30 B + D	2.048 Mbps	
Hybrid interface	A + C	Analog voice and up to 16-kbps data	Used during the transition to ISDN

FIGURE 10-8   Typical ISDN interfaces.

Individual channels may be offered separately in some instances, to comply with regulatory requirements in the United States and other countries. For example, a customer might be able to lease 35 B-channels and 6 D-channels. However, it is expected that most customer-premises equipment will be designed to take advantage of either the basic-rate or primary-rate interfaces. A comparison of typical ISDN interfaces is shown in Fig. 10-8.

ISDN EQUIPMENT FUNCTIONS AND REFERENCE POINTS

The equipment in an ISDN network and attached to an ISDN network is classified by the functions that it performs. We consider here only the customer-premises equipment, not the details of the central office in the ISDN environment. On the customer's premises, there is both ISDN *Terminal Equipment*, or *TE*, and *Network Termination equipment*, or *NT*.

There are different types of ISDN Terminal Equipment. In this case, the word *terminal* does not refer only to the dumb, smart, or intelligent terminals discussed so far in this book. Instead, terminal equipment in the ISDN nomenclature refers to any device attached to the end of an ISDN circuit. This device could be a dumb terminal, but it could also be a telephone, a personal computer, or any device attached to the ISDN network that transmits or receives voice, data, or other information.

Terminal equipment that is compatible with the ISDN network is known as *Terminal Equipment Type 1*, or *TE1*. An ISDN-compatible digital telephone, an ISDN-compatible personal computer port, and an ISDN-compatible workstation are all examples of TE1. A device that is not compatible with ISDN, such as an RS-232-C dumb terminal, is known as *Terminal Equipment Type 2*, or *TE2*. This equipment can be attached to an ISDN network only by using a special *Terminal Adapter*, or *TA*, which acts as a converter between the TE2 and the ISDN network.

The TE1, or TE2/TA combination, is attached to the Network Termination equipment, as illustrated in Fig. 10-9. The point between the Network Termination equipment and the TE1 or TA is known as the *S reference point*. The point between the TE2 and the TA is known as the *R reference point*.

There are also several different types of Network Termination equipment. They provide functions similar to those found in the lower layers of the ISO-OSI model, and some users need only certain functions. *Network Termination 1* equipment, or *NT1*, provides only OSI Layer 1 (Physical Layer) functions, including the electrical and physical termination of the network on the customer's premises. The NT1 function allows the rest of the customer-premises equipment to be isolated from the technology used in the local loop. For example, if the local exchange carrier currently uses twisted pair wire for local loops, an NT1 compatible with this transmission medium can be used. If

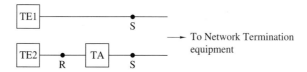

FIGURE 10-9   ISDN Terminal Equipment.

fiber optic local loops later become available, only the NT1 needs to be changed, since it is the only equipment that attaches directly to the circuit.

There is no exact equivalent of the NT1 in the analog telephone network in our homes today; however, consider the box in our house where the phone company's local loop is connected to our house's telephone wiring. This box, terminating the public network circuit, is the rough equivalent of the NT1, though it performs fewer functions. The NT1 is similar in function to the CSU discussed in Chapter 4.

Network Termination 2 equipment, or *NT2*, can provide OSI Layers 2 and 3 (Data Link and Network Layer) functions, including concentration and switching, if needed. LANs, PBXs, and other controllers are examples of NT2 equipment. While residential users would rarely need their own NT2 equipment, business users would, for the economical and practical reasons previously explained.

Finally, *Combined Network Termination 1 and 2*, or *NT12*, contains both NT1 and NT2 functions in a single device. Some economies can be gained by purchasing a single device that performs both functions, but if the local loop transmission technology changes, the entire NT12 may need to be replaced. Though the NT12 is less flexible than separate NT1 and NT2 devices, some users may choose NT12 for economical reasons.

The relationship between the Network Termination equipment is shown in Fig. 10-10. The point between the NT1 and the rest of the ISDN network is known as the *U reference point*. The point between the NT1 and the NT2 (if an NT2 is used) is known as the *T reference point*. If an NT1 is used without an NT2, the S and T reference points coincide where the NT1 is connected directly to the terminal equipment.

In the United States, both TE and NT are usually considered customer-premises equipment. Outside the United States, however, the local exchange carrier almost always provides the NT1 function. Even in the United States, the customer usually has the option of leasing some of the NT functions from the local exchange carrier.

The current ISDN standards specify that the S and T reference points require two twisted pairs for transmission, while the U reference point requires one pair for the BRI and two pairs for the PRI. The exact nature of transmission at the S, T, and U reference points is clearly defined in the ISDN standards. The standard at the R reference point depends on the interface standard of the TE2.

Understanding the details of the ITU(CCITT) S, T, and U reference point standards is not as important as understanding the functions performed by the TE1, TE2, TA, NT1, NT2, and NT12. In an ISDN environment, customer-premises equipment is

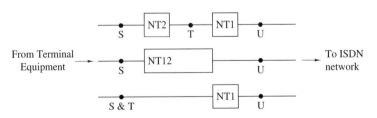

FIGURE 10-10   ISDN Network Termination equipment.

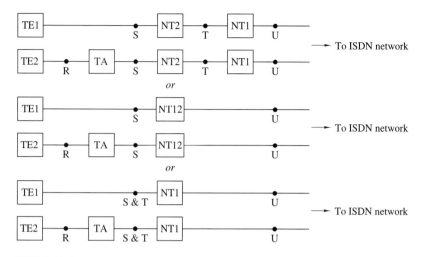

FIGURE 10-11   Interconnecting ISDN Terminal Equipment and Network Termination equipment.

classified according to this terminology. Examples of interconnection of various combinations of equipment are shown in Fig. 10-11.

CIRCUIT AND PACKET SWITCHING IN ISDN

The B-channels in an ISDN network are circuit switched, but D-channel messages are packet switched. D-channel signaling messages that pass between central offices and users in the network are placed in packets according to certain protocols.

All of the switches in an ISDN network are interconnected by a packet switched network to exchange signaling information. If a user wants to place a call from San Francisco to New York, the appropriate call-request packet is sent from the user through the D-channel to the packet-switched signaling network. If the user in New York answers the phone, a call-connect packet returns on the signaling network, and a B-channel is enabled by the network to support this call. This B-channel is circuit switched and remains active for the duration of the call, while the signaling occurred in the separate packet-switched signaling network.

It is also technically possible for users to send data messages on the D-channel if spare bandwidth is available, but not all carriers offer this service. The predominant use today of the D-channel is to carry the network's signaling messages.

PBXS, LANS, AND ISDN

Although an ISDN public network can provide the features of a PBX, and at a bandwidth approaching that of a LAN, both PBXs and LANs will still play an important role in an ISDN world. For example, even though an ISDN central office can provide

PBX features like call forwarding and caller identification, it shares the same fundamental inefficiency found in Centrex service. If internal calls must be processed through the central office, a local loop is required for each desk. The central-office charges would be greater than the charges if a PBX were used to minimize the number of central-office lines. However, many PBXs can interface to ISDN, typically through the primary-rate interface.

Similarly, some users require high-bandwidth data transmission. The same ISDN inefficiency discussed previously applies here as well. Users needing high bandwidth for local data communications may still use a LAN; however, the LAN often contains gateways to the ISDN network, so LAN users can access devices located off the LAN when necessary.

ISDN SERVICES

While an integrated digital network is a sound technical concept, there is little reason for users to discard existing analog equipment in the interests of technical purity alone. To motivate users to support a new type of network, special user services are included in addition to digital transmission.

ISDN's signaling capabilities are significantly superior to those of today's public network. The D-channel can carry information about the call's destination, the calling party, billing instructions, and other information. This signaling is passed throughout the ISDN network, so the central office at the destination knows not only who is being called, but also where the call came from. The central office can relay this information on the D-channel to the customer with an ISDN digital phone.

In an ISDN world, when the telephone rings, the phone displays information about the caller, like "(516)-555-1234 John Smith." The user can then choose to answer or ignore the call. In addition, the user could send instructions to the central office to block all calls from John Smith, or to forward them to an answering service.

Another example of an often-cited ISDN feature is similar to the PBX camp-on feature. When calling a friend across the country, if we hear a busy signal, we can touch a button on our digital phone that instructs our central office that we really want to reach our friend. Our central office then sends special signaling information to our friend's central office, asking it to inform our central office when our friend is off the phone, so that our call can be placed again automatically.

ISDN signaling is carried between switches in the network according to the standard known as *Signaling System 7*, or *SS7*. This standard for network signaling, developed in 1984, is already in widespread use throughout the United States. SS7 information includes the call's origin and destination phone number, as well as instructions for the network handling the call. In most cases today, SS7 is used only between switches in the network. If a call is being placed to an ISDN subscriber, the SS7 signaling information is translated to the appropriate D-channel format before transmission to the end user.

This signaling technology is often used to assist in call routing. For example, a chain of retail outlets advertises a central, toll-free phone number. A potential customer calls this number and is automatically routed to the nearest store. The network signaling messages identify the caller, and based on the caller's phone number, either public or private switching equipment can route the call to the proper store.

Most end users today still utilize analog phones. While almost all central and toll offices have the capability to pass on signaling information, few subscribers today are able to take advantage of it. Some analog customers today subscribe to a *Caller ID* service, enabling them to use their existing analog phones with a special display to indicate the number—or sometimes the name and number—of the party calling them. These devices are not ISDN phones, and they provide only a single feature similar to one of the many found in ISDN. The ISDN network carried the signaling message to the central office, making it possible for the information to be delivered to the user using Caller ID.

The availability of these services has sparked many interesting discussions in the United States about the use of telecommunications technology. Many customers have raised questions about their privacy rights and would prefer not to be identified as the calling party. There have been numerous proposed approaches to solve these issues. This debate is one example of the type of societal issues that ISDN will continue to confront during its deployment.

Using ISDN for residential Internet access is another popular application. In some regions, ISDN pricing is very reasonable, and it has caught on for Internet access, as well as for remote access to the corporate LAN. In other areas, however, the cost of ISDN is still prohibitive. One recent ISDN service is particularly interesting for accessing the Internet or the corporate LAN. Known as *Always On/Dynamic ISDN*, or *AODI*, it uses the ISDN D-channel to send up to 9600 bps of data packets to the Internet or corporate LAN. When user demand exceeds 9600 bps, B-channels are then connected to provide higher bandwidth, and the data flow switches to the B-channels. When the traffic drops below 9600 bps, it is switched back to the D-channel again. This creative use of the available ISDN bandwidth allows a continual connection to the data network over the available D-channel, without tying up the network's B-channels when they are not needed. This system results in lower connection charges from the carrier and increased network efficiency. It is one example of how ISDN is being used to meet the needs of applications that were not even considered during its original development.

An endless number of features can be provided to the customer with ISDN. The extensive signaling capabilities provided in ISDN allow new features to be added later simply by modifying the software in the existing central-office switches.

NATIONAL ISDN

ISDN implementation in the United States has been facilitated by the introduction of the *National ISDN* standards. These are Bellcore standards designed to ensure the consistent deployment of ISDN in a user's entire private network, regardless of carrier or equipment manufacturer. National ISDN-*N*, where *N* is the number of the standard, can be thought of as a snapshot of ISDN's technology as it evolved and was implemented. It captures an agreed-upon set of ISDN features, provides necessary implementation details, and freezes these features and details long enough for vendors, providers, and users to deploy networks. A few months or years later, the next set of features are agreed upon, and improvements are deployed. For example, the first version, National ISDN-1, has already been deployed, as has National ISDN-2. Plans for deploying future National ISDN versions are already under discussion. In Europe, a similar standard, known as *EuroISDN*, defines a set of features implemented there.

VIDEO AND ISDN

There are many different standards committees working on developing ideal methods for transmitting moving images as well as still images. One committee working on moving pictures, or video, is ISO's *Moving Pictures Expert Group*, or *MPEG*. The group provides a variety of standards with different quality levels. One example is the *MPEG II* standard, which offers varying degrees of quality based on the bit rate used. While uncompressed broadcast-quality video might require 21 Mbps bandwidth, on average, the MPEG II compression technique reduces this requirement to only 7 Mbps. Neither the basic-rate nor the primary-rate interface of ISDN can provide the bandwidth required for true broadcast-quality video.

Broadcast quality, however, is not required for successful videoconferencing. Many users have found existing ISDN interfaces suitable for videoconferencing applications, and equipment is available using ISDN's basic-rate interface. Typically, the equipment uses both B-channels in a basic-rate interface to carry the video and audio signals. Primary-rate videoconferencing is also available, utilizing 23 B-channels.

In a typical videoconference, most of the picture is composed of stationary items, like the table and the wall. Typically, the only moving items are people's mouths, arms, and heads. Most videoconferencing equipment takes advantage of this lack of great movement and transmits only the changing parts of the picture, allowing reasonable transmission on a basic-rate interface. If participants start moving around the room, there is usually a perceptible degradation of quality.

Use of a primary-rate instead of a basic-rate interface improves the situation but still falls far short of the 7 Mbps needed for broadcast quality video. Many users do not require broadcast-quality and are satisfied with a speed somewhere between the basic-rate and primary-rate interfaces. The term $N \times 64$, or *multirate ISDN*, has evolved to describe the usage of multiple B-channels for a single connection. While theoretically any number of B-channels can be associated in multirate ISDN, some channel combinations are more commonly used than others. For example, six B-channels, for a total of 384 kbps, is very popular. Some examples of common channel combinations, and the names used to refer to them, are shown in Fig. 10-12. Multirate ISDN can also be used to carry any type of data, including the video example discussed here.

Service name	Number of B-channels	Data rate
H0	6	384 kbps
H11	24	1.536 Mbps
H12	30	1.920 Mbps

FIGURE 10-12   Some common channel combinations in multirate ISDN.

Clearly, ISDN is useful for videoconferencing applications, but it is not considered suitable for broadcast video. As compression technology improves, so will the quality of video transmission, but most experts believe that a higher bandwidth than that associated with ISDN will be necessary to fully develop video applications.

THE REALITIES OF ISDN

ISDN is based on already-proven technologies. For example, the basic-rate interface is similar to that used by many PBX manufacturers in their digital phones today. The 23B+D version of the primary-rate interface is similar to the T-1 carrier scheme used in the United States. Almost all of the ISDN features are already being used in digital PBXs, so their operation is well understood. National ISDN and EuroISDN are making slow but steady progress.

Will ISDN evolve from a set of international standards into a worldwide telecommunications network? Or will ISDN be the next RS-449, a standard that provides for everything, but fails to gain widespread acceptance? For ISDN to be fully implemented, new customer-premises equipment and transmission equipment will need to be purchased or existing equipment modified. Existing digital central offices and toll offices can certainly be modified to accommodate ISDN. But who will pay for ISDN?

In some countries, the government strictly regulates the telecommunications industry and sometimes also runs the public network. In these cases, the government could simply insist that all communications equipment in that country conforms to ISDN, and the standard could be implemented quickly. The government, and ultimately the citizens, would bear the expense of the conversion.

In the United States, however, it is likely that the FCC and PUCs will require common carriers to continue to offer basic telephone service at reasonable prices. While ISDN technology is being used extensively by the carriers in their internal networks, ISDN is still just one of the many options customers have for accessing the public network.

Simple economics will dictate how fast ISDN is implemented in customer-premises equipment in the United States. For example, the primary-rate interface is almost identical to T-1 carrier; the main difference is that one of the 24 channels is used for signaling instead of data transmission. Assuming that it continues to be priced reasonably close to the T-1 transmission offerings, the ISDN primary-rate interface will continue to be a very attractive alternative to T-1. By giving up one of the 24 data channels, the customer gains incredible signaling power for the other 23 channels. A customer with PBXs at two locations can tie them together with an ISDN primary-rate circuit; the signaling passed between the two PBXs over the ISDN signaling channel makes it appear to users that they are on a single PBX.

The basic-rate interface may be only of limited appeal to business users. In Centrex-type installations, in which the central office provides the switching function for a customer, the basic-rate interface is a reasonable method of providing digital voice and data service to the desktop.

PBX customers, however, may have already invested in their PBX vendor's own proprietary desktop data interfaces that perform functions similar to those provided by the basic-rate interface. These PBXs will likely be compatible with ISDN interfaces to the central office, but may still use proprietary digital interface standards internally.

Some PBX vendors, however, will also choose the ISDN basic-rate service for transmission between the PBX and the desktop.

Finally, residential telephone users make up the biggest unknown for ISDN. Will we welcome basic-rate service in our homes? Is there a need for a second channel for data in most residences? Clearly, many professionals would benefit from remote access to their corporate LAN. Home-based businesses could also benefit from high-speed access. But do most purely residential users need a data channel? Only a minority of today's telephone customers takes advantage of custom calling services, such as call waiting and call forwarding. Will ISDN's services be any more attractive to residential users? Until the growth of the Internet, ISDN was largely a failure in the residential market. It definitely offers a higher speed connection to the Internet than do dial-up phone lines, but other options for digital connection to the Internet, discussed later, surpass ISDN in speed. For now, ISDN does not appear to be a significant force in the residential market.

When home computers were originally introduced, in the 1970s, manufacturers touted the computer as an information organizer that would be widely used to store recipes and help manage the household. Over time, however, many people decided that it was easier to keep recipes in a book or card file. Similarly, ISDN advocates now believe that we will use the data channel to send instructions from our office computer to our home, to turn on the air conditioner, to ask our VCR to record that television show we forgot to program, and to transfer computer files so that we do not have to carry a briefcase. Will we actually use ISDN for these purposes?

Considering the fact that less than half of American bank customers regularly use their automated teller machines and that an even smaller percentage of Americans understands how to program their home VCRs, there is certainly some doubt as to who will use all of this ISDN technology. Only time will tell whether users will find a need for, and be willing to pay for, ISDN functions at home.

ISDN will probably have to stand on its own merits in the United States. The FCC and PUCs are not likely to let the local exchange carriers use existing telephone service revenues to subsidize ISDN. Either the carrier's shareholders or the initial ISDN customers are bearing the cost of ISDN implementation. Ironically, these initial customers will not reap the full benefits of ISDN services, because many of these services depend on both the called and calling party's use of ISDN-compatible equipment.

Clearly, ISDN can provide functional advantages to certain residential and business users at a reasonable cost within existing technology. For the residential market, ISDN is serving as one option for connecting to the office LAN and for Internet access. However, with higher bandwidth options already available, ISDN will probably not widely penetrate the residential market.

DIGITAL SUBSCRIBER LINE SERVICES

The need to connect residences and businesses to the Internet, or to remotely attach them to the company LAN, caused increased demand for digital connections. While ISDN is one alternative, another technology is *Digital Subscriber Line*, or *DSL*. Originally developed by Bellcore, DSL was intended to deliver high-speed digital connections over copper cable from the central office to the residential or business user without the expensive repeaters found in T-1 lines. DSL was offered in many variations, hence the term *xDSL*, where the *x* defines the type of service being offered. All operate over twisted pair wire, and not all variations and speeds are offered in all areas.

Asymmetric Digital Subscriber Line, or *ADSL*, offers a transmission path that is of a higher speed in one direction than in the other. The central office sends data to the user of the ADSL line with a higher speed than the user sends data to the network. Applications like residential Internet access can certainly benefit from this arrangement, since in most cases, the majority of data flows from the Internet to the user. ADSL is available at speeds ranging from 1.5 to 9 Mbps in the high-speed direction and 16 to 640 Kbps in the low-speed direction, over a single twisted pair. One popular combination is 6.1 Mbps/640 kbps for specific distances and over certain-quality wire. *Rate-Adaptive Digital Subscriber Line*, or *RADSL*, simply scales back the speed of ADSL based on the quality of the wire and the distance between the user and the central office. A newer version of ADSL, known as *Universal Asymmetric Digital Subscriber Line*, or *UADSL*, and also as *ADSL Lite*, *DSL Lite*, and *G.Lite*, is an attempt to standardize ADSL deployment across all carriers, since early implementations had so many speed and transmission differences. It operates using a 1.544 Mbps/384 Kbps combination.

High-bit-rate Digital Subscriber Line, or *HDSL*, offers 1.544 Mbps or 2.048 Mbps transmission in both directions, but requires two twisted pairs; *HDSL2* is a recent version of HDSL that operates at the same speeds and distances as HDSL does, but over a single twisted pair. *Single-line Digital Subscriber Line*, or *SDSL*, offers speeds ranging from 384 Kbps all the way to HDSL speeds, but over shorter distances, using only a single twisted pair. One application of HDSL, HDSL2, and SDSL is to connect businesses to the Internet.

Very-high-bit-rate Digital Subscriber Line, or *VDSL*, offers even higher speeds, but is asymmetric, with the high speeds ranging from 12.96 to 51.84 Mbps and the low speeds from 1.6 to 2.3 Mbps. Its distance is very limited, and one popular application of it is as a local connection to a higher speed fiber optic network.

There are numerous other xDSL versions, all with their own speeds and distance limitations, and the technology is continually improving. No single DSL choice is clearly superior to the others. Rather, it is a question of matching the transmission speed with the user's application. Also, all of these DSL versions simply provide a digital pipe from the central office to the user. Once the data reaches the central office, the carrier must then pass it to the data network (e.g., the Internet) using the B-channels in the ISDN network or some other means.

CABLE MODEMS

Another possibility for local access to data networks like the Internet is provided by *cable modems*. Most cable modems operate by taking some of the bandwidth available on a cable television system away from television signals and dedicating it instead to data traffic. On some older analog cable television networks, data signals are modulated onto sine waves, much like traditional modems do, and placed on some of the existing analog system channels. The transmission speed of these modems is much higher than that of conventional modems, because they are not limited by the 3000 Hz bandwidth of the telephone line. Newer digital cable television systems, with digital cable converter boxes, actually send the television signals, and the user's data, on separate digital channels on the system. These digital cable modems are not truly modems at all, but more like the Digital Service Units (DSUs) described in Chapter 4.

Using these various techniques, competing technologies offer many different speeds. In most cases, the transmission speed to the subscriber is much higher than the transmission speed to the network. Some combinations offered by cable modem vendors include 10 Mbps/768 Kbps, 27 Mbps/1.5 Mbps, 27 Mbps/2 Mbps, 30 Mbps/1.9 Mbps, 30 Mbps/2 Mbps, and 30 Mbps/2.56 Mbps. In many cases, the bandwidth in a neighborhood is shared, just like in an office LAN, so the user never has access to all of the bandwidth. There is always the risk that a neighbor may be downloading huge amounts of data, slowing down the entire neighborhood network, but cable system providers can monitor this usage and place reasonable restrictions on customers to prevent abuse. Similarly, like on a LAN, anyone electronically monitoring the cable with test equipment can see the data sent by anyone else on this particular network. To maintain privacy, conventional encryption technology can be used for any sensitive data.

Cable networks can also dedicate channels for voice transmission, offering an alternative to the local telephone company for telephone service. Cable television networks offer one possibility for combining voice, broadcast video, and data on a single connection to the residence. The ability to send high-quality video in both directions, as in videoconferencing, requires more bandwidth than today's cable television systems provide to cable modems. Another network, known as *Broadband ISDN*, offers even more promise in this area.

BROADBAND ISDN

The basic-rate and primary-rate ISDN interfaces were once considered extremely high-bandwidth interfaces. However, with improvements in transmission technology and the advent of fiber optic cables, much faster transmission rates are now possible. An even faster class of ISDN interface standards, referred to as *Broadband ISDN*, or *BISDN*, is currently being developed by the ITU(CCITT) to handle much higher transmission speeds. When compared to this new BISDN, the basic-rate and primary-rate ISDN interfaces are sometimes called *Narrowband ISDN*. However, Narrowband ISDN still provides a higher effective bandwidth than that of today's existing analog telephone facilities.

BISDN is already widely available to business users. The extremely high bandwidth of BISDN permits digitized video signals to be transmitted, as well as digitized voice and data. BISDN could eventually integrate our telephone and cable television networks into a single network delivering information to businesses and residences.

The business applications of BISDN would include inexpensive high-quality videoconferencing. Digital video telephones would cost no more than a small television set does today. Residential applications could revolutionize entertainment. Rather than going to the video store to rent a movie, a BISDN user would call the video store's computer, scan a catalog of available movies on the television screen, and make a selection.

The rental fee would be automatically deducted from the user's bank account, and the movie would be transmitted to the home from the video store.

With BISDN, many office workers could effectively work at home and could even attend meetings through videoconferencing. Other work could be performed on their home computer and transferred to their boss, who might also be at home. The telephone would still exist for everyday voice conversations.

Compared to today's analog service, Narrowband ISDN simply adds a data channel and signaling, uses digital voice transmission, and provides additional services. BISDN, on the other hand, could actually revolutionize the way in which we communicate. For this reason, many people believe that BISDN will eventually achieve greater residential penetration than Narrowband ISDN will. Many feel that Narrowband ISDN will be used mainly by businesses and that most residential users will not be interested. BISDN, however, may provide such clear advantages to residential users that it will be hard to resist. On the other hand, many see BISDN as a technology primarily for use by carriers building their wide area networks. A further discussion of BISDN technology will clarify its usefulness.

BROADBAND ISDN TRANSMISSION MEDIA

As discussed in Chapter 2, the trend towards deregulation in the telecommunications and cable television industries should speed up the deployment of combined voice and video networks. The timetable for widespread implementation of BISDN will be accelerated by deregulation. The infrastructure necessary to be successful in this market is significant, so the more companies—and, hence, the more capital committed to its deployment—the sooner BISDN will be widely deployed.

Fiber optic cable has been replacing copper cable in many of these companies' long-distance lines for years because it is an affordable method of transmitting a very high bandwidth. Recognizing that a high-bandwidth infrastructure is the key to success in the BISDN market, some local phone companies and cable companies are already extending their fiber optic networks to locations that are very near to the customers. When the fiber optic cable reaches the customer premises, it is often called *fiber to the premises*, or *fiber to the home* in residential applications.

Most networks utilize fiber optic cable for much of the distribution, but return to copper cable of some form before reaching the customer premises. Copper cable can support high bandwidths, but for much shorter distances than fiber optic cable can. Most of the distribution schemes take advantage of this fact and do not demand the use of fiber optic cable to every phone jack and cable box. While rewiring the network is difficult enough, rewiring customer premises makes it even more difficult to sell new services. Therefore, both phone and cable companies will probably use the existing copper wiring inside residences and businesses and switch to fiber only after leaving the building.

Fiber to the curb is the term used to describe one approach taken by phone companies, where fiber optic cable is used to connect the central office to a section of a particular street. A special device then converts the optical signals to electrical signals for transmission to the customer on ordinary twisted pair wire. *Fiber to the neighborhood* describes a similar approach taken by cable television companies. This method is sometimes called *fiber to the feeder* or *fiber to the vault*. In this scheme, the fiber optic cable reaches only as far as the neighborhood and does not reach each customer's street. In this case, the device converting the optical signals to electrical ones serves the entire neighborhood, typically transmitting this electrical signal to the customers over coaxial cables. There are other hybrid distribution schemes being used, and all seek to balance the benefits of fiber optics with the economic reality of already-installed copper cable in customer premises.

ASYNCHRONOUS TRANSFER MODE

The transmission technology used to implement BISDN is *Asynchronous Transfer Mode*, or *ATM*. Although this is not the only technology suitable for BISDN, it is the one that was chosen by all major standards committees. ATM technology can also be used as a transmission technology for purposes other than BISDN. ATM does not require any fixed channel rate, or speed. Instead, it describes how to fragment data into fixed-size chunks, or *cells*, so that voice, video, data, or any other information can be sent over the same network.

For example, a user might subscribe to ATM at 45 Mbps, similar to the T-3 rate, or might instead choose a speed of several hundred Mbps or even many gigabits per second, or Gbps. The higher the bandwidth of the link, the greater the number of cells that can be transmitted. Though fiber optic cable is not required, the higher bandwidth that it affords is clearly an advantage for any network trying to carry video transmission or other demanding applications. There are many standards using twisted pair wire for a limited distance at speeds up to 100 Mbps and beyond, which suggest that twisted pair wire will play a significant role in future networks. However, some *multimedia* applications may outstrip twisted pair's capability. For example, would the users be satisfied with broadcast-quality video, or would they prefer something closer to *High-Definition Television*, or *HDTV*? Regardless of the underlying physical transmission media used, ATM can be the format, or protocol, used to transmit the cells.

Why was ATM selected for BISDN by all major standards bodies? Much of this acceptance can be credited to the work of the *ATM Forum*, a group of member companies, organizations, and users whose sole purpose is to promote the rapid development and deployment of the ATM specification. Founded in October 1991, this group has grown quickly, and it works with national and international standards bodies to encourage ATM activities. Some ATM specifications have been agreed upon in months, whereas prior networking committees have often taken years to settle detailed implementation issues.

Major standards bodies, such as ISO, ITU(CCITT), and ANSI have recognized ATM as the standard of choice for BISDN. Inevitably, there will be another standard as yet unknown that will offer additional promise and performance. But for now, it appears that ATM will be the standard ushering us into the BISDN era.

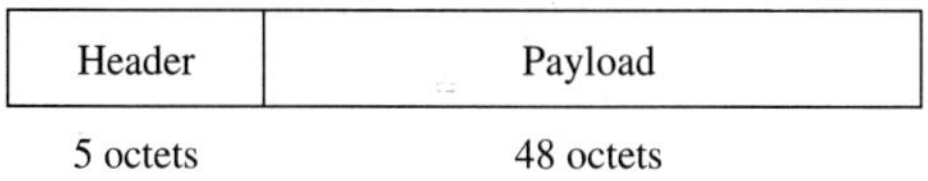

Header	Payload
5 octets	48 octets

FIGURE 10-13   An ATM cell.

ATM CELLS

The fundamental building block of an ATM link is a 53-byte cell. In ATM, and in telecommunications in general, bytes are often referred to as *octets*. The word *cell* is just a different name for a group of data bits, just as the words *packet* and *frame* are used in other standards. The word *cell* is generally used only with respect to the 53 bytes found in ATM.

The 53-byte cell is made up of two parts, the *header* and the *payload*, as shown in Fig. 10-13. The header consists of 5 octets, and the payload consists of the remaining 48 octets. Depending on the type of data being sent, the 48 octets may contain additional overhead to help partition and reassemble longer messages, so that the user may be able to utilize as few as 44 octets of each cell.

There are different types of headers, depending on the endpoints on each link. For example, one type of header is used at the *User–Network Interface*, or *UNI*, where customer-premises equipment connects to a provider network. Another type of header is used at the *Network–Network Interface*, or *NNI*, where two provider networks are connected together. While the detailed formats of the headers are not important for our discussion, it is important to know that there are different formats, depending on the type of interface.

PHYSICAL TRANSMISSION IN ATM

The asynchronous part of ATM does not refer to the physical transmission of the bits. In fact, the bits are transmitted synchronously. Rather, it refers to the fact that the arrival of the next cell is not at a predictable, fixed rate, much as characters arrive at any time in asynchronous data transmission.

How is it possible to send a synchronous bit stream composed of asynchronously arriving cells? Consider the bit stream to be continuous, but the data sporadic. There are two methods used to maintain the continuous bit stream. If no user data needs to be transmitted, then either a special pattern of bits representing an idle line can be sent or idle cells can be transmitted. The receiver gets a continuous stream of bits, some of it cells containing user payloads and others representing idle time, either in the form of idle bits or idle cells. The physical transmission medium can impose other overhead bits to separate timing from data and to help position cells within the continuous bit stream.

Many different telecommunications network standards for transmitting data at high speeds would be suitable for carrying ATM cells. Already mentioned was the T-3 rate of 45 Mbps. The *Synchronous Optical Network* standard, or *SONET*, is an ANSI

Rate	OC	STS	SDH
51.84 Mbps	OC-1	STS-1	n/a
155.52 Mbps	OC-3	STS-3	STM-1
622.08 Mbps	OC-12	STS-12	STM-4
1.24416 Gbps	OC-24	STS-24	STM-8
2.48832 Gbps	OC-48	STS-48	STM-16
9.95328 Gbps	OC-192	STS-192	STM-64

FIGURE 10-14 Some synchronous transmission standards.

standard commonly discussed as a transmission method for ATM. Line speeds in SONET are usually designated by the term *Optical Carrier-N*, or *OC-N*, where N × 51.84 Mbps is the speed of the line. For example, *OC-1* refers to a 51.84 Mbps speed, *OC-3* refers to 155.52 Mbps, and *OC-12* refers to 622.08 Mbps. OC-3 is literally the combination of three OC-1 signals, and OC-12 is made up of twelve OC-1s. The electrical equivalent of the OC-*N* signals is referred to as *Synchronous Transport Signal-N*, or *STS-N*. The data carried is the same in both cases, but when it is in optical form, we use the OC-N label, and we reserve STS-N for the electrical transmission. When a circuit is being used as a single channel, we add a "c," for *concatenated*, to the end of the label. For example, OC-3c means that we use the entire bandwidth of 155.52 Mbps as a single channel, rather than as three separate 51.84 Mbps channels.

These OC-N/STS-N signals are similar to the ITU(CCITT) standard known as *Synchronous Digital Hierarchy*, or *SDH*. The lowest multiple available in SDH is 155.52 Mbps. These signals are labeled as *Synchronous Transport Module-N*, or *STM-N*, where N is the number of multiples used. For example, the OC-3 speed of 155.52 Mbps would be the equivalent of an *STM-1*. The relationships between some common speeds and the standards that apply are shown in Fig. 10-14.

SONET and SDH provide physical transmission paths on which ATM cells can be transmitted, but can also be used to transfer information in other formats, including traditional circuit-switched digital voice. SONET and SDH, however, provide conveniently available high-speed paths that offer the bandwidth needed for advanced applications. There are numerous other standards, including T-1, T-3, 25 Mbps, and 100 Mbps standards, that could also serve as the physical pipe carrying ATM cells. Undoubtedly, many other standards will evolve, especially at the UNI, to meet the widely varying bandwidth demands of users. ATM can operate at any speed, making it a very flexible technology that can fit any application, and can take advantage of future improvements in transmission methods.

ROUTING CELLS IN AN ATM NETWORK

In Chapter 8, we discussed packet switching networks in detail. Some of the characteristics of traditional packet switching networks that made voice transmission impractical were the long delays and the uncertainty of route. Since packet #3 might arrive before packet #2, an additional delay might occur at the destination while the packets are resequenced.

ATM does not have this resequencing problem, since all cells follow the same route. There are also several assumptions in ATM that help reduce the delay to a bare minimum. First, it is assumed that the underlying transmission media is digital in nature and is relatively error free. Therefore, ATM does not require the link-error recovery found in protocols like X.25. The lowest layer of the network assumes that the data arrives without errors and relies on higher layers at the source and destination to rectify any problems with data integrity, if necessary. Some basic error checks are performed on the header to ensure that the cell is not misrouted, but the user data is not checked inside the ATM switches.

With the assumption of no payload errors and the guarantee that all cells follow the same route, the major remaining causes for delay are travel distance and the time spent in each node of the network. The travel distance cannot be avoided and would be present in a traditional circuit-switched network as well. So the key is to minimize the routing time at each node. ATM switches accomplish this by establishing the route for cells at the beginning of each conversation. Once the routing decision is made for a call, the individual switches can be preprogrammed with instructions for handling cells for the duration of the conversation. When cells do arrive at an ATM switch, the switching can be performed mostly by hardware, because the routing decision has been made in advance and stored in a table in each switch. The ATM switch checks the header of the incoming cell, and based on this header, looks up the correct port on which to transmit the cell on the next leg of its journey. As the cell is transmitted, the header can be modified at each step, to point to the correct entry in the table in the following switch.

The header consists of *Virtual Channel Identifiers*, or *VCIs*, and *Virtual Path Identifiers*, or *VPIs*, which are modified as necessary by each node in the network to ensure proper transmission of the cell to its destination. Rather than each node making an independent routing decision, as in traditional packet switching, the nodes simply follow their preprogrammed instructions and modify the VPIs and VCIs accordingly as they transmit the message.

In some ways, ATM is similar to the frame relay method discussed in Chapter 8. They both assume inherently reliable physical networks and therefore have minimal error recovery in the network. However, ATM relies on fixed cell sizes, while frame relay allows for various frame lengths. ATM also has different data formats to accommodate a wide variety of message types, including voice, video, and data, while frame relay is largely a data transport mechanism. One significant difference between an ATM network and a frame relay network is that ATM is very well suited to carry *isochronous* traffic. In the case of voice traffic, this means that the approximate timing between cells, as well as the order of the cells, is maintained as the cells flow through the network. If 53-byte cells were placed into the network at a certain rate, they would come out at roughly the same rate, in exactly the same order. If the cells had a 3 msec gap between them when they entered an ATM network, they would have approximately a 3 msec gap when they leave the network. While a frame relay network with little or no traffic might perform this way by chance, an ATM network has special timing mechanisms to increase the likelihood that this performance happens. This factor makes ATM networks ideally suited to voice and video communications.

VIDEO TRANSMISSION AND ATM

While ATM might provide an infrastructure for transmitting video, it says little about how to turn video images into ones and zeroes. The MPEG standard discussed earlier in this chapter is an excellent example of a digitization technique for video that will be carried on ATM networks. Since ATM is scalable in terms of speed, it certainly could accommodate video signals of varying quality, depending on the bandwidth the user is willing to pay for. While compression techniques and algorithms may improve, this improvement does not affect ATM itself, because the digitized video is merely the payload carried on the ATM network.

ATM AND THE OSI MODEL

One can think of ATM as providing service at least at Layers 1 and 2 of the OSI model. However, some higher layer activities, like routing, do occur on an ATM network as well. Most users treat ATM as a physical link, ignoring the internals of the network, and add higher layer protocols to ensure the integrity of the network. If the user is comfortable with the reliability of the digital links, then OSI Layers 1 and 2 can be considered satisfied by ATM and the underlying links, and only OSI Layers 3 and 4 need to be considered to complete the transport picture. One good example of ATM use is to interconnect LANs with routers using an ATM network between them; TCP/IP can then be used as the OSI Layers 4 and 3 protocols, with ATM as the underlying service for OSI Layers 2 and 1.

ATM LAYERS

The ATM standard itself describes its functions in three layers, as shown in Fig. 10-15. These layers are not identical to the first three layers of the OSI model. The lowest layer is the *Physical Layer*, where the cells are actually transmitted. This layer is similar to OSI Layer 1, although it transmits cells, rather than individual bits. The cells transmitted over a standard such as SONET make up this Physical Layer. The next layer is the *ATM Layer*, which is responsible for handling the mechanics of cell transport. This job includes separating cells from different connections, reading and interpreting the headers, and routing information. The ATM Layer is responsible for manipulating the VPI and VCIs as the cells travel through the network to direct them to their destination. The highest layer is the *ATM Adaptation Layer*, or *AAL*, which breaks down user data into 48-octet payloads so that it can be packaged into cells and then reassembles the cells into the original data stream at the destination. The AAL may also perform other functions, depending on the service required of the ATM network.

ATM CAPACITY ISSUES

Theoretically, an ATM network could accommodate any mix of voice, video, and data traffic, as long as the user does not exceed the bandwidth of the physical link to the

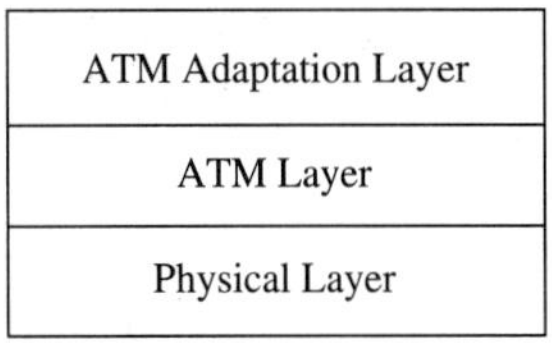

| ATM Adaptation Layer |
| ATM Layer |
| Physical Layer |

FIGURE 10-15   Layers in ATM.

network. It can even handle a source of data that varies in speed, often referred to as *variable bit rate* data.

ATM is particularly useful when combining data from many sources. For example, a user with a 64 kbps voice connection, a 10 Mbps Ethernet data stream, and a 7 Mbps compressed video transmission would have no problem breaking these messages into ATM cells and transmitting them on the same 45 Mbps ATM link. A large pipe, through which users can transmit data at varying rates, provides *bandwidth on demand*. ATM exhibits this characteristic in theory, but in practice, there are limitations.

The network may have the bandwidth to receive all of these messages over the initial pipe, but the capability to transmit them across the entire network can be limited by other factors. For example, a highway on-ramp might support 60 cars per minute entering an empty highway. But at rush hour, there might already be so many cars on the highway that only 10 per minute can enter and find a place on the highway. So network capacity may not always be available, even though your link to the network may have the available bandwidth.

To understand ATM's capacity issues, it is useful to contrast ATM with traditional voice networking, like T-1, or even Narrowband ISDN's B-channel service, both of which require the establishment of fixed channels. These 64 kbps channels are reserved for an entire call, whether or not anyone is talking or anything is being transmitted. Similarly, several of these 64 kbps channels are sometimes grouped together to provide medium-quality videoconferencing. In both cases, these are circuit-switched connections. Once a call is established, the channel is allocated and the bandwidth is reserved.

Rather than establishing fixed B-channels for the duration of the voice or video call, ATM simply accepts cells on one side of the network and delivers them to the other side. A video call would naturally generate many more cells than a voice call would. The variable bandwidth demand of ATM is harder to predict than the simple 64 kbps required for a voice connection in traditional networks, so the carriers running the network are faced with an interesting dilemma. Should the network be sized to accommodate low-bandwidth voice calls, high-bandwidth video calls, or both at the same time? In between are data calls, requiring a wide range of bandwidth, from a simple electronic mail message to a database file containing many megabytes. This classic statistical multiplexing problem is not caused by ATM, but by the variability of the traffic requirements. The network used must be prepared for any combination of traffic from 64 kbps up to the speed of the physical link, perhaps as high as many gigabits per second.

ATM TARIFF ISSUES

Pricing ATM appropriately is a problem plaguing many carriers hoping to deliver commercially viable service. While traditional networks priced voice calls based on distance, connection time, and time of day, ATM must also consider the type of service provided. For example, a video call will clearly cost more than a voice call, but the price will not be directly proportional to the number of bits transmitted.

A two-hour movie, transmitted using MPEG II video and requiring 7 Mbps, is approximately 50.4 gigabits. Assuming a $3.00 charge to view this movie results in a cost of roughly six cents per gigabit. With voice at 64 kbps, you could speak for four hours and 20 minutes before reaching 1 gigabit. No one expects the carriers to offer this voice call for six cents, because the number of bits transmitted is only one of the many factors that will be part of ATM rates.

Carriers will need to strike a balance between call setup, quality of service or bandwidth, call duration, and time-of-day usage charges. One possibility is the notion of the bandwidth contract, where users pay a certain rate to guarantee availability of a given bandwidth, but can burst to higher speeds when there is additional demand and the network has space available. Premium rates could be charged for bursting above your guaranteed rate at high traffic times.

Issues such as traffic, congestion control, and tariffs will probably be refined during deployment of these networks. Clearly, today's approaches to traffic, congestion control, and tariffs as used in circuit-switched networks are not appropriate to handle the wide range of bandwidth possible in the ATM networks of the future.

THE INFORMATION SUPERHIGHWAY

What is the *information superhighway* so often discussed in the media today? To some, it is the promise of Broadband ISDN, with its possibility for efficient sharing of bandwidth to allow for cost-effective transmission of voice, video, and data. To others, the information superhighway is today's Internet, with its wide array of databases attached to a relatively low-speed network. Will ATM networks extend to residences, or will cable modems, DSL services, and Narrowband ISDN provide local access to wide area networks? The answer to this question depends largely on the speeds and services the users demand and the prices charged by the competing telephone and cable companies.

As the 21st century begins, there is no need to choose between IP and ATM networks. In fact, it is clear that the two will coexist for some time. Most voice carriers have chosen ATM as the transmission technology behind their voice networks. IP has been chosen by local area and wide area networks as the standard for data communications networks. IP network standards continue to evolve and eventually will offer many of the features for guaranteeing bandwidth that isochronous ATM networks do. Conceivably, we could continue forever with separate networks for voice, video, and data communications, but most people expect the technologies to continue to converge.

There are definitely two strong points of view in the industry on the direction that this *convergence* will take, though probably neither technology will conquer the other. If we were starting with a blank piece of paper and no networks existed, ATM would clearly win, since it carries all types of traffic with ease. Since IP networks are widely deployed today, however, the problem is not so easy. If data traffic were to continue to grow to the point that it was far greater than voice or video traffic, it might be practical to base the world's communications networks solely on IP. A small portion of the IP networks could be set aside to carry voice and video traffic. Since IP doesn't provide the features required to reliably carry isochronous traffic in its current IPv4 implementations, newer versions would need to be deployed and equipment changed or reprogrammed. Alternatively, IP could be used as the local access technology for data users, with the IP datagrams stuffed into ATM cells over the wide area networks that carried voice, video, and data traffic. Voice technology could utilize ISDN as the local access technology, while carriers could convert the B-channels to ATM cells for the wide area. Real networks are being deployed today utilizing all of these techniques.

Of all the emerging technologies discussed in the broadcast and print media in the last two decades, no three words have been so often misunderstood and misinterpreted as "the information superhighway." It is precisely the vagueness of the term that allows readers to use their imaginations to project almost any network applications onto these words. To the nontechnical, the words may conjure up the possibility of instant access to libraries around the world. To those already accustomed to computers and databases, this image seems a trivial exercise, so they imagine instead that integrated video and data communications between multimedia workstations will take place over the information superhighway.

Interestingly enough, most people discuss what is at the end of the highway, rather than the highway itself. The exciting new multimedia databases that can be accessed from the information superhighway are typical examples and garner much more public attention than IP protocols or any ATM congestion-control scheme ever will. This new marvel of technology, a high-bandwidth network, is not as impressive to the general public as what gets attached to it.

In a sense, we have returned to the origin of telecommunications. Surely, neither Samuel Morse nor Alexander Graham Bell was able to interest the general public in the voltages on their transmission lines. Rather, it was the potential uses of the information that could now be transmitted that acted as the motivating force to lay the infrastructure for the new technologies. Just as users of early telephones could not even begin to imagine the pervasive role of telecommunications in today's world, we cannot predict all of the applications of a Broadband ISDN network.

So, as standards committees continue to ponder the future of data communications, new technologies are sure to emerge. The driving force behind the implementation of these networks of the future will be the potential applications rather than the technology itself.

SUMMARY

As the 21st century begins, telecommunications and data communications are converging. Both customer-premises equipment and transmission facilities are increasingly using digital technology. Digital PBXs are being used to integrate voice and data with digital phones. LANs and PBXs can be connected to packet switching networks, frame relay networks, and IP networks, allowing communications among devices attached to any of them. In addition, transmission of still images, using fax, or moving images, using video, once performed only by analog transmission methods, can now be done digitally. Digital transmission of voice is possible by using a digitizing method known as pulse code modulation, or PCM. In PCM, an analog signal is typically converted to a 64 kbps digital signal, using 8000 samples per second and eight bits per sample.

High-bandwidth digital transmission facilities are playing a major role in communications today. The T-1 standard, developed by AT&T, provides a 1.544 Mbps digital path now available from almost all of the common carriers. T-1 carrier can provide 24 channels, each able to carry 64 kbps of digitized voice or 56 kbps of data over two twisted pairs; analog transmission of 24 voice channels would require 24 pairs of wires.

Even with the added expense of repeaters and digital transmission equipment, T-1 is an economical alternative for users with high-volume communications traffic. There are several different methods for carrying signaling information using T-1 carrier. The T-1 channels can also be broken down into several lower speed channels by submultiplexing. In addition, voice and data compression can further increase the effective bandwidth of T-1 circuits. Finally, there are higher speed digital transmission facilities than T-1, such as T-1C and T-3, providing 48 and 672 channels, respectively.

The Integrated Services Digital Network, or ISDN, is a set of standards for a digital network carrying both voice and data communications. The ITU(CCITT) led the international standards development effort, specifying both interface standards for connecting to the public network and network services. ISDN provides different types of transmission paths, known as channels. The B-channel, or bearer channel, is a 64 kbps digital channel for digitized voice or data. The D-channel is a 16 kbps or 64 kbps digital channel used for signaling information and sometimes for low-priority data packets. The A-channel is similar to today's analog voice circuits, and the C-channel provides a low-speed 16 kbps data channel for use with low-speed devices.

The basic-rate interface includes 2 B-channels and 1 D-channel and is intended for residential or individual business users; this interface provides voice and data communications, as well as extensive signaling capability, for an individual user. The primary-rate interface contains 23 or 30 B-channels and 1 D-channel and is aimed primarily at larger business users. The 23 B+D version is intended for use in North America and Japan, where the 1.544 Mbps T-1 carrier is already prevalent, and the 30 B+D version is intended for use in Europe, where 2.048 Mbps transmission equipment currently exists. The hybrid interface contains both an A-channel and a C-channel and provides analog phone users with some of the benefits of ISDN.

Equipment attached to an ISDN network is classified into two basic categories: Terminal Equipment (TE) and Network Termination equipment (NT). In addition, several reference points are defined where various NT and TE devices are interconnected. Terminal equipment compatible with ISDN is known as TE1; terminal equipment not compatible with ISDN is known as TE2 and can be attached to an ISDN network using a Terminal Adapter, or TA. The R reference point is between the TE2 and TA, and the S reference point is between the TE1, or TA, and NT equipment. The NT equipment providing OSI Layer 1 services and terminating the network circuit on the customer's premises is known as NT1; OSI Layer 2 and 3 services, providing concentration and switching if needed, can be provided by NT2. Both the NT1 and NT2 functions can be combined in a single device, known as NT12. The point between the NT1 and NT2 (if an NT2 is used) is known as the T reference point; if no NT2 is used, then the S and T reference points coincide where the NT1 is directly connected to the Terminal Equipment. The U reference point occurs where the NT1 connects to the rest of the ISDN network.

PBXs and LANs can take advantage of an ISDN network's digital transmission facilities. However, to further motivate users to support ISDN, special services are provided. Many of these services are based on the extra signaling information available in the D-channel. The Signaling System 7, or SS7, is used to pass this information through the ISDN network. ISDN services can include call waiting, call forwarding, calling-party identification, camp-on, and message notification.

It is clear that ISDN can provide functional advantages to certain business users at a reasonable cost within existing technology. ISDN is already being implemented in the United States through National ISDN and in Europe through EuroISDN, though mainly for business users. Always On/Dynamic ISDN, or AO/DI, is particularly useful for remote access to corporate LANs or the Internet. The real potential of the residential market is not yet understood, and a completely digital telephone network may never be realized.

Digital Subscriber Line, or DSL, provides numerous ways to connect the user to the central office by digitally using twisted pair wire. Speeds vary from hundreds of kbps all the way to many Mbps, depending on the transmission option chosen. Many DSL implementations are asymmetric, offering higher transmission speeds from the central office to the user than in the other direction. Most cable modems also offer an asymmetric, high-speed data connection, typically offering speeds as high as 30 Mbps in the high-speed direction and a few Mbps in the low-speed direction. Both DSL and cable modem services are ideal for connecting residential users to the Internet or to the corporate LAN.

Broadband ISDN, or BISDN, an even-faster class of interface standards, is currently being deployed. BISDN, which can handle higher transmission speeds, can easily carry digitized video transmission, along with digitized voice and data. A mixture of fiber optic and copper cable is being used for BISDN. The transmission technology that is used to implement BISDN is Asynchronous Transfer Mode, or ATM. ATM fragments data into fixed-size chunks, or cells, so that voice, video, data, or any other information can be sent over the same network. The ATM Forum is promoting the rapid development and deployment of the ATM specification. ISO, ITU(CCITT), and ANSI have all recognized ATM as the standard of choice for BISDN.

The 53-octet ATM cell is made up of a 5-octet header and a 48-octet payload. One type of header is used at the User–Network Interface, or UNI, where customer-premises equipment connects to a provider network. Another type of header is used at the Network–Network Interface, or NNI, where two provider networks are connected together.

In ATM, the bits are transmitted synchronously, although the cells may not always arrive at a fixed rate. Synchronous Optical Network, or SONET, is an ANSI standard commonly discussed as a transmission method for ATM. Line speeds in SONET are usually designated by the term Optical Carrier-N, or OC-N, with electrical equivalents referred to as Synchronous Transport Signal-N, or STS-N. These OC-N and STS-N signals are similar to the ITU(CCITT) standard known as Synchronous Digital Hierarchy, or SDH. Other transmission methods are also possible.

ATM establishes the route for cells at the beginning of each conversation. When cells arrive at an ATM switch, the switching can be performed mostly by hardware, since the routing decision has been made in advance and stored in a table residing in each switch. Based on the header of the incoming cell, the ATM switch looks up the correct port on which to transmit the cell on the next leg of its journey. The header consists of Virtual Channel Identifiers, or VCIs, and Virtual Path Identifiers, or VPIs, which are modified as required by each node in the network to ensure proper transmission of the cell to its destination. ATM networks have special timing mechanisms that make them ideal for isochronous traffic.

ATM provides service at least at Layers 1 and 2 of the OSI model, though some higher layer activities, such as routing, are included. The ATM standard itself describes its functions in three layers: the Physical Layer, the ATM Layer, and the ATM Adaptation Layer, or AAL. A cell relay network such as ATM presents a variety of capacity, traffic, and tariff issues far different from those encountered with a circuit-switched network. ATM and IP networks will continue to coexist for years to come.

TERMS FOR REVIEW

AAL
A-channel
ADSL
ADSL Lite
Always On/Dynamic ISDN
AO/DI
Asymmetric Digital
  Subscriber Line
Asynchronous Transfer
  Mode
ATM
ATM Adaptation Layer
ATM Forum
ATM Layer
Bandwidth on Demand
Basic-rate interface
B-channel
Bearer channel
BISDN
BRI
Broadband ISDN
Cable modem
Caller ID
C-channel
Cell
Channel
Combined Network
  Termination 1 and 2
Common-channel signaling
Concatenated
Convergence
D-channel
Digital phone
Digital Subscriber Line

Digitized
DSL
DSL Lite
DS-1
EuroISDN
Fiber to the curb
Fiber to the feeder
Fiber to the home
Fiber to the neighborhood
Fiber to the premises
Fiber to the vault
Fractional T-1
Frame
Framing bit
G.Lite
G.711
HDSL
HDSL2
HDTV
Header
High-bit-rate Digital
  Subscriber Line
High-Definition Television
Hybrid interface
In-band signaling
Information superhighway
Integrated Services Digital
  Network
Integrated voice/data
  terminal
ISDN
Isochronous
IVDT
Loading coil

Moving Pictures Expert
  Group
MPEG
MPEG II
Multimedia
Multirate ISDN
N × 64
Narrowband ISDN
National ISDN
Network–Network Interface
Network Termination
  equipment
Network Termination 1
Network Termination 2
NNI
NT
NT1
NT2
NT12
OC-N
OC-1
OC-3
OC-12
Octet
Optical Carrier-N
Out-of-band signaling
Payload
PCM
Physical layer
PRI
Primary-rate interface
Pulse code modulation
R reference point
RADSL

Rate-Adaptive Digital
   Subscriber Line
Robbed-bit signaling
S reference point
Sample
SDH
SDSL
Signaling System 7
Single-line Digital
   Subscriber Line
SONET
SS7
STM-1
STM-N
STS-N
Submultiplexing
Synchronization
Synchronous Digital
   Hierarchy
Synchronous Optical
   Network

Synchronous Transport
   Module-N
Synchronous Transport
   Signal-N
T reference point
T-1C
T-1 carrier
T-1 multiplexer
T-1/D1
T-1/D2
T-1/D3
T-1/D4
T-1/D5
T-3
TA
TE
TE1
TE2
Terminal Adapter
Terminal Equipment
Terminal Equipment Type 1

Terminal Equipment Type 2
30 B + D
23 B + D
2 B + D
U reference point
UADSL
UNI
Universal Asymmetric Digital
   Subscriber Line
User–Network Interface
Variable bit rate
VCI
VDSL
Very-high-bit-rate Digital
   Subscriber Line
Video transmission
Virtual Channel Identifier
Virtual Path Identifier
VPI
xDSL

EXERCISES

10-1. What are some examples of digital customer-premises equipment?

10-2. Explain how pulse code modulation can be used to digitize voice.

10-3. What is the total bandwidth of a T-1 circuit? What portion of this bandwidth is dedicated to framing and synchronization?

10-4. What are the advantages of using a T-1 circuit instead of 24 analog leased lines for PBX-to-PBX communications?

10-5. Why is submultiplexing sometimes used with T-1?

10-6. What are the names, functions, and bandwidths of the major ISDN channels?

10-7. What are the two major digital interfaces specified in the ISDN standards? What combination of channels are used in each? What are their intended functions?

10-8. Compare the different types of ISDN Terminal Equipment and their functions.

10-9. How do the functions of the various types of ISDN Network Termination equipment correspond to the lower layers of the OSI model?

10-10. Why is a service like caller name identification possible in ISDN, but not in today's analog public network?

10-11. What is the major difference between Narrowband and Broadband ISDN?

10-12. What is ATM? What are the layers of ATM?

10-13. What is DSL? What makes ADSL different than a traditional digital phone line?

10-14. What is a cable modem?

A P P E N D I X

The Binary Number System

In the binary number system, all numbers are represented using only zeroes and ones. Computers typically use the binary number system to represent information, because it is easy for computer hardware to represent an off/on, or 0/1 condition.

The binary number system is based on powers of two, while the more familiar decimal number system is based on powers of ten. There are many charts available for converting decimal numbers to binary numbers, and vice versa. However, they are crutches that most people can do without. Like multiplication tables, they are a useful learning tool, but no one wants to have to consult a multiplication table every time they want to multiply.

Fortunately, converting numbers between the binary number system and decimal number system is an easy task. We first examine the decimal number system, and then the binary number system.

In the decimal number system, the digits 0, 1, 2, 3, 4, 5, 6, 7, 8, and 9 are used to represent all numbers. Each place or position in a number has a value that is a power of ten. The value of the first place is 1 or 10^0, the value of the second is 10 or 10^1, the value of the third is 100 or 10^2, the value of the fourth is 1000 or 10^3, and so on. For example, in the decimal number system, the number 5048 is really 5 times 1000, plus 0 times 100, plus 4 times 10, plus 8 times 1.

In the binary number system, numbers are represented in the same way, but powers of two are used for the places, and only a 0 or a 1 is used for each digit. Each place or position in a number has a value that is a power of two. The value of the first place is 1 or 2^0, the value of the second is 2 or 2^1, the value of the third is 4 or 2^2, the value of the fourth is 8 or 2^3, and so on. For example, in the binary number system, the number 1011 is 1 times 8, plus 0 times 4, plus 1 times 2, plus 1 times 1.

We consider only binary numbers up to eight bits long to simplify our discussion, although the same principles are applicable for any size number. In an eight-bit binary number, the place values are as follows:

Digits								
Values	128	64	32	16	8	4	2	1
Powers	2^7	2^6	2^5	2^4	2^3	2^2	2^1	2^0

The eight-bit number 10010110 could be placed in these positions this way:

Digits	1	0	0	1	0	1	1	0
Values	128	64	32	16	8	4	2	1
Powers	2^7	2^6	2^5	2^4	2^3	2^2	2^1	2^0

This number could be converted to decimal simply by multiplying the digits by the values and adding the results:

$(1 \times 128) + (0 \times 64) + (0 \times 32) + (1 \times 16) + (0 \times 8) + (1 \times 4) + (1 \times 2) + (0 \times 1) =$
128   +   0   +   0   +   16   +   0   +   4   +   2   +   0   =   150

For another example, consider the binary number 11101101:

Digits	1	1	1	0	1	1	0	1
Values	128	64	32	16	8	4	2	1
Powers	2^7	2^6	2^5	2^4	2^3	2^2	2^1	2^0

This number could be converted to decimal simply by multiplying the digits by the values and adding the results:

$(1 \times 128) + (1 \times 64) + (1 \times 32) + (0 \times 16) + (1 \times 8) + (1 \times 4) + (0 \times 2) + (1 \times 1) =$
128   +   64   +   32   +   0   +   8   +   4   +   0   +   1   =   237

Using eight bits, the binary number system can represent decimal numbers from 0 to 255. 0 in decimal converts to eight zeroes in binary, and 255 converts to eight ones in binary. Anything larger requires more bits. Any binary number can be converted to a decimal number using the addition and multiplication technique shown above.

Converting decimal numbers to binary numbers requires only subtraction, and a simple decision: Is one number greater than or equal to another? For example, to convert the decimal number 185 to binary form, we must start at the left of our binary number form shown below:

Digits								
Values	128	64	32	16	8	4	2	1
Powers	2^7	2^6	2^5	2^4	2^3	2^2	2^1	2^0

We then ask the question "Is 185 greater than or equal to 128?", the value of the digit on the left of our form. The answer is yes, so we need 128 in the number 185, and we use a 1 for that digit, as shown below:

Digits	1							
Values	*128*	*64*	*32*	*16*	*8*	*4*	*2*	*1*
Powers	2^7	2^6	2^5	2^4	2^3	2^2	2^1	2^0

We then subtract 128 from 185, leaving us with 57. We now ask the question, "Is 57 greater than or equal to 64?", the value of the next digit. The answer is no, so we don't need 64 in the number 185, and we use a 0 for this digit, as shown below:

Digits	1	0						
Values	*128*	*64*	*32*	*16*	*8*	*4*	*2*	*1*
Powers	2^7	2^6	2^5	2^4	2^3	2^2	2^1	2^0

Since we didn't use 64, there is no subtraction necessary. We then ask the question, "Is 57 greater than or equal to 32?", the value of the next digit. The answer is yes, so we need 32 in the number 185, and we use a 1 for that digit, as shown below:

Digits	1	0	1					
Values	*128*	*64*	*32*	*16*	*8*	*4*	*2*	*1*
Powers	2^7	2^6	2^5	2^4	2^3	2^2	2^1	2^0

We then subtract 32 from 57, leaving us with 25. We now ask the question, "Is 25 greater than or equal to 16?", the value of the next digit. The answer is yes, so we need 16 in the number 185, and we use a 1 for this digit, as shown below:

Digits	1	0	1	1				
Values	*128*	*64*	*32*	*16*	*8*	*4*	*2*	*1*
Powers	2^7	2^6	2^5	2^4	2^3	2^2	2^1	2^0

We then subtract 16 from 25, leaving us with 9. We now ask the question, "Is 9 greater than or equal to 8?", the value of the next digit. The answer is yes, so we need 8 in the number 185, and we use a 1 for this digit, as shown below:

Digits	1	0	1	1	1			
Values	*128*	*64*	*32*	*16*	*8*	*4*	*2*	*1*
Powers	2^7	2^6	2^5	2^4	2^3	2^2	2^1	2^0

We then subtract 8 from 9, leaving us with 1. We now ask the question, "Is 1 greater than or equal to 4?", the value of the next digit. The answer is no, so we don't need 4 in the number 185, and we use a 0 for this digit, as follows:

Digits	1	0	1	1	1	0		
Values	*128*	*64*	*32*	*16*	*8*	*4*	*2*	*1*
Powers	2^7	2^6	2^5	2^4	2^3	2^2	2^1	2^0

Since we didn't use 4, there is no subtraction necessary. We now ask the question, "Is 1 greater than or equal to 2?", the value of the next digit. The answer is no, so we don't need 2 in the number 185, and we use a 0 for this digit, as shown below:

Digits	1	0	1	1	1	0	0	
Values	*128*	*64*	*32*	*16*	*8*	*4*	*2*	*1*
Powers	2^7	2^6	2^5	2^4	2^3	2^2	2^1	2^0

Since we didn't use 2, there is no subtraction necessary. We now ask the question, "Is 1 greater than or equal to 1?", the value of the next digit. The answer is yes, so we need 1 in the number 185, and we use a 1 for this digit, as shown below:

Digits	1	0	1	1	1	0	0	1
Values	*128*	*64*	*32*	*16*	*8*	*4*	*2*	*1*
Powers	2^7	2^6	2^5	2^4	2^3	2^2	2^1	2^0

We then subtract 1 from 1, leaving us with 0, so we know we have accounted for all of the values in the number 185. If our result is not zero at this point, we know that we made an error in our calculation, or the number we chose is too large to be represented in eight bits (greater than the decimal number 255).

Based on our calculations, the binary number 10111001 is the equivalent of the decimal number 185. As a double check, let's convert it back to decimal:

$$(1 \times 128) + (0 \times 64) + (1 \times 32) + (1 \times 16) + (1 \times 8) + (0 \times 4) + (0 \times 2) + (1 \times 1) =$$
$$128 \quad + \quad 0 \quad + \quad 32 \quad + \quad 16 \quad + \quad 8 \quad + \quad 0 \quad + \quad 0 \quad + \quad 1 \quad = \quad 185$$

Converting between the binary and decimal number systems is a matter of following a simple set of rules. It allows us to easily convert between the decimal world we are familiar with, and the binary world of computers.

For those who prefer to use a chart rather than performing the simple calculations, a conversion chart is provided for the decimal numbers from 0 to 255.

CONVERTING BETWEEN THE DECIMAL AND BINARY NUMBER SYSTEMS

Binary	Dec.	Binary	Dec.	Binary	Dec.	Binary	Dec.	Binary	Dec.
00000000	0	00110101	53	01101010	106	10011111	159	11010100	212
00000001	1	00110110	54	01101011	107	10100000	160	11010101	213
00000010	2	00110111	55	01101100	108	10100001	161	11010110	214
00000011	3	00111000	56	01101101	109	10100010	162	11010111	215
00000100	4	00111001	57	01101110	110	10100011	163	11011000	216
00000101	5	00111010	58	01101111	111	10100100	164	11011001	217
00000110	6	00111011	59	01110000	112	10100101	165	11011010	218
00000111	7	00111100	60	01110001	113	10100110	166	11011011	219
00001000	8	00111101	61	01110010	114	10100111	167	11011100	220
00001001	9	00111110	62	01110011	115	10101000	168	11011101	221
00001010	10	00111111	63	01110100	116	10101001	169	11011110	222
00001011	11	01000000	64	01110101	117	10101010	170	11011111	223
00001100	12	01000001	65	01110110	118	10101011	171	11100000	224
00001101	13	01000010	66	01110111	119	10101100	172	11100001	225
00001110	14	01000011	67	01111000	120	10101101	173	11100010	226
00001111	15	01000100	68	01111001	121	10101110	174	11100011	227
00010000	16	01000101	69	01111010	122	10101111	175	11100100	228
00010001	17	01000110	70	01111011	123	10110000	176	11100101	229
00010010	18	01000111	71	01111100	124	10110001	177	11100110	230
00010011	19	01001000	72	01111101	125	10110010	178	11100111	231
00010100	20	01001001	73	01111110	126	10110011	179	11101000	232
00010101	21	01001010	74	01111111	127	10110100	180	11101001	233
00010110	22	01001011	75	10000000	128	10110101	181	11101010	234
00010111	23	01001100	76	10000001	129	10110110	182	11101011	235
00011000	24	01001101	77	10000010	130	10110111	183	11101100	236
00011001	25	01001110	78	10000011	131	10111000	184	11101101	237
00011010	26	01001111	79	10000100	132	10111001	185	11101110	238
00011011	27	01010000	80	10000101	133	10111010	186	11101111	239
00011100	28	01010001	81	10000110	134	10111011	187	11110000	240
00011101	29	01010010	82	10000111	135	10111100	188	11110001	241
00011110	30	01010011	83	10001000	136	10111101	189	11110010	242
00011111	31	01010100	84	10001001	137	10111110	190	11110011	243
00100000	32	01010101	85	10001010	138	10111111	191	11110100	244
00100001	33	01010110	86	10001011	139	11000000	192	11110101	245
00100010	34	01010111	87	10001100	140	11000001	193	11110110	246
00100011	35	01011000	88	10001101	141	11000010	194	11110111	247
00100100	36	01011001	89	10001110	142	11000011	195	11111000	248
00100101	37	01011010	90	10001111	143	11000100	196	11111001	249
00100110	38	01011011	91	10010000	144	11000101	197	11111010	250
00100111	39	01011100	92	10010001	145	11000110	198	11111011	251
00101000	40	01011101	93	10010010	146	11000111	199	11111100	252
00101001	41	01011110	94	10010011	147	11001000	200	11111101	253
00101010	42	01011111	95	10010100	148	11001001	201	11111110	254
00101011	43	01100000	96	10010101	149	11001010	202	11111111	255
00101100	44	01100001	97	10010110	150	11001011	203		
00101101	45	01100010	98	10010111	151	11001100	204		
00101110	46	01100011	99	10011000	152	11001101	205		
00101111	47	01100100	100	10011001	153	11001110	206		
00110000	48	01100101	101	10011010	154	11001111	207		
00110001	49	01100110	102	10011011	155	11010000	208		
00110010	50	01100111	103	10011100	156	11010001	209		
00110011	51	01101000	104	10011101	157	11010010	210		
00110100	52	01101001	105	10011110	158	11010011	211		

Glossary

AAL *See* ATM Adaptation Layer.

Access method Means used to allow local area network users to transmit data.

Access Point A type of wireless LAN attached to a wired LAN using regular protocols, but utilizing a special Medium Access Control on the wireless part of the LAN.

A-channel The analog voice channel in ISDN.

Acknowledgment Typically used in protocols, it is sent by the receiving device to the transmitter to confirm successful receipt of data.

ACK0 In BSC, the control character indicating an acknowledgment.

Active monitor The station on a token ring network responsible for watching for the token and for generating a new token if the token is lost.

Ad hoc A type of wireless LAN containing only wireless users with no underlying wired LAN technology.

Adaptive bridge A type of bridge that can learn the locations of users and deliver messages accordingly based on their Layer 2 address. Also known as a learning bridge.

ADCCP *See* Advanced Data Communications Control Procedures.

Address Typically used to identify different devices, either in a polling and selecting environment or in a local area network.

Address Field The part of an SDLC frame containing the eight bits representing the identity of the Secondary station.

ADSL *See* Asymmetric Digital Subscriber Line.

ADSL Lite *See* Universal Asymmetric Digital Subscriber Line.

Advanced Data Communications Control Procedures (ADCCP) A bit-oriented ANSI protocol.

Advanced Mobile Phone Service (AMPS) A popular analog cellular system used in the United States, South America, Australia, China, and other countries.

Agent The remote partner to a central station, or manager, in a network management protocol.

Algorithm A set of instructions for performing a task.

Always On/Dynamic ISDN (AO/DI) Integrated Services Digital Network option that allows a continual D-channel connection, with the option to substitute higher bandwidth B-channels as traffic increases.

AM *See* Amplitude Modulation.

American National Standard Code for Information Interchange (ASCII) The ANSI seven-bit character code, with an eighth bit for parity checking.

American National Standards Institute (ANSI) An umbrella organization for all standards organizations in the United States. These organizations can submit standards to ANSI for acceptance as a national standard.

American Telephone & Telegraph (AT&T) Now a long-distance company, researcher, and equipment manufacturer; formerly, the parent company of the Bell System, which also included many local phone companies.

Amplitude The strength of an electronic signal (in volts), or the volume of a tone (in decibels).

Amplitude modulation (AM) Transmission of information by varying the volume of a tone (the amplitude of a sine wave).

Amplitude shift keying (ASK) Another name for amplitude modulation.

AMPS *See* Advanced Mobile Phone Service.

Analog A signal that can vary infinitely over a given range, like voice.

Analog cellular Traditional cell-based wireless telephone service, in which the signals are transmitted to users in analog form.

Analog test equipment Devices used to diagnose voice-grade telephone circuits.

ANSI *See* American National Standards Institute.

Answer-only modem A type of modem that can only receive calls.

AO/DI *See* Always On/Dynamic ISDN.

Applet Applications software that downloads when needed; typically used with a browser.

Application Layer Layer 7, the highest layer of the OSI model; it provides access to the network to the end user.

Application-level firewall A firewall that screens messages only for a particular application, like electronic mail.

Application Program In SNA, a software program running on a Host Processor that communicates through an SNA network.

Applications software User programs running on a host computer, such as word-processing programs, spreadsheets, and accounting programs.

Area code Three-digit code used in the public network to route calls to a particular geographical area.

ARPANET The packet switching network used to connect U.S. government computing facilities.

ARQ *See* Automatic Repeat Request.

ASCII *See* American National Standard Code for Information Interchange.

ASK Amplitude shift keying. *See* Amplitude modulation.

Asserted state The state of an RS-232-C control signal when it is ON, raised, or true.

Asymmetric Digital Subscriber Line (ADSL) A digital access technology that provides a link from the user to the central office over twisted pair wire that is higher speed in one direction than in the other.

Asymmetric keys An encryption technique that uses a different key to encrypt a message than is used to decrypt the message.

Asynchronous Transfer Mode (ATM) A technology used to fragment data into cells so that voice, video, data, or any other information can be sent over the same network. ATM is used to implement BISDN.

Asynchronous transmission Method of data transmission requiring start and stop bits.

AT&T *See* American Telephone & Telegraph.

AT&T Premises Distribution System AT&T's method for wiring office buildings with standard cable.

ATM *See* Asynchronous Transfer Mode.

ATM Adaptation Layer (AAL) The third layer in ATM, it breaks down user data into 48-octet payloads so that it can be packaged into cells and reassembles them at the destination; it can perform other functions, depending on the service required.

ATM Forum A group of member companies, organizations, and users whose sole purpose is to promote the rapid development and deployment of the ATM specification.

ATM Layer The second layer in ATM, it is responsible for handling the mechanics of cell transport.

Attendant Operator of a PBX console.

Automatic repeat request (ARQ) An error-control method in which the receiving device detects an error in data transmission and asks for a retransmission of the block of data.

Availability The ratio of uptime to the total of uptime and downtime.

Backoff The length of time a device waits after a collision occurs before attempting retransmission.

Balanced transmission A method of sending data requiring two wires, as in RS-422-A.

Bandwidth The carrying capacity of a circuit, usually measured in bits per second for digital circuits or Hertz for analog circuits.

Bandwidth on demand A term describing a large pipe through which users can transmit data at varying rates.

Baseband transmission Transmission of a data signal directly on a wire.

Basic-rate interface (BRI) The preferred method for attachment to ISDN by individual users; it includes two B-channels, one for digitized voice and one for data, and one D-channel for signaling.

Basic service element (BSE) A feature or service provided by the local exchange carrier to the public, as part of Open Network Architecture.

Baud rate The number of possible signal changes in a second; sometimes equivalent to the bit per second rate, but not always.

Baudot code One of the first character codes, it uses five bits to represent characters.

BCC In BSC, a block check character used for error detection.

BCD *See* Binary Coded Decimal.

B-channel The bearer channel in ISDN, it carries 64 kbps of digitized voice or data.

Bearer channel *See* B-channel.

Bell 103/113 AT&T's 300 bps frequency modulation method, now widely accepted as an industry standard.

Bell 212A AT&T's 1200 bps dibit phase-shift keying method, now widely accepted as an industry standard; it falls back to the Bell 103/113 300 bps frequency modulation method when communicating with Bell 103/113 modems.

Bell Communications Research The research arm of the RBOCs formed after divestiture, also known as Bellcore.

Bell Labs The research arm of AT&T.

Bell Operating Company (BOC) Individual local exchange carrier, previously owned by AT&T before divestiture.

Bell System The name used to designate the combination of the Bell Operating Companies and AT&T's long-distance business before it was broken up by divestiture.

Bellcore *See* Bell Communications Research.

BERT *See* Bit error rate test.

Best-effort delivery As found in IP, the network attempts to deliver the packet but does not guarantee that the packet will not be lost.

Binary Coded Decimal (BCD) An early character code used internally by computers to represent information.

Binary number system A numeric system based on powers of two; therefore, all numbers are represented using only the digits 0 and 1.

Binary Synchronous Communications (BSC) IBM's character-oriented (or byte-oriented) half duplex, stop-and-wait ARQ protocol.

BISDN *See* Broadband ISDN.

Bisync *See* Binary Synchronous Communications.

Bit A binary digit, either a 1 or a 0.

Bit error A transmission error in which a 1 is received as a 0, or vice versa.

Bit error rate test (BERT) An industry standard measure of reliability, it is the ratio of the number of bit errors detected to the total number of bits received.

Bit interleaving A time-division multiplexing method in which each time slot contains a bit from each channel.

Bit-oriented protocol A protocol using single bits for communicating control information.

Bits per second (bps) A typical measurement of data speed, it is the number of bits transmitted (or received) in a second.

BLERT *See* Block error rate test.

Block A group of characters, or bytes.

Block error rate test (BLERT) An industry-standard measure of reliability, it is the ratio of the number of block errors detected to the total number of blocks received.

BOC *See* Bell Operating Company.

Bps *See* Bits per second.

Branch port The low-speed port of a multiplexer, usually attached to the terminal or front-end processor.

Breakout box Test equipment used to monitor the interface status, determine if a device is a DTE or DCE, modify interfaces, and test cables.

Break-up The divestiture of the Bell Operating Companies from AT&T.

BRI *See* Basic-rate interface.

Bridge A device that connects two or more networks and operates at Layer 2 of the OSI model.

Broadband ISDN (BISDN) A set of interface standards being developed by the ITU(CCITT) for high-speed transmission.

Broadband transmission A transmission method in which data is modulated on a carrier signal, such as a sine wave.

Broadcast A message sent to all users on a network.

Broadcast message Data intended for multiple users, as on a multidrop circuit.

Browser Software that allows a user to view information, typically information stored in the HTML format.

BSC *See* Binary Synchronous Communications.

BSE *See* Basic Service Elements.

Buffering Holding data temporarily, usually until it is properly sequenced, as in packet switching networks, or until another device is ready to receive it, as in front-end processors.

Bus network A network topology in which all devices are connected to a single cable.

Busy signal A signal provided by the central office to the user indicating that the called party is already using the phone.

Busy token A pattern of bits used to indicate that another station is already using the token passing network.

Byte A group of bits, usually eight.

Byte interleaving A time-division multiplexing method in which each time slot contains a byte from each channel.

Byte-oriented protocol A protocol using entire bytes for communicating control information.

Cable extension A wireless LAN technique that uses a special hub to substitute radio transmission for cabling to the users, while using the original Medium Access Control protocol.

Cable modem An access technology that dedicates channels on a cable television system to data transmission, it is usually used to provide Internet access.

Call-back device Data security equipment used with dial-up modems that calls back users to verify their location.

Caller ID A service available with analog telephone lines that allows users to see the phone number of the incoming caller on a special display.

Carriage return A special character used to send a terminal's cursor or printer's head to the left margin.

Carrier Detect (CD) *See* Data Carrier Detect.

Carrier sense multiple access (CSMA) A collision-avoidance contention method often used with local area networks, it requires the transmitting device to check if the network is free before transmitting.

Carrier sense multiple access/collision detection (CSMA/CD) A contention method often used with local area networks, it requires the transmitter to check if the network is free before transmitting and continue monitoring to determine if there is a collision during transmission.

Carrier signal An electronic signal used to modulate data in broadband transmission, usually a sine wave.

Category I The RS-449 signals that require two wires, allowing for RS-422-A transmission.

Category II The RS-449 signals that require only a single wire and a common return and that use RS-423-A transmission.

Cathode ray tube (CRT) Another name for a terminal.

CBDS *See* Connectionless Broadband Data Service.

CC *See* Control codes.

C-channel The low-speed data channel in ISDN, carrying up to 16 kbps.

CCITT *See* Consultative Committee on International Telephone and Telegraph.

CD Carrier Detect. *See* Data Carrier Detect.

CDDI *See* Copper Distributed Data Interface.

CDMA *See* Code Division Multiple Access.

CDPD *See* Cellular Digital Packet Data.

Cell When used in wireless communications, a cell is a zone served by a particular transmitter. When used in ATM, it is a data packet containing 53 bytes, including a 5-byte header and 48-byte payload.

Cell relay Another name for the technique used in ATM.

Cellular A wireless communications technique that divides an area into cells, each served by a transmitter; calls are handed from one cell to the next as users move.

Cellular Digital Packet Data (CDPD) A wireless data service that sends packet data over the existing analog cellular network while providing added functions, like error detection and correction.

Central office The local exchange carrier's office where the central-office switch is located and that provides power, routing, and signaling functions for the user.

Central-office switch The device in the central office that provides the power, routing, and signaling functions for the user.

Central-office trunk A local loop between the central office and a PBX.

Central processing unit (CPU) Often used as another name for a host computer, it actually refers only to the heart of the host computer.

Centralized control A control method in which a single device runs a network.

Centrex Service with which the local exchange carrier handles both external and internal calls for a customer.

Channel Transmission path used in ISDN; available in various sizes.

Channel interface The high-speed port of a front-end processor that connects directly to the host computer's high-speed input/output channel.

Channel service unit (CSU) The device terminating the common carrier's digital circuit on the customer's premises.

Character A letter of the alphabet, number, punctuation mark, or a special key used by different terminals; also includes special codes used by devices to communicate.

Character code Methods of representing characters, typically with ones and zeroes.

Character interleaving Another name for byte interleaving.

Character-oriented protocol Another name for byte-oriented protocol.

Chassis ground The RS-232-C pin used to connect cable shields to the electrical ground.

Checksum An error-checking method in which bits are added before and after transmission and then compared.

Cipher text Data that has been encrypted for transmission.

Circuit switching Establishing a path and reserving resources for the duration of a connection regardless of whether or not any transmission actually takes place; e.g., in the telephone network, in which a call is connected and channels set aside in both directions even if no one is talking.

Clear text Data that is not encrypted.

Clear to Send (CTS) The RS-232-C control signal generated by the DCE indicating that the DTE can transmit data.

Client/server An architecture in which portions of a program operate on a local workstation, with centralized databases operating on a shared server.

Closed user group (CUG) A security measure often used in packet switching networks, it restricts access to a certain set of users.

Cluster Controller Device used in SNA to allow several Workstations a single point of access to the network.

CMIP *See* Common Management Information Protocol.

CNM *See* Communications Network Management.

Coax *See* Coaxial cable.

Coaxial cable A transmission medium consisting of a single wire in the center, surrounded by a core of insulating material with an outer conductive wrapping, covered by an insulating sheath.

Code conversion To translate from one character code to another, thereby allowing certain incompatible devices to communicate.

Code Division Multiple Access (CDMA) A digital cellular standard used in the United States, it shares channels with the analog AMPS system.

Collect calls A packet switching and public network service that bills call costs to the called party.

Collision The result of two devices transmitting at the same time, usually causing data to be lost.

Collision avoidance A contention technique in which devices check if the network is free before transmitting.

Collision detection A contention technique in which devices check whether collisions occur during transmission.

Collision Domain A part of a network where users share a transmission media and could accidentally talk simultaneously.

Combined Network Termination 1 and 2 (NT12) ISDN equipment combining the Network Termination 1 and Network Termination 2 functions.

Common carrier Company providing voice and/or data communications transmission services to the general public.

Common-channel signaling A method in which a separate channel is used for signaling bits.

Common Management Information Protocol (CMIP) An ISO protocol for network management that is far richer than SNMP, but less widely used.

Common return A single wire serving as a shared path for returning electrical signals, as in RS-423-A transmission.

Communications architecture A manufacturer's strategy for connecting its host computers, terminals, and communications equipment; it defines the elements necessary for data communications between devices.

Communications Controller In SNA, a device responsible for routing data through a network and controlling the communications links.

Communications Controller Node An SNA node containing a Communications Controller.

Communications line control Rules for sharing a communications path.

Communications Network Management (CNM) A series of IBM tools for managing networks.

Communications server A device that provides local area network users access to resources located off the network and vice versa, through modems or other communications circuits.

Concatenated The combination of several channels into a single channel, as in a SONET OC-Nc circuit.

Concentrator Another name for a port-sharing device.

Conditioned line A type of leased line suitable for high-speed data transmission, requiring extra hardware and available at an added cost.

Connectionless A term used to describe the process of delivering each piece of data independently, without establishing a connection.

Connectionless Broadband Data Service (CBDS) A European service similar to Switched Multimegabit Data Service.

Connection-oriented A term used to describe the process of establishing a physical or virtual connection, rather than just delivering individual pieces of data independently.

Consultative Committee on International Telephone and Telegraph (CCITT) An international telecommunications standards organization, whose members include regulating bodies from member countries, representatives from leading companies, and representatives from other organizations. *See* International Telecommunications Union.

Contention Method used to share a communications path.

Continuous ARQ An automatic repeat request method in which the transmitter continues sending data blocks without waiting for acknowledgment messages, until a set number of unacknowledged blocks have been sent or a negative acknowledgment is received.

Control character Character used in character codes to perform special functions.

Control codes (CC) ASCII characters used to convey control information in protocols.

Control Field The part of an SDLC frame containing control information.

Control information In a protocol, the data sent to perform polling, selecting, ARQ, and error checking, as well as to convey status information to devices.

Control key A specific key on a terminal that will cause a special character to be generated when struck in conjunction with another key on the terminal.

Control signal In RS-232-C and RS-449, the pins indicating the status of a given connection.

Control station In BSC, the single station that can communicate with all of the other (Tributary) stations.

Convergence The combination of voice and data technologies on today's networks.

Copper Distributed Data Interface A copper version of Fiber Distributed Data Interface.

Cordless The simplest type of wireless communications; it typically consists of a handset and base station using radio waves between them instead of cable.

Corporation for Open Systems (COS) A nonprofit corporation consisting of major host computer manufacturers, whose purpose is to facilitate the implementation of OSI.

COS *See* Corporation for Open Systems.

CPE *See* Customer-premises equipment.

CPU *See* Central processing unit.

CRC *See* Cyclical redundancy check.

Crossover Function performed by DCEs in a communications circuit, taking the transmitted data from one DTE and delivering it to the other DTE for reception.

CRT *See* Cathode ray tube.

CSMA *See* Carrier sense multiple access.

CSMA/CD *See* Carrier sense multiple access/collision detection.

CSU *See* Channel service unit.

CTS *See* Clear to Send.

CUG *See* Closed user group.

Customer-premises equipment (CPE) Devices used at the customer site, either leased or owned.

CX *See* Data Carrier Detect.

Cycle A full repetition of a sine wave, including one peak and one valley.

Cycles per second A measure of frequency, the number of cycles of a sine wave in a second.

Cyclical parity A parity checking method designed to detect two sequential bit errors in a byte.

Cyclical redundancy check (CRC) A sophisticated version of a checksum, it uses a complex mathematical formula combining division and addition to detect errors.

DA *See* Destination Address.

Dash In Morse code, a long beep used to send characters.

Data Carrier Detect (DCD) The RS-232-C control signal generated by the DCE indicating that the DTE should expect to receive data at any time.

Data circuit-terminating equipment (DCE) The type of interface typically found on modems and some multiplexers.

Data communications The exchange of digital information between two devices using an electronic transmission system.

Data compression devices Equipment that allows more data to be transmitted per second than the speed of the link would normally allow.

Data conversion Protocol and/or code conversion.

Data Encryption Algorithm (DEA) The name used by ANSI for the Data Encryption Standard.

Data Encryption Standard (DES) A standard, general purpose encryption algorithm using secret keys developed by IBM and later adopted by the National Institute of Standards and Technology.

Data Link Layer Layer 2 of the OSI model, it is responsible for ensuring error-free, reliable transmission of data.

Data rate The speed at which bits are transmitted and received, usually measured in bits per second, or bps.

Data Rate Select (DRS) The RS-232-C control signal used by devices to change each other's speed.

Data Set Ready (DSR) The RS-232-C control signal generated by the DCE to indicate that it is powered on and ready to begin communications.

Data terminal equipment (DTE) The type of interface usually found on terminals, host computers, and printers.

Data Terminal Ready (DTR) The RS-232-C control signal generated by the DTE to indicate that it is powered on, on-line, and ready to begin communications.

Data transport network A general term describing a system that carries data communications, like local area networks and packet switching networks.

Datagram An individual data packet, as in IP.

Dataphone Digital Service (DDS) AT&T's four-wire, digital data communications service operating at speeds ranging from 2400 bps to 64 kbps.

Datascope A type of data communications test equipment that provides all of the functions of a breakout box and also provides a display screen for monitoring data and analyzing protocols; it can also trap events and sound alarms and can be programmed for complex simulations.

DB9 A 9-pin connector, available in male and female versions, defined in the ISO standard 4902 and in the RS-449 standard, and used with the secondary channel of the RS-449 interface.

DB25 A 25-pin connector, available in male and female versions, defined in ISO standard 2110, and often used with the RS-232-C interface.

DB37 A 37-pin connector, available in male and female versions, defined in ISO standard 4902 and in the RS-449 standard, and used with the primary channel of the RS-449 interface.

DCD *See* Data Carrier Detect.

DCE *See* Data circuit-terminating equipment.

D-channel In ISDN, the signaling channel, carrying 16 kbps or 64 kbps, depending on circuit type.

DDD network *See* Direct distance dial network.

DDS *See* Dataphone Digital Service.

DEA *See* Data Encryption Algorithm.

Decoder circuit The part of a modem's circuitry that translates incoming square waves to an internal representation of ones and zeroes.

Decryption The decoding, or descrambling, of received data.

Default A term often used to describe a customer's standard long-distance carrier.

Demand Priority A transmission scheme that allows certain traffic to be transmitted on a high priority basis.

Demodulation Converting analog signals back to digital form.

Demodulator circuit The part of a modem's circuitry that converts analog signals back to digital form.

DES *See* Data Encryption Standard.

Destination Address (DA) In IP, a 32-bit field indicating the location to which the datagram is to be delivered. In Ethernet, the 48-bit field indicating the location to which the frame is to be delivered.

Destination node In the OSI model, it is the host computers at each end of a connection, often used to describe the transmitting and receiving computers that implement the higher layers; in a packet switching network, it is the node attached to the DTE that is receiving the data.

DF *See* Don't fragment flag.

Dial tone A signal provided by the central office to the user indicating that it is ready to accept digits.

Dial-up A telephone circuit connection that requires the user to place a new call each time, allowing destination flexibility.

Dibit modulation A technique for modulating two bits for every baud or signal change.

DID trunk *See* Direct inward dial trunk.

Digital A way of representing information using ones and zeroes.

Digital cellular A new type of wireless telephone service, in which the signals are transmitted to users in digital form.

Digital certificate A type of digital signature used to verify the authenticity of a file, often for downloaded software.

Digital circuit Special lines provided by the common carriers that are suitable for transmitting data directly in square wave form without modulation.

Digital PBX A computer that treats telephones and trunks as specialized input and output devices; voice is either digitized in the phone or at the PBX, and voice as well as data communications can be switched.

Digital phone A device that digitizes voice and is attached to either a digital PBX or an ISDN-type public network.

Digital postmark A method of verifying the time and date a message was sent, based on a digital signature and with the help of a trusted third party.

Digital service unit (DSU) A device connected between the user's DTE and the common carrier's digital circuits, which are typically terminated by a channel service unit.

Digital signature A method of verifying message authenticity or sender identification by encrypting with a secret key and decrypting with a public key.

Digital Subscriber Line (DSL) A broad title covering an array of digital access technologies connecting the central office to the user with twisted pair wire.

Digital transmission Sending data in square wave form rather than by using modulation over analog circuits.

Digitize To convert voice to ones and zeroes, or digital form.

Direct distance dial (DDD) network Another name for the public network.

Direct inward dial (DID) trunk A local loop between the central office and a PBX allowing for automatic call routing, in which the central office signals the PBX to indicate the called party's extension.

Display station Another name for a terminal.

Distributed control A design for spreading the responsibility of running a network throughout the attached devices, as in some local area networks.

Distributed Processor In SNA, a device similar to a Host Processor, though more limited in function.

Divestiture The breakup of the Bell System, whereby AT&T lost its local phone companies, but kept its long-distance business, Bell Labs, and Western Electric.

Domain In SNA, a System Services Control Point and all of the devices it controls.

Don't fragment (DF) flag In IP, a one-bit flag in the flags field indicating that the datagram should not be fragmented further.

Dot In Morse code, a short beep used to send characters.

Double encrypted When a message is encrypted with the sender's secret key and the receiver's public key and is decrypted with the sender's public key and the receiver's secret key, to provide both data confidentiality and authenticity.

Downlink The satellite dish receiving information from the satellite.

Downtime The time when a system or network is unavailable.

Driver circuit The part of a modem's circuitry that translates the modem's internal representation of ones and zeroes to square waves at the appropriate voltage levels.

DRS *See* Data Rate Select.

DS-1 The standard specifying the electrical characteristics for 1.544 Mbps transmission over four wires, as in T-1 transmission.

DSL *See* Digital Subscriber Line.

DSL Lite *See* Universal Asymmetric Digital Subscriber Line.

DSR *See* Data Set Ready.

DSU *See* Digital service unit.

DTE *See* Data terminal equipment.

DTMF *See* Dual-tone multifrequency dialing.

DTMF register Equipment that can recognize DTMF digits.

DTR *See* Data Terminal Ready.

Dual-tone multifrequency (DTMF) dialing Also known as Touch-tone, a dialing method using two simultaneous tones of different pitches to represent digits.

Dumb modem Modem that performs only modulation and demodulation, but is not able to dial calls; the user needs a separate phone to dial the calls, or a PBX can automate the process.

Dumb terminal A terminal that receives data from a host computer and displays it on its screen, but is unable to change or modify the data; similarly, any data typed into the keyboard is sent directly to the host computer without major modifications.

E-1 carrier A standard for 2.048 Mbps digital transmission often used in Europe; it is similar to the T-1 standard more commonly used in North America.

EBCD *See* Extended Binary Coded Decimal.

EBCDIC *See* Extended Binary Coded Decimal Interchange Code.

Echo canceller Device used to remove echoes from conversations on voice-grade lines by actually subtracting the echo before it reaches the user.

Echo checking An error-detection method in which the receiver repeats everything received to the transmitting device.

Echo suppressor Device used on voice-grade lines to prevent echoes by allowing transmission in only one direction at a time, in a half duplex fashion.

Echo testing Another name for loopback testing.

ECSA *See* Exchange Carriers Standards Association.

EIA *See* Electronic Industries Association.

EIA-232-D A revision to RS-232-C, its new features are seldom implemented.

EIA-232-E A revision of EIA-232-D, its new features are seldom implemented.

800 number Another name for a toll-free number.

Electronic Industries Association (EIA) A standards organization representing many manufacturers in the U.S. electronics industry.

Electronic mail A messaging method in which text, files, images, and any data storable on a computer can be transmitted to another user.

Email *See* Electronic mail.

Encryption Scrambling or coding data for transmission.

Encryption device Equipment that scrambles or codes data for transmission.

End office Another name for a central office.

End User In SNA, the parties on the end of each LU–LU session, including Application Programs and people at Workstations.

Enhanced service provider (ESP) In Open Network Architecture, a company that delivers a special function or service to the customer through the public network.

ENQ In BSC, the control character used as an enquiry.

Enquiry In a protocol, when a device asks permission to send data.

EOT In BSC, the control character signifying the End of Transmission.

Equal access Ability to choose a default long-distance carrier and still access all other long-distance carriers by using a simple dialing method.

Error detection Determining that one or more bits changed from a 1 to a 0, or vice versa, during transmission.

Error detection and correction Determining which bits changed from a 1 to a 0, or vice versa, during transmission and changing the bits back to their original form.

Error detection with a request for retransmission Determining that one or more bits changed from a 1 to a 0, or vice versa, during transmission and asking that the block of data be repeated.

Error detection with flagging Determining that one or more bits changed from a 1 to a 0, or vice versa, during transmission and notifying the user of the error.

ESP *See* Enhanced service provider.

ETACS *See* European Total Access Communications System.

Ethernet The CSMA/CD bus local area network originally used by Xerox, DEC, and Intel and now by many other vendors as well.

ETX In BSC, the control character signifying the end of actual user data.

EuroISDN The regional implementation of ISDN used in Europe.

European Total Access Communications System (ETACS) A popular analog cellular standard used primarily in Europe.

Even parity An error-detection method requiring an even number of ones in each byte.

Exchange Carriers Standards Association (ECSA) A standards organization consisting of telephone equipment manufacturing companies, formed after the AT&T divestiture to continue work on standards previously developed by the Bell System.

Expert system A type of artificial intelligence computer software tool often used in network management to help isolate and diagnose problems.

Extended ASCII A version of the ASCII character code providing eight data bits, allowing for graphics or foreign language characters, but at the expense of the parity bit.

Extended Binary Coded Decimal (EBCD) The predecessor of the Extended Binary Coded Decimal Interchange Code.

Extended Binary Coded Decimal Interchange Code (EBCDIC) An eight-bit character code developed by IBM.

External PAD A PAD located on the user's premises, outside a packet switching network.

External Transmit Clock (XTC) The RS-232-C Timing Signal generated by a DTE that times its own data transmission.

Facsimile (Fax) A method of sending still images, like a printed page, over telephone lines.

False state The state of an RS-232-C control signal when it is OFF or lowered.

Fast Ethernet The version of the IEEE 802.3 network that operates at 100 Mbps, it is simply the original version operating 10 times faster.

Fax *See* Facsimile.

FCC *See* Federal Communications Commission.

FCS *See* Frame Check Sequence Field.

FDDI *See* Fiber Distributed Data Interface.

FDM *See* Frequency-division multiplexing.

FE *See* Format effectors.

FEC *See* Forward error correction.

Federal Communications Commission (FCC) The body regulating all interstate communications in the United States.

Federal Information Processing Standards (FIPS) A set of specifications that must be met to supply the U.S. government with computing and data communications equipment.

FEP *See* Front-end processor.

Fiber Distributed Data Interface (FDDI) A high-speed local area network using fiber optic cable to form an inner and outer token ring suitable for mainframe computer communications and other applications.

Fiber optic cable A high-bandwidth transmission medium allowing data to be transmitted by shining a light through a special glass fiber.

Fiber to the curb One of many cabling approaches used to combine fiber optic cable for long distances with copper cable for short distances, it utilizes fiber to the customer's street and copper to the customer's premises.

Fiber to the feeder One of many cabling approaches used to combine fiber optic cable for long distances with copper cable for short distances, it utilizes fiber to reach somewhere in the neighborhood of the customer and copper to the customer's premises. It is also known as fiber to the vault or fiber to the neighborhood.

Fiber to the home A cabling approach in which fiber optic cable connects a central office or cable television company directly with the customer's home. It is also known as fiber to the premises.

Fiber to the neighborhood One of many cabling approaches used to combine fiber optic cable for long distances with copper cable for short distances, it utilizes fiber to reach somewhere in the neighborhood of the customer and copper to the customer's premises. It is also known as fiber to the vault or fiber to the feeder.

Fiber to the premises A cabling approach in which fiber optic cable connects a central office or cable television company directly with the customer's premises. It is also known as fiber to the home.

Fiber to the vault One of many cabling approaches used to combine fiber optic cable for long distances with copper cable for short distances, it utilizes fiber to reach somewhere in the neighborhood of the customer and copper to the customer's premises. It is also known as fiber to the feeder or fiber to the neighborhood.

Figures A special character in the Baudot character code indicating that future transmission will be from the Upper Case set of characters.

File server A shared storage device for local area network users, typically in the form of a personal computer with a high-volume disk, attached to the network.

File Transfer Protocol (FTP) Part of the TCP/IP Protocol Suite, it allows remote viewing of file directories as well as transfer of files in either direction across a TCP/IP network.

FIPS *See* Federal Information Processing Standards.

Firewall A technique used to screen messages passing between two networks to protect against security breaches or the spreading of certain error conditions.

Firewire *See* IEEE 1384.

Firmware encryption An encryption method in which software containing the algorithm, or the keys, can be stored on preprogrammed chips in an encryption device.

Flag In SDLC, the pattern of eight bits beginning each frame.

Flags field In IP, a 3-bit field containing one unused bit, the don't fragment flag, and the more fragments flag.

Flow-control negotiation A packet switching service allowing DTEs to specify the size of the packet and other parameters.

FM *See* Frequency modulation.

Foreign exchange A voice communications service offered by common carriers for business users that want phone numbers in areas other than their actual location.

Format effectors (FE) The ASCII control characters that perform special functions on printers and terminals.

Forward error correction (FEC) Another name for error detection and correction.

Four-wire communications Communicating over two pairs of wires; this term is often incorrectly used as a synonym for full duplex, as full duplex communications no longer requires four wires.

Fractional T-1 A carrier service offered for customers that do not need all 24 channels available in T-1.

Fragment In IP, a new datagram that is actually a piece of a larger datagram.

Fragment offset field In IP, a 13-bit field used to number a datagram fragment for later reassembly.

Frame A block of data sent using a protocol, like BSC or SDLC, or a group of bits representing data from many channels, as in T-1 transmission.

Frame Check Sequence (FCS) field In many protocols, the part of the frame containing the CRC error-checking bits.

Frame ground Another name for chassis ground.

Frame Level The second level of the ITU(CCITT) X.25 standard, it conforms to the ITU(CCITT) LAP-B Protocol.

Frame relay A technique used in data transport networks in which error checking is performed end to end, instead of on each individual link.

Framing bit In T-1 transmission, a bit used for synchronization and sometimes for error checking.

Free token A pattern of bits on a token passing network, indicating that the network is available for use.

Frequency The pitch of a tone, or the number of cycles per second of a sine wave.

Frequency division A local area network contention method based on the frequency-division multiplexing technique.

Frequency-division multiplexing (FDM) A multiplexing method in which devices continually share the bandwidth of the link by dividing the communications circuit into many separate frequencies, or channels.

Frequency modulation (FM) Transmission of information by varying the pitch of a tone (the frequency of a sine wave).

Frequency shift keying (FSK) Another name for frequency modulation.

Front end Another name for a front-end processor.

Front-end port Another name for the line interfaces of a front-end processor.

Front-end processor (FEP) A device acting as a communications assistant for the host computer, handling all communications with terminals and other devices and allowing the host computer to concentrate on calculations.

FSK Frequency shift keying. *See* Frequency modulation.

FTP *See* File Transfer Protocol.

Full duplex communications A simultaneous, two-way communications path.

G.711 The ITU(CCITT) standard for digitized voice signals upon which V.90 modems are based.

G.Lite *See* Universal Asymmetric Digital Subscriber Line.

Gateway A device used to connect two separate networks that use different communications methods.

Gbps *See* Gigabits per second.

GEO *See* Geosynchronous-earth orbit.

Geosynchronous-earth orbit (GEO) A satellite that orbits at approximately 22,230 miles above the earth.

Get A type of SNMP message sent from the manager to the agent to request configuration or status information.

Gigabit Ethernet The version of the IEEE 802.3 network that operates at 1 Gbps, it includes some additional changes to allow transmission to be 100 times faster than the original Ethernet.

Gigabits per second (Gbps) A billion bits per second.

Global System for Mobile (GSM) A digital cellular standard first deployed in Europe, it is now in use throughout the world.

GND Ground. *See* Chassis ground.

Go-back-N continuous ARQ A type of automatic repeat request in which transmission continues until too many frames are unacknowledged or until a negative acknowledgment is received; the frame in error, and all succeeding frames, must be retransmitted.

Group 1 An early ITU(CCITT) fax standard, it was purely analog, offered 100 lines per inch of resolution, and took approximately six minutes to transmit a typical page.

Group 2 An early ITU(CCITT) fax standard, it was purely analog, offered 100 lines per inch of resolution, and took approximately three minutes to transmit a typical page.

Group 3 A commonly used ITU(CCITT) fax standard, it converts the image to digital form and compresses it before transmission; it typically operates at 4800 or 9600 bps, offers 200 lines per inch of resolution, and takes under a minute to transmit a typical page.

Group 4 An advanced ITU(CCITT) fax standard, it converts the image to digital form, operates at speeds up to 64 kbps, and offers 400 lines per inch of resolution.

GSM *See* Global System for Mobile.

Half duplex communications An alternating transmission path that goes two ways, but only one direction at a time.

Hamming code A method devised by Richard Hamming for detecting a single bit error in a byte and correcting it with 100% accuracy.

Handshaking The interaction of control signals between devices.

Hardware encryption Encryption and decryption of data using a separate device; the algorithm is changed by purchasing a new device.

HDLC *See* High-level Data Link Control.

HDSL *See* High-bit-rate Digital Subscriber Line.

HDSL2 A version of HDSL that operates at the same speeds and distances, but over a single twisted pair.

HDTV *See* High-Definition Television.

Header In most protocols, it is the beginning of a package of data used for routing. For example, in ATM, the first five octets of a cell are known as the header. In IP, the first 20 bytes (plus any options bytes) make up the header.

Header checksum field In IP, the 16-bit field used to verify if the header contains any errors.

Hertz Another name for cycles per second.

High-bit-rate Digital Subscriber Line (HDSL) A digital access technology that provides a link from the user to the central office over two twisted pairs that runs the same speed in both directions, typically 1.544 Mbps or 2.048 Mbps.

High-Definition Television (HDTV) A standard for very high-quality television transmission, far superior to traditional broadcast quality.

Higher layers Layers 4 though 7 of the OSI model (the Transport, Session, Presentation, and Application Layers).

High-level Data Link Control (HDLC) The ISO bit-oriented protocol, similar to SDLC, but with some additional features.

High-Performance Serial Bus *See* IEEE 1384.

High-Speed Token Ring The new version of the IEEE 802.5 network that operates at speeds above 16 Mbps, including 100 Mbps and above.

High-usage intertoll trunk Trunk connecting toll offices that can carry many conversations simultaneously.

Historical logging A security method providing a complete recording of all data passed through a particular device.

Hop A step in delivering messages in a network. In packet networks, like IP networks, each handoff to the next router is a hop; in terrestrial microwave transmission, a repeater station is used for each hop.

Hop counter Typically, a field in a protocol that is incremented or decremented with each step in routing to track the number of routing steps.

Host computer The heart of a data communications network, it can perform numerical calculations, store and retrieve data, and perform a variety of tasks known as applications.

Host identifier (Hostid) Part of the Network Layer address in IP, it uniquely describes a particular host on a network. The network itself is identified by the netid.

Host Node In SNA, a node containing a Host Processor.

Host Processor The SNA term for a host computer.

Hostid *See* Host identifier.

Howler signal The signal sent by the central office to the user to indicate that the phone has been left off the hook.

HSTR *See* High-Speed Token Ring.

HTML *See* HyperText Markup Language.

HTTP *See* HyperText Transfer Protocol.

Hub A device used to simplify wiring of bus or ring networks by using a physical star topology while maintaining the original logical bus or ring.

Hybrid interface An ISDN interface that combines the A-channel and C-channel, providing a user with analog voice and low-speed data, along with access to some of the ISDN services.

HyperText Markup Language (HTML) A document format that links items in a hierarchical fashion, it can link text, audio, video, image, or any collection of items to allow for easy browsing.

HyperText Transfer Protocol (HTTP) A protocol used with TCP/IP to transfer information, typically data prepared in the HTML format.

Hz Hertz. *See* Cycles per second.

IBM International Business Machines Corporation.

IBM Cabling System IBM's method for wiring office buildings with standard cable.

IBM PC Network An IBM local area network available in baseband and broadband CSMA/CD versions.

IBM Token Ring Network An IBM local area network using token passing on a baseband, star-wired ring, similar to the IEEE 802.5 standard.

Identification field In IP, the 16-bit field used to identify the original datagram so that the fragments can later be reassembled together.

IEC *See* Interexchange carrier.

IEEE *See* Institute of Electrical and Electronics Engineers.

IEEE 802 An IEEE local area network standards committee, made up of several subcommittees.

IEEE 802.1 A standard providing an overview of local area networks, methods for connecting networks, and systems management.

IEEE 802.2 A Logical Link Control standard for local area networks.

IEEE 802.3 A CSMA/CD bus Medium Access Control standard for local area networks.

IEEE 802.4 A token bus Medium Access Control standard for local area networks.

IEEE 802.5 A token ring Medium Access Control standard for local area networks.

IEEE 802.6 A metropolitan area network Medium Access Control standard for local area networks.

IEEE 802.7 An advisory subcommittee on using broadband transmission in local area networks.

IEEE 802.8 An advisory subcommittee on using fiber optics in local area networks.

IEEE 802.9 An advisory subcommittee on integrating voice and data in local area networks.

IEEE 802.11 An example of a special protocol used in wireless LANs.

IEEE 1384 A data communications interface designed to connect peripherals to desktop computers, it operates at speeds up to 400 Mbps and is also known as High Performance Serial Bus, or Firewire.

IETF *See* Internet Engineering Task Force.

I-Frame *See* Information Format Frame.

IHL *See* Internet Header Length field.

In-band signaling Interspersing signaling bits with user data, instead of transmitting signaling on a separate channel.

Incoming calls only A packet switching network service allowing DTEs to accept calls, but not place them.

Independent Telephone Company (ITC) Local exchange carriers not formerly controlled by AT&T before divestiture.

Information Field In SDLC, the part of the Information Frame containing user data.

Information Format Frame (I-Frame) In SDLC, the type of frame used to send and receive user data.

Information separators (IS) In ASCII, the control characters used by host computers in storing and retrieving data.

Information superhighway A high-bandwidth network providing cost-effective transmission of voice, video, and data; it will probably be based on BISDN.

Information Systems Network (ISN) AT&T's combination of local area network and packet switching network transmission methods to provide connections to a wide variety of devices.

Input/output channel The high-speed port of a host computer, usually connected to a front-end processor.

Institute of Electrical and Electronics Engineers (IEEE) A professional organization of engineers, consisting of specialized societies whose committees prepare standards in their area of specialty.

Integrated Services Digital Network (ISDN) An evolving set of standards for a digital network carrying both voice and data communications.

Integrated voice/data terminal (IVDT) A device, usually attached to a PBX, combining the capabilities of a digital phone with those of a terminal.

Intelligent terminal A programmable smart terminal.

Interexchange carrier (IEC) Another name for a long-distance company.

Interexchange circuit (IXC) Another name for an intertoll trunk, as well as the link-connecting nodes in a packet switching network.

Interface The point at which one device connects to another.

Inter-LATA call A call between two local access transport areas, also known as a long-distance call.

Intermediate node The device between two communicating host computers that implements the lower layers of the OSI model.

Internal PAD A PAD located inside a packet switching node.

International Baudot A version of the Baudot code with a sixth bit added for parity checking.

International Standards Organization (ISO) A standards organization in which each member country is represented by its own national standards organization.

International Telecommunications Union (ITU) The parent organization of the ITU-T (formerly CCITT). An international telecommunications standards organization, whose members include regulating bodies from member countries, representatives from leading companies, and representatives from other organizations.

International Telecommunications Union–Telecommunications Standardization Sector (ITU–T) The official name that the CCITT now uses to describe its activities and new standards. Usually referred to simply as "ITU."

Internet When the "I" is capitalized, the Internet is a popular wide area network using TCP/IP protocols. When the "i" is in lowercase, an internet can be any collection of connected networks.

Internet Engineering Task Force (IETF) An international organization dedicated to the evolution and smooth operation of the Internet.

Internet Header Length field (IHL) In IP, the 4-bit field used to indicate the length of the header, in 32-bit increments.

Internet Protocol (IP) A part of the TCP/IP Protocol Suite, it operates at Layer 3 of the OSI model, the Network Layer, routing individual packets, known as datagrams.

Internet Service Provider A company operating a packet switching network based on IP protocols, attached to other IP networks, as part of the global Internet.

Internetworking Connecting two or more separate networks.

Interoffice trunk (IOT) A communications circuit connecting two central offices in a local area.

Intertoll trunk A communications circuit connecting two toll offices.

Intranet The servers and applications attached to a company's TCP/IP-based network that are accessible only to internal users.

Inverse multiplexer A device used to combine the bandwidth of two or more communications circuits to meet high-bandwidth requirements.

Inward WATS trunk Another name for a toll-free number.

IOT *See* Interoffice trunk.

IP *See* Internet Protocol.

IP Security protocol (IPSec) A protocol used to allow secure private networking across insecure public data networks.

IPSec *See* IP Security protocol.

IPv4 The current version of Internet Protocol that is most widely deployed.

IPv6 A new version of the Internet Protocol that offers many enhancements; however, it may be years before it changes the networking landscape.

IS *See* Information separators.

ISDN *See* Integrated Services Digital Network.

ISN *See* Information Systems Network.

ISO *See* International Standards Organization.

ISO Standard 2110 A standard describing the DB25 connectors.

ISO Standard 4902 A standard describing the DB37 and DB9 connectors.

Isochronous A type of data traffic in which data order and timing is critical, as in real-time communications like voice and video.

ISP *See* Internet Service Provider.

ITC *See* Independent Telephone Company.

ITU *See* International Telecommunications Union.

ITU-T *See* International Telecommunications Union–Telecommunications Standardization Sector.

IVDT *See* Integrated voice/data terminal.

IXC *See* Interexchange circuit.

Key A specific set of codes used by an encryption algorithm to encode data and by a decryption algorithm to decode data.

Key system A customer-premises equipment solution to small business telecommunications needs; it eliminates the inefficiencies of Centrex, but is smaller and less sophisticated than a PBX.

Keyboard The part of a terminal where data is entered by the user.

LAN *See* Local area network.

LAN Switch A device that creates a true star network and in which data is delivered to the appropriate user only based on the destination address; it is also known as a switching hub.

LAP-B *See* Link Access Procedure-Balanced.

LAPM *See* Link Access Procedure for Modems.

LATA *See* Local access and transport area.

Layer Division according to function as found in the OSI model; *See* also Application Layer, Presentation Layer, Session Layer, Transport Layer, Network Layer, Data Link Layer, and Physical Layer.

Layer 2 switching A device that delivers messages based on their Layer 2 address (e.g., Ethernet MAC address).

Layer 3 switching A device that delivers messages based on their Layer 3 address, (e.g., IP address).

Layer 4 switching A device that delivers messages based on their Layer 3 address (e.g., IP address) but is aware of the Layer 4 protocol being used (e.g., TCP) and handles, routes and prioritizes the Layer 3 packet accordingly.

Learning bridge A type of bridge that can learn the locations of users and deliver messages accordingly based on their Layer 2 address. Also known as an adaptive bridge.

Leased line Circuit rented from the common carriers for a flat monthly fee, with no usage charge per call.

Least cost routing A PBX system feature that chooses the least expensive trunk for a given call at a particular time of day.

LEC *See* Local exchange carrier.

LED *See* Light-emitting diode.

LEO *See* Low-earth orbit.

Letters A special character in the Baudot character code indicating that future transmission will be from the Lower Case set of characters.

Light-emitting diode (LED) A small light bulb, about an eighth of an inch in diameter, typically found on a breakout box.

Limited-distance modem Another name for a short-haul modem.

Line discipline Another name for a protocol.

Line feed A special character used to send a terminal's cursor or printer's head to the next line.

Line interface The low-speed port on a front-end processor that is typically attached to terminals.

Line of sight The requirement that in terrestrial microwave transmission, there be no obstructions between two dish antennas.

Line splitter A device that allows many terminals to share one front-end port and that is located remotely from the front-end processor.

Link A communications circuit.

Link Access Procedure-Balanced (LAP-B) The ITU(CCITT) bit-oriented protocol similar to SDLC.

Link Access Procedure for Modems (LAPM) The ITU(CCITT) standard for modem error correction, also known as V.42.

Link level protocol A set of rules precisely defining methods for communicating over a communications circuit, or link.

LLC *See* Logical Link Control.

Loading coil Device used in some analog telephone circuits to improve voice quality at longer distances.

Local access and transport area (LATA) A geographical region where the local phone company provides the user with entry, or access, to the public network and carries or transports calls.

Local analog loopback test A modem diagnostic technique that can be performed with a modem, a cable, and a terminal.

Local area network (LAN) A privately owned data communications system that provides reliable high-speed, switched connections between devices in a single building, campus, or complex.

Local exchange Another name for the central office.

Local exchange carrier (LEC) Another name for the local phone company that provides service inside the LATA.

Local loop The pair of wires that runs from the central office into our home or business.

Logical Link Control (LLC) The IEEE 802.2 subcommittee standard relating to local area network functions like error checking and reliability.

Logical Unit (LU) In SNA, the Network Addressable Unit that is the End User's access point to the network.

Long-distance call Another name for an inter-LATA call.

Loopback plug A special connector used to perform echo testing with an asynchronous dumb terminal.

Loopback testing A diagnostic technique in which transmitted data is returned to the sender for comparison with the original message.

Low The state of an RS-232-C control signal when it is off or false.

Low-earth orbit (LEO) A satellite that orbits at approximately a few hundred miles above the earth.

Lower Case The portion of the Baudot character code used for the letters of the alphabet.

Lower layers Layers 1 through 3 of the OSI model (Physical, Data Link, and Network Layers).

LU *See* Logical Unit.

MAC *See* Medium Access Control.

Mainframe Host computer usually serving a large organization.

MAN *See* Metropolitan area network.

Management Information Base (MIB) The common set of information needed to manage a network, as described in SNMP.

Manager The central station partner of the remote agent in a network management protocol.

Manufacturing Automation Protocol (MAP) A user-defined networking standard originally developed by General Motors.

MAP *See* Manufacturing Automation Protocol.

Mark In RS-232-C, transmission of a 1, using an electrical signal between –3 and –15 volts.

Mark parity An error-detection method in which the parity bit is always a 1.

Maximum transmission unit (MTU) The longest message allowed on a particular network.

Mbps Millions of bits per second.

MCI One of many common carriers offering a variety of services.

Mean time between failures (MTBF) The average time between network failures, or uptime.

Mean time to repair (MTTR) The average time required to diagnose and correct a problem, or downtime.

Medium Access Control (MAC) A group of IEEE standards relating to local area network access methods, describing how devices share time on a network.

Medium-earth orbit (MEO) A satellite that orbits a few thousand miles above the earth.

MEO *See* Medium-earth orbit.

Mesh network A network topology in which each device is connected by a cable to every other device in the network.

Metropolitan area network (MAN) The IEEE 802.6 standard describing Medium Access Control for networks spanning a city.

MF *See* More fragments flag.

MFJ *See* Modified Final Judgment.

MIB *See* Management Information Base.

Microcellular A type of cellular system using small zones, such as areas of a building.

Microcom Network Protocol (MNP) A commercial modem protocol licensed by Microcom to many vendors to perform error correction and sometimes compression, depending on the version of the protocol.

Microcomputer Host computer usually serving only a single user.

Microsegmentation Using a LAN switch with only one station is connected to each port.

MIME *See* Multipurpose Internet Mail Extensions.

MI/MIC lead *See* Mode indicator lead.

Minicomputer Host computer usually serving a group of users, such as a department or a division.

MNP *See* Microcom Network Protocol.

MNP 5 The first version of MNP to provide the data compression feature.

Mode indicator (MI/MIC) lead A pair of wires connected to a dumb modem; when closed by a PBX, they cause the modem to begin communicating with a remote modem.

Modem A device that performs modulation and demodulation, allowing data communications to occur in analog form over telephone circuits.

Modified Final Judgment (MFJ) The edict requiring AT&T to divest itself of the Bell Operating Companies.

Modulation Converting digital signals to analog form for transmission.

Modulator circuit The part of a modem's circuitry that performs modulation.

Modulo-8 As used in protocols like SDLC, the ability to transmit up to seven frames without waiting for an acknowledgment message.

Modulo-128 As used in protocols like SDLC, the ability to transmit up to 127 frames without waiting for an acknowledgment message.

More fragments (MF) flag In IP, a single bit in the flags field used to indicate that this is not the last of the fragments of a particular datagram.

Morse code A character code used in telegraph transmission, in which long and short tones are used to represent characters.

Moving Pictures Expert Group (MPEG) An ISO committee providing a variety of standards for video transmission.

MPEG *See* Moving Pictures Expert Group.

MPEG II One of the Moving Pictures Expert Group's standards that provides varying degrees of quality based on the bit rate used.

MTBF *See* Mean time between failures.

MTTR *See* Mean time to repair.

MTU *See* Maximum transmission unit.

Multicast A message sent to a group of users on a network; sometimes it is sent to everyone, but ignored by those not in the group.

Multidrop A configuration in which several terminals are directly attached to, and share, a single communications line leading to a single front-end or host computer port.

Multimedia A term commonly used to describe applications or transmissions containing some combination of voice, video, image, and data.

Multiplexer (Mux) A device used to allow a single communications circuit to take the place of several parallel ones; often used to allow several remotely located terminals to communicate with several front-end processor ports over a single circuit.

Multipurpose Internet Mail Extensions (MIME) A set of enhancements beyond SMTP that allow for a variety of items, including text, executable files, audio, video, and binary files, to be exchanged in electronic mail messages.

Multirate ISDN The usage of multiple B-channels for a single connection, also known as N × 64.

Multispeed A capability found in many modems allowing them to communicate at different speeds.

Mux *See* Multiplexer.

NAK In BSC, the control character signifying a negative acknowledgment.

Narrowband ISDN The ISDN standard currently being implemented, including the basic-rate, primary-rate, and hybrid interfaces; *See* Integrated Services Digital Network.

National Bureau of Standards (NBS) *See* National Institute of Standards and Technology.

National Electrical Code A widely used standard for electrical wiring and safety practices.

National Institute of Standards and Technology (NIST) The federal standards organization in the United States; it produces the Federal Information Processing Standards. It was formerly known as the National Bureau of Standards (NBS).

National ISDN A series of Bellcore standards that ensure consistent deployment of ISDN regardless of carrier or equipment manufacturer.

National Security Agency (NSA) A federal agency that has adopted the Data Encryption Standard for protecting sensitive, but not classified, information.

NAU *See* Network Addressable Unit.

NBS *See* National Bureau of Standards.

Netid *See* Network identifier.

Netview IBM's host-computer-based network management software.

Netview/PC IBM's personal computer-based network management software that allows any device conforming to IBM's standard set of protocols to transmit network management information to Netview.

Network A group of interconnected, communicating devices.

Network Addressable Unit (NAU) In SNA, a device with a unique address to which data is routed.

Network computer A host with very little processing power and designed to run thin clients, it is the modern day equivalent of a dumb terminal.

Network control The network management function acting as the network "boss," allowing for the activation and deactivation of network components and features.

Network identifier (Netid) Part of the Network Layer address in IP; it uniquely describes a particular network. The specific host on the network is described by the hostid.

Network Layer Layer 3 of the OSI model; it is responsible for setting up the appropriate routing of messages throughout a network.

Network management Ensuring consistent reliability and availability of a network, as well as timely transmission and routing of data, it can be performed by dedicated devices, by host computers, by people, or by some combination of all of these.

Network monitoring The network management function acting as the network "watchdog" that constantly checks on the network and reports on any problems.

Network statistical reporting The network management function acting as the network "statistician" that pinpoints which parts of a network are being utilized and how often.

Network Termination (NT) equipment In ISDN, equipment providing functions similar to those found in the lower layers of the OSI model.

Network Termination 1 (NT1) In ISDN, the equipment providing only OSI Layer 1 (Physical Layer) functions, including the electrical and physical termination of the network on the customer's premises.

Network Termination 2 (NT2) In ISDN, the equipment providing OSI Layers 2 and 3 (Data Link and Network Layer) functions, including concentration and switching, if needed.

Network troubleshooting The network management function acting as the network "diagnostician" that assists in isolating and diagnosing problems.

Network–Network Interface (NNI) The ATM interface specification describing how to connect two provider networks.

Newsgroup A popular Internet application in which users post, review, and subscribe to information on an electronic bulletin board system.

NIST *See* National Institute of Standards and Technology.

NNI *See* Network–Network Interface.

Node In SNA, the component or device interconnected by the SNA network; in a packet switching network, the device that switches and routes calls at each location.

NSA *See* National Security Agency.

NT *See* Network Termination equipment.

NT1 *See* Network Termination 1.

NT2 *See* Network Termination 2.

NT12 *See* Combined Network Termination 1 and 2.

Null modem cable A special cable used to connect two DTEs together in RS-232-C, it simulates the operation of two DCEs and the network between them.

Numbering In a packet switching network, the method of tracking the proper sequence of packets.

N × 64 The usage of multiple B-channels for a single connection, also known as Multirate ISDN.

OC-1 An OC-N signal operating at 51.84 Mbps.

OC-12 An OC-N signal operating at 622.08 Mbps.

OC-3 An OC-N signal operating at 155.52 Mbps.

OC-N *See* Optical Carrier-N.

Octet Another name for a byte in telecommunications.

Odd parity An error-detection method requiring an odd number of ones in each byte.

OFF The state of an RS-232-C control signal when it is false or low.

Off-hook The status of a phone that has been picked up; also the signal sent by the user to the central office when the phone is picked up.

Office code The three-digit prefix that designates the destination central office.

ON The state of an RS-232-C control signal when it is asserted, raised, or true.

ONA *See* Open Network Architecture.

On-hook The status of a phone that has been hung up; also, the signal sent by the user to the central office when the phone is hung up.

100BASE-T An Ethernet standard for baseband transmission at 100 Mbps over twisted pair wiring.

100VG-AnyLan An emerging IEEE 802.12 local area network standard for 100 Mbps transmission using a demand-priority scheme.

Open Network Architecture (ONA) The post-divestiture FCC requirement that all network services be divided into basic service elements and be made available separately to enhanced service providers.

Open Systems Interconnection (OSI) model The International Standards Organization's set of standards that breaks down the task of computer communications into seven independent layers, each with its own tasks; *see* Lower layers, Higher layers.

OpenView A Hewlett-Packard network management product that supports a wide variety of protocols.

Operator The person running the console of a PBX.

Optical Carrier-*N* (OC-*N*) The SONET designation used with fiber optic signals, it supports speeds of 51.84 Mbps and above.

Options field In IP, the optional area of the header used to extend the protocol beyond its original definition.

Originate/answer modem A type of modem that can place calls and answer calls.

Originate-only modem A type of modem that can only place calls.

OSI model *See* Open Systems Interconnection model.

Outgoing calls only A term used to describe a packet switching network service that allows DTEs to place calls, but not accept them.

Out-of-band signaling A method of sending signaling bits on a separate channel, rather than sending them interspersed with the data.

Outward WATS trunk A type of PBX trunk that connects to a discounted long-distance service.

Overhead Nondata bits or characters necessary for transmission, error detection, or use by protocols.

Overlay A term used to describe the use of two or more area codes in a single geographic region.

Packet Block of data, including addressing, routing, and numbering information.

Packet assembler disassembler (PAD) A device used to connect a packet switching network with equipment that does not perform packet formatting.

Packet-filtering A technique used in firewalls in which packets are screened based on their origin, destination, and type of data.

Packet Level In packet switching networks, the X.25 level providing for network-level addressing and call connection.

Packet switching network (PSN) Network providing a switched service in which data is sent in packets through nodes over various routes and is recombined at its destination in the proper sequence.

Packetized Description of data that is divided into packets.

PAD *See* Packet assembler disassembler.

Padding In IP, it is used in conjunction with the options field to ensure that the header length rounds up to a 32-bit increment.

Parallel/serial conversion Changing data from parallel to serial form and vice versa.

Parallel/serial converter A device that changes data from parallel to serial form and vice versa.

Parallel transmission A method of transmission in which all of the bits in a byte are sent at once on separate wires.

Parity bit A bit reserved for error detection in the parity checking method.

Parity checking A method of error detection in which a single bit is added by the transmitter and checked by the receiver to determine if errors occurred; *see* Even parity, Mark parity, Odd parity, and Space parity.

Password The most common form of security, it requires the user to enter a secret set of characters to access information or systems.

Payload The 48 bytes of an ATM cell used to carry the user data, it can actually contain up to 4 overhead bytes, resulting in as few as 44 bytes available for user data.

PBX *See* Private branch exchange.

PCM *See* Pulse code modulation.

PCS *See* Personal Communications Service.

Peer level In the OSI model, the corresponding layers on two communicating host computers—for example, the Network Layers on each computer.

Period The length of time of a complete cycle of a sine wave.

Peripheral Node In SNA, a single Workstation, or a Cluster Controller with several Workstations.

Personal Communications Service (PCS) A telecommunications service in which calls follow a user from place to place. It can include a mix of wired and wireless telephones.

Personal computer Host computer usually serving only a single user.

Personal identification number (PIN) The password used with an automated teller machine.

P/F bit The bit in the SDLC control frame that can be used for polling by the Primary station or to indicate the final frame of transmission by the Secondary station.

PGP *See* Pretty Good Privacy.

Phase modulation (PM) Transmission of information by varying the phase of a sine wave.

Phase shift keying (PSK) Another name for phase modulation.

Physical Layer In the OSI model, it is Layer 1, the lowest layer, responsible for the transmission of bits; it is always implemented in hardware. In ATM, it is responsible for the transmission of cells.

Physical Level The lowest level of X.25, it describes the actual interface, which conforms to the ITU(CCITT) V.24/V.28 standard and is similar to RS-232-C.

Physical Unit (PU) In SNA, the Network Addressable Unit that manages and monitors a node's resources.

PIN *See* Personal identification number.

Plain text Another name for clear text.

Plug-in Typically a small application, or applet, that downloads to a browser when needed.

PM *See* Phase modulation.

Point of presence (POP) The point at which a long-distance call is handed from the local exchange carrier to the interexchange carrier.

Point-to-Point Protocol (PPP) A Layer 2 protocol used for sending IP packets, or other packets, over a serial link like a telephone line, it provides error detection and allows dynamic address assignment.

Polling The method used by a host computer or front-end processor to ask a terminal if it has data to send.

POP *See* Point of presence.

Port-sharing device A device that allows many terminals to share a single front-end port and is located near the front-end processor; it is often called a concentrator.

Postal, telephone, and telegraph (PTT) administration Government agencies in many countries that regulate and often also operate the public network.

PPP *See* Point-to-Point Protocol.

Prefix Another name for an office code.

Presentation Layer Layer 6 of the OSI model, it provides format and code conversion services.

Presubscription The method by which a customer selects a default long-distance carrier.

Pretty Good Privacy A very widely used encryption software product, it supports numerous algorithms.

PRI *See* Primary-rate interface.

Primary station In SDLC, the single device or station that communicates with all of the other (secondary) stations.

Primary-rate interface (PRI) The preferred method for attachment to ISDN by PBXs and LANs, it consists of 23 or 30 B-channels for user data and digitized voice and 1 D-channel for signaling.

Print server A shared printing device for local area network users, typically in the form of a personal computer with a high-speed printer, attached to the network.

Priority backoff A backoff method in which each device on a network has a different backoff time, providing those with lower times a higher priority in using the network.

Private branch exchange (PBX) A telecommunications switching system owned by the customer, it acts as an in-house central office with advanced features and capabilities.

Processing unit The intelligent part of a front-end processor, it is actually a special-purpose computer programmed for communications functions.

Protective ground Another name for chassis ground.

Protocol A set of rules precisely defining the methods used to communicate.

Protocol analyzer Another name for a datascope.

Protocol conversion Translating data from one protocol to another.

Protocol converter A device that performs protocol conversion.

Protocol field In IP, the eight-bit field indicating the protocol being carried in the datagram (e.g., TCP).

PSK Phase-shift keying. *See* Phase modulation.

PSN *See* Packet switching network.

PTT *See* Postal, telephone, and telegraph administration.

PU *See* Physical Unit.

Public key An asymmetric key published in a directory; typically used for encryption, in conjunction with a secret key used for decryption.

Public network The telephone network, also called the direct distance dial network, accessed when using a home telephone.

Public packet switching network A packet switching network owned and operated for customers by service providers.

Public utilities commission (PUC) The regulating body of each state responsible for regulating intrastate phone service.

PUC *See* Public utilities commission.

Pulse code modulation (PCM) A method of digitizing normal telephone conversation.

Pulse dialing A dialing method in which a switch is opened and closed at the end of the local loop at a fixed rate of speed; also known as rotary dialing.

Pure time-division multiplexing A time-division multiplexing method in which the transmission speed of the trunk port is at least as great as the sum of the speeds of the branch ports, guaranteeing enough bandwidth to handle the attached devices' maximum transmission.

Quadrature amplitude modulation A modulation method used in the ITU(CCITT) V.22 bis standard that combines changes in phase and amplitude to send four bits with each baud.

R reference point In ISDN, the point between the TE2 and the TA.

RADSL *See* Rate-Adaptive Digital Subscriber Line.

Raised state The state of an RS-232-C control signal when it is on, asserted, or true.

Random access A contention method allowing devices to transmit whenever they please.

Random backoff A backoff method in which each device picks a random amount of time to wait before retransmitting after a collision.

Rate-Adaptive Digital Subscriber Line (RADSL) A digital access technology that provides a link from the user to the central office over twisted pair wire that is higher speed in one direction than in the other, its rate varies depending on the transmission line's length and quality.

RBOC *See* Regional Bell Operating Company.

RC *See* Receive Clock.

RD *See* Received Data.

Receive Clock (RC) The RS-232-C timing signal generated by the DCE to time synchronous data transmission from the DCE to the DTE.

Receive Common One of the RS-423-A signal returns.

Received Data (RD) The RS-232-C data signal received by the DTE from the DCE.

Receiver Not Ready (RNR) In SDLC, the Control Field message indicating a temporary busy condition.

Receiver Ready (RR) In SDLC, the Control Field message indicating that data has been successfully received and that more data can be sent.

Recommended Standard (RS) The designation used by EIA to describe its communications specifications.

Regional Bell Operating Company (RBOC) Any of seven holding companies, each a collection of local Bell Operating Companies, formed after divestiture to permit the new BOCs to remain efficient and achieve economies of scale.

Regional Holding Company (RHC) Another name for a Regional Bell Operating Company.

REJ *See* Reject.

Reject (REJ) In SDLC, the Control Field message indicating that a retransmission of data is necessary.

Reliability The ability of a network to pass data without errors, often measured using a bit or block error rate test.

Remote bridge A type of bridge used to connect networks at two or more locations.

Remote digital loopback test A modem diagnostic technique that can test the phone line itself as well as parts of the modem; it requires two modems, a terminal, a phone line, and a cable.

Remote intelligent controller A device, similar to a line splitter, that can also perform some front-end processor functions.

Remote Network Monitoring (RMON) A LAN management MIB created by the IETF, it is commonly used with SNMP; RMON1 operates on lower layer (MAC) addresses, while RMON2 recognizes higher layer addresses and protocols.

Repeater Device used to keep a digital signal strong and recognizable over long distances.

Request to Send (RTS) The RS-232-C control signal generated by the DTE to ask permission to transmit data.

Resequencing A function performed by destination packet switching nodes to arrange received packets in their proper order before transmitting them to the DTE.

Resolution A measure of image quality, often in lines per inch.

Resource Reservation Protocol (RSVP) A protocol used to reserve bandwidth in an IP network.

Response time Though its definition varies with each application, it often refers to the total amount of time it takes a message to travel from the terminal to the host computer, plus the processing time at the host computer, plus the travel time of the reply.

Reverse charging Another name for collect calls.

RHC Regional Holding Company. *See* Regional Bell Operating Company.

RI *See* Ring Indicator.

Ring Indicator (RI) The RS-232-C control signal generated by the DCE to alert the DTE that a remote device wants to initiate communications.

Ring network A network topology in which all devices are connected in a continuous loop.

Ringback signal A signal provided by the central office to the caller to indicate that the called party's phone is being rung.

Ringing signal A signal provided by the central office to the called party to cause the telephone to ring.

Rlogin A protocol used with UNIX-based computers to provide remote login capabilities.

RMON *See* Remote Network Monitoring.

RMON1 *See* Remote Network Monitoring.

RMON2 *See* Remote Network Monitoring.

RNR *See* Receiver Not Ready.

Robbed-bit signaling A common T-1 signaling method in which a bit is occasionally stolen from a channel to carry signaling information.

Rotary dialing Another name for pulse dialing.

Rotary register A device in the central office that can detect the opening and closing of a switch at the end of the local loop; used in rotary, or pulse, dialing.

Route optimization Another name for least cost routing.

Router Similar to a bridge, but includes OSI Layer 3 intelligence.

RR *See* Receiver Ready.

RS *See* Recommended Standard.

RS-232-C One of the most common interface standards for data communications in use today, it is an EIA standard defining exactly how ones and zeroes will be transmitted, including voltage levels needed and other electronic signals necessary for communication.

RS-422-A An EIA standard describing a method of balanced transmission that can be used for RS-449 Category I signals.

RS-423-A An EIA standard describing a method of unbalanced transmission used for RS-449 Category II signals.

RS-449 An EIA standard describing the mechanical and functional characteristics of the DTE/DCE interface and specifying the RS-422-A and RS-423-A standards for transmission.

RSA A public key encryption algorithm widely used in electronic messaging systems, it is named after its inventors: Rivest, Shamir, and Adelman.

RSVP *See* Resource Reservation Protocol.

RTS *See* Request to Send.

Run length encoding A method of digitally compressing an image to reduce fax transmission time.

S reference point In ISDN, the point between the Network Termination equipment and the TE1 or TA.

SA *See* Source Address.

Sample A snapshot of a signal at a given moment, as used to digitize voice in pulse code modulation.

Satellite An orbiting vehicle often used for communications.

Satellite dish A special antenna used to transmit signals to or receive signals from a satellite.

Satellite transmission Use of an orbiting satellite to repeat signals to all antennas in view of the satellite.

Screen The part of a terminal where received data is displayed.

SCTS *See* Secondary Clear to Send.

SDCD *See* Secondary Data Carrier Detect.

SDH *See* Synchronous Digital Hierarchy.

SDLC *See* Synchronous Data Link Control.

SDSL *See* Single-line Digital Subscriber Line.

Sealed message A type of message that cannot be modified by an unauthorized party.

Secondary Clear to Send (SCTS) The RS-232-C Clear to Send signal for the secondary channel.

Secondary Data Carrier Detect (SDCD) The RS-232-C Data Carrier Detect signal for the secondary channel.

Secondary Received Data (SRD) The RS-232-C Received Data signal for the secondary channel.

Secondary Request to Send (SRTS) The RS-232-C Request to Send signal for the secondary channel.

Secondary station In SDLC, a device or station that communicates with the primary station; there can be several secondary stations.

Secondary Transmitted Data (STD) The RS-232-C Transmitted Data signal for the secondary channel.

Secret key A type of encryption code that is not publicly known.

Secret message A secure message that is encrypted so that it cannot be understood by an unauthorized party.

Secure channel A communications link that is known to be safe from intrusion or eavesdropping.

Secure/Multipurpose Internet Mail Extensions (S/MIME) Extensions to the MIME protocol that provide public key encryption features.

Secure Sockets Layer protocol (SSL) A protocol that allows common protocols in IP networks, like HTTP, Telnet, and FTP, to transmit securely using public key encryption techniques.

Segment A piece of a LAN, usually that was part of a larger LAN previously; in Ethernet, typically it encompasses a single collision domain.

Segmentation The result of breaking a LAN into smaller pieces.

Segmenting The process of breaking a LAN into smaller pieces.

Selecting Method used by a host computer or front-end processor to ask a terminal if it is ready to receive data.

Selective repeat continuous ARQ A type of automatic repeat request whereby transmission continues until a negative acknowledgment is received, and only the frame with the error is repeated.

Send Common One of the RS-423-A signal returns.

Sequenced message A message protected against undetected loss or repetition by numbering.

Serial Line Internet Protocol (SLIP) A Layer 2 protocol used for sending IP packets over a serial line, it offers no error detection and cannot be used with non-IP protocols.

Serial transmission A method of transmission in which the bits in a byte are sent one after the other on the same wire.

Service level The criterion for acceptable network performance.

Session In SNA, a communications path through a network.

Session Layer Layer 5 of the OSI model, it requests that a logical connection be established or terminated, and it handles logon and password procedures.

Set A type of SNMP message sent from the manager to the agent to change the configuration or settings on a remote device.

SFD *See* Start-of-Frame Delimiter.

SFDM *See* Statistical frequency-division multiplexing.

S-Frame *See* Supervisory Format Frame.

SG *See* Signal Ground.

Short-haul modem A modem that transmits data over twisted pair wire over a limited distance on a customer's premises, but not through telephone company central offices.

Signal Ground (SG) The RS-232-C ground that acts as a zero-volt reference for all other signals.

Signal Quality Detect (SQ) The RS-232-C control signal asserted by the DCE when it perceives that transmission is of a high quality and that no errors are occurring.

Signaling In the telephone network, information sent between devices, or between devices and users, to convey status and information, like dialed digits, busy signals, and ringing.

Signaling System 7 (SS7) A standard for network signaling developed in 1984 and already in widespread use in the United States, it plays a key role in ISDN.

Signed message A message that includes proof of the sender's identity.

SIM *See* Subscriber Identity Module.

Simple Mail Transfer Protocol (SMTP) A part of the TCP/IP Protocol Suite, it provides a universal format for exchanging electronic mail.

Simple Network Management Protocol (SNMP) Originally a part of the TCP/IP Protocol Suite, it describes methods for exchanging a common set of network management information; in its second version (SNMPv2), it also includes support for non-IP protocols.

Simplex communications A one-direction communications path.

Sine wave An electronic representation of a pure tone; it is a signal that repeats indefinitely its pattern of peaks of equal height and valleys of equal depth.

Single-line Digital Subscriber Line (SDSL) A digital access technology that provides a link from the user to the central office over a single twisted pair that is the same speed in both directions, at speeds up to 1.544 Mbps or 2.048 Mbps.

SLIP *See* Serial Line Internet Protocol.

Smart card A credit-card-sized device typically containing a customer's identification and authentication information, among other items.

Smart modem A modem that can accept dialing instructions from the user and dial the call, as well as perform the necessary modulation and demodulation.

Smart terminal A terminal that sends extra information to a host computer beyond what the user types, typically using a protocol containing error checking and addressing information.

SMDS *See* Switched Multimegabit Data Service.

S/MIME *See* Secure/Multipurpose Internet Mail Extensions.

SMTP *See* Simple Mail Transfer Protocol.

SNA *See* Systems Network Architecture.

Sniffer A type of protocol analyzer used to troubleshoot LANs.

SNMP *See* Simple Network Management Protocol.

SNMPv2 *See* Simple Network Management Protocol.

Software encryption A method of programming the encryption algorithm and keys into a host computer or intelligent terminal without the use of separate encryption devices.

SOH In BSC, the character indicating the start of the header.

SolarisNet Manager A Sun Microsystems network management product that supports a wide variety of protocols, it was formerly known as SunNet Manager.

SONET *See* Synchronous Optical Network.

Source Address (SA) Another name for the return address on a data communications network. In IP, it is the 32-bit field indicating the originator of the IP datagram. In Ethernet, it is the 48-bit field indicating the originator of the Ethernet frame.

Source routing One of several methods used by bridges to ensure that there is only one active path between two users.

Source routing transparent One of several methods used by bridges to ensure that there is only one active path between two users.

Space In RS-232-C, sending a zero, using an electrical signal between +3 and +15 volts.

Space parity An error-detection method in which the parity bit is always a 0.

Spanning tree protocol One of several methods used by bridges to ensure that there is only one active path between two users.

Spectrum A Cabletron network management product that supports a wide variety of protocols.

Spread spectrum A wireless transmission technology in which voice is broken into pieces and sent on several channels simultaneously.

SPRINT One of many common carriers offering a variety of services.

SQ *See* Signal Quality Detect.

Square wave A signal that alternates between two voltage levels almost instantaneously.

SRD *See* Secondary Received Data.

SRTS *See* Secondary Request to Send.

SSCP *See* System Services Control Point.

SSL *See* Secure Sockets Layer protocol.

SS7 *See* Signaling System 7.

Stamped message A message whose receipt by the correct party is guaranteed.

Standards organization Group or committee that devises specifications or standards for a particular industry or country.

Standby monitor In a token ring network, a station that is ready to take over the monitoring function for the active monitor, if necessary.

Star network A network topology in which each user is connected to a center point and all data is routed through that point.

Star-wired bus network A logical bus network created using wiring in a physical star configuration in conjunction with a hub.

Star-wired ring network A logical ring network created using wiring in a physical star configuration in conjunction with a hub.

Starlan Network AT&T's star network for connecting personal computers in an office environment.

Start bit In asynchronous transmission, the bit sent before each character (always a 0).

Start–stop transmission Another name for asynchronous transmission.

Stat mux A device that performs multiplexing using statistical methods like statistical time-division multiplexing.

Station Another name for a device on a LAN, or an end point on a link in the BSC and SDLC protocols.

Station feature PBX function controlled by and performed for the individual user.

Station line The circuit between a PBX and individual user's phones.

Statistical frequency-division multiplexing (SFDM) A multiplexing method continually changing the allocation of channels to accommodate the demands and needs of the attached devices.

Statistical logging A security method providing a record of which users accessed particular ports and at what times.

Statistical time-division multiplexing (STDM) A multiplexing method continually changing the allocation of time slots to accommodate the demands and needs of the attached devices.

STD *See* Secondary Transmitted Data.

STDM *See* Statistical time-division multiplexing.

STM-1 An STM-N signal operating at 155.52 Mbps.

STM-N *See* Synchronous Transport Module-N.

Stop bit In asynchronous transmission, the bit or bits sent after each character (always a 1).

Stop-and-wait ARQ A type of automatic repeat request in which transmission halts after each block, until an acknowledgment is received.

STS-N *See* Synchronous Transport Signal-N.

STX In BSC, the character indicating the start of user data.

Subarea In SNA, a Subarea Node and the resources that node controls.

Subarea Node In SNA, a Host Node or Communications Controller with its attached Workstations.

Submultiplexing A method of dividing an already-multiplexed channel into smaller channels.

Subscriber Identify Module (SIM) A device used by a customer to identify himself or herself to a GSM phone.

SunNet Manager *See* SolarisNet Manager.

Supercomputer An extremely fast host computer dedicated to extensive mathematical calculations.

Supervisory Format Frame (S-Frame) In SDLC, the type of frame used to transfer control information, including acknowledgment of the accurate receipt of data.

Switch A device that routes calls to different locations, such as a PBX or central office.

Switched Multimegabit Data Service (SMDS) A connectionless service designed to internetwork LANs and offered by many carriers today in North America.

Switched service A type of service requiring that a connection be made to different locations each time, as in the public telephone network or a packet switching network.

Switching hub A device that creates a true star network for which data is delivered to the appropriate user based only on the destination address; it is also known as a LAN switch.

Switching node In a packet switching network, the device that routes communications.

Symmetric keys An encryption technique using the same key to encrypt and decrypt a message.

SYN In BSC, the sync characters transmitted before the start of actual data.

Sync character In synchronous transmission, the special character sent at the beginning of a block to allow the receiver to adjust to the speed of the transmitting device.

Synchronization In T-1 transmission, the timing function provided by the framing bit.

Synchronous Data Link Control (SDLC) IBM's bit-oriented, full duplex, go-back-N continuous ARQ protocol.

Synchronous Digital Hierarchy (SDH) A CCITT digital transmission standard similar to SONET, it operates at speeds of 155.52 Mbps and above.

Synchronous Optical Network (SONET) A popular ANSI standard for digital transmission, it operates at speeds of 51.84 Mbps and above.

Synchronous transmission A transmission method using special characters and clock signals for timing.

Synchronous Transport Module-N (STM-N) The SDH designation used to describe signals, it supports speeds of 155.52 Mbps and above.

Synchronous Transport Signal-N (STS-N) The electrical equivalent of SONET's Optical Carrier-N signals.

System feature PBX functions performed and controlled for the entire system.

System Services Control Point (SSCP) In SNA, the Network Addressable Unit that monitors and controls a network's resources.

Systems Network Architecture (SNA) IBM's communications architecture that connects a wide variety of devices, it is highly flexible and versatile.

T reference point In ISDN, the point between the NT1 and NT2.

T-1 carrier AT&T's standard for 1.544 Mbps digital transmission over two twisted pairs.

T-1 multiplexer A device that divides the 1.544 Mbps of T-1 bandwidth into 24 separate channels of digitized voice or data.

T-1C A 3.152 Mbps digital transmission standard offering 48 channels.

T-3 A 44.736 Mbps digital transmission standard offering 672 channels.

TA *See* Terminal Adapter.

Tandem office A switch used by the local exchange carrier to route calls between central offices in the same LATA.

Tandem trunk A circuit connecting a central office to a tandem office.

Tap The point at which devices connect to a bus network.

Tariff A complete description of a common carrier's service, including the rate charged for that service.

TASI *See* Time assignment speech interpolation.

TC *See* Transmit Clock.

TCP *See* Transmission Control Protocol.

TCP/IP *See* TCP/IP Protocol Suite.

TCP/IP Protocol Suite A collection of protocols originally designed for use on a network connecting U.S. government agencies with universities performing research, it covers a wide variety of tasks likely to be performed on an open network. *See also* Transmission Control Protocol, Internet Protocol.

TCT *See* Toll-connecting trunk.

TD *See* Transmitted Data.

TDM *See* Time-division multiplexing.

TDMA *See* Time-Division Multiple Access.

TE *See* Terminal Equipment.

TE1 *See* Terminal Equipment Type 1.

TE2 *See* Terminal Equipment Type 2.

Technical and Office Products (TOP) A user-defined local area network standard developed by Boeing Computer Services, using a CSMA/CD bus network.

Telecommunications The exchange of information, usually over a significant distance and using electronic equipment for transmission.

Telecommunications Act of 1996 Legislation designed to increase competition in the industry.

Telenet The original name of a public packet switching network now operated by SPRINT.

Telnet Part of the TCP/IP Protocol Suite, it is a protocol that provides a universal method for accessing a remote host computer through a TCP/IP network.

10BASE-F An Ethernet standard for baseband transmission at 10 Mbps over fiber optic cable.

10BASE-T An Ethernet standard for baseband transmission at 10 Mbps over twisted pair wiring.

Terminal A device permitting users to communicate with a computer, it typically contains a screen and a keyboard; more generally, any device at the end of a communications circuit is sometimes considered a terminal, as in ISDN.

Terminal Adapter (TA) In ISDN, a device connected between the Terminal Equipment Type 2 and the Network Termination equipment.

Terminal Equipment (TE) In ISDN, customer-premises equipment attached to the ISDN network that transmits or receives voice, data, or other information. Examples are digital telephones, host computers, dumb terminals, and smart terminals.

Terminal Equipment Type 1 (TE1) In ISDN, Terminal Equipment that is compatible with the ISDN network.

Terminal Equipment Type 2 (TE2) In ISDN, Terminal Equipment that is not compatible with the ISDN network and can be connected to the network only through a Terminal Adapter.

Terminal handler Another name for an external PAD.

Terrestrial microwave A medium for transmission of data that uses radio waves over relatively short distances, using dish antennas with a clear line of sight between them.

Thin client User software that is very simple, requiring little processing power.

30B + D The European version of the ISDN primary-rate interface.

Throughput A measure of effective network transmission speed, it is the net bandwidth of a network.

Throughput class negotiation A packet switching network service allowing DTEs to negotiate for a certain bandwidth on a virtual circuit.

Tie trunk A telephone circuit connecting two PBXs.

Time assignment speech interpolation (TASI) A method of sharing an intertoll trunk, in which a communications path is allocated a few milliseconds after sound is detected; this method is suitable for voice communications, but can damage data transmission.

Time division A local area network contention method based on the time-division multiplexing technique.

Time-Division Multiple Access (TDMA) A transmission technology used in digital cellular telephone systems in which users share time on a transmission channel.

Time-division multiplexing (TDM) A method of allowing lower speed channels to share time on a high-speed communications circuit by allocating separate time slots to each channel.

Time slot The time reserved for a particular channel's communications in time-division multiplexing.

Time to live field In IP, the eight-bit field indicating the number of hops over which the datagram may be routed before it is discarded; it is usually set initially and is decremented with each hop.

Token A pattern of ones and zeroes with a special meaning in token-passing networks, typically used to control access to the networks.

Token bus A local area network using a bus topology and token passing, as in the IEEE 802.4 standard for Medium Access Control.

Token passing Using a token, typically either a free token or a busy token, to regulate access to a network.

Token ring network A local area network using a ring topology and token passing, as in the IEEE 802.5 standard for Medium Access Control or the IBM Token Ring Network.

Toll call Another name for a long-distance, or inter-LATA, call.

Toll-connecting trunk (TCT) A telephone circuit between the toll office and the central office.

Toll-free number A service in which the called party agrees to pay the charges for all calls, also known as inward WATS.

Toll office The switching office of a long-distance carrier.

TOP *See* Technical and Office Products.

Topology The form, or physical shape, of a network.

Total length field In IP, the 16-bit field indicating the total length of the datagram in bytes; it's value cannot exceed 65,535 bytes.

Touch-Tone dialing Another name for dual tone multifrequency dialing.

Transfer rate of information bits (TRIB) The ANSI formula for calculating throughput, it is the average rate at which users can expect the network to transport actual information bits to their destination.

Transmission Control Protocol (TCP) Part of the TCP/IP protocol suite, it operates at Layer 4 of the OSI model, the Transport Layer, and it ensures reliable delivery of the user's message.

Transmission Group In SNA, the communications Links between Subarea Nodes.

Transmission medium The physical path for carrying information, such as twisted pair wires, coaxial cable, fiber optic cable, terrestrial microwave, and satellite transmission methods.

Transmit Clock (TC) The RS-232-C timing signal generated by the DCE to time synchronous data transmission from the DTE to the DCE.

Transmitted Data (TD) The RS-232-C data signal sent by the DTE to the DCE.

Transparent A term often used to describe pure time-division multiplexing, because its functions are not visible to the user.

Transparent bridge A type of bridge typically used to connect Ethernet networks.

Transparent data mode In BSC, a method used to send control characters as data.

Transponder The device on a satellite that receives signals from uplink stations and transmits them to downlink stations.

Transport Layer Layer 4 of the OSI model, it is responsible for isolating the function of the lower layers from the higher layers.

Trap An SNMP message sent by the agent to inform the manager of specific events being monitored at the remote device.

Tree network A network topology similar to a bus network, but sometimes with many different branches off the main bus.

Trellis coding A technique used in conjunction with quadrature amplitude modulation in high-speed modems, usually 4800 bps and above, that relies on a special error-correction process.

TRIB *See* Transfer rate of information bits.

Tributary station In BSC, a device or station that communicates with the single Control station.

Triple DES A form of the Data Encryption Standard used for high-security transactions, the algorithm is actually executed three times to complicate code-breaking efforts.

True state The state of an RS-232-C control signal when it is asserted, ON, or raised.

Trunk A line or circuit connecting two switches.

Trunk port The high-speed port of a multiplexer, usually attached to the communications circuit.

Tunnel The encapsulation of data inside a protocol so that it can pass through a network, and the removal of that protocol at the far side of the network.

23B + D The North American and Japanese version of the ISDN primary-rate interface.

Twinax *See* Twinaxial Cable.

Twinaxial cable A cable similar to coaxial cable, but with two inner conducting wires.

Twisted pair Typically used in a local loop, it consists of two wires continuously twisted throughout its entire length.

2B + D The ISDN basic-rate interface.

Two-wire communications Communicating over a single pair of wires; this term is often incorrectly used as a synonym for half duplex; however, both half duplex and full duplex transmission can now occur over two wires.

Tymnet The original name of a public packet switching network now operated by MCI.

Type of service field In IP, the eight-bit field indicating the type of handling the source is requesting the network provide for this datagram.

UADSL *See* Universal Asymmetric Digital Subscriber Line.

UDP *See* Universal Datagram Protocol.

U-Frame *See* Unnumbered Format Frame.

U reference point In ISDN, the point between the NT1 and the rest of the ISDN network.

Unbalanced transmission A method of sending data requiring one wire for data and a common return wire or reference that can be shared with other signals, as in RS-423-A.

UNI *See* User–Network Interface.

Unicast A message sent to one of the users on a network; sometimes it is sent to everyone but ignored by those it is not addressed to.

United States Digital Cellular (USDC) A digital cellular standard used throughout the United States, it shares channels with the analog AMPS system and uses TDMA technology.

Universal Asymmetric Digital Subscriber Line (UADSL) An attempt to standardize ADSL deployment across all carriers, it operates at 1.544 Mbps/384 kbps; it is also known as ASDL Lite, DSL Lite, and G.Lite.

Universal Datagram Protocol (UDP) A Layer 4 protocol used to send individual IP packets, or datagrams.

Universal Serial Bus (USB) A data communications interface designed to connect peripherals to desktop computers, it commonly operates at 12 Mbps.

UNIX A computer operating system commonly used in open networks.

Unnumbered Format Frame (U-Frame) In SDLC, the type of frame used for special functions, including establishing connections, reporting procedural problems, and special cases of data transfer.

Unreliable service As found in IP, packets can be lost and the protocol does not retransmit them.

Uplink The satellite dish transmitting data to the satellite.

Upper Case The portion of the Baudot character code used for the numbers and punctuation marks.

Upper layers Another name for the higher layers of the OSI model.

Uptime The time when a system or network is available.

USB *See* External Transmit Clock.

USDC *See* United States Digital Cellular.

User–Network Interface (UNI) The ATM interface specification describing how to connect customer premises equipment to a provider network.

V.10 The ITU(CCITT) equivalent of the ANSI RS-423-A standard.

V.11 The ITU(CCITT) equivalent of the ANSI RS-422-A standard.

V.21 The ITU(CCITT) standard for 300 bps modulation, similar to the Bell 103/113 standard popular in the United States.

V.22 The ITU(CCITT) standard for 1200 bps modulation, similar to the Bell 212A standard popular in the United States.

V.22bis The ITU(CCITT) standard for 2400 bps modulation, it is widely used throughout the world.

V.24 The ITU(CCITT) equivalent of the signals in the ANSI RS-232-C standard.

V.28 The ITU(CCITT) equivalent of the voltage levels in the ANSI RS- 232-C standard.

V.32 The ITU(CCITT) standard for 4800 and 9600 bps modulation, it is widely used throughout the world.

V.32bis The ITU(CCITT) standard for 14.4 kbps modulation, it is widely used throughout the world.

V.34 The ITU(CCITT) standard for 28.8 and 33.6 kbps modulation, it is widely used throughout the world.

V.42 The ITU(CCITT) standard for modem error correction, also known as LAPM.

V.42bis The ITU(CCITT) standard for modem data compression.

V.90 The ITU(CCITT) standard for 56 kbps modulation, it offers 56 kbps in one direction and 33.6 kbps in the other.

Variable bit rate A source of data whose speed can change during transmission.

VCI *See* Virtual Channel Identifier.

VDSL *See* Very-high-bit-rate Digital Subscriber Line.

VDT *See* Video display terminal.

Version field In IP, the four-bit field used to indicate the version of IP being used.

Very-high-bit-rate Digital Subscriber Line (VDSL) A digital access technology that provides a link from the user to the central office over twisted pair wire that is higher speed in one direction than in the other; it provides very high speeds, but extremely short distances, so it is often used for a short connection to an existing fiber network.

Video display terminal (VDT) Another name for a terminal.

Video transmission The transmission of moving images, it can be performed using analog or digital techniques.

Virtual Channel Identifier (VCI) The part of the ATM header that designates a particular channel for a single connection.

Virtual circuit A circuit that appears to the user like a permanent connection, it simply ensures that data is appropriately routed, using the network's resources only when data is transmitted.

Virtual Path Identifier (VPI) The part of the ATM header that designates a grouping of channels.

Virtual Private Network Creating a tunnel through a public network, typically with secure protocols, to create a safe path for corporate data to travel inside of the publicly shared network.

Voice call multiplexing A method of sharing an intertoll trunk in which there is no additional risk of losing voice or data.

Voice grade circuit A standard telecommunications circuit.

VPN *See* Virtual Private Network.

VPI *See* Virtual Path Identifier.

WACK In BSC, the control character indicating that the device is temporarily busy but will be ready soon.

WAN *See* Wide area network.

WATS *See* Wide area telecommunications services.

Wave division multiplexing A transmission technique used in fiber optic cables in which different colors of light are used to carry data on separate channels.

WDM *See* Wave division multiplexing.

Western Electric AT&T's equipment manufacturing organization.

Wide area network (WAN) A network covering a large geographical area, such as a packet switching network.

Wide area telecommunications services (WATS) A bulk-rate, long-distance service for business users with high call volume.

Wireless The use of communications equipment without cabling.

Workstation The SNA term for a terminal.

World Wide Web The collection of publicly accessible information stored on servers connected to the Internet, it is usually in HTML format and read with browser software.

X.3 The ITU(CCITT) standard for the functions and parameters of an internal PAD.

X.25 The ITU(CCITT) standard for connecting a DTE to a packet switching network.

X.28 The ITU(CCITT) standard for connecting a DTE to an internal PAD in a packet switching network.

X.29 The ITU(CCITT) standard for communications between an internal PAD and the remote host computer.

xDSL A broad title covering the various types of digital access technologies, known as Digital Subscriber Line, that connect the central office with the user using twisted pair wire.

XON/XOFF ASCII control characters that can be used to start and stop host computer transmission, respectively.

XTC *See* External Transmit Clock.

Bibliography

A general listing of data communications books is provided first, followed by a suggested reading list of books and articles for each chapter in this text.

GENERAL DATA COMMUNICATIONS BOOKS

Abrams, Marshall, and Ira. W. Cotton, eds., *Computer Networks: A Tutorial* (4th ed.). New York, NY: IEEE Computer Society Press, 1984.

Black, Uyless D., *Computer Networks: Protocols, Standards, and Interfaces* (2d ed.). Upper Saddle River, NJ: Prentice Hall, Inc., 1993.

Black, Uyless D., *Data Communications and Distributed Networks* (3d ed.). Upper Saddle River, NJ: Prentice Hall, Inc., 1993.

The Executive Guide to Data Communications (Vol. 8). New York, NY: McGraw-Hill Publications Company, 1987.

Fitzgerald, Jerry, *Business Data Communications: Basic Concepts, Security, and Design* (3d ed.). New York, NY: John Wiley & Sons, 1990.

Folts, Harold C., ed., *McGraw-Hill's Compilation of Data Communications Standards* (3d ed.). New York, NY: McGraw-Hill Inc., 1986.

Freeman, Harvey A., and Kenneth J. Thurber, eds., *Local Network Equipment*. New York, NY: IEEE Computer Society Press, 1985.

Glover, I. A., and P. M. Grant, *Digital Communications*. Upper Saddle River, NJ: Prentice Hall, Inc., 1998.

Helmers, Scott A., *Data Communications: A Beginner's Guide to Concepts and Technology*. Upper Saddle River, NJ: Prentice Hall, Inc., 1989.

Lam, Simon S., ed., *Tutorial: Principles of Communication and Networking Protocols*. New York, NY: IEEE Computer Society Press, 1984.

Martin, James, *Telecommunications and the Computer* (3d ed.). Upper Saddle River, NJ: Prentice Hall, Inc., 1990.

Roden, Martin S., *Analog and Digital Communications* (4th ed.). Upper Saddle River, NJ: Prentice Hall, Inc., 1996.

Sherman, Ken, *Data Communications: A Users Guide* (3d ed.). Upper Saddle River, NJ: Prentice Hall, Inc., 1989.

Sklar, Bernard, *Digital Communications: Fundamentals and Applications.* Upper Saddle River, NJ: Prentice Hall, Inc., 1988.

Stallings, William, *Business Data Communications* (2d ed.). New York, NY: Macmillan Publishing Company, 1994.

Stallings, William, *Data and Computer Communications* (5th ed.). New York, NY: Prentice Hall, Inc., 1997.

Tanenbaum, Andrew S., *Computer Networks* (3d ed.). Upper Saddle River, NJ: Prentice Hall, Inc., 1996.

CHAPTER 2: UNDERSTANDING TELECOMMUNICATIONS

Borsook, Paulina, "Specter of Incompatibility Raised About ONA Offerings," *Data Communications*, November 1987.

Bradsher, Keith, "Can Cellular Phone Companies Agree on a New Standard for Transmission?" *The New York Times*, September 16, 1990.

Garg, Vijay, K. Smolik, and Joe Wilkes, *Applications of CDMA in Wireless Personal Communication.* Upper Saddle River, NJ: Prentice Hall, Inc., 1997.

Graham, John, *The Facts on File Dictionary of Telecommunications.* New York, NY: Facts on File Publications, 1983.

Green, James Harry, *The Dow Jones-Irwin Handbook of Telecommunications.* Homewood, IL: Dow Jones-Irwin, 1986.

Messmer, Ellen, "FCC Divides U.S. for New Wireless Providers," *Network World*, September 27, 1993.

Moffett, R. H., "Echo and Delay Problems in Some Digital Communications Systems," *IEEE Communications*, August 1987.

Rappaport, Theodore S., *Wireless Communications: Principles & Practice.* Upper Saddle River, NJ: Prentice Hall, Inc., 1996.

Rey, R. F., ed., *Engineering and Operations in the Bell System* (2d ed.). Murray Hill, NJ: AT&T Bell Laboratories, 1983.

Ricci, Fred J., *Personal Communications Systems Applications.* Upper Saddle River, NJ: Prentice Hall, Inc., 1997.

Telecommunications and You (2d ed.). White Plains, NY: International Business Machines Corporation, 1987.

Wolfson, Joel R., "Computer III: The Beginning or the Beginning of the End for Enhanced Services Competition," *IEEE Communications*, August 1987.

CHAPTER 3: BASIC DATA COMMUNICATIONS CONCEPTS

Data Communications Concepts (2d ed.). White Plains, NY: International Business Machines Corporation, 1987.

Touring Datacomm, A Data Communications Primer. Cupertino, CA: Hewlett-Packard Company, 1983.

CHAPTER 4: DATA INTERFACES AND TRANSMISSION

Black, Uyless D., *Physical Level Interfaces and Protocols.* Washington, DC: IEEE Computer Society Press, 1988.

Boyd, Robert S., "Commercial Satellites Launch 'Unwired Planet,'" *The San Jose Mercury News*, May 18, 1997.

Cochrane, P., and Mike Brain, "Future Optical Fiber Transmission Technology and Networks," *IEEE Communications Magazine*, November 1988.

Cochrane, P., Heckingbottom, R., and David Heatley, "The Hidden Benefits of Optical Transparency," *IEEE Communications Magazine*, September 1994.

Connecting to Your Computer. Cupertino, CA: Hewlett-Packard Company, 1984.

Ferguson, David D., "New Digital Network Service Capabilities," *Proceedings of the IEEE International Conference on Communications*, 1987.

Folts, Harold C., "A Powerful Standard Replaces the Old Interface Standby," *Data Communications*, May 1980.

Greene, Tim, "Wave Division Multiplexing (WDM): Follow the Light," *Network World*, September 7, 1998.

Hansen, Richard C., "AT&T's Digital Network Evolution," *Proceedings of the IEEE International Conference on Communications*, 1987.

Johnson, Johna Till, and James K. Hurd, "High Speed Modems: A Price Worth Paying?" *Data Communications*, July 1993.

Kaiser, P., Midwinter, J., and Sadakuni Shimada, "Status and Future Trends in Terrestrial Optical Fiber Systems in North America, Europe, and Japan," *IEEE Communications Magazine*, October 1987.

Nagel, Suzanne R., "Optical Fiber—The Expanding Medium," *IEEE Communications*, April 1987.

Pahlavan, K., and Jerry L. Holsinger, "Voice-Band Communication Modems—A Historical Review: 1919–1988," *IEEE Communications Magazine*, January 1988.

Palais, Joseph C., *Fiber Optic Communications* (4th ed.). Upper Saddle River, NJ: Prentice Hall, Inc., 1998.

Pelton, Joseph N., *Wireless and Satellite Telecommunications: The Technology, the Market and the Regulations.* Upper Saddle River, NJ: Prentice Hall, Inc., 1994.

Politi, C., and John A. Stein, "VSATS Give Corporate Networks a Lift," *Data Communications*, February 1991.

Pruitt, James B., "The Real Case For Microwave," *Computer and Communications Decisions*, August 1987.

Putman, Byron W., *RS-232 Simplified.* Englewood Cliffs, NJ: Prentice Hall, Inc., 1987.

Senior, John M., *Optical Fiber Communications: Principles and Practice* (2d ed.). Upper Saddle River, NJ: Prentice Hall, Inc., 1992.

Wilkens, William B., "Standards for Communications," *IEEE Communications Magazine*, July 1987.

CHAPTER 5: IMPROVING DATA COMMUNICATIONS EFFICIENCY

Boyd, Joseph A., "Communications Cost-Containment Through High Technology," *Journal of Telecommunications Networks*, Summer 1982.

Hoffman, Darlane, "Squeezing Line Costs via Data Compression," *Data Communications*, August 1987.

CHAPTER 6: DATA INTEGRITY AND SECURITY

Abrams, M. D., and Albert B. Jeng, "Network Security: Protocol Reference Model and the Trusted Computer System Evaluation Criteria," *IEEE Network*, April 1987.

Bellovin, S. M., and William R. Cheswick, "Network Firewalls," *IEEE Communications Magazine*, September 1994.

Branstad, Dennis K., "Considerations for Security in the OSI Architecture," *IEEE Network*, April 1987.

Chokhani, Santosh, "Toward a National Public Key Infrastructure," *IEEE Communications Magazine*, September 1994.

Denning, D. E., and Miles Smid, "Key Escrowing Today," *IEEE Communications Magazine*, September 1994.

Folts, Hal, "Open Systems Standards," *IEEE Network Magazine*, April 1987.

Ford, Warwick, *Computer Communications Security*. Upper Saddle River, NJ: Prentice Hall, Inc., 1994.

Hellman, Martin E., "Commercial Encryption," *IEEE Network*, April 1987.

Kluepfel, Henry M., "Securing a Global Village and Its Resources," *IEEE Communications Magazine*, September 1994.

Newman, D. B. Jr., Omura, J. K., and Raymond L. Pickholtz, "Public Key Management for Network Security," *IEEE Network*, April 1987.

Salamone, Salvatore, "Internetwork Security: Unsafe at Any Node?" *Data Communications*, September 1993.

Zorpette, Glenn, "Breaking the Enemy's Code," *IEEE Spectrum*, September 1987.

CHAPTER 7: ARCHITECTURES AND PROTOCOLS

Bass, Charlie, "Data Networks' Endangered and Protected Species," *Data Communications*, October 1987.

Black, Uyless D., *Data Link Protocols*. Upper Saddle River, NJ: Prentice Hall, Inc., 1993.

Bonnet, Luther, *SNA Fundamentals*. Chicago, IL: Science Research Associates, An IBM Company, 1987.

Carlson, David E., "Bit-Oriented Data Link Control Procedures," *IEEE Transactions on Communications*, April 1980.

Communicating with IBM. Hewlett-Packard Company, 1984.

Conrad, James W., "Character-Oriented Data Link Control Protocols," *IEEE Transactions on Communications*, April 1980.

General Information: Binary Synchronous Communications (3d ed.). White Plains, NY: International Business Machines Corporation, 1970.

Lam, Simon S., "Data Link Control Procedures," W. Chou, ed., *Computer Communications, Vol. 1: Principles*, Englewood Cliffs, NJ: Prentice Hall, Inc., 1983.

Martin, J., with Kathleen Kavanagh Chapman, *SNA: IBM's Networking Solution*. Upper Saddle River, NJ: Prentice Hall, Inc., 1987.

Rothberg, Michael, "The Architecture Battle," *Computer & Communications Decisions*, January 1988.

Stallings, William, ed., *Tutorial: Computer Communications: Architectures, Protocols, and Standards*. New York, NY: IEEE Computer Society Press, 1985.

Stix, Gary, "Special Report: Heeding a Call to Distribute," *Computer Decisions*, January 1987.

Stix, Gary, "Special Report: Peer Pressure," *Computer & Communications Decisions*, January 1988.

Synchronous Data Link Control Concepts (4th ed.). White Plains, NY: International Business Machines Corporation, 1986.

Systems Network Architecture, Concepts and Products (4th ed.). White Plains, NY: International Business Machines Corporation, 1986.

Systems Network Architecture, Formats (9th ed.). White Plains, NY: International Business Machines Corporation, 1987.

Systems Network Architecture, Technical Overview (3d ed.). White Plains, NY: International Business Machines Corporation, 1986.

Weissberger, Alan J., "Bit Oriented Data Link Controls," *Computer Design*, March 1983.

CHAPTER 8: DATA TRANSPORT NETWORKS

Backes, Floyd, "Transparent Bridges for Interconnection of IEEE 802 LANs," *IEEE Network*, January 1988.

Bertsekas, D., and Robert Gallager, *Data Networks* (2d ed.). Upper Saddle River, NJ: Prentice Hall, Inc., 1991.

Bhushan, Brij, "A User's Guide to Frame Relay," *Telecommunications Magazine*, July 1990.

Boscak, L., and Charles Hedrick, "Problems in Large LANs," *IEEE Network*, January 1988.

Bosack, Leonard, "Using Bridges and Routers to Manage Larger Networks," *LAN Technology*, February 1989.

Chao, H. J., Ghosal, D., Saha, D., and Satish K. Tripathi, "IP on ATM Local Area Networks," *IEEE Communications Magazine*, August 1994.

Comer, Douglas E., *Internetworking with TCP/IP (Volume 1): Principles, Protocols, and Architecture* (2d ed.). Englewood Cliffs, NJ: Prentice Hall, Inc., 1991.

Cooper, Edward, *Broadband Network Technology: An Overview for the Data and Telecommunications Industries*. (2d ed.). Upper Saddle River, NJ: Prentice Hall, Inc., 1991.

Costa, Janis Furtek, *Planning and Designing High Speed Networks*. Upper Saddle River, NJ: Prentice Hall, Inc., 1994.

Cotton, Ira W., "Technologies for Local Area Computer Networks," *Computer Networks*, November 1980.

Cox, T., and Frances Dix, "SMDS: The Beginning of WAN Superhighways," *Data Communications*, April 1991.

Csenger, Michael, "Two Vendors Plan Products Based on 100Base-VG Technology," *Communications Week*, September 20, 1993.

Dixon, Roy C., "Lore of the Token Ring," *IEEE Network Magazine*, January 1987.

Dixon, R. C., and Daniel A. Pitt, "Addressing, Bridging, and Source Routing," *IEEE Network*, January 1988.

Farowich, Steven, "Communicating in the Technical Office," *IEEE Spectrum*, April 1986.

Folts, Hal, "Open Systems Standards," *IEEE Network Magazine*, January 1987.

Francett, Barbara, "MAP Confronts the Real World," *Computer and Communications Decisions*, November 1987.

Gerla, Mario, "High-Speed Local Area Networks," *IEEE Spectrum*, August 1991.

Goldberg, Glenn, "Unshielded Twisted-Pair Wiring Can Overcome Ethernet Cabling Woes," *Computer Technology Review*, Fall 1987.

Johnson, Howard W., *Fast Ethernet: Dawn of a New Network*. Upper Saddle River, NJ: Prentice Hall, Inc., 1996.

Johnson, Johna Till, "Wireless Data: Welcome to the Enterprise," *Data Communications*, March 21, 1994.

Kaminski, Michael A., Jr., "Protocols for Communicating in the Factory," *IEEE Spectrum*, April 1986.

Kehoe, Brendan P., *Zen and the Art of the Internet*. Upper Saddle River, NJ: Prentice Hall, Inc., 1993.

Kummerle, K., and M. Reiser, "Local-Area Communication Networks—An Overview," *Journal of Telecommunication Networks*, Winter 1982.

Langdal, James, "Systems Integrators' MAP to the Promised LAN," *Systems & Software*, October 1985.

Lerner, S., and Joel Bion, "The Well-Managed LAN," *LAN Magazine*, June 1989.

Lindstrom, Annie, "Birmingham Users Turn to SMDS," *Communications Week*, May 17, 1993.

Making the LAN Connection, Hewlett-Packard Company, 1984.

Malamud, Carl, *Exploring the Internet*. Upper Saddle River, NJ: Prentice Hall, Inc., 1993.

Markov, J. D., and N. C. Strole, "Token-Ring Local Area Networks: A Perspective," *Proceedings of COMPCON F82*, 1982.

McNamara, John E., *Local Area Networks*. Burlington, MA: Digital Press, 1985.

Metcalfe, R. M., and David R. Boggs, "Ethernet: Distributed Packet Switching for Local Computer Networks," *Communications of the ACM*, July 1976.

Miller, Arthur, "From Here to ATM," *IEEE Spectrum*, June 1994.

Networking with X.25. Hewlett-Packard Company, 1985.

Pitt, Daniel, "Standards for the Token Ring," *IEEE Network Magazine*, January 1987.

Ross, Floyd E., "Rings are 'Round for Good!" *IEEE Network Magazine*, January 1987.

Rybczybski, Antony, "X.25 Interface and End-to-End Virtual Circuit Service Characteristics," *IEEE Transactions on Communications*, April 1980.

Saltzer, J. H., Clark, D. D., and Kenneth T. Pogran, "Why a Ring," *The Proceedings of the Seventh Data Communications Symposium*, 1981.

Satz, Greg, "Combining Level 2 Bridging and Level 3 Routing," *The Proceedings of the Systems Design and Networks Conference*, May 1989.

Seifert, Rich, *Gigabit Ethernet: Technology and Applications for High Speed Lans*. Reading, MA: Addison Wesley Longman, Inc., 1998.

Seifert, William, "Bridges and Routers," *IEEE Network*, January 1988.

Sevcik, Peter, "Going Global," *Network World*, September 19, 1988.

Shah, A., and G. Ramakrishnan, *FDDI: A High Speed Network*. Upper Saddle River, NJ: Prentice Hall, Inc., 1994.

Sharma, Roshan L., "Interconnecting LANs," *IEEE Spectrum*, August 1991.

Shimada, Karl, "Fast Talk About Fast Ethernet," *Data Communication*, March 21, 1994.

Stallings, William, "Beyond Local Networks," *Datamation*, August 1983.

Stallings, William, ed., *Tutorial: Local Network Technology*. New York, NY: IEEE Computer Society Press, 1985.

Steenstrup, Martha, *Routing in Communications Networks*. Upper Saddle River, NJ: Prentice Hall, Inc., 1995.

Strole, Norman C., "The IBM Token-Ring Network—A Functional Overview," *IEEE Network Magazine*, January 1987.

Tangney, B., and Donald Mahony, *Local Area Networks and Their Applications*. Upper Saddle River, NJ: Prentice Hall, Inc., 1988.

Willett, Michael, "Token-Ring Local Area Networks—An Introduction," *IEEE Network Magazine*, January 1987.

CHAPTER 9: NETWORK MANAGEMENT

Boyd, R. C., and Alan R. Johnston, "Network Operations and Management in a Multi-Vendor Environment," *IEEE Communications*, July 1987.

Cameron, W. H., LaCerte, C., and J. F. Noyes, "Integrated Network Operations Architecture and its Application to Network Maintenance," *IEEE Communications*, August 1987.

Chiu, D. M., and Ram Sudama, *Network Monitoring Explained: Design and Application*. Chichester, England: Ellis Horwood, 1992.

Data Communications Testing. Colorado Springs, CO.: Hewlett-Packard Company, 1980.

Fisher, Lawrence M., "Having a Network Nightmare? Let the Software Take Over," *The New York Times*, September 18, 1994.

Rose, Marshall T., *The Simple Book: An Introduction to Management of TCP/IP-based Internets* (2d ed.). Upper Saddle River, NJ: Prentice Hall, Inc., 1993.

Rosenberg, Robert, "Are Users Up in the Air Over Network Management?," *Data Communications*, December 1987.

Salazar, A. C., Scarfo, P. J., and R. J. Horn III, "Network Management Systems for Data Communications," *IEEE Communications Magazine*, August 1987.

Taylor, Floyd, "Data Comm Testing," *Computer/Electronic Service News*, October 1982.

Terplan, Kornel, *Communications Network Management* (2d ed.). Upper Saddle River, NJ: Prentice Hall, Inc., 1992.

Voruganti, Ram Rao, "A Global Network Management Framework for the '90s," *IEEE Communications Magazine*, August 1994.

CHAPTER 10: DIGITAL TELECOMMUNICATIONS

Armbruster, H., and Gerhard Arndt, "Broadband Communication and Its Realization with Broadband ISDN," *IEEE Communications Magazine*, November 1987.

Ballart, R., and Yau-Chau Ching, "SONET: Now It's the Standard Optical Network," *IEEE Communications Magazine*, March 1989.

Black, Uyless D., *Emerging Communications Technologies*. Upper Saddle River, NJ: Prentice Hall, Inc., 1994.

Borsook, Paulina, "'U' Marks the Critical Spot for User Interface to ISDN," *Data Communications*, October 1987.

Brunet, Craig J., "Hybridizing the Local Loop," *IEEE Spectrum*, June 1994.

Chen, Po, "How to Make the Most of ISDN's New LAPD Protocol," *Data Communications*, August 1987.

Chen, T. M., and David G. Messerschmitt, "Integrated Voice/Data Switching," *IEEE Communications Magazine*, June 1988.

Chester, Jeffrey A., "The Price is Right for T1 Communications," *Infosystems*, April 1987.

Cheung, Nim K., "The Infrastructure for Gigabit Computer Networks," *IEEE Communications Magazine*, April 1992.

Chu, N. N. Y., and P. B. Deleski, "ISDN Readiness Assessment," *Proceedings of the IEEE International Conference on Communications*, 1987.

Day, Andrew, "International Standardization of BISDN," *IEEE LTS—The Magazine of Lightwave Telecommunications Systems*, August 1991.

Delisle, D., and Lionel Pelamourgues, "B-ISDN and How it Works," *IEEE Spectrum*, August 1991.

DePrycker, Martin, *Asynchronous Transfer Mode* (2d ed.). Chichester, England: Ellis Horwood, 1993.

DSL Source Book (2d ed.). Paradyne Corporation, 1999.

Falek, J. I., and Mary A. Johnston, "Standards Makers Cementing ISDN Subnetwork Layers," *Data Communications*, October 1987.

Fischer, W., Wallmeier, E., Worster, T., Davis, S. P., and Andrew Hayter, "Data Communications Using ATM: Architectures, Protocols, Resource Management," *IEEE Communications Magazine, August 1994.*

Guinn, Donald E., "ISDN: Is the Technology on Target?" *IEEE Communications Magazine*, December 1987.

Herman, J. G., and Mary A. Johnston, "ISDN When? What Your Firm Can Do in the Interim," *Data Communications*, October 1987.

Kemezis, Paul, "What Price ISDN? First Cost Details Bared," *Data Communications*, August 1987.

Kovarik, K., and Payam Maveddat, "Multi-Rate ISDN," *IEEE Communications Magazine*, April 1994.

Lane, James, "ATM Knits Voice, Data on Any Net," *IEEE Spectrum*, February 1994.

Mier, Edwin E., "Are Analog Local Loops Too 'Dirty' for ISDN?" *Data Communications*, July 1987.

Pancha, P., and Magda El Zarki, "MPEG Coding for Variable Bit Rate Video Transmission," *IEEE Communications Magazine*, May 1994.

Pandhi, Sushil N., "The Universal Data Connection," *IEEE Spectrum*, July 1987.

Partridge, Craig, *Gigabit Networking*. Reading, MA: Addison-Wesley, 1994.

Perry, Tekla S., "Telephone Challenges: A Plethora of Services," *IEEE Spectrum*, July 1990.

Powers, J. T. Jr., and Henry H. Stair II, *Megabit Data Communications: A Guide For Professionals*. Upper Saddle River, NJ: Prentice Hall, Inc., 1990.

Pruitt, James B., "Stepping Up to T-3," *Computer and Communications Decisions*, November 1987.

Ruiu, Dragos, "Testing ATM Systems," *IEEE Spectrum*, June 1994.

Russotto, Thomas V., "The Integration of Voice and Data Communications," *IEEE Network Magazine*, October 1987.

Sazegari, Steven A., "Network Architects Plan Broadening of Future ISDN," *Data Communications*, July 1987.

Skrzypczak, Casimir S., "The Intelligent Home of 2010," *IEEE Communications Magazine*, December 1987.

Stallings, William, ed., *Advances in ISDN and Broadband ISDN*. New York, NY: IEEE Computer Society Press, 1992.

Stallings, William, ed., *Broadband Switching*. New York, NY: IEEE Computer Society Press, 1991.

Stallings, William, *ISDN and Broadband ISDN with Frame Relay and ATM* (3d ed.). Upper Saddle River, NJ: Prentice Hall, Inc., 1995.

Stallings, William, ed., *Tutorial: Integrated Services Digital Networks (ISDN)*. New York, NY: IEEE Computer Society Press, 1985.

Strauss, Paul R., "Small is Beautiful: New T1 Muxes Stress Savings," *Data Communications*, January 1988.

Strauss, Paul R., "Squeeze Play: Carriers Quietly Trying Compressed Voice; Users Could Soon Squeeze Big Savings," *Data Communications*, July 1987.

Tang, W. Victor, "ISDN—New Vistas in Information Processing," *IEEE Communications Magazine*, November 1986.

Tanzillo, Kevin, "ATM Users Don't Need to Worry About Data Eavesdroppers," *Communications News*, July 1994.

Verma, Pramode K., ed., *ISDN Systems: Architecture, Technology, and Applications*. Upper Saddle River, NJ: Prentice Hall, Inc., 1990.

Vickers, B. J., and Tatsuya Suda, "Connectionless Service for Public ATM Networks," *IEEE Communications Magazine*, August 1994.

Watanabe, Hitoshi, "Integrated Office Systems: 1995 and Beyond," *IEEE Communications Magazine*, December 1987.

Weinstein, Stephen B., "Telecommunications in the Coming Decades," *IEEE Spectrum*, November 1987.

Index